COMMUNICATION:

GENERAL SEMANTICS PERSPECTIVES

Communication: General Semantics Perspectives

Based on the Eleventh International Conference on General Semantics—
"A Search for Relevance,¹⁹⁶⁸"

Compiled and Edited by
LEE THAYER
The University of Iowa

Associate Editors

ELWOOD MURRAY
Director, Institute of General Semantics

CHARLOTTE S. READ
New York, New York

PAUL HUNSINGER
President, International Society for
General Semantics

KENNETH G. JOHNSON
University of Wisconsin–Milwaukee

Advisory Editors

D. DAVID BOURLAND, JR.
Information Research Associates, Inc.

RUSSELL JOYNER
Executive Director, International Society
for General Semantics

S. I. HAYAKAWA
San Francisco State College

LLOYD MORAIN
San Francisco, California

SPARTAN BOOKS

NEW YORK • WASHINGTON

Library of Congress Catalog Card No. 73–80437
Standard Book Number 87671–702–4

Printed in the United States of America

Sole Distributors in Great Britain, the British
Commonwealth, and the Continent of Europe:

MACMILLAN & COMPANY, LTD.
Little Essex Street
London, W. C. 2

Contributors

J. Samuel Bois
Viewpoints Institute, Inc.
Los Angeles, California

George A. Borden
Pennsylvania State University

D. David Bourland, Jr.
Information Research Associates, Inc.
Washington, D.C.

James M. Broadus
Transylvania College
Lexington, Kentucky

Deems M. Brooks
Florida State University at
   Tallahassee

Cecil J. Coleman
State University College
   at Geneseo, New York

Alan P. Frederickson
Evergreen, Colorado

Alfreda S. Galt
The Lifwynn Foundation
Westport, Connecticut

Sister Margaret Gorman
Newton College of the Sacred Heart
Newton, Massachusetts

Hanno Hardt
The University of Iowa

S.I. Hayakawa
San Francisco State College

Kenneth G. Johnson
University of Wisconsin–Milwaukee

Wendell Johnson
(until his death in 1965)
The University of Iowa

Dwight R. Kauppi
University of Minnesota

M. Kendig
Institute of General Semantics
Lakeville, Connecticut

Stanley Krippner
Maimonides Medical Center
Brooklyn, New York

Ervin Laszlo
State University College at
   Geneseo, New York

Laura L. Lee
Northwestern University

Howard F. Livingston
Pace College
Pleasantville, New York

Harry E. Maynard
General Semantics Foundation
New York, New York

Patrick Meredith
University of Leeds
   England

Thomas E. Miller
University of Missouri
   at Kansas City

Maurice B. Mitchell,
Chancellor, University of Denver

Charles H. Morgan
Hughes Aircraft Company
Fullerton, California

Elwood Murray
University of Denver

Thomas J. Pace, Jr.
Southern Illinois University

Sue Ann Pace
Southern Illinois University

Neil Postman
New York University

Walter Probert
University of Florida

Robert P. Pula
Baltimore, Maryland

Thaddeus J. Pula
Westinghouse Electric Corporation
Baltimore, Maryland

Anatol Rapoport
University of Michigan

Allen Walker Read
Columbia University

Charlotte S. Read
New York, New York

Karen L. Ruskin
Lockheed-California Company
Burbank, California

Bernard Sarachek
University of Missouri
  at Kansas City

Bent Stidsen
University of Pennsylvania

Mel Thistle
National Research Council of
  Canada

Donald E. Washburn
Edinboro State College
Edinboro, Pennsylvania

Albert Upton
Whittier College
Whittier, California

EDITOR'S PREFACE

The task of compiling and editing this collection of papers was an assignment that I undertook with some misgivings. The reasons for these misgivings, and for finally accepting the responsibility of bringing this volume into being, are undoubtedly germane to the way it should be described and introduced here.

I am not a general semanticist. In fact, I had come to identify myself, in a dichotomous (Aristotelian?) way, as belonging in the tradition of the critics of general semantics rather than the disciples.[1] Less than a year before the conference on which this book is based, I wrote the following to Professor Emeritus Elwood Murray of the University of Denver, then Director of the Institute of General Semantics.

> . . . I distrust any intellectual movements which become cults. . . . a great many general semantics folk attribute to themselves and to the general semantics "movement," and particularly to Korzybski, a lot of ideas that were developed in other disciplines both before and after Korzybski. Many of your publications seem to me to be more like forums for people who cite only each other, and acclaim a handful of messiahs, than scholary journals given over to the evolution of an open, viable discipline or body of knowledge. . . . I sense a serious . . . closedness in the "movement." . . . If those who share general semantics convictions do not relate their comprehensions to the work that has gone on and is going on . . . in perhaps a dozen other fields that overlap the interests of the general semanticist, then it seems to mé that the "movement" is destined to languish in its own adoration and ingrown-ness.[2]

Yet I knew that general semantics has had over the years considerable appeal for some extremely intelligent scientists and scholars highly respected within their own disciplines. And, as I wrote to Professor Murray, "I agree fully with you about the importance of general semantics—in terms of its far-reaching implications for man and for the nature of his individual and social existence."

How was one to understand these apparent contradictions? It seemed to me there had to be some reasons that were not readily obvious.

My major criticisms of the present state of general semantics—that it is for many of its central spokesmen more of a religion than an intellectual discipline; that its disciples often exhibit a kind of "intellectual imperialism"; that it is static, closed, and proprietary; that it is myopic and naive*—have not changed essentially with the additional contact I have had with it, through its proponents and dissidents, during the development and editing of this book.

But some of those inobvious reasons for the apparent contradictions in its appeal to a few, yet its scorn by many, in its potential yet its relative lack of significant influence, became somewhat more obvious. In my view those reasons have a relevance that exceeds that of any pro or con argument. And, for the most part, they seem to me to be closely related to the phenomenon of scientism.

SCIENTISM

The remarkable achievements of science are but one part of its spectacular history in the twentieth century. A by-product of perhaps equal or greater import is the phenomenon of scientism.

Scientism is pseudoscience, bureaucratized science, parodized science. Scientism deifies the methods and the trappings of science. Its ideologies are its techniques; the primary if not the sole justification for inquiry is the elegance and the current popularity of the techniques employed.

Given the interlocking nature of the evolution of a body of scientific knowledge, only so much useful "sciencing" can be done. But its caricatures in scientism can and have evolved and proliferated without limit. Where science may be viewed as one of the finest of the fine arts, scientism is basically political and economic.

Like a cancer, scientism has fed upon the growing status and prestige of science. Nowhere is this more apparent than in academe. Where mathematics used to be an adequate index of a course of study, it has become obvious that mathematical *sciences* is politically and budgetarily a more potent term. The study of management is giving way to the management *sciences*; the study of psychology and sociology and related fields to the behavioral *sciences;* and the study of politics and of rhetoric to political *science* and the speech *sciences* or communication *sciences.*

This desire to appear scientific, to identify oneself and one's intellectual endeavors as scientific, has achieved the proportion of a cultural mania.

---

* Such criticisms could, of course, be levelled at a great many of the disciplines and movements concerned with some part-aspect of human behavior and its by-products.

Its underlying assumptions have become so deeply imbedded that we no longer recognize them as assumptions. As Harley Shands observed recently, ". . . scientific method is itself the kind of one-sided, eccentric application of symbolic method that we would characterize as neurosis were it found in a patient complaining of distress."[3] Scientism is the common neurosis of our time. While philosophy departments have decreased in size and political potency on our campuses, departments of computer *sciences* have emerged and grown to formidable size and power.

This is not an adequate description of the phenomenon of scientism. But it may perhaps suffice as the backdrop for identifying one major reason for the apparent contradictions in the present state of general semantics.

The philosophical issues involved in determining whether a given idea or family of ideas (a discipline) is useful, or whether it is scientific, were raised long before the logical positivists took them up as points of departure. But those issues were most starightforwardly resolved by logical positivism. And, as Hanno Hardt points out, in his paper in this volume, what is important for us to remember is that this was the intellectual milieu in which Korzybski nurtured his own ideas.

The fundamental contradictions in the nature and the state of general semantics were thus built into it at the outset by Korzybski himself. It seems obvious that Korzybski's scien*tistic* posture, at least in *Science and Sanity,* implied his intention that his general semantics would evolve into a first-order science (if not *the* science of the sciences). Korzybski's formulations do not comprise a set of tools for further inquiry (a theory), however, but a rationale for establishing methods for improving individual and social hygiene.

General semantics is substantively a *hygienic* discipline, not a scientific one. Korzybski gave it the mantle of science by the *style* of his posture and his exposition. But in doing so he endowed general semantics with a fundamental contradiction: it must be a *normative* science in the sense that the essential parameters are given. It is left to the general semanticist only to discover or create ways of "doing" general semantics that fit those essential parameters and the philosophy from which they evolved. No way was provided for *disproving* its formulations. To understand it, you must buy it. To the extent you haven't "bought" it, it's assumed you simply don't understand it.

We are all familiar with the fact that courses of study that might be directly useful or beneficial to our everyday lives are generally looked upon as below the dignity of an academic enterprise—particularly a scientific one. Most home economics departments have disappeared from university curriculums in the last two decades, as have other vocational and avocational courses of study. It is an okay thing to teach someone how to be a good scientist. But we are not likely, in the near future, to see courses that attempt to teach college students how to be good lovers.

The hierarchies of prestige and power today are largely determined by competitive scientism: the more scientistic a school or department can appear to be relative to the others, the higher in the hierarchy it rises. Even psychology, which might originally have been the study of man, has, in order to survive, become psychologism, wherein what counts is not the relevance of the inquiry, but the elegance of the design.

This circumstance confronts the general semanticist of today with the following dilemma: in order to fulfill the promise of general semantics, it must be made scientific. Yet it is in basis not a scientific discipline but a hygienic discipline; its real value and potential are eroded as it is scientized. At the same time, there is very little place for a hygienic discipline in contemporary academe; the low status of hygienic disciplines largely obviates their significance and/or their influence.

The picture that emerges is one which reflects more upon the pathologies of postpositivist scientism than it does upon the legitimacy or the relevance of general semantics. Those who would defend the ideologies of general semantics appear to us as belonging to an idiosyncratic minority—not for substantive but for quantitative reasons. If the underlying philosophies of scientism had been grasped by only a few stalwart defenders of that faith, then scientism would today be the totem of a cult rather than a way of life for millions.

We ought not dismiss general semantics solely on the basis of the "holier-than-thou" stance of scientism. At the same time, those who believe general semantics has something to say ought not sell out for a more prestigious place in the scientistic hierarchy.

I took on the task of compiling and editing this volume in part because I hoped it might in sum justify those two "oughts." In one sense, and whatever the inadequacies of general semantics may be, the dilemma of the general semanticist today is in part attributable to the neurosis of scientism, which is pervasively embedded in our academic and intellectual ways of life.

There is one further source of contradiction that should be considered here before moving on to a description of the purposes and organization of the book.

General semantics was given its present shape and form at a time when a science of man—indeed a *unified* science of man—was beginning to be thought of as not only desirable but possible. Not unlike the inventors or fathers of many other disciplines or hybrids of the time, Korzybski may have on occasion thought of general semantics as the panacea, the discipline around which all others could be synthesized into a final science of man.

This posture likely invested the movement with two weaknesses.

First, any attempt to build a synthesizing discipline is not a scientific enterprise, but a political or at best a philosophical one.

Second, it introduces a paradox. Science necessarily simplifies. Yet, unless we assume the ultimate aim of human life to be simplification, we must either remake human existence to fit this necessary end of science, or recognize the nature and extent of the irrelevance of science to the infinite possibilities for man and his social and symbolic environments.[4]

The paradox is easily illustrated by example. The aim of a "science" of cake baking, for example, would be to find the ultimate formula for baking the ultimate cake. The tangible product of this science of cake baking would be a single recipe. Yet we know that part of the pleasure of cake baking (and cake eating, to be sure) stems from the almost infinite possibilities for discovering or creating variety. The aims are fundamentally incompatible.

In my opinion, the ultimate values and the relevancies of general semantics inhere in its potential for stimulating man's variety and diversity, not in its potential as an integrator of a science of man. Is the end of human life to be that condition in which each of us extensionalizes in exactly the same way? If each of our maps fit the territory exactly, and hence was indistinguishable from the others, could we possibly look upon that as an ultimate human achievement?

What Korzybski (and some of his followers) called for indirectly is a condition of life in which every man is perfectly adapted to his environment—and hence necessarily perfectly controlled by it. Such a science of man would be his ultimate dehumanization.

What are the alternatives to "time-binding"? If to conceive of something in a certain way, or to say something about something, is time-binding, then the alternative is to avoid thinking or talking about things in *some* way—which is tantamount to not thinking or talking about them at all. Indexing is, of course, a useful practical *technique* for reminding oneself and others who adopt the technique that a concept or a comment about something does not accurately reflect its process nature, but it is hardly a *theoretical* alternative to the necessiy of time-binding in thinking about or talking about a process world. If we were to remodel our languages after the languages of science, we would necessarily remodel man in the image of science.

The general semantics of *Science and Sanity* comprises an incomplete philosophical tract on certain language-related conditions of man and his societies.* That is both its weakness and its strength. On the one hand, general semantics isn't a science, and efforts to scientize it cannot but further depreciate it. On the other hand, because it can be actualized only as a practical philosophy, it is destined to occupy an inferior status in our scientistic culture.

To the extent that general semantics could succeed in its scientific aspirations, it would necessarily have to turn its propositions to the impoverishment of man. To the extent that it fails, whatever value it has as a practical philosophy or as a hygienic discipline is lost.

I undertook the task of compiling and editing this volume in part with the hope that these basic paradoxes and dilemmas might be made more obvious to both the proponents and the opponents of general semantics, as well as to those who have had no previous contact with it. I take this as no justification or legitimation of general semantics. But if the price we are paying for scien*tism* is the stillbirth of every conflicting ideology, then that price may be too high.

Read as a practical philosophy, understood as a hygienic discipline, general semantics has something of value to offer both directly and by default. I hope this diverse collection of papers will, in sum, suggest something of both its potential human usefulness and its basic human dilemma.

RATIONALE AND ORGANIZATION OF THE BOOK

The meeting out of which this volume grew was the International Conference on General Semantics, held in Denver, August 5–9, 1968. Having as theme ". . . a Search for Relevance,[1968]" the broad spectrum of interests and intellectual orientations represented at the conference was due largely to the prodigious efforts of its instigator and program chairman, Elwood Murray. Murray has devoted much of his time in recent years to the task of bringing about some significant ecumenism among the several disciplines whose subject matters are relevant to the study of man and the nature of his existence. That conference and this book are both a consequence of his untiring pursuit of that task.

Our conception of this book has changed several times.

It was inevitable that the possibility of publishing a full set of proceedings would be considered. But with over two hundred papers, panels, and workshops, and with the great variations in intellectual orientations involved, a "proceedings" seemed hardly feasible—or useful.

The criterion question raised by the editorial committee was, "How can we best let others know what is going on in general semantics and related

---

* The trick of trying to enhance its scientific significance through advertisements of endorsement betrays some of the hucksterism that has surrounded it from its inception.

xii

areas today?" This led to the difficult decision and process of selecting from the conference those papers and discussions that might be most representative.

Finally, given that it is rarely possible for all of those whose work and thought are most representative of their field to attend such conferences, the editors decided to solicit contributions from a number of scholars who did not present papers at the conference itself.

Thus, in order to satisfy a number of criteria that the editors felt important, this volume in its published form contains several papers that were first presented at the conference (or elsewhere prior to the conference)—some revised or rewritten for publication, as well as a number of papers that were contributed in keeping with both the theme of the conference and our desire to present as representative a picture as possible of what is going on in general semantics and related areas at this time.

Since the two kinds of contributions are not distinguished in the text, it may be helpful to distinguish them here (see also list of contributors):

Papers Selected from the Conference	Papers Contributed after the Conference
Borden	Bois
Bourland, Morgan, & Ruskin	Gorman
Broadus	Hardt
Brooks and T. Pace	W. Johnson
Coleman	Kendig
Frederickson	Maynard
Galt	Miller and Sarachek
Hayakawa	Murray
K. Johnson	S. Pace
Kauppi	Probert
Krippner	C. Read
Laszlo	Stidsen
Lee	Thistle
Livingston	Upton
Meredith	
Mitchell	
Postman	
R. Pula	
T. Pula	
Rapoport	
A. Read	
Washburn	

Deciding how best to organize a volume such as this is always a difficult problem. A number of possibilities were considered. But it would be pertinent here only to describe briefly the way in which the book is organized in its published form.

It is always appropriate that the "Formulations" of a philosophy such as general semantics be reconsidered, discussed, analyzed, etc. The first section of the book is given over to this end. It is my opinion that the analysis Hardt makes of an underlying issue in Korzybski's posture is the sort of analysis that would contribute greatly to the health and viability of any philosophical discipline or ideology, and is the sort of analysis that has been largely lacking in the general semantics movement. A comparison of Charlotte Read's and Murray's papers in this first section should clearly reflect the contradictory trends toward traditionalism and ecumenism beginning to come alive in general semantics today. Sister Gorman's and Marie Kendig's papers should perhaps be read or reread in the context of the Rapoport paper and discussion in the second section of the book. Broadus', Johnson's, and Robert Pula's papers all deal with "neglected formulations, " and could therefore profitably be read together.

The second section, "Applications," is intended to represent some of the applications that can be made of general semantics ideas and techniques, as well as some of the kinds of research that can be carried out in the context of those ideas or techniques—e.g., the Bourland *et al.* paper and the Livingston paper and its discussion. Laura Lee's paper and Sue Pace's paper should perhaps be read together, since both deal with the development of language capabilities and incapabilities. The papers by Kauppi. Krippner, Probert, Stidsen, and Washburn suggest the broad range of phenomena to which general semantics orientations may be relevant—from clinical psychology to the analysis of drug-induced states, to law, to economic reasoning, to the comprehension and enjoyment of literature. I would single out Stidsen's paper particularly as an example of the more fruitful kinds of applications of general semantics principles that could be made totally outside the impetus toward scientism. Stidsen applies a basic general semantics concept to the evolution of thought in economics with intriguing results, and with the further implication that general semantics might be well suited to application as a speculative philosophy. I see the Coleman paper and Thistle's contribution as extremely unique kinds of applications of general semantics philosophies—the one to the nature of a common human circumstance, the other to the characterization of broad cultural phenomena. Thaddeus Pula describes in his paper *how* he uses and *what* he uses of general semantics in the training of electrical engineers. Hayakawa's, Maynard's, and Rapoport's papers, and the discussion of Rapoport's paper, should be taken together in the context of the conference and its theme. They provide various perspectives on the question of how and whether general semantics is relevant to today's world.

There are inevitably "Variations" on any theme. The third section of the book is intended to capture the spirit of some variants of general semantics. Represented are such thinkers as Bois, Wieman (Brooks and Pace paper), Burrow (Galt paper), and Wendell Johnson, all of whom had some allegiance to general semantics, but all of whom developed formulations at some variance with the more traditional Korzybski-ites. The Laszlo and Meredith papers represent attempts to go beyond the more basic formulations with the help of concepts and approaches from other disciplines. Miller and Saracheck offer an example of how the humanism implicit in the philosophy of general semantics can be indirectly applied in developing a case study approach to manager (human) development. Frederickson's paper was one of three prepared by the members of the Denver Jazz Club, and presented during the "Evening of Jazz" night at the conference. Mitchell's paper is adapted from his opening talk before the conference. Upton's paper should probably be read as a uniquely Upton-esque variation on semantics and general semantics, and Borden's as an example of the many attempts being made in the communication field to bring more order to its evolution.

The Appendix by Charlotte Read on Korzybski is being reprinted here because the editors felt it would be relevant to the overall aim of the book.

COMMUNICATION AND GENERAL SEMANTICS

My own paper at the conference was entitled "Communication: Meta-science of the Sciences." It is not included in this volume primarily because it does not relate directly to general semantics. However, some of the issues implied by this and other exclusions should probably be noted.

Scholars, researchers, and philosophers of many disciplinary persuasions having interest in some part of the phenomena of human communication, by whatever terms, for the most part go their own ways, substantively oblivious to aech other. The three international symposia on communication sponsored by the Center for the Advanced Study of Communication under my direction [5] have been but one attempt to bring about a synergistic rapprochement among such scholars, researchers, and philosophers. In spite of such efforts, perspectives continue to proliferate and to develop independently of each other.

The obstacles, in my opinion, are not the proverbial communication problems, but are essentially political in nature. Somewhat like the world language problem, the ultimate question is: "Whose concepts and terminologies are going to win out?" Will all of the wide-ranging interests in human communication phenomena extant today by whatever terms be subsumed under communication, or semiotics, or general semantics, or symbolic interactionism, or psycholinguistics, or linguistic anthropology, or the behavorial sciences—or what? No discipline can retain its sovereignty when it incorporates with another or other disciplines in pursuit of common goals.

Which language shall we speak? At the conference on which this book is based, general semantics was the language most universally spoken. There were very few aliens who described themselves as communication scholars or as semioticians. If one speaks of the same phenomenon in different languages and from different philosophical bases, is he talking about the same thing? I think not.

The issue is a crucial one. Although we never discussed it directly, I'm sure Elwood Murray has wondered, as I have: If a volume of this sort is put together and edited by a nongeneral semanticist, by, in fact, an alien from the field of communication, would any of the obstacles inherent in this issue be at all softened or set aside?

My own bias is to study, and to develop a conceptual framework for studying human communication,[6] borrowing as freely from other fields of study as seems useful to the conduct of the inquiry. My own bias is that one ought to study the processes of human communication—whether they be called communication or not—not the structure or the concepts of the disciplines set up to study the process. Communication is a process word —as ambiguous as it may be; general semantics is not.

The other editors do not necessarily agree with me. Even so, it should be noted that the title of this volume, *Communication: General Semantics Perspectives,* is in no way an attempt to subsume general semantics *under* communication. It is merely to suggest that there are a wide variety of perspectives on the *processes* we often refer to as human communication (or contingent on those processes in some way), and that the concepts and formulations of general semantics provide one of those perspectives.

ACKNOWLEDGEMENTS

The associate and advisory editors selected by the conference committee, and by the officers of the Institute of General Semantics and the International Society for General Semantics, the professional associations that cooperated to bring about the conference and to assist in the development of this book, were extremely helpful to me at all stages of the compilation and editing task. I wish to publicly extend my appreciation for their significant contributions here.

Special thanks are due Laura Lee and Charlotte Read for their unreserved and timely assistance when requested.

All of the editors join me in extending our gratitude to all of the contributors to this volume, especially those who had to operate under the pressures of time to prepare (or repair) manuscripts.

We extend our thanks to all of those copyright holders who have given us permission to include copyrighted material, and for permission to reprint in this volume papers which have been published elsewhere.

A special note of thanks should go to the publisher, Spartan Books, and its editors, for the courage if not the foresight to see the need for and the value of a book of this nature.

The Universities of Iowa and Denver contributed resources and facilities, as well as assistance of various kinds, without which the preparation of this book would have been greatly hampered.

And, for the many things that ultimately make the difference between pleasure and pain in the task of editing a volume such as this, a final loving gesture of thanks to my silent partner in all things, Nancy Thayer.

—Lee Thayer
Iowa City, Iowa, July 1969

REFERENCES

1. See also, Chapter 23, "General Semantics, Etc.," in Martin Gardner's *In the Name of Science*, New York: Putnam's, 1952; and Anatol Rapoport, "General Semantics: Its Place in Science," *ETC: A Review of General Semantics*, Vol. XVI, No. 1, Autumn, 1958.
2. Some parts of that letter were printed in the March 1968 *IGS News*, with a response by Charlotte Read. A further reference to that exchange appears in M. Kendig's paper in this volume.
3. Shands, Harley C. "Crystallized Conflict: Semiotic Aspects of Neurosis and Science," *Perspectives on Communication*, Carl E. Larson and Frank E. X. Dance (eds.), Speech Communication Center, University of Wisconsin–Milwaukee, 1968, p. 142.
4. Compare with Chapter 13, "Questions for a Science of Man," in Rollo May's *Psychology and the Human Dilemma*, Princeton, New Jersey: D. Van Nostrand, 1967; and Abraham Maslow, *The Psychology of Science*, New York: Harper & Row, 1966.
5. The proceedings of the first symposium are published as *Communication: Theory and Research*, Springfield, Illinois: C C Thomas, Publishers, 1967; and those of the second symposium as *Communication: Concepts and Perspectives*, New York: Spartan Books, 1967. The proceedings of the third symposium, held in

the late summer of 1968 and following a quite different format, are still in process and may or may not be published.

6. Representative and somewhat more current for any reader who might be interested are "On Communication and Change: Some Provocations," *Systematics,* Vol. 6, No. 3, December, 1968; "Communication: *Sine qua non* of the Behavioral Sciences," *Vistas in Science,* ed. D. L. Arm, Albuquerque: University of New Mexico Press, 1968; and *Communication and Communication Systems,* Homewood, Illinois: R. D. Irwin, 1968.

INTRODUCTION

ELWOOD MURRAY

M OST of the papers in this volume were selected from the program of
the International Conference on General Semantics held in Denver,
Colorado, August 5–9, 1968, which explored the theme "A Search for Relevance."

Relevance to what? There is no relevance without something to be relevant to—without the specifics of time and circumstance. To what are you
and I relevant now? As persons? In our work? With our associates? Involved in these questions is the importance that persons and groups attribute to themselves and to each other. To ask about relevance is to raise
those questions that are vital to so many people today: Who am I? What
am I? Why am I?

These are only the beginning questions that the semantic indexing of relevance indices. We are led to inspect the growing obsolescence of almost
everything we have built. We are led to question what almost every person
has been and is now doing. These questions revive in new urgency the possibilities Norman Cousins implied some twenty-five years ago in his volume, *Modern Man Is Obsolete*.

"Education," in almost its whole range as an institution, was a major
concern of the 1968 International Conference on General Semantics. Included in this field was the concern over the relevance of large areas of
what is being taught—the false, half-true and out-dated information with
which curricula are crammed, and the failure to teach students to understand their own learning, evaluating, and communicating behaviors.

The ratio of information to useful and valid knowledge has become
gravely impaired, lopsided, and dangerous. We continue to live amid ignorance, superstition, and violence.

The quest for relevant knowledge is the central activity of science. The
search continues for relationships of one thing to another thing; of one organ in the body to another organ; of one person, group, institution, or society to another person, group, institution, or society. The great challenge
to education is not only to transmit these relevancies, but to give learners

the means to explore changing relevancies, and to prevent self-delusion in respect to what they "know."

How is relevance ascertained? How may hidden and obscure relevancies be perceived? How may the attribution of false relevancies be prevented? How may people be equipped to perceive relevance so that they may be competent in the midst of the greatest of complexities, confusion, and chaos? What must be done to bring an ordering into our perceptions of events and an improvement in the logics that we use?

To answer these questions general semanticists would ask that education emphasize an orientation to language behaviors and those premises that would bring language behaviors into a closer isomorphism with the universe in which we live. This orientation constantly seeks hidden and complex relationships, i.e., relevancies. We must constantly search for order, function, and structure both within ourselves and within our physical and social symbolic environments. The environments that man creates and perpetuates are proving the most difficult to understand and control. Thus, the timeliness and the significance of a conference such as the one from which this volume emerged.

There is paradox in the study and application of general semantics. While Alfred Korzybski warned us that his work was incomplete and certainly no panacea, we have been told that some students continue to act as if it were. Offsetting this, is research underway in applying general semanics to critical social problems, and research upon general semantics, which we believe will eventually strengthen the discipline.

To date, the complete application of non-Aristotelian methodology to writing about general semantics has been rare indeed, for it requires a genius able to combine poetic insight with scientific rigor. To the extent that these conditions are not fulfilled, the papers in this collection contradict that which they purport to advance. Yet, we must live with this sort of frustration for a long time to come. Even toward those papers that seem the least "non-Aristotelian," the general semanticist must be flexible enough to appreciate the ideas and insights that they provide.

In this volume, there are some criticisms of general semantic. This is no more than we ask of others; namely, that they *apply* general semantics, that they evaluate their evaluations, and doubt their certainties as they doubt others whose certainties differ. These are constructive activities, indeed, where there is capability of so doing.

Some critics claim that general semantics tends to appropriate other approaches to education and learning, that it aspires to leadership in a whole array of "related methodologies" emerging from scientific activities in the realm of communication. Some may not be aware of the fact that hundreds of teachers and members of other professions incorporate general semantics in their work. This criticism comes from a few scholars who would keep their discipline "pure" and pristine, and encapsulated in their terminological barriers! Let us say that any such "leadership" activity there might be has fallen into our laps because: (1) Many leaders in those "related methodologies" fail to take cognizance of developments in parallel "movements" *relevant* to their own work. In this, they exclude what general semantics could contribute to their own disciplines. (2) Many communication theorists continue to dichotomize and to look at only a part of that most dynamic of human behaviors—what we label the evaluating-communicating process.

Undoubtedly, we have been unable to fulfill all of the great opportunities and challenges. Do we really care whether cybernetics, psycholinguistics, group dynamics, general systems, or general semantics, etc., becomes predominate or subordinate—as long as our mutual quests are furthered? What is crucial today is that we begin to learn from each other. It is hoped that this book will contribute to that end.

EDUCATION, A SEARCH FOR RELEVANCE [1968]

PAUL HUNSINGER

I T is difficult to select a good theme for a conference. The theme should be specific enough so that it will interest the participants, and yet not so specific that people who wish to contribute papers are limited or handicapped. The theme should provide a framework for the diverse parts of the conference, and should also be attractive enough so that it can be used for the necessary promotion of the conference.

The tentative theme for the conference, from which this book emerged, at the time of the first announcement was "A Search for Structure[1968]." Structure is one of the most basic concepts in general semantics. There are over 800 pages in Korzybski's *Science and Sanity* devoted to structure.

In the fall of 1967, the board of the International Society for General Semantics met in San Francisco to select the official theme for the conference. The idea of using "structure" as a theme for the conference was discussed in detail, but it seemed too rigid, and would not lend itself to the many interests of the people who would be asked to contribute papers. Dr. Elwood Murray, the Program Chairman, felt that "structure" would be the best theme for the conference, but he too was disturbed by the idea that it might not be broad enough. The idea of general semantics and the search for structure did become an integral part of the program, and several excellent papers were developed along these lines.

During the conversations regarding the theme, there were numerous suggestions. We needed to emphasize the idea that the papers should be relevant to what is happening now, rather than relevant to the situation when general semantics was first developed by Alfred Korzybski many years ago. The conference should be relevant to the interests of communication scholars as well as relevant to the interests of those who have more of an applied interest in general semantics.

After the theme was agreed upon by the Board of the International Society for General Semantics, it was discussed in more detail by Harry Maynard, the other Cochairman of the conference, and myself, and the theme was expanded to "Education, a Search for Relevance[1968]." This broader topic encompassed the idea that the purpose of education is the quest for what is relevant in the *here* and *now*. During the course of the development of the conference, there were times when the theme was shortened to "Relevance[1968]" because of the natural tendency to shorten titles but the major emphasis was on the total theme throughout its planning and programming.

Some strong attacks on general semantics were made during the conference. Respected scholars pointed out that general semantics is no longer relevant to what is happening in the dynamic present. The most notable "attack" is the paper by Anatol Rapoport, which is included in this volume with prepared commentaries. One of the most heated sessions of the conference came after Rapoport's paper was read. His questioning of the relevance of general semantics to what is happening today in the world is thought provoking; but perhaps this questioning identifies some of the failures to exploit general semantics' *potential relevance* to current affairs rather than its *nonrelevance*. At the same time, there was strong sentiment that general semantics is relevant to what happens in the present—including the war in Vietnam and our problems at home.

Thus, it seems that the theme of the conference was well chosen. But if the questions raised are to be fully meaningful, the search for relevance must continue. This book represents a continuation of that search.

Contents

EDITOR'S PREFACE vii

INTRODUCTION xix
Elwood Murray

EDUCATION, A SEARCH FOR RELEVANCE 1968 xxiii
Paul Hunsinger

PART I.   FORMULATIONS

1. STRUCTURE AND CIRCULARITY AS NEGLECTED FORMULATIONS   3
James M. Broadus

2. GENERAL SEMANTICS TODAY 11
Margaret Gorman

3. GENERAL SEMANTICS AND SCIENTIFIC ETHICS 15
Hanno Hardt

4. INVARIANCE UNDER TRANSFORMATION 23
Kenneth G. Johnson

5. A NOTE BY M. KENDIG 29
M. Kendig

6. DEVELOPING FORMULATIONS OF GENERAL SEMANTICS 33
Elwood Murray

7. NEGLECTED FORMULATIONS 43
Robert P. Pula

8. TOWARD A SENSE OF UNITY 55
Charlotte S. Read

PART II. APPLICATIONS

9. A Semantic Experiment: Searching for Undefined Terms   63
    D. David Bourland, Jr.   Charles H. Morgan
                    Karen L. Ruskin

10. Relevance: General Semantics and a True Believer   73
                    Cecil J. Coleman

11. A Search for Relevance [1968]   85
                    S. I. Hayakawa

12. The Application of General Semantics to the Classifi-
    cation of Mentally Retarded   89
                    Dwight R. Kauppi

13. Psychedelic Experience and the Language Processes   95
                    Stanley Krippner

14. The Relevance of General Semantics to the Develop-
    ment of Sentence Structure in Children's Language . 117
                    Laura L. Lee

15. The Effects of Instruction in General Semantics on the
    Reading of Poetry 123
                    Howard F. Livingston

Comments on Dr. Livingston's Paper 127
        Neil Postman, Kenneth G. Johnson, Charlotte S. Read

16. General Semantics and Today's World 131
                    Harry E. Maynard

17. Genetic Transfer of Verbal Learning Disabilities 139
                    Sue Ann Pace

18. Some Reflections on Law-Language 145
                    Walter Probert

19. General Semantics as an Educative Tool in the Electri-
    cal Curriculum 151
                    Thaddeus J. Pula

xxvi

20. THE QUESTION OF RELEVANCE 163
        Anatol Rapoport

COMMENTS ON DR. RAPOPORT'S PAPER 176
        Allen Walker Read, D. David Bourland, Jr.

REPLY BY ANATOL RAPOPORT 184

21. GENERAL SEMANTICS AND ECONOMICS: SOME SPECULATIONS .. 189
        Bent Stidsen

22. THE NATURE OF PARADOX 203
        Mel Thistle

23. THE EXTENSIONAL WORLD OF FRANÇOIS RABELAIS 217
        Donald E. Washburn

PART III.   VARIATIONS

24. A MEDITATION ON WIGO 227
        J. Samuel Bois

25. RELEVANT AREAS OF RESEARCH IN HUMAN COMMUNICATION.. 233
        George A. Borden

26. CREATIVE INTERCHANGE, HENRY NELSON WIEMAN'S CONTRI-
    BUTION 243
        Deems M. Brooks   Thomas J. Pace, Jr.

27. JAZZ IMPROVISATION 251
        Alan P. Frederickson

28. TRIGANT BURROW: AN ALTERED APPROACH TO UNSANITY 255
        Alfreda S. Galt

29. SPEECH DISORDERS OF THE FLUENT 261
        Wendell Johnson

30. MULTILEVEL FEEDBACK THEORY OF MIND 267
        Ervin Laszlo

31. THE STRUCTURE OF COMMUNICATION 297
        Patrick Meredith

32. MANAGEMENT BY UNDERSTANDING 305
Thomas E. Miller   Bernard Sarachek

33. OVER-, UNDER-, AND MISCOMMUNICATION IN OUR SOCIETY ... 323
Maurice B. Mitchell

34. ON THE "MATTER" OF FRESHMAN ENGLISH 331
Albert Upton

PART IV.   APPENDIX

ALFRED KORZYBSKI: HIS CONTRIBUTIONS AND THEIR HISTORICAL
DEVELOPMENT 339
Charlotte S. Read

Part I

FORMULATIONS

James M. Broadus is Professor of Education and Chairman of the Department of Education and Physical Education at Transylvania College, Lexington, Kentucky. A native of Alabama, he received his A.B. and M.A. from the University of Alabama and his Ph.D. from Johns Hopkins University. He has been a member of several IGS Summer Seminar-Workshop teams.

1

STRUCTURE AND CIRCULARITY AS NEGLECTED FORMULATIONS

JAMES M. BROADUS

EXCEPT for *Science and Sanity,* books written about general semantics often fail to consider these two formulations that are central to any other considerations.

In the inadequate index to *Science and Sanity,* "structure" is accorded 170 references, more than any other single item, and many of the 170 are ff.'s. Its closest competitor is 108 for "abstracting and abstractions," followed by "language" with 95. Six of the ten parts of *Science and Sanity* include the word "structure" in their titles. Concern with structure is evident throughout.

Obviously, Korzybski did not neglect this formulation. Why do so many of the rest of us? It has not been completely ignored, but the indexes for Hayakawa's *Language in Thought and Action,* Lee's *Language Habits in Human Affairs,* and Johnson's *People in Quandries* have *no* entries for "structure."

These three widely read books may reveal the difficulty of treating structure on a "popular" level. It undoubtedly places something of a strain on any writer to try to explain everything at once and in simple terms.

However, it seems to me that somehow "structure" deserves better treatment than it has received. While being all encompassing, while remaining elusive, and while apparently failing to yield the simple delight and beauty associated with sudden "insight," I believe we cannot escape the responsibility for trying to restructure Alfred Korzybski's "structure" in our own nervous systems. Here are a few of Korzybski's uses of "structure."

3

We start with the negative $\bar{A}$ premise that words are *not* the un-speakable objective level, such as the actual objects outside of our skin *and* our personal feelings inside our skin. It follows that the only link between the objective and the verbal world is exclusively structural, necessitating the conclusion that the only content of all 'knowledge' is structural. Now structure can be considered as a complex of relations and ultimately as multi-dimensional order.[1]

Since 'knowledge,' then, is not the first order un-speakable objective level whether an object, a feeling.; structure, and so relations, becomes the only possible content of 'knowledge' *and of meanings.*[2]

If facts cannot be covered by given linguistic forms and methods, new forms, new structures, new methods are invented or created to cover the structure of facts in nature.[3]

. . . with our present low development and the lack of structural researches, we still keep an additive A language, which is, perhaps, able to deal with additive, simple, immediate, and comparatively unimportant issues, but is entirely unfit structurally to deal with principles which underlie the most fundamental problems of life.[4]

Linguistic and semantic researches show that the structure of all languages can, and *must,* be made similar to empirical structures; and then, also, the rest of humans can, and probably will, behave in a less silly and futile way than they have done in the past and are doing in the present.[5]

It is desirable to introduce consciously and deliberately *terms* of a *structure* similar to the structure of human knowledge, of our nervous system, and of the world, involving appropriate *s.r.*[6]

Are these uses of the word *structure* similar to the commonly accepted understanding of the word?

Turning to *Webster's Collegiate Dictionary,* 5th ed., we see "structure" defined as follows:

1: manner of building; form; construction   2: something constructed or built, as a building, a dam, a bridge   3: arrangement of parts, of organs, or of constituent tissues or particles, in a substance or body   4: figuratively, the interrelations of parts as dominated by the general character of the whole . . .

Even by dictionary definition there is no need for disturbing the structure that I hold for the Korzybskian use of the word *structure.* I particularly like the implication that there must be a structurer. Things, buildings, dams, etc., are not built without a builder. This definition also strikes a familiar note with *relation,* as in interrelation and as in relationship. The phrase, "dominated by the general character of the whole" surely brings recognition and agreement.

Most modern psychologists now accept, as Korzybski did, the proposition that the organism operates as a whole.

And "From the organism-as-a-whole, point of view structural ignorance must result in some semantic defectiveness."[7]

Harry Weinberg claims:

> The structure-as-a-whole has characteristics not found in any of the parts, and these non-additive characteristics are perhaps the key ones which "touch off" the feeling of beauty. But these "wholeness" characteristics cannot be pointed to, cannot be directly observed, cannot be discovered by analysis, for analysis, which is a concentration on the elements of a structure, immediately destroys the wholeness characteristics. The perception of structure-as-a-whole is of a higher level of abstraction than is perception of the elements of the structure, and the characteristics of this level, as would be expected, have different characteristics.[8]

Stuart Chase acknowledges his structure of Korzybskian structure by recounting the easy-to-understand analogy of map-territory:

> *If we wish to understand the world and ourselves, it follows that we should use a language whose structure corresponds to physical structure.* To this cardinal point Korzybski returns again and again. He cites the helpful illustration of a map. One cannot climb mountains or drive motorcars on a map, but it is a mighty useful aid in both activities. To be an aid, the map must have a structure similar to the territory on which we are to walk or drive. The trails and roads must bear similar relations, the towns must come in similar order to the actual trails, roads, and towns.[9]

To be valuable, the map must have a predictable relationship to the territory it is describing. This relationship is paramount in the search for structure.

According to Korzybski, the difficulty is in the search, not in the structure.

> Structure, then, becomes the only possible content of all knowledge; and all scientific technicalities, admittedly laborious and difficult, become only a necessary tool in the search for structure, with little, if any, intrinsic value, and are unnecessary for 'knowledge' as soon as in a given case the structure is discovered. This structure is always simple and can be given to children.[10]

If Korzybski is correct in saying that structure is the sole content of all knowledge, and I certainly find this position a fruitful one, and if knowledge has anything to do with predictability, then it seems that structuring and restructuring must be ongoing if we are to move toward less unsanity.

This includes the restructuring of the language we use to describe the structures. Structure becomes the only link we have to connect our verbal processes with empirical data.

Some order resulting from ordering, and some relations resulting from relating, precede the structuring leading to structure. Structure results from structuring; structures result from building, from our attempts to get along in this world, to evaluate, to determine values and value systems, to reach guidelines for decision making, etc.

Structure results when we transact, interact with our environments, when we reach some "conclusions" about what is "out there." We assume that structures of some sort—probably of many sorts—do happen "out there," and we hopefully build our inner structures to reflect as closely as possible the structures outside ourselves. We try to create maps that give some predictability to our transactions with the territory. We try to make maps that lead to evaluations about the territory, which allow transactional sanity.

And we must consider the probability of structures within structures. Thus, I have, in my nervous system, some structure for my automobile's engine, another structure for the whole car, including that of the engine; both being a part of the structure I hold for the problem of air pollution, increasing incidence of lung cancer, etc.

As each structure-as-a-whole is altered, thus changes the larger structure-as-a-whole. Since we are continually bombarded with raw materials for structural rearrangement, we expect to find some of our structures more stable than others.

As the scientist, with more reinforcing data, feels increasing confidence in his statements, thus our structures are structured more or less firmly depending on the consistency in the signals we receive from "out there." Lack of consistency is, of course, compounded by the reinforcing talk we carry on with ourselves about the inevitability of change, about the "bad luck" we experience, about the "mistreatment" we receive at the hands of others, about the "goodness of Mother Nature," etc.

Korzybski states:

> If we think *verbally,* we act as biased observers, and project onto the silent levels the structure of the language we use, and so remain in our rut of old orientations, making keen, unbiased, observations and creative work well-nigh impossible.[11]

In his "Introduction" to *Science and Sanity*, 2nd Ed., Korzybski wrote: ". . . any language involves structural assumptions which build up a *system of orientations* that may be racial, national, personal, etc." [12]

Since we all grow up in the society of our times, we assimilate the orientations of our culture—orientations that may be better suited to a former time.

As new "knowledge" (structure) is gained, it is our responsibility to reorient our personal structures. As long as things "out there" and "in there" change, structure will change.

Each structurer has to start with the raw materials he finds about himself. But we can get no assurance as to the order and relation of the raw materials as used by each builder. Thus, we can only guess about the resulting structure for each person.

Should we attempt to change our structures? For me, the question becomes a purely academic one if the process universe goes on. But if we are in some part the *active* (not merely passive) architects of the structures we carry around in our nervous systems, the *direction* of the change remains, at least in part, the responsibility of the architect, of the structurer.

Yet I must remember that you are a part of my universe, the same universe about which I build structures. When you move about in our universe, which contains those environments that we share, I assume you are behaving in accordance with the structures you have built. And I am further aware of your behavior—even your being there changes our process universe (the environmental transactions) from which I construct my structures. You may change my environment. I'm getting some new data from "out there." I am restructuring.

There are very few structures that do not involve circularity; in fact, many structures are primarily circular ones. The pattern formed, if we stand far enough away from a situation and see the overall structure of it, would show circularity as usually an integral part of that structure.

I have no argument with the designation of circularity as a neglected formulation. References in the literature are sparse indeed. The index of *Science and Sanity* carries only four entries under "circularity of knowledge." But it seems to me that this formulation is a very essential part of the formulations making up general semantics.

Berelson and Steiner offer ample evidence that the study of circularity is far more than an academic exercise. In their description of the characteristics of prejudice, they stress the circularity of self-image. Self-image or knowledge of self is an important component of "knowledge," and thus a part of the circle leading to and resulting from "knowledge."

These are some of the findings reported by Berelson and Steiner.

People typically do not appreciate how prejudiced they in fact are.

People prejudiced against one ethnic group tend to be prejudiced against others. [Prejudice tends to be generalized, although it is not usually directed equally at all ethnic groups.]

. . . stereotypes are quite resistant to change, although changing social and economic conditions can lead to shifts over a long period of time.

The common stereotypes of the society tend to be copied unconsciously in the mass media of communication.

The stereotype as a whole sets the emotional tone for the several traits within it.[13]

We set up our structure—our evaluations—we evaluate our evaluations, adjust to the results so as to remain comfortable, and proceed to pour back into the "vicious circle" an approving evaluation of the evaluation, i.e., our prejudices.

I want to know who I am. I listen. I hear some things about me and my kind. I don't very much like what I hear. I hear the same "bad" thing again and again and again. I still don't like it, but it's better than not being anything special. Yes, I guess that is how I am. I'll work very hard at being what I am. I am what I am. If the voices of authority have something to say about my image, it must have some validity, and I should accept it in my quest for self-understanding.

An individual over a period of time accepts the image placed on him by society, thus reinforcing society's image of him.

Korzybski seems to use "circularity" in at least two related but slightly different ways. He refers to circularity in the functioning of the nervous system, and to circularity as man-in-process, in transaction with his environments. Let us consider the following briefly.

Our present* knowledge of the nervous system is limited as regards its complexities and possibilities, but we know many structural facts which seem to be well established. One of these is that the human nervous system is more complex than that of any animal. Another is that the human cortex is of later origin than, and in a way an outgrowth from, the more central parts of the brain (which establishes a structure of *levels*). A third is that the interconnection of the parts of the nervous system is *cyclic*. A fourth is that the velocity of nerve currents is *finite*. The last fact is of serious structural importance, and, as a rule, disregarded.[14]

In a $\bar{A}$ ∞-valued system we reject the 'is' of identity; we cannot confuse orders of abstractions; we cannot identify words with the un-speakable objective levels or inferences with descriptions, and we cannot identify the different abstractions of different individuals. This semantic state of proper evaluation results in discrimination between the different orders of abstrac-

---

* (1933) Please note the word of caution here.

tions; *an automatic delay is introduced**—the cortex is switched completely into the nervous circuit. The semantic foundation is laid for 'higher mentality' and 'emotional balance.' [15]

Korzybski gave some extensional devices (indexes, dates, quotes, and hyphens) that one could use to react extensionally. In explaining them, he said:—

> In non-Aristotelian orientations, these extensional devices should be used habitually and permanently, with a slight motion of the hands to indicate absolute individuals, events, situations, etc., which change at different dates, also different orders of abstraction, etc. Thus thalamic factors become involved, *without which the coveted thalamo-cortical integration cannot be accomplished.*[16]

More recent information about brain function (particularly that about the reticular formation) indicates that Korzybski's caution regarding limited knowledge (in 1933) about the human nervous system was well taken. The later information also supports Korzybski's intuition that some such integrative device must be present in the brain.

The reticular formation supplies the "missing link." Now circularity—integration—between the thalamus and the cortex has a neurological basis.

In 1957 it was reported:

> So it would seem that in the waking state the RAS (reticular activating system) plays a part, in combination with the cortex, in focusing attention and probably in many other mental processes. . . . The astonishing generality of the RAS gives us a new outlook on the nervous system. Neurologists have tended to think of the nervous system as a collection of more or less separate circuits, each doing a particular job. It now appears that the system is much more closely integrated than had been thought.[17]

The implications of such an integration seemed of great importance to Korzybski.

> Before we can be fully human and, therefore, 'sane,' as a 'normal' human being should be, we must first know how to handle our nervous responses —a circular affair.
> A non-Aristotelian system must not disregard this *human-natural-history structural fact* of the inherent circularity of all physiological functions which in any form involve human 'knowing.' [18]

The other use of circularity is made clear by reference to the structural differential. One may "plug in" the peg to the event level and to the object level. Not only do we experience what is "out there," but we talk to our-

---

* The italics indicated here are mine.

selves about the experience, and then we sometimes, as a result of the experience *and* the subsequent talking, proceed to transact with the process level—we change things.

Korzybski reassures us.

> We had already encountered the inherent circularity in the structure of human knowledge, which admittedly is semantically disconcerting if not faced boldly. But, when recognized, this circularity is not only not vicious, but even adds to the interest and beauty of life and makes science more interesting.[19]

So we assume that things are "out there." We transact with some of them. We have some reactions to the transaction. We talk about the transaction and/or about the event. Sometimes, through talking about our experiences, we change the tone, the depth, and even the content of the experience. We, as a part of the process universe, influence that which influences us, which we influence, which influences us, etc., etc., etc.

REFERENCES

1. Korzybski, Alfred. *Science and Sanity: An Introduction to Non-Aristotelian Systems and General Semantics,* 4th ed. Lakeville, Conn.: International Non-Aristotelian Library Publishing Co., 1958, p. 20. Distributed by the Institute of General Semantics.
2. *Ibid.,* p. 22
3. *Ibid.,* p. 172.
4. *Ibid.,* p. 265.
5. *Ibid.,* p. 365.
6. *Ibid.,* p. 179.
7. *Ibid.,* p. 552.
8. Weinberg, Harry. *Levels of Knowing and Existence.* New York: Harper & Row, 1959, p. 133.
9. Chase, Stuart. *The Tyranny of Words.* New York: Harcourt, Brace & World, 1938, p. 80.
10. Korzybski, *op. cit.,* p. 544.
11. ———, *Manhood of Humanity,* 2d ed. Lakeville, Conn.: International Non-Aristotelian Library Publishing Co., 1950, p. xlix. Distributed by the Institute of General Semantics.
12. *Ibid.,* p. xix.
13. Berelson, Bernard and Steiner, Gary A. *Human Behavior: An Inventory of Scientific Findings.* New York: Harcourt, Brace & World, 1964, pp. 501–504.
14. Korzybski. *Science and Sanity,* p. 161.
15. *Ibid.,* p. 425.
16. *Ibid.,* p. xlviii.
17. French, J. D. "The Reticular Formation," *Scientific American,* Vol. 196, pp. 59, 60.
18. Korzybski. *Science and Sanity,* p. 12.
19. *Ibid.,* p. 220.

Sister Margaret Gorman is Professor of Psychology at Newton College of the Sacred Heart, Newton, Massachusetts. She
is author of *The Educational Implications of the Theory of
Meaning and Symbolism of General Semantics,* which was later
republished under the title, *General Semantics and Modern
Thomism,* with an introduction by S. I. Hayakawa.

2

GENERAL SEMANTICS TODAY

MARGARET GORMAN

ALTHOUGH the problem of communication in its widest sense is considered by many to be the chief problem in every area—international,
economic, religious, racial, educational, political, industrial, interpersonal
as well as intrapersonal—the place of general semantics as a theory of
communication in relation to these problems is *not* so generally recognized.

When efforts at communication are blocked at San Francisco State College, where the editor of *ETC.,* the general semantics quarterly, is acting
President, we can ask if this is not symbolic of the deeper problems of
communication now troubling us.

The original message of Korzybski had been: "The map is not the territory"; "be aware of the levels of abstraction"; "nothing is identical, or the
same." Now, many years after Korzybski's book was first published in
1933, these principles are so accepted that they have almost become proverbs.

Perhaps because we are now so aware (thanks to general semantics) of
the "map" and the "levels of abstraction," the dangers of the deeper problems of communication can be brought to the surface. We are acutely
aware that words mean different things to different people. "Democratic" to
students and to administrators means quite different things. "Church"
means one thing to the bishops of America and/or the Italian curia; it
means another thing, no doubt, to dissenting priests and young adults.
There is agreement *on the lack of agreement* on what words mean. This
agreement is due, no doubt, in part to the work of general semanticists
working directly as general semanticists or as, or with, professionals in
other fields.

11

But there always is the further question—how *far* is consensus needed? How to achieve it? How free are we to impose our meanings on others? General semantics can answer *"how"* do we disagree? but not "how far" *can* we disagree?

"How" depends on the "what" a thing is; but "how far" depends on the "why." Somehow there has been explicit denial by general semanticists of even the existence of the "why" question because it is, they have said, meaningless, because it is not scientific, because a preoccupation with finality, purpose, or goal is Aristotelian.* Yet, in time, general semanticists have to face that question: "how far?"

Currently one of the foremost leaders of general semantics is facing the question, "How far can violence go on a university campus?" His answer, while it appears to be absolute (and, as absolute, it would be a contradiction of general semantic principles), is, I think, in the finest sense, *relative* or *relational*. Violence must be considered in *relation* to the function (or goals) of a university, to the rights, which grow out of the *goals*, of each student as a human being, etc.

So general semantics may have warned us about the confusion over the map—different maps—and their relation to the territory. We have passed that stage now. We are asking not about the *map* but *about the territory*: how we relate to it and where do we want it to lead us? We are not asking for *different meanings* but *whether there is a meaning,* and how we can make something meaningful. We are asking this of schools and churches about democracy, peace, and freedom. We are asking for goals, or for direction, or for limits to our violence and movement.

The students at Harvard, like other students, have said in substance that their goal is "community." They seek to build a "community." Does *community* come from communication, or does communication only occur in a community? Is a community built, or drafted like a resolution, or treaty, or contract, or constitution is drafted? A community cannot be built on words. It is built on respect for persons as persons. It is basically nonverbal. A community is not a map; it is the territory. It implies faith and trust and love and hope. These are nonverbal, non-point-at-able, "nonmappable." General semantics can help me be aware that my *words* are not the answer. But general semantics cannot give me *the answer*. General semantics helps me in conversation with the outer world; it does not help in dialogue with the inner world. This does not mean there is no answer, or that general semantics is wrong.

---

* Compare with the paper by Hanno Hardt, Chapter 3.—Editor.

It only leads me to ask if we are not at a stage "beyond" general semantics? Perhaps the Paris peace talks need the principles of general semantics so that real communication can begin. Then the other question must be faced. Not *"how* shall we talk with each other," but "what are our goals?" How far can each of us go? How much can each of us give? General semanticists used to say that these were *meaningless* questions. Can they still say that today?

I am grateful to general semantics for challenging my maps, for helping me converse with the outer world. The world of man's hopes and fears and goals and loves are his inner world where he works out his deepest meanings, and asks the "why," not the "how" or "what" questions. At least now general semantics no longer seems to deny these problems. Those who ask them need help from general semanticists to clarify their *maps.* In turn, I ask of them, where do we go with the "why" and the "how far" questions?

Hanno Hardt, a native of Germany, studied law at Kiel and Heidelberg universities before receiving his M.A. and Ph.D. from Southern Illinois University. He is Assistant Professor of Journalism, University of Iowa, and the author of several articles on mass media in both German and United States journals.

3

GENERAL SEMANTICS AND SCIENTIFIC ETHICS

HANNO HARDT

WHEN Alfred Korzybski wrote *Manhood of Humanity* in 1921, he developed a theory of man and culture that became the basis for the teachings of general semantics throughout his career. In his major work, *Science and Sanity,* Korzybski utilized the philosophical framework of the nature of man in his design of a science of neurosemantic and neurolinguistic reactions of man to his semantic environment, and proposed that unconscious assumptions about language and reality must be the main concern of any problem-solving mechanism.

He stressed, in particular, the scientific aspects of general semantics, and throughout his writings recognized science and scientific approaches to the study of man as the only legitimate modes of inquiry.

However, the difficulties of this approach became quite obvious in Korzybski's discussion of ethics. One often hears that everything seems to be a matter of semantics. This paper suggests some limits to the therapeutic effects of general semantics by tracing Korzybski's view of man, and the role of general semantics in providing society with a program or directive that could help clarify contemporary thoughts on human conduct and individual responsibility.

Korzybski's school of general semantics has generally been linked to logical positivism, the Vienna Circle, and the Polish school of analytical philosophy,[1] although it has also been held that Korzybski utilized ideas and concepts of many different individuals.[2]

His major contribution to philosophy, and the basis for his general semantics was the definition of man as a "time-binder," which he developed in *Manhood of Humanity*. It was the time-binding capacity of man that distinguished him from the plant and animal life around him. Korzybski called it the only natural criterion, and felt that it could be found "to embrace the whole of the natural laws, the natural ethics, the natural philosophy, the natural sociology, the natural economics, and the natural governance, to be brought into the education of time-binders." He added that "everything which is really 'time-binding' is in the Human Dimension; therefore, it will represent every quality that is implied in such words as—good, just, right, beautiful." [3] Time-binding was also described as the unique survival mechanism of human beings," [4] which meant that problems of human survival became problems of communication, and general semantics offered a scientific approach to the solution of these problems.

Korzybski also outlined modes of ethical behavior of the time-binding class, stressing the importance of the law of human nature. He said:

> . . . to live ethically is to live in accordance with the law of human nature, and when it is clearly seen that man is a natural being, a part of nature literally, then it will be seen that the law of human nature—the only possible rules for ethical conduct—are no more supernatural and no more man-made than is the law of gravitation, or any other natural law.[5]

And he admitted that one of the greatest difficulties in the search for ethics has been the misconception of the nature of man based on the limited solutions of Aristotelian philosophy, and Euclidean and Newtonian science.

Korzybski was convinced that the zoological solution that described the animal nature of humans had led to grave consequences in the social sciences, ethics, law, and economics since it applied animal logic that had resulted in "animal" ethics and a survival-of-the-fittest theory not suited for human beings. He seemed to voice Thomas H. Huxley's notion that the law of survival of the fittest, while an appropriate and important evolutionary hypothesis in the biological sciences, was not an ethical principle, but that man must do his best to overcome the law of the jungle to establish ethical ideals.[6] Korzybski declared that survival of the fittest for man must mean survival in time, which he defined in terms of "intellectual or spiritual competition, struggle for excellence." [7]

He also rejected the notion of the mythological nature of man (man as a mixture of "animality and divinity") as void of natural law, and said that "scientifically judged, they are mythological absurdities—muddle-headed chattering of crude and irresponsible metaphysics—well-meaning, no doubt, but silly and deadly in their effects upon the interests of mankind, vitiating ethics, law, economics, politics, and government." [8]

Korzybski proposed, instead, a scientific concept or definition of man in which questions of ethics became questions of fact, thus taking ethics into the realm of scientific inquiry. He emphasized the application of mathematical philosophy and rigorous scientific thinking to discover the "secret and source of ethics."[9] This was a familiar trend in 19th- and early 20th-century philosophy when the ideas of scientific philosophy made their rounds in Europe. Moritz Schlick, a prominent member of the Vienna Circle whose ideas on the philosophy of language are very similar to those of general semantics,[10] explored the question of scientific ethics. He concluded that if there are ethical questions that have meaning, and are therefore capable of being answered, then ethics is a science, and he viewed ethics as a system of knowledge that could be explored scientifically.[11] In Korzybski's framework of human engineering, ethics as a study of what is good or bad became whatever agreed or disagreed with the natural activity of the "civilization-producing" energies of humanity.[12]

However, this view was by no means undisputed, and the question of whether one could scientize ethics and should do so, even if it were possible, remained. As for Korzybski, part of the answer underlying his comments toward the end of his career was that the progress of general semantics and its application to the contemporary world problems was slow, that the "obstacles were serious," and that it was not a simple task "to make the necessary revisions of existing theories." [13]

But much earlier there had been a realization among philosophers that all problems are not merely verbal, and thus could be treated empirically. This was particularly true in the case of ethical questions and the development of ethical systems.

The existence of nonverbal problems was recognized by Ludwig Wittgenstein, one of Korzybski's sources, who claimed that "ethics is supernatural, and our words only will express facts." He summarized his ideas about ethics by pointing out that:

> . . . ethics so far as it springs from the desire to say something about the ultimate meaning of life, the absolute good, the absolute valuable, can be no science. What it says does not add to our knowledge in any sense. But it is a document of a tendency in the human mind which I personally cannot help respecting deeply, and I would not for my life ridicule it.[14]

Part of this notion was reiterated by Schlick who said that a system of scientific ethics could not establish a hierarchy of moral order since criteria for absolute values were lacking.[15]

Rudolf Carnap excluded ethical statements from scientific inquiry since they were beyond empirical methods of verification, an idea that is also reflected in the thinking of A. J. Ayer.[16] Jan Lukasiewicz, whose many-valued logic was used by Korzybski in the construction of his "non-Aristotelian" system, admitted in 1946 that he could not provide a system of scientific philosophy.[17] And Tadeusz Kotarbinski developed the concept of an ethics independent of scientific philosophy, and aimed at providing a broad guide for moral conduct in everyday life.[18]

Korzybski's emphasis on the time-binding characteristics of mankind led to an undue emphasis on semantics and the optimistic view that all problems can be solved because they are semantic problems. His statement: "man's achievement rests upon the use of symbols. For this reason we must consider ourselves as a symbolic class of life, and those who rule the symbols, rule us,"[19] has been regarded as a distortion of the role of language in society, and a misinterpretation of the relationship between language and reality. In his critical analysis of general semantics, Albrecht Neubert wrote that man in his social and economic habitat acts and reacts without realizing the nature of his actions, and that Korzybski's statement that "all our human institutions follow the structure of our language, but we never think of that," should be reversed. This argument is based on dialectical materialism which in assessing the relationship of language and society demands as an objective criterion the recognition of material, social relationships as existing, but not perceived as such.[20] Neubert's criticism was directed toward Korzybski's statement that productivity is the materialization of the time-binding capacity of human beings that unduly emphasized communicative abilities.

In addition, man is not helplessly exposed to his "semantic environment," but must realize that this environment is created by the historical, social, and economic forces of society. And as the environment changes so does the language; words and meanings of words can and do change under different social or cultural conditions. The point has been made that the continuity of language is only possible because of its ability to change.[21] The problem is further complicated by the fact that general semantics expects the same behavior from mankind that it expects from an individual. Its theoretical value is thus reduced to a subjective-empirical level at which "verbal maps" do not reflect accurately the patterns of changing society, and which makes subjective, emotional experiences of reality the aim of knowledge.[22]

When genuine problems that can be scientifically formulated become semantic problems, and when philosophical problems such as questions of ethics and ethical systems become merely verbal, they will share the imperfection of language. Finally, thought processes are reduced to language, and reflect its imperfections as well.

Furthermore, in its treatment of language, the system of general semantics seemed unable to distinguish, for instance, between accidental word associations on the basis of specific, individual experiences in learning situations, and the universal *Erkenntniswert* of words. Although a word, as such, is not to be confused with the concrete thing ("the word is not the thing") or a relationship in the environment, it can express knowledge that is deep, rich in content, and true in its reflection of reality.[23]

These shortcomings of Korzybski's theories are based on his failure to present in *Science and Sanity* a scientifically sound blueprint for the solution of both philosophical and pragmatic questions of everyday life. Adam Schaff called the book "morbid and marked by monomania" and "a strange mixture of *Dichtung und Wahrheit*," and left little doubt about his opinion of Korzybski's scientific standards.[24] Anatol Rapoport characterized *Science and Sanity* as the obscure work of a dilettante, and added that it was not based on empirical research.[25]

Margaret Schlauch commented, "To say that man is a 'time-binding animal' because he has memory does not justify the claim to an Einsteinian approach. It is rather an attempt to conceal truism behind pretentious terminology." [26]

The dangers of general semantics as a unique problem-solving device were also recognized by Barbara Herrnstein Smith, who referred to general semantics as "the poor man's logical positivism," thus reflecting upon the process of leveling and oversimplification, which had been applied to a sophisticated school of philosophy that reflected man's consciousness of language in the twentieth century.[27]

Korzybski's view of man and his development of an ethical system was an ideal; it failed because of the absence of rigorous methods of scientizing his philosophy of the law of human nature. His flight from the world of nonverbal problems did not produce a workable solution to ethical and moral questions. Those members of the Vienna Circle and the Polish school of analytical philosophy who studied the problems of scientific philosophy extensively had realized the dilemma of scientific ethics decades ago. Perhaps general semantics today has reached the end of a dead-end street in its search for solutions to all problems of life.*

Years ago it was suggested that:

> . . . semantics and sanity are connected, without doubt, and the valid relations between them will be explored in due time. The authentic investigation will be made . . . by persons actuated by a social philosophy more generous

---

* See the paper by Anatol Rapoport, Chapter 20.—EDITOR.

than any evinced by current writers on the subject. Such a study must be made, at the very least, by those who are not seeking escape from the actuality of nonverbal problems. It must be made by students who accept the existence of our material world, with everything in it that is unpleasing to us now; and who are willing to fuse theory and practice in realistic efforts toward its amelioration. For such students, the lore of semantics will become an instrument of social progress instead of a technique of social evasion.[28]

Or to paraphrase Lukasiewicz again, the work that is waiting for future general semanticists is gigantic, but will have to be done by minds much more powerful than any that have ever existed before on earth.

REFERENCES

1. The Vienna Circle came into being in the early 1920's. It consisted of men like Moritz Schlick, Rudolf Carnap, Otto Neurath, Herbert Feigl, Friedrich Waismann, Edgar Zisel, Victor Kraft, Philipp Frank, Karl Menger, Kurt Gödel, and Hans Hahn.
   Among the most prominent members of the Polish school of analytical philosophy are Alfred Tarski, Maria Kokoszynska, Leon Chwistek, Jan Lukasiewicz, Kazimierz Ajdukiewicz, Tadeuz Kotarbinski, and Stanislaw Lesniewski.
2. Korzybski dedicated *Science and Sanity* to the works of 55 individuals which have "greatly influenced my enquiry."
3. Korzybski, Alfred. *Manhood of Humanity*. New York: E. P. Dutton & Company, 1921, p. 70.
4. Hayakawa, S. I. "The Aims and Tasks of General Semantics: Implications of the Time-Binding Theory," *ETC.*, VIII, p. 243.
5. Korzybski. *Manhood of Humanity*, p. 14.
6. Huxley, Thomas H. *Evolution and Ethics* (1893). Cited by Brand Blanshard, in *Reason and Goodness*. London: Allen & Unwin, 1961, p. 381.
7. Korzybski. *Manhood of Humanity*, p. 147.
8. *Ibid.*, p. 87.
9. *Ibid.*, p. 13.
10. According to Anatol Rapoport in "General Semantics and the 'Behavioral Sciences,' " *ETC.*, XIII, p. 57, who said that Schlick's ideas on the philosophy of language "bear a close affinity to those of general semantics."
11. Schlick, Moritz. *Problems of Ethics*. New York: Prentice-Hall, Inc., 1939, p. 1.
12. Korzybski, *Manhood of Humanity*, p. 194.
13. Quoted in an editorial, *"Release of Atomic Energy," ETC*, III, p. 144.
14. Wittgenstein, Ludwig. "Lecture on Ethics," *Philosophical Review*, LXXIV, 1954, pp. 7–12.
15. A discussion of Schlick's concept of ethics by Victor Kraft, in *Der Wiener Kreis*. New York: Springer Verlag, 1968, p. 168.
16. *Ibid.*, p. 167.
17. Skolimowski, Henryk. *Polish Analytical Philosophy*. London: Routledge & Kegan Paul, 1967, p. 71.
18. *Ibid.*, pp. 81–84.

19. Korzybski, Alfred. *Science and Sanity: An Introduction to Non-Aristotelian Systems and General Semantics,* 4th ed. Lakeville, Conn.: International Non-Aristotelian Library Publishing Co., 1958, p. 76. Distributed by the Institute of General Semantics.
20. Neubert, Albrecht. *Semantischer Positivismus in den USA.* Halle: Max Niemeyer Verlag, 1962, p. 264.
21. *Ibid.,* p. 296.
22. *Ibid.,* p. 278.
23. *Ibid.,* p. 271. For penetrating criticism see Max Black, "Korzybski's General Semantics," *Language and Philosophy.* New York: Cornell University Press, 1949.
24. Schaff, Adam. *Introduction to Semantics.* London: Pergamon Press, 1964, pp. 93–94.
25. Rapoport, Anatol. "What is Semantics," in S. I. Hayakawa, *Language, Meaning and Maturity.* New York: Harper & Row, 1954, p. 6.
26. Schlauch, Margaret. "Semantics as Social Evasion," *Science and Society,* 6:4, 1942, pp. 318–19.
27. Smith, Barbara Herrnstein. "The New Imagism," *Midway,* 9:3, 1969, p. 35.
28. Schlauch, *op. cit.,* p. 330.

Kenneth G. Johnson is Associate Professor and Chairman of the Department of Mass Communication, University of Wisconsin–Milwaukee. He has his Ph.D. in Chemistry, M.S. in Journalism, and Ph.D. in Mass Communication, all from the University of Wisconsin. He has been a member of the staffs of the IGS Summer Seminar-Workshops since 1960.

4

INVARIANCE UNDER TRANSFORMATION *

KENNETH G. JOHNSON

THOSE of us who teach general semantics or write about it do a pretty good job, it seems to me, of emphasizing the relativity of human observations, of stressing change, of insisting on the importance of dating to indicate an awareness of the process character of "reality." Some of our students, I'm afraid, come away with a few quick clichés—"everything is relative;—the only thing we can be sure of is change;—that's *your* opinion" (implying it therefore has little value)—untempered by a deeper understanding of Korzybski. The result is likely to be a kind of nihilism—a denial that there is any basis for agreement, any reason for preferring one opinion over another, one theory over another.

Perhaps we have to go back and emphasize one of the neglected formulations of Korzybski, that of "invariance under transformation." Like indexing, the notion of invariance under transformation is borrowed from mathematics, but generalized by Korzybski into a method of evaluation that can be applied to all areas of human concern.

A whirlpool provides a dramatic illustration of invariance under transformation. The transformation—the change—is obvious. From moment to moment we can see the change. Yet some aspect, the "something" we call "whirlpool," remains invariant, unchanged, or relatively so.

You and I are like whirlpools—different from moment to moment, yet somehow the same—transformed, yet in some way invariant.

In teaching the extensional device called "dating," we are likely to emphasize change; indeed, Korzybski introduced it for that purpose—to emphasize an aspect of the "territory" that is often overlooked in our map-

---

* Compare with paper by Ervin Laszlo, Chapter 30.—EDITOR.

making. But when we say "George [1968] is not George [1965]," we are not only calling attention to change; we continue to use the term "George" to imply something invariant. We are saying, in effect, that "George has changed, but George is still George." Something has remained invariant in spite of transformations.

We must be careful here not to interpret "invariance" as "permanence," for we are often talking about the *relative* invariance we perceive in the world around us.

> In general terms, the structure of the external world is such that we deal always on the objective levels with absolute individuals, with absolute differences. The structure of the human nervous system is such that it abstracts, or generalizes, or integrates., in higher orders, and so finds similarities, discovering often invariant (sometimes relatively invariant) relations.[1]
>
> Thus, a process of being iron, or a rock, or a table, or you, or me, may be considered, for practical purposes, as a temporal and average invariance of function on the sub-microscopic level. Under the action of other processes, the process becomes structurally transformed into different relational complexes, and we die, and a table or rock turns into dust, and so the invariance of this function vanishes.[2]

The only absolute invariance we are likely to find is in a self-contained system such as pure mathematics. And as Einstein said, "As far as the laws of mathematics refer to reality, they are not certain; and as far as they are certain, they do not refer to reality." [3]

It would be well to distinguish between what I shall call "invariance by definition" and "invariance under transformation."

When we create a category, we look for certain similarities (invariants), and ignore differences. Our category is then defined in terms of the invariants. If our definition is operational, we should be able to distinguish clearly those items that belong within that category (have these invariant characteristics) from those that do not.

An operational definition tells us *what to do* and *what to observe* to bring the invariant characteristics or effects within our experience. The invariants pointed out in the operational definition are not assumed to be there to begin with, but are a product of our operations and our (selective) perceptions—an interaction between the observer and the observed.

The process of defining or categorizing, though an important, sometimes critical, first step, in itself adds little to our knowledge. A more powerful notion is that of "invariance under transformation," in which we deal not only with definitions but with relationships.

When we record with a tape recorder, vibrations in the air are transformed into movements of a diaphragm that are transformed into electrical impulses that are transformed into magnetic impulses that are transformed into magnetic patterns. When we play back the recording, a series of transformations takes place that result in vibrations in the air very similar to those we recorded. A high fidelity recording could be described as one in which there is a maximum invariance throughout these transformations. Yet we might find it difficult to specify what remains invariant, except to say "certain relationships."

But let us begin with a simpler example of invariance under transformation taken from mathematics:

> Let us take as an example, for instance, the transformation of a set of integers 1, 2, 3. Let us suppose that the given law of transformation is given by the function $y = 2x$. The result would be the manifold of even integers 2, 4, 6. We see that integers are transformed into integers; therefore the characteristic of being an integer is preserved; in other words, this characteristic is an invariant under the given transformation $y = 2x$, but the values of the integers are not preserved.[4]

So far we are dealing with the "rules of the game" of a self-contained system. But if we can establish correspondence between mathematical quantities and physical quantities (measurements of the external world), we can establish a similarity of structure between nonverbal and verbal levels, based on invariance of relations that are found or discovered in both.

Probably the simplest kind of structural correspondence is illustrated by house numbers. In this case, the invariant *order* of the houses can readily be mapped with a number system that consists of an invariant *ordered* series.

At a more complex level, a physicist may take a number of measurements of the time it takes an object to fall certain distances. He may notice that distance appears to be a *function* of time. If he then establishes a correspondence between the physical measurements and the mathematical quantities, he finds that the *same relations* hold for the physical quantities as for the corresponding mathematical quantities. He has established a similarity of structure between the nonverbal and the verbal (mathematical, in this case) world. The relationship (first established by Galileo) may be expressed $D = \frac{1}{2}gt^2$ where g is a constant. This relationship proved to be invariant *within certain limits*.[5]

> The law of gravity is a higher-order abstraction, and like all higher-order abstractions, it is static. Based upon many highly accurate observations, it is a summary and idealization (generalization) of certain invariances in relationships among objects we can discern by ignoring or controlling certain in-

dividual differences, such as wind velocity, pressure, etc. Thus we can apply it to falling bullets, or falling water, or falling leaves; it is an invariant under transformation. On the verbal level, these laws of nature, like the equations of pure mathematics, are absolutely invariant under transformation. When applied to the non-verbal world, they are relatively invariant, and have a very high degree of probability of being correct and a wide and accurate range of predictability.[6]

A series of right triangles provides another example of invariance of relations. Let us assume that each triangle differs in some respect (size, shape) from the others. But they would all be called "right triangles" (invariance by definition), and certain relationships hold for all of them: The square of the hypotenuse is equal to the sum of the squares of the other two sides $(h^2 = a^2 + b^2)$—relationships that remain invariant under transformation.

So far my examples have been chosen from mathematics because mathematics has proven to be a highly effective language for expressing and manipulating relationships. Korzybski considered it the only language that, at present, has a structure similar to that of the world and the human nervous system. However, the search for invariance, for order amid seeming chaos, is not confined to scientists or mathematicians. We all have a longing—no, a need—for stability, for predictability, for invariance in a changing world. When we ask, "Will drug x cure disease y?" we are seeking an invariant relationship. When we ask, "Should a child be taught to read before he goes to school?" we are seeking an invariant relationship between certain actions on our part (teaching), and certain long-range benefits. (In this case the "benefits" would have to be defined operationally before we could begin to answer the question.)

> The attempts to make less exact sciences (like psychology) more exact have been mainly attempts to find invariants with which to build operational definitions. The so-called intelligence quotient (I.Q.) is a familiar example. "Intelligence" is quite an old concept in psychology, but its usefulness has been questionable because no operational definition of it has ever been given, so that one was never sure just what to observe to be aware of intelligence. The I.Q., on the other hand, is easy to define operationally: give such and such a test and compute the score. The meaningfulness of the I.Q., however, depends on its invariance. To the extent that it is invariant (and it is within limits), the I.Q. measures "something," and thus is at least meaningful. To the extent that the score enables a psychologist to predict *other* things about the individual, for example, the ease with which he will perform certain tasks *other* than those in the I.Q. test, the I.Q. is useful.[7]

Usefulness, in this case, as in the case of most generalizations, depends upon an invariant relationship that makes predictions possible. And, like many operational definitions, this definition involves measurements (test scores) that lend themselves to expressing relationships and to being manipulated with the powerful tools of mathematics.

> Scientific abstractions point to invariants which ordinarily would not have been observed. For example, no amount of passive observation, no matter how astute, could have established the invariance underlying such seemingly diverse processes as respiration of animals, burning of substances, and rusting of iron. Yet there is a process underlying all of these—oxidation. On the basis of the discovery of such invariants, predictions can be made. The fulfillment of the prediction tests the stability of the invariant.[8]

Obviously, the search for "invariance under transformation" began long before the term was invented. What, then, is the advantage of such a cumbersome term? "Invariance under transformation"—like the terms *order, relations, structure,*—is a nonelementalistic term; that is, it can be used equally well in talking about the external world, the human nervous system, or our symbol systems. The tape recorder mentioned earlier provides an excellent example of invariance under transformation in the external world. Studies of perception explore invariance under transformation in the human nervous system. A lexicographer is directly concerned with invariance under transformation within our symbol system. But the profound impact of this notion lies in the fact that it permits us to talk about relations in the external world in a language *similar in structure* to that external world; that is, it provides the kind of language that enables us to make verbal "maps" that are similar in structure to the "territory."

> It seems that *relations,* because of the possibility of discovering them and their invariance in *both* worlds, are, in a way, more 'objective' than so-called objects. We may have a science of 'invariance of relations,' but we could not have a science of permanence of things. . . .[9]

What I am suggesting, then, is that we rediscover and reexamine this neglected formulation. Perhaps we can use it in teaching our students ways of seeking agreement, reasons for preferring one opinion over another, methods of evaluating one theory against another.

REFERENCES

1. Korzybski, Alfred. *Science and Sanity: An Introduction to Non-Aristotelian Systems and General Semantics,* 4th ed. Lakeville, Conn.: International Non-Aristotelian Library Publishing Co., 1958, p. 263. Distributed by the Institute of General Semantics.
2. *Ibid.,* p. 285.

3. *Ibid.,* p. 66.
4. *Ibid.,* p. 286.
5. Einstein's law of gravity is far more general. That is, it expresses a relationship that remains invariant under groups of transformations.
6. Weinberg, Harry L. *Levels of Knowing and Existence.* New York: Harper & Row, 1959, p. 205.
7. Rapoport, Anatol. *Operational Philosophy.* New York: Harper & Row, 1953; John Wiley & Sons, Inc., 1965, p. 28.
8. *Ibid.,* p. 28.
9. Korzybski, *op cit.,* p. 285.

5

A NOTE BY M. KENDIG [1]

M. KENDIG

I WOULD very much go along with Lee Thayer's negative reactions (or evaluations) [2] in regard to the "general semantics *movement*" as exhibited in the journal *ETC.,* and in the behaviors of many persons who call themselves "general semanticists." In my lexicon, "movement" falls in the class of pejorative terms. Such has been the course of "popularization" (pejorative) of the discipline during the past 20 years (1947 to date) that the last thing I would call myself is a "general semanticist." I haven't the vaguest notion what the term represents to a person who uses it. I would have to question him/her in a rather thoroughgoing way.

After 34 years of study, training and self-training, editing, and teaching, I feel only mildly secure or justified in labeling myself a "non-Aristotelian," or to make it more limited, a "Korzybskian." So far as my experience goes, I would guess that I have known about 30 individuals who have in some degree adequately, by my standards, mastered this highly general, very simple, very difficult *system* of orientation and *method* of evaluating—reversing as it must *all* our "cultural conditioning," neurological "canalization," etc.[3]

Learning to *un*learn, for me, best describes the process of learning the discipline theoretically (verbally) and organismically. It is a very tough continuous "fight" to maintain a high degree of conditionality, against identification. So far as I know, this mechanism functions for the survival of all types of organisms except humans, i. e., a symbolic class of life. But here I must stop or I'll be involved in explicating dimensionality in time-binding theory, etc.

To me the *great error* Korzybski made—and I carried on, financial necessity—and for which we pay the price today in such criticisms as Dr. Thayer's, consisted in not restricting ourselves to training very thoroughly a *very few* people who would be competent to utilize the discipline in various fields and to train others. We should have done this before encouraging anyone to "popularize" or "spread the word" (horrid phrase), in societies for general semantics, by talking *about* general semantics instead of learning, using, etc., the methodology to *change* our essential epistemologic assumptions, premises, etc. (unconscious or conscious), i.e., the *un*learning basic to learning to learn.

Yes, large numbers of people do enjoy making a philosophy of general semantics; it saves the pain of rigorous training in a methodology so simple and general and limited that it sounds obvious when *said,* yet so difficult. The more you struggle to *use* it, the deeper the difficulties become, the more you become aware of them.

Here's one example of a "general semanticist" who "knows all about it." He might say, to put words in his mouth: "Because I am a scientist—a mathematical biophysicist, a researcher and all that—I don't have to train myself in such baby stuff.[4] Poor old Korzybski is out-of-date, but his stuff is good for the ignorant man in the street, and my do-gooder friends are democratically helping such by philosophizing about g.s., and making it easy by saying it all in 'everyday' language, etc." That summarizes some attitudes this scientist might exhibit in his talkings and writings regarding general semantics according to my long observations.

Now what are we talking about when we speak of Korzybski's non-Aristotelian system and general semantics? We are talking about the principles of nonidentity and nonelementalism; we are talking about training in nonidentity, that is, *consciousness of abstracting,* the *orders of abstractions,* the mechanism of *multiordinality,* the use of the "operators" called the *extensional devices*/techniques, etc. I believe that these terms stand for what we may call Korzybski's originations. (Otherwise, as he clearly says over and over, his work is *not* original, it depends on, is drawn from, the work of many many men of many many generations—one could say sweepingly all the "thinkings" of the West, the Indo-Europeans, i.e. time-binding.) Korzybski synthesized and systematized some of this "knowledge," past and present, for his purposes. But I'm "fighting" a different battle here, though not unrelated to my example.

Neurolinguistically-evaluationally, Korzybski based his *system* on the denial of the validity of the *IS of Identity* as a form of representation. The map is *not* the territory it represents. (The *IS of Predication* becomes a *special case* of the *IS of Identity.*)

The map analogy applies not only to language as such, but includes what we call our perceptions, our thinkings, our conscious and unconscious reactions, all goings-on in our nervous system or, better, the totality of our organism-as-a-whole reacting/interacting electrodynamically with environments. This complex whole we call the silent unspeakable levels—the territory. Thus Korzybski's crisp summary—"Whatever you say something *is*, it *is not.*"

Now we get to my example: This distinguished "general semanticist" in the July, 1967, issue of *Scientific American,* (p. 50), writes:

> More recently, Alfred Korzybski, the founder of the "non-Aristotelian" system called "general semantics," based his system on the theory that a fundamental contradiction exists between language and reality. "Whatever you say *about* something," Korzybski used to say, "it is not." (The Moroccan scholar's remark [above] about the diagonal of a square is in a way an expression of this attitude.)

First: Obviously, (I assume), you see the difference: Korzybski said, "Whatever you say something *Is,* it is not"— a generalized denial of the *"Is of Identity."* He is reported to have said, "Whatever you say *about* something, it is not." It seems to me that any careful reader of the above quote would label Korzybski as pretty much an idiot. Most people I have met, on questioning, would agree that something they were telling me *about* was not the happening they were describing. However, if I throw a piece of universe (I call an apple) at a John Smith and ask, "What did I throw at you?" (provided he understands English)—maximum probability—I can predict that, in about 9 out of 10 cases, he will *say* "It *is* an apple."

NOTES

1. This short note was prepared in January and February, 1968, and was "inspired" by a letter from Elwood Murray. It was not written for publication, but was contributed in response to the Editor's query, to appear only as an unfinished, offhand note.
2. An apparently similar letter to Thayer about the same time prompted his reply by letter, which is printed, in part, in the March, 1968, IGS *News,* and this is the gist of what I refer to here as his negative reactions (or evaluations).
3. Legitimate *all,* I believe, on deeper levels of analysis.
4. See Korzybski's "Letter to Co-Workers, September 1934." Supplement I, p. 5. Alfred Korzybski. *Collected Papers,* 1969.

Elwood Murray received his Ph.D. from the University of Iowa in 1931. He became Director of the Institute of General Semantics in 1967, and Emeritus Professor and Director, School of Speech, University of Denver in 1962. He is past President of the National Society for the Study of Communication, a Fellow of the American Speech and Hearing Association, and Institute of General Semantics, and author of several books including *The Speech Personality* and *Integrative Speech.*

6

DEVELOPING FORMULATIONS OF GENERAL SEMANTICS

ELWOOD MURRAY

CLAIMED only as an introduction, the fountainhead for general semantics remains in Alfred Korzybski's massive volume, *Science and Sanity.*[1] As an enrollee in Korzybski's intensive seminars, I remember that we were warned that the work was incomplete; that what had been presented would need to change as the various science source areas changed. But with Korzybski and his immediate successors, such as M. Kendig and Charlotte Read, there was an equal and justifiable concern that the work be studied deeply, that time be taken to assimilate it; that there be no attempt at teaching unless thoroughly internalized. Korzybski was heard to say that his chief enemies were his students, some of whom tended to go completely overboard in enthusiasm, others of whom angrily rejected his ideas, while neither group had more than a superficial acquaintance with the work.

Among what might be called the first generation of general semantics scholars were S. I. Hayakawa,[2] Wendell Johnson,[3] Irving J. Lee,[4] Francis Chisholm,[5] J. Samuel Bois,[6] Harry L. Weinberg,[7] and Elwood Murray.[8] Their textbooks are widely used today to introduce general semantics. There were many others whose work and lives were also affected by their exposure to the direct teaching of Korzybski. There was considerable mutual influence among those who attended the Korzybski seminar-workshops together.

Nevertheless, as was to be expected, these scholars interpreted Korzybski in light of their own backgrounds and interests. As comparisons of their writings with each other and with *Science and Sanity* were made, the inevitable question arose—*whose* general semantics? This question is a sort of measure of the distance the discipline has to go to become a science. For instance, there is great agreement among medical textbooks on smallpox. There are practically no differences among them within a specific decade. Although there will be lags, sometimes of several years, such textbooks change substantially only as research provides new and significant data.

In the main, general semantics textbooks supplement each other in interesting and valuable ways. With *Science and Sanity* as their basic reference, and without undue redundancy, they are substantially in agreement on what are called the basic formulations of general semantics. Undue redundancy was avoided by the use of original illustrations with new concreteness and fresh explanatory matter. At the same time, little has been done by these authors and other researchers to "fill out" the formulations by drawing on relevant findings from the other, particularly the behavioral, sciences.

We need only to mention *Psychological Abstracts* as one illustration of neglect of massive available resources of research findings relevant to general semantics. Hundreds of research findings from the various "schools" of psychology and psychiatry have been appearing for decade after decade under the rubrics of sensation, perception, cognition, language, personality, speech disorders, etc. Of particular importance are many developments in the journals concerned with general systems, cybernetics, information theory, group dynamics, organization theory, game theory, psycholinguistics, the existential, phenomenal, and, in fact, all of the exploding organismic and evolutionary "movements" that have been underway for many years. These activities, not incompatible with general semantics, are all in the same deep river bed out of which general semantics evolved. Our failure to keep abreast of the developments in these areas continues to deprive general semantics of the effectiveness it might have in the unifying of the diverse activities and disciplines concerned with human development.

No one knows, at present, the potential of these diverse efforts, for the amelioration of human problems, if they could be brought into a unity through the general semantics methodology of ordering, relating, and evaluating.

Translating the findings from those areas with objectives similar to general semantics for the use of general semanticists and the common communication process is a formidable task. There is opposition from the phalanx of "pure" scientists who resent any disturbance to the structures by which their disciplines are fortified. Oddly, there is resistance from "pure" general semanticists who fear "contamination" of *their* discipline. The former do not recognize the advantages that would come to their disciplines if their work could be viewed at operational levels free from verbal identification. The latter seem to be working in contradiction to the openness and extensionality that general semantics purportedly enables. Both contribute to the perpetuation of the compartmentalization and elementalization they deplore. Scholars, whatever their major interests, should obtain rigor without absolutism.

While specialized scholars may succeed in breaking through verbal barriers into an awareness of nonverbal operations and relationships in their particular areas, some of them tend to remain narrowly limited in much of what they can do. For instance, Skinnerian behavioralists have a very esoteric terminology in respect to language and language disorders. Some of them have been known to be derisive of Rogerian approaches. If they could come closer to operational levels by applying extensional devices to their terminologies, communication might be improved—to their mutual benefit.

Within the textbooks mentioned, there is general agreement on the basic formulations. There is less agreement on the priorities among them, and the emphasis to be placed upon each. None of the authors has attempted to exhaust all of Korzybski's formulations. There remain large areas that have not been explicated such as to permit general application.

Stated positively, at least as taught by this writer, these are the key formulations: proper evaluating (with improvement of predictability), delay of reaction, consciousness of abstracting; map-territory and word-fact correspondences; nonidentification, nonallness, multiordinality, self-reflexiveness, extensional devices, extensional-intensional orientations, ordering of abstractions, circularity and natural order of evaluation, search for order, function, structure. Time-binding seems to me the overriding formulation of the entire system.

Central to these "formulations" is a potent device originally called the structural differential, and then vastly oversimplified by some teachers by being called an "abstraction ladder," a distortion repudiated by Korzybski. The structural differential grossly outlines the series of abstracting behaviors that occur in the sense organs and brain between an environment and statements generated about it—from input through transformations into language.

As a schema or diagram of the interactions of persons with an environment, it is a valuable device to remind us that we are always abstracting in our knowledge-getting and evaluating. This *consciousness of abstracting* has a tendency to slow down impulsiveness and to induce one to correct his premises.

The structural differential takes on a more substantial form as the formulations mentioned above are connected one with the other. Each formulation focuses on behaviors that are a part of the processes of abstracting and verbalization. As a total unified phenomenon, taken together, they may be considered as a general semantics model. The stress upon the integration of these formulations within the structural differential is a recent development which came with the advent of the current communication theories.

Each formulation describes a group of behaviors that occur within the structure of human evaluating-communicating behaviors. By no means is there a claim that all of this together makes more than a fairly initial description of the process. For this reason, general semanticists have usually been open to contributions from all other related theories, methodologies, and research findings from other disciplines to permit as complete a description as possible. The most that is claimed is that these formulations all bear on highly important, and often neglected, aspects of communicating-evaluating. They bring many phenomena not ordinarily noticed into clinical accessibility.

Note that the word *formulation* is used instead of the word *concept* or *category*. This usage seems necessary to prevent one's thinking that the structural differential with the associated formulations constitute the "conceptual framework of general semantics." "Formulation" seems a more accurate description of the focusing and organizing of behaviors concerned in what has long been called concept, percept, idea, or category. These words tend to atomize and make static what is exceedingly dynamic and transforming. To the extent that it is practical, the entire vocabulary for describing human behavior should be modified to eliminate terms with static and allness implications, in favor of those with more dynamic and relational implications. For instance, perception would become perceiving; knowledge would become knowing, etc. Action and relating words would be emphasized. Words ending with *-ing* seem more accurate.

The quality of writing and speaking often improves as there is avoidance of language with elementalistic and atomistic implications. In the hands of great writers, science has poetic characteristics, and poetry manifests the exactitudes of science. Robert Oppenheimer is an example of the former. Quality usually improves with the elimination of the "is" of identification and of predication.

Every science must evolve new terminology as it is applied and tested. For instance, research in neurology concerning the cerebellum and thalamic areas of the brain has been giving more attention to the reticular formation. The reticular formation is apparently vital to a large group of phenomena related to emotions and to control—matters that are central to language behaviors and general semantics. In growing out of and being dependent upon many sciences, general semantics necessarily must be concerned with advances over a wide range of knowledges. To keep up with research relevant to general semantics is a formidable task indeed. Then there is that reluctance on the part of scholars to "tamper" with the work of other scholars—especially with anything as massive as Korzybski's interdisciplinary venture.

But innovation has been underway, nevertheless, since the work was introduced. Korzybski did not bring the so-called extensional devices together for a unified treatment until the second edition of *Science and Sanity* (1941). The textbooks of S. I. Hayakawa, Wendell Johnson, Irving J. Lee, and Francis Chisholm had their own versions of the structural differential. Differing in details from the diagram in *Science and Sanity,* they were, nevertheless, potent in their effectiveness. Korzybski's last paper, an article on perceptual processes, referred to an adaptation by Chisholm of the diagram Korzybski had used in his seminars for some years.

An example of change through the use of the formulations is that of "semantic reaction." In replacing the word "meaning" with "semantic reaction," teachers were helped to become aware of phenomena in the human brain that words induce. Meaning, one of the oldest terms used by teachers of communication, has wasted incalculable effort as a consequence of its vagueness, and of its false implication of something inherent within, and carried by, words. With the advent of consciousness of abstracting and multiordinality, it became possible to talk about the "meaning of meaning," and other previously intractable problems with coherency. This greater scope given to semantic reaction, if the writer's memory is correct, began to be used about the same time by Johnson, Hayakawa, and Lee.

Considerable impediments have come from what appear to the average reader as contradictions in *Science and Sanity.* For example, Koryzbski spoke of the extreme simplicity of a non-Aristotelian system based on the denial of the *is of identity.* He repeatedly said that his work was extremely *general,* and extremely *limited.* M. Kendig has pointed out that the verbally oriented person often jumps to the conclusion that this is a contradiction. And it is anything *but* simple to the reader who is unconsciously victimized by the verbal entrapments of the language. He may fail to apprehend the continuum from identification to consciousness of abstracting. Textbook writers have the difficult task of avoiding such blockages as they attempt to explain these matters. Teachers have found themselves driven more and more to nonverbal demonstrations.

At the heart of general semantics is the map-territory, word-facts formulation. A statement is to its facts as a map is to its territory. The measure of the adequacy of maps is their correspondence to their territory. Similarly with words, their suitability depends upon their correspondence to their fact-territories. Whether geographic or verbal, a perfect map or statement would have point-to-point correspondence with the fact-territory. Upon this correspondence depends the predictability of word-maps. From this formulation Korzybski derived his three non-Aristotelian premises: namely, that the map (or word) is not its territory; that the map (or word) is not all; that maps (or words) are self-reflexive (they are used to talk about themselves).

This formulation has been extended to apply to those assumptions or premises that people hold concerning what they talk about. Such assumptions, whether they be unconscious or not, may be compared with maps, and as such need constant correction as the fact-territories they represent change. General semantics is frequently explained as a discipline to bring such assumptions into better correspondence with that which exists, and to keep language behaviors in better correspondence with the assumptions. With the failure of correspondence, predictability breaks down followed by various disorders of communication, by misevaluations, and not infrequently *un*sane, if not insane, behavior.

The map-territory formulation becomes more precise and useful with the incorporation of "isomorphism" as a major formulation. However, the map-territory analogy must be retained to illustrate structural similarity, which is a definition of isomorphism. This modification of map-territory relationships into isomorphism permits the general semantics methodology to be brought directly to the service of the communication process and communication theory—an area which at present is much in flux and incomplete. This formulation grows out of the viewing of the communication process as a series of transformations in the human brain and nervous system as the person abstracts from his environments through several transformations into his language behaviors. What Korzybski mentioned concerning invariance, and invariance under transformation, has been rather neglected by teachers.* The communication process, described as a series of invariant isomorphic transformations, implies complete and perfect communication. This, of course, is impossible, since the correspondence of an assumption or a statement cannot be completely point-to-point. But the ex-

---

* See the paper by Kenneth G. Johnson, Chapter 4.—EDITOR.

tent or degree of isomorphism introduces relativity, and hence some practicability into what may be expected of language correspondence.

A further benefit of wide implication in the introduction of isomorphism as a major formulation comes out of the just beginning exchanges with the highly multidisciplinary group of scholars in the Society for General Systems Research.[9] This group, as is true of general semanticists, is hesitant in defining their purposes. Their most prevalent definition of general systems is that it is the search for and study of isomorphisms!*

Helpful in describing the circularity and interplay between higher order abstractions and their fact-phenomena are terms from cybernetics, such as *feedback*. Feedback must go on between *A* and *B* if they are to correct each other's assumptions, and avoid the difficulties that occur when their differing orders of abstraction encounter each other. When properly joined with feedforward, the abstracting proceeds according to given purposes.

Emerging from the space sciences into great importance for both general semantics and communication philosophy are the formulations of entropy and negentropy. They have been broadened in application in social systems and organization theory. For communication, entropy refers to the loss of organization and clarity of information between input and output as messages are transmitted from person to person and group to group. For general semantics, it became valuable as a "container" of the neurosemantic disorders that prevent coherence of statements and proper evaluation.

Of all the "ideas" and statements that are generated for possible utterance at a given moment, symbolic formation goes forward by inhibiting those statements not relevant or otherwise inappropriate. Negation of entropy has a counterpart in the farmer who removes the weeds that interfere with the growing seed.

Further, general semantics has a potential contribution to make to the great problem of unification of proliferating knowledges through the ordering of abstractions that are encountered in the libraries. Students who are able to apply extensional devices (use of indexes, dates, etc., hyphens, and quotes) tell us that their confusions and discomforts tend to lessen. That "integration" that does occur results from the mental indexing and dating they employ as they envisage the content of the volumes at operational and relational levels. This ability would be a boon to education if sufficient teachers would bring it about in their students.

If cybernetics and general semantics would join in their deeper levels, I predict that the revolution in college curricula, which is so long overdue,

---

* A joint conference of scholars to explore in depth relationships of the two disciplines is pending for 1970.

might come much faster. Most liberal arts programs are concerned with the development of the whole-person-in-his-situation-as-a-whole. This has always also been a major aim of general semantics. General semantics claims that the process of learning and maturing is enhanced through the development of the extensional orientation. Social cybernation, which deals with control and regulation of organisms by negative feedback (Norbert Wiener), brings a scientific approach into the formation and persistence of purposes and the amelioration of the pathologies of purpose so widespread today. It happens that education in either general semantics or cybernation principles requires a greater width and depth of curriculum, from Art to Zoology, than is required in most universities for the baccalaureate degree today. Is the joining of these two disciplines as the basic framework of all knowledges feasible? Would this joining release the new competencies in evaluating and living which are demanded by the changes with which our students must cope?

There is another very important change that eventually might be adopted by general semantics scholars. For consideration some years hence, I suggest that the label general semantics might be relabeled as a branch of morphology (the study of structure), namely Isomorphics (the study of similarity of structures), or Isomorphology. This label might free general semantics for its full functioning. This science would, as general semantics potentially could, serve all other disciplines, especially those concerned with their epistemologies and the communication of their disciplines.

This is a time in which all of our institutions are undergoing intense scrutiny and criticism. Perhaps no one of our activities are functioning at its optimum. General semantics, we are certain, has never reached its optimum, let alone fulfilled its potential. That optimum would be reached when the posture of science becomes generally adopted in the learning and living of all individuals. And this, of course, requires that general semantics be applied to general semantics.

I have been able to suggest only a few of the developments that are feasible to undertake. Reports on other developments are presented in this volume, and will emerge from the Conference on Research Designs in General Semantics[10] held earlier this year.

The demise of general semantics has been predicted by some persons ever since it was launched some thirty-six years ago. We predict that it is going to be an increasingly lively corpse as the larger number of competent scholars now available engage themselves in the opportunities for research which general semantics continues to open. They will find themselves "where the action is."

REFERENCES

1. Korzybski, Alfred. *Science and Sanity: An Introduction to Non-Aristotelian Systems and General Semantics.* Lakeville, Conn.: International Non-Aristotelian Library Publishing Co., 1st ed., 1933; 4th ed., 1958. Distributed by the Institute of General Semantics.
2. Hayakawa,, S. I. *Language in Thought and Action.* New York: Harcourt, Brace & World, 1939.
3. Johnson, Wendell. *People in Quandaries.* New York: Harper & Row, 1945.
4. Lee, Irving, J. *Language Habits in Human Affairs.* New York: Harper & Row, 1941.
5. Chisholm, Francis. *Introductory Lectures on General Semantics.* Lakeville, Conn.: Institute of General Semantics, 1945.
6. Bois, J. Samuel. *Art of Awareness.* Dubuque, Iowa: Wm. C. Brown, Co., 1966.
7. Weinberg, Harry L. *Levels of Knowing and Existence.* New York: Harper & Row, 1959.
8. Murray, Elwood; Phillips, Gerald; and Truby, David. *Speech: Science–Art.* Indianapolis: Bobbs-Merrill, 1969.
9. See also Anatol Rapoport and Ludwig von Bertalanffy, eds., *Yearbooks* of the Society for General Systems Research, Ann Arbor, Mich., beginning in 1955.
10. Proceedings to be published by Gordon and Breach, New York, New York, 1969.

Robert P. Pula received his B.A. in 1958 from Loyola College in Baltimore, Maryland. Presently he is a high school teacher in the Baltimore Public School System, and he also teaches reading improvement for various government agencies such as NASA and FCC.

7

NEGLECTED FORMULATIONS

ROBERT P. PULA

FUNCTION *

THERE are many reasons why *Science and Sanity* (*S&S*) has attracted-repelled its readers, not the least of which is its "embarrassing" richness. There are enough suggestions sprinkled throughout *S&S* to engage a population of researchers for generations to come. That Korzybski anticipated many lines of inquiry (cybernetics, logotherapy, neurolinguistics, etc.) is obvious to anyone who has read *S&S* carefully. As J. S. Bois has noted, " . . . earnest workers in the sciences of man cannot help but say things that fit with the Korzybskian viewpoint." It is not surprising, then, that from such a plethora of formulations, some worked out in detail as *sine qua nons* of his system (e.g., *semantic reactions*), some merely surfacing only to sink back into the ongoing surge of thematic development (e.g., the relevance of combinations of higher order thinking processes)—it is not surprising that some of these formulations have been "neglected," especially by admitted popularizers of general semantics. One such neglected formulation is *function*.

With characteristic boldness, Korzybski generalized the notion of mathematical function into a principle of neurolinguistics. Before discussing that translation, let me review the notion of function as it is used in mathematics.[1]

Stated very simply and very commonsensically, a *function* labels something that happens if something else happens: if so, then so. If two (or more) factors (called *variables*) are *related* to each other in such a way

---

* The word *function* is used here most often in its mathematical sense. Occasionally it is used in its less restricted "everyday" sense to mean *purpose* or *activity*.

that if you change one of them (the *independent* variable) you change the other/s (the *dependent* variable/s), the factors are said to be *functions* of each other. Edna Kramer has stated the principle very nicely:

> Mathematics is forever and again a study of different *functions*. When we remark that "price control is a function of the state," or "Mrs. Smith's bridge parties are boring functions," the term is not being used in a mathematical sense. But if we say that the weight of an object is a function of its physical and chemical composition, that health is a function of nutrition, that Hitler wrote that the justification of the use of the most brutal weapons is always a function of fanatical belief, that Mr. Brown's treatment of his employees is a function of his moods, which, in turn, are functions of the activity of the stock market, then we are being mathematical.[2]

Once we have established (or *decided*) that a factor (y) is a function of a factor (x), we can establish the *value* of y by knowing (or *deciding*) the value of x.

Korzybski gives these simple mathematical illustrations of functional operations:

> ... $y = x + 3$. If we select the value 1 for x our $y = 1 + 3 = 4$. If we select $x = 2$, then $y = 2 + 3 = 5$.
>
> Let us take a more complicated example, for instance: $y = x^2 - x + 2$. We see that for $x = 1, y = 1 - 1 + 2 = 2$; for $x = 2, y = 4 - 2 + 2 = 4$; for $x = 3, y = 9 - 3 + 2 = 8$.[3]

In mathematical notation, a function is expressed: $y = f(x)$, and is read, "y equals f (or function) of x" or "y depends on x," or "the value of y varies as the value of x varies," etc.

The function (relationship) $y = f(x)$, once values (numerical or otherwise) have been assigned, becomes *itself* a value; i.e., the entire expression may then be used as a unit of value in further calculations.

Let us go to Courant and Robbins for some additional insight into the role of the function notion in mathematics and pursuits, such as physics, where mathematics serves as the language of precision:

> The concept of function enters whenever quantities are connected by a definite physical relationship. The volume of a gas enclosed in a cylinder is a function of the temperature and of the pressure on the piston. The atmospheric pressure as observed in a balloon is a function of the altitude above sea level.[4]
>
> The concept of function is of the greatest importance, not only in pure mathematics but also in practical applications. Physical laws are nothing but statements concerning the way in which certain quantities depend on others when some of these are permitted to vary. Thus the pitch of the note emitted by a plucked string depends on [i.e., *is a function* of: R.P.P.] the length,

weight, and tension of the string, the pressure of the atmosphere depends on the altitude, and the energy of a bullet depends on its mass and velocity. The task of the physicist is to determine the exact or approximate nature of this functional dependence.[5]

A mathematical function is simply a law governing the interdependence of variable quantities.[6]

As is to be expected, mathematicians and physicists focus differently with regard to function. Mathematicians see function simply as the expression of relatedness, with no necessary cause-effect implications. Physicists are interested in the cause-effect relationship of specific factors expressed as quantities.

This is the attitude ordinarily taken if one *applies* mathematics to physics or engineering.[7]

On the basis of the notion of *mathematical* function, Bertrand Russell formulated the notion of the *propositional* function. Korzybski gives this definition of a propositional function:

. . . an ∞-*valued* statement, containing one or more variables, such that when single values are assigned to these variables the expression becomes, in principle, a *one-valued* proposition.[8]

We may replace the term "∞-*valued*" with the term "*empty*" to get an intuitive grasp of the relationship between a propositional function and a proposition; thus, when a propositional function (which is "empty") is "filled" (i.e., *values* are *assigned* to the variables), the propositional function becomes a proposition. In other words, the "meaning" of the proposition is a *function* of the values assigned to the variables of the propositional function. The propositional function, then, is "meaning–*less*" until we "fill in" some "meaning," at which point we have not a propositional function, but a *proposition* (i.e., a definite statement of some sort), which may be said to be either true or false. Propositional functions are like empty symbolic buckets (arrangements of possible "meaning") that become "meaningful" (i.e., *propositions*) when we fill up the buckets.

Those who have struggled with the "new math," which has been around for a century, will recognize the similarity between the propositional function and the "empty set" of set theory. The circularity and plenum or manifold-like quality of human knowledge is again demonstrated:

The theory of aggregates underlies the theory of function. An aggregate, or manifold, or set, is a system such that: (1) it includes all entities to which a certain characteristic belongs [sometimes called a *class*]; (2) no entity without this characteristic belongs to the system; and (3) any entity of the system is permanently recognizable as distinct from other entities.

The separate entities [members of the set], which belong to such a collection, system, aggregate, manifold, or set are called elements. We assume the possibility of selecting at pleasure, by a definite process or law, one or more elements of any aggregate A, which would form another aggregate B,.

The above few lines express how the human 'thought' processes work, and how languages were built up . . . and so the mathematical theories are not expressed in the usual antiquated 'psychological' *terms,* although they describe one of the *most important psycho–logical processes.*[9] [Italics and parenthetical expressions are mine: R.P.P.]

Now we must go one step farther, to a yet "higher" and certainly broader order of abstraction, to mention Keyser's notion of a *doctrinal function.* (You see how the spiral grows: ever "outward" and "upward," feeding on itself to grow beyond itself, each "higher" level depending on (being a *function* of) its "lower" relatives: a process that may be called "semantic cannibalism.") Here is part of Korzybski's discussion:

A manifold of interrelated propositional functions, usually called postulates, with all the consequences following from them, usually called theorems, has been termed by Keyser a *doctrinal function.* A doctrinal function, thus, has no specific content, as it deals with variables, but establishes *definite relations* between these variables. In principle, we can assign many single values to the variable terms, and so generate many doctrines from *one* doctrinal function.[10]

We can simplify this for ourselves by recalling the caveat, "From premises, conclusions follow."

There is yet one more stage (one yet "higher" order of abstraction) to "visit" before we can move on to consider what Korzybski has done with this. The next level is that of the *system-function*:

. . . if we take any *system,* an analysis will discover that it is a whole of related doctrinal functions. As this situation is the most frequent, and as 'thinking,' in general, represents a process of relating into higher order relational entities, which are later *treated as complex wholes,* it is useful to have a term which would symbolize doctrinal functions of higher order, which are made up of doctrinal functions of lower orders. We could preserve the terminology of 'higher' and 'lower' order; but as these conditions are always found in all *systems,* it seems more expedient to call the higher body of interrelated doctrinal functions, which ultimately produce a system —*a system–function.* At present, the term 'system–function' has been already coined by Doctor H. M. Sheffer; but, to my knowledge, Sheffer uses his 'system–function' as an equivalent for the 'doctrinal function' of Keyser, For the reasons given above, it seems advisable to limit the term 'doctrinal function' to the use as introduced by Keyser, and to enlarge the meaning of Shaffer's term 'system–function' to the use suggested in the present work, this natural and wider meaning to be indicated by the insertion of a hyphen.[11]

Enough has been presented, I hope, to give the "nonmathematical" reader at least an "intuitive" grasp of the mathematical notions. If not, you might try looking at a photograph of a section of brain tissue in any book on neurophysiology. There is an especially good one for our purpose in D. A. Sholl's *The Organization of the Cerebral Cortex*, Plate 3, showing a section of the sensory motor cortex of a cat. If you can imagine those neurons *animated*, seeming to move like the elements in a painting by Jackson Pollack or Piet Mondrian, you may get a "feel" for sets, combinations of sets, etc.

Since Korzybski's system is "circular," i.e., relational, each subformulation dovetailing or being practically coextensive with all others, many of them can be expressed as functions.[12] At this point, I want to stress that the mathematical notion of function seems to have been one of the key trigger-elements that culminated in the formulation of that *system–function* called general semantics.

Korzybski's *reaction* to having *internalized* the mathematical notion of function may be suggested in this way:

> If language is a function of brain, then by studying language, we can learn something about brain-function. Apparently, as brain varies (evolution), so does language vary: $L = f(B)$; as language varies (culture), so does brain vary: $B = g(L)$

If language and brain are functions of each other, and if language (like other brain "products") serves to assist the organism to transact with "its" "environment" (i.e., survive), then the language should bear a structure similar to the structure of the nonlinguistic "environment." That is, language-worth (efficiency) is a function of the language's relation to the nonverbal world as we understand it at a given date: $L_e = f(r[L:W])$—

If a given language does *not* bear a positive structural relation to the nonverbal world, and remembering that language is a brain-function, and that *the organism functions as a whole,* then the organism will not be adjusted to its nonverbal "environment." This adjustment of the organism-environment continuum is what we mean by the term *sanity.* Stated as a positive function, we may say (let S stand for *sanity*):

$$S = f(L_e)$$

and

$$L_e = g(S)$$

There are many languages with varying degrees of positive relatedness to various aspects of the nonverbal world. Most vernaculars, at least among the Indo-European group, bear a *negative* relatedness to the nonverbal world; that is, the structures of these languages are *not* similar to the structure of the world that they presume to describe. There is one language, however, which *when applied* is seen to bear a high degree of positive relatedness to the nonlinguistic "environment." When a *negative* relatedness is discovered between this language and the nonlinguistic "environment" (the nonverbal world), *this* language is revised to achieve *positive* relatedness, so that at any given date this language is the best we have from the structural point of view. This language is, of course, mathematics.

Since mathematics, too, is a product of the brain, and since, because of its economy of expression it is easier to study its structure, study of mathematical structure should give us insight into two subjects of profound importance for man's survival:

1) brain function–structure
2) linguistic (vernacular) revision.

Much of the work in cybernetics seems to support many of Korzybski's suggestions.[13] However, cybernetics is also increasingly showing the difficulty of finding *values* to assign to the variables of the functions suggested here so simply by a "nonmathematical" general semanticist. Here is a recent statement of the problem by Jagjit Singh:

> In the cerebral cortex of man . . . a single axon of a neuron may influence as many as five thousand others, and each neuron on the average holds within its . . . grasp about 100 somas of other neurons. The ten billion neurons of the human nervous system thus form a meshwork with about one thousand billion internal synapses. There are therefore several hundred times more neural connections in the living brain than there are people on the earth.[14]

Singh points out that with the brain having so many units, we cannot expect to construct an analysis that would bear a one-to-one correlation to those units. (One would not expect that from a *model,* anyway). However·

> If it is true that the connection schemes according to which the living brain develops are determined only by certain broad parameters of growth, then there is some hope that the performance of such a system might be analyzed in terms of these parameters. The analysis might aim at elucidating the main types of behavior patterns.[15]
>
> Unfortunately, no statistical theory able to take in its stride even some of the more salient features of brain function exists at present. What we do

have are speculative fragments with varying degrees of marginal plausibility.[16]

We can see, then, that while the research to verify, modify, or reject the Korzybskian notion of *function* as applied to "thinking" is being carried out, it is far from having arrived at a point where some reasonably secure supportive statement-at-a-given-date can be made. The function–notion remains at the level of eminent plausibility: one of the most brilliant hunches of the twentieth century's emerging science of man.

MULTIORDINALITY

A careful reading of *Science and Sanity* will show that, except for such notable examples as the justly famous map-territory analogy, that 800-page work is singularly free of metaphors, simile, etc., in the commonly understood literary and poetic senses of those terms. There is a radical, head-on *literal–ness* about Korzybski's analyses that does not allow of compromise at the level of analysis, and *at the level of application*—particularly the application that takes place in training situations. Some of the popularizers of Korzybski's system have forgotten this or have simply chosen to ignore it; whatever the reason, the results have been similar: in making Korzybski "palatable," they have made his system less operative.

This is the sense in which I see *multiordinality* as a "neglected formulation." It has not been so much neglected as it has been slighted by insufficient rigor in statement, and insufficient vigor in application.

At the level of application, i.e., in training situations where we have some control, we have been neglectful, too—at least in recent years. This neglect has been expressed at both levels mentioned above—statement and application. Some people who teach general semantics manifest a readiness to emphasize either the verbal or the nonverbal approach in the training of students. Sometimes this emphasis becomes quite polar (either-or) and we find general semantics being taught as just another way to *talk* ("philosophize") about things (as in some academic environments) without much concern for *changing the behavior* of the person doing the talking; or we find general semantics being taught almost solely through application (exercises) at the expense of verbal coherence.

Obviously, both approaches are needed; they are *functions* of each other. What the "verbal" general semanticists seem to forget is the necessity for *practice* if the system is to be internalized. What the "nonverbal" general semanticists seem to forget is that, for all their practice, when their students leave the training situation, they can be expected to continue to "talk to themselves." The trainer has an obligation to provide a clear set of formulations *for the student to tell to himself* when he leaves the training environment. Failure to do this may be one reason why we commonly see people who have been "in general semantics" for many years still very confused about basic formulations. These confused verbal systems often find expression in amorphous yet pained behavior.

It seems to me that an instructor who consistently operates on either side of this disastrous dichotomy is only "half" a general semanticist.

In the first part of this paper, I discussed the neglected formulation *function*. That is a neglected formulation in an almost total sense. It is seldom discussed in books on general semantics—not, in my experience, in *courses* on general semantics. *Multiordinality,* on the other hand, *does* get introduced, particularly in the more recent explications. Of the early "big four" (Chase, Hayakawa, Johnson, and Lee) only Johnson's *People in Quandaries* has indexed references to multiordinality. The more recent works by Bois (*Explorations in Awareness; The Art of Awareness*), and Weinberg (*Levels of Knowing and Existence*) emphasize multiordinality of terms as important. But even where multiordinality is discussed, the discussions are not significant in proportion to the whole book in which they appear. And the emphasis nowhere approaches the intensity of Korzybski's original statement. Multiordinality, examined from several points of view, is well represented in the generally inadequate index of *Science and Sanity*. An especially succinct statement is:

> Analysis finds that certain of the most important terms we use; such as, 'yes,' 'no,' 'true,' 'false,' 'all,' 'fact,' 'reality,' 'existence,' 'definition,' 'relation,' 'structure,' 'order,' 'number,' 'is,' 'has,' 'there is,' 'variable,' 'infinite,' 'abstraction,' 'property,' 'meaning,' 'value,' 'love,' 'hate,' 'knowing,' 'doubt,' may apply to all verbal levels, and in each particular case may have a different content or meanings and so *in general no single content or meaning*. I call such terms *multiordinal terms (m.o.)*. The definition of such terms is always given in other *m.o.* terms preserving their fundamental multiordinality. In other words, a *m.o.* term represents a many-valued term. If the many values are identified, or disregarded, or confused, we treat a fundamentally many-valued term as one-valued, and we must have every kind of paradox through such an identification. All known paradoxes in mathematics and life can be manufactured by the disregard of this fundamental multiordinality. Vice versa, by formulating the general semantic problem of multiordinality, we gain means to discriminate between the many meanings, and so assign a single meaning in a given context. A *m.o.* term represents a variable in general, and becomes constant or one-valued in a given context, its value being given by that context.[17]

What needs to be stressed *in a most uncompromising way* is that *m.o.* terms *have no general meaning.* If the *m.o.* terms "mean" *different things* at different levels of abstraction, they "mean" *nothing* if the level of abstraction is not clear. The *m.o.* term, so common in our everyday language, is thus a "first cousin" of the propositional function: it has *no* value until a value is *assigned* consciously by a writer or speaker, or *discovered* by a reader or listener by examining the *context* in which the word is used. The "meaning" of a *m.o.* term is a function of level of abstraction; level of abstraction is a function of context.

Examination of a word in context reveals two related *but different* aspects of words: (1) the *level of abstraction* at which the word is being used (*m.o.*); (2) the particular *dictionary definition* that can be assigned to the word (multimeaning). These two, multiordinality and multimeaning, are often confused. Let's examine them.

Once we have established the "meaning" of the term in question by examining the context and consulting the dictionary ("meaning" in the traditional sense) we may then examine the term to see if it has the multiordinal character. If it has, then *only awareness of its level of abstraction* can give us a secure notion of what its user "meant" when he used it.

Example: The word *house* can be used in many ways (multimeaning) depending on the word's referent, and the form (part of speech) in which it is being used:

> *House* the equipment. (verb)
> Visit the White *House.* (noun)
>   etc.

The same can be shown for the word *love*:

> *Love* thy neighbor. (verb)
> John is in *love.* (noun)

Now, while *house* and *love* share the multimeaning character, they do not (in normal usage) share the *m.o.* character. It is characteristic of *m.o.* terms that they can be applied to themselves; i.e., *multiordinal terms are self-reflexive.* Thus while I am not likely to "house my house of love," I may very well "love my love of houses."

Note that, in addition to being self-reflexive, the *m.o.* term (as Bois has pointed out in *The Art of Awareness*) does not change its *dictionary* meaning; both *loves* as used above would be *defined* in the same way; but since they "occupy" different levels of abstraction, they do not "mean" the same thing. My love of houses may be called (and in general semantics literature usually is) a *first order* love. My love of my love is called a *second order* love. In other words, my second order love is *about* (refers to) my first order love. Obviously, these loves are different, even though the verbal form in which they are expressed is similar.

The "sameness" in form of *m.o.* terms is the prime source of the confusion that they cause. Korzybski observed that, because the words *look* and *sound* alike, and because we tend to *identify* levels of abstraction, we often respond to the words *as though* their "meanings" were the same. This is true, too, in problems of multimeaning; but here examination of context will usually suggest what is intended by the speaker or writer. (I recognize, but am not discussing here, the problem of multimeaning as a function of unique nervous systems.)

Simple examination of context, then, is not enough to avoid the snares of *m.o.* terms. What is needed is specific training to develop in students an ongoing, vital, operative *consciousness of multiordinality*. Avoidance of "paradoxes" * in particular, and achievement of sane evaluating in general, are impossible without consciousness of multiordinality. The neglect of this formulation by general semanticists, then, is not only surprising, it is dangerous.

REFERENCES

1. This review is based on Alfred Korzybski's *Science and Sanity: An Introduction to Non-Aristotelian Systems and General Semantics.* Lakeville, Conn.: International Non-Aristotelian Library Publishing Co., 4th ed., 1958, Chapter XVI, Distributed by the Institute of General Semantics; and on Richard Courant's and Herbert Robbins' *What is Mathematics?* New York: Oxford University Press, 1963.
2. Kramer, Edna. *The Main Stream of Mathematics.* New York: Fawcett, 1961, p. 134.
3. Korzybski, *op. cit.,* p. 136.
4. Courant and Robbins, *op. cit.,* p. 272.
5. *Ibid.,* p. 275.
6. *Ibid.,* p. 276.
7. *Ibid.*
8. Korzybski, *op. cit.,* p. 136.
9. *Ibid.,* p. 281.
10. *Ibid.,* p. 144.
11. *Ibid.,* p. 145.
12. See D. D. Bourland, Jr. "Introduction to a Structural Calculus: A Postulational Statement of Alfred Korzybski's Non-Aristotelian Linguistic System," *General Semantics Bulletin,* Nos. 8, 9, 1952.
13. See Harry L. Weinberg, "Structure and Function in Cybernetics," *Levels of Knowing and Existence.* New York: Harper & Row, 1959; and Paul A. Ptacek,

---

* See the paper by Mel Thistle, Chapter 22.—EDITOR.

"Computers as an Extension of Man's Neuro-Linguistic Functioning or as Extra-Neuro-Linguistic Aids," *General Semantics Bulletin,* Nos. 26, 27, 1960, pp. 27–30.
14. Singh, Jagjit. *Great Ideas in Information Theory, Language and Cybernetics.* New York: Dover, 1966, p. 132.
15. *Ibid.,* p. 315.
16. *Ibid.,* p. 316.
17. Korzybski, *op. cit.,* p. 753, cf. pp. 439–41.

8

TOWARD A SENSE OF UNITY

CHARLOTTE S. READ

S OME formulations in Korzybskian general semantics may appear contradictory at first glance. Emphasis on the separation of aspects of processes may lead to misunderstandings, and increase our feelings of dichotomy, unless we can sense the deeper relatedness. I would like to share with you some of my theoretical reflections, some ways of considering Korzybski's formulations that I have felt a need to clarify for myself, and some approaches that I believe can lead to a deeper sense of functioning as a totality-in-the-environment, or what I refer to in my title as "a sense of unity."

We make the separations of *verbal* and *nonverbal*, and yet, more deeply, we find that they cannot be separated. We speak of "delayed reactions," while we extol the importance of becoming more "spontaneous." Can these seemingly contradictory statements be resolved? Is it necessary to behave rigidly sometimes, to reverse the natural order of evaluation, as one writer on general semantics has recently said? [1]

We are familiar with Korzybski's insistence that "the word is not the thing": "whatever we *say* something *is* obviously *is not* the 'something' on the silent levels." [2] He also says in the same paper: ". . . even though it becomes necessary to investigate different aspects of the processes of abstracting for purposes of analysis, we should be aware that these different aspects are parts of one whole continuous process of normal human life." [3]

On the one hand, we have stressed the importance of getting the feel of differentiating the *verbal* and *nonverbal*, and, on the other hand, it is also important to get the feel that verbal aspects are only one among numerous others in a total situation before us.

Whoever has worked at reaching the "silent level," where we stop the in-

55

cessant verbal chattering in our heads, where we come to more inner quiet, knows how difficult this is. Although Korzybski considered this as the first step in becoming conscious of abstracting, hardly anyone so far has dealt with it more than cursorily in general semantics literature. People sometimes ask, "How can we really become silent on nonverbal levels when we know, from years of conditioning in our culture, that our language is a part even of every perception?" We can learn gradually not to let our talking or "verbal thinking" get in the way of our acting and reacting, and thus be involved more directly.

There seems no doubt about the extreme importance of getting quiet without our usual inner verbalizing. The emphasis it is given by many of the world's great men throughout the centuries (especially as an important part of Eastern philosophies where it has been studied deeply) indicates its central role in the age-old problems of language in relation to experiencing. Particularly in this respect, I consider Korzybski's theory a significant link between East and West.

I believe, however, that it would be helpful also to emphasize letting our language be an important part of the total situation when we are speaking. For instance, we say that we can "speak *about*" an experience, but that the words *about* it are not *it*. We may say that the experience and the speaking *about* it are on different orders of abstraction. This way of stating it, appropriate perhaps at times, does not give enough recognition to the more inclusive process of "letting the experience come to words." Speaking *about* something is different from "speaking the experience," where the speaking is a part of the whole happening. Every therapist, every actor and speech teacher, and many others know how important it is for our words to be connected to our feelings. We can tell, if we are attuned to it, whether they are "genuine," whether they come from our depths. It often requires considerable training before our words and feelings come together in one expression—when we are not "phony," but "wholehearted."

In each of his seminars, and in his many writings, Korzybski emphasized the organism-as-a-whole-in-its-environment approach, and it seems to me worthwhile to consider how this bears on the verbal/nonverbal differentiation. We may choose not to speak, but stay open and in touch with a situation. Or we may remain too rigid, believing that we have to become "bottled up" trying not to speak. Or, if we want to speak, we may aim to bring our verbalizings as clearly and closely to our experiencing as we can. Does this have something to do with the stress being laid these days on being "authentic"? I believe it does.

This seems to me to be a part of a larger possibility—that of being open to a wider range of awareness.

In an article on "extra-verbal techniques," we read:

> The natural order of abstracting must be reversed at certain times. We have to do a large number of activities in prescribed ways; we have to hold certain actions or movements back for our safety; or we have to attend to only certain sensations and not others for some special reasons, but we do not have to behave rigidly all the time. Rigidity does not have to become a habit. There are many hours during the day in which we can let go, and let each level operate as it was meant to operate. Then what happens happens.[4]

This statement creates a two-valued dichotomy of rigidity *versus* the natural order of abstracting; it implies that it is *necessary* to behave rigidly part of our day, and when we walk out of the office (or wherever it is that we "have to be" rigid), we can then "be natural." This seems to me a misunderstanding. Even though we may want to hit our boss because he has made certain demands, we do not do it. We may reassess the situation, and include other factors (perhaps he is sick, perhaps we love his daughter, perhaps we don't want to lose our job, perhaps he is not aware of certain facts, etc.). We may decide, not by making efforts to hold back but by reevaluating the situation, that we will go along with him without anger. Or we may decide that the happening is important enough to risk losing our job and react in anger. Or we may find another alternative. I am *not* saying we ought not to get angry and express it, if at all appropriate, to the person responsible. The point I want to make is that we can react to the data that we allow to come to our awareness, including future possible factors. We evaluate their relative importance; we do not *have* to be rigid about it.

We become aware, as in the transactional point of view, that the various factors in a situation must be viewed as being present in the situation together, verbal and nonverbal. Dewey and Bentley's use of the term *transaction* conveys this attitude:

> The knowing-known taken as one process in cases in which in older discussions the knowings and knowns are separated and viewed as in interaction. The knowns and the named in their turn taken as phases of a common process in cases in which otherwise they have been viewed as separated components, allotted irregular degrees of independence, and examined in the form of interactions.[5]

Korzybski's construction of orders of abstracting, multiordinality, etc., are not a part of the transactional psychology structure. Nevertheless, Arthur Bentley in *Knowing and the Known* was prompted to write:

Fusion of "symbol" and "entity" is what Russell demands, and confusion is what he gets. With an exhibit as prominent as this in the world, it is no wonder that Korzybski has felt it necessary to devote so much of his writings to the insistent declaration that the word is *not* the thing.[6]

What about "delayed reactions" and "spontaneity?" Are these contradictory? This seems also related to the foregoing problem. The importance of allowing so-called "spontaneous" actions, without blocking, is well-known in psychotherapeutic practice, and in present-day behavioral sciences, etc. This is a necessary first step toward healthier behavior when a person has become too blocked. "Spontaneity" has now become a fetish, a sort of "sacred cow." "There is nothing so rigid," said one serious worker in the field, "as programmed spontaneity." However, the aim is to allow action that happens naturally without our own interference, without different messages in us to move in different directions—where we have been able to reach a more "total" functioning without inner conflicts. Does "delaying" our reactions in the Korzybskian sense interfere with this healthy process? I do not believe so. In *Science and Sanity,* Korzybski explicitly mentioned the undesirability of suppressing our reactions.[7]

As I understand the process of "delaying reactions," it involves coming actually fully (as fully as possible) in contact with a given situation. This process of getting closer may take a fraction of a second, or much longer. The delay takes place not by blocking or suppressing, but by getting more closely in touch through "silence on the objective level." Then there is the possibility that our evaluations will not be severely distorted by our identifications or past associations. Then, coming face to face with the situation, we are not avoiding it but are open to it, physiologically and psychologically. We then have a better chance of responding more appropriately.

In the areas I have mentioned, one of the common factors is the ability to allow as much into our awareness as possible, as a basis from which to evaluate and act. The practice of "allowing" rather than making unnecessary efforts, of becoming more fully awake with a quiet alertness, seems an important ingredient in becoming conscious of abstracting.

The understanding of the *circularity of knowledge* helps us to get the feel of the relatedness of the whole continual process of experiencing, verbalizing, generalizing, inferring, and projecting. Out of this sense of unity, of functioning as a "totality," we may feel more freedom to act, to live.

REFERENCES

1. Payne, Buryl, "Extra-verbal Techniques and Korzybskian Formulations," *ETC.,* Vol. XXV, No. 1 (March, 1968).

2. Korzybski, Alfred. "The Role of Language in the Perceptual Processes," *Perception: An Approach to Personality,* by Robert Blake, Glenn Ramsey, *et al.* New York: Ronald Press, 1951, p. 172.
3. *Ibid.*
4. Payne, *op. cit.,* p. 14.
5. Dewey, John; and Bentley, Arthur. *Knowing and the Known.* Boston: Beacon Press, 1949, p. 304.
6. *Ibid.,* p. 220.
7. Korzybski, Alfred. *Science and Sanity: An Introduction to Non-Aristotelian Systems and General Semantics.* Lakeville, Conn.: International Non-Aristotelian Library Publishing Co., 1st ed., 1933, 4th ed., 1958, p. 421. Distributed by the Institute of General Semantics.

Part II

APPLICATIONS

D. David Bourland, Jr., received his A.B. in Mathematics from Harvard in 1951, and his M.B.A. from the Harvard Business School in 1953. He was the last holder of a Korzybski Fellowship for study at the Institute of General Semantics under the direction of Korzybski (1949–50). He is currently President of Information Research Associates, Inc., of San Diego and Washington D.C.; Trustee of the Institute of General Semantics since 1967; and Editor of the *General Semantics Bulletin.*

Charles H. Morgan is now a member of the professional staff of Hughes Aircraft Company at Fullerton, California. He has done extensive work in the field of Naval Communications. He is Editorial Assistant for the *General Semantics Bulletin,* and a specialist in technical writing.

Karen L. Ruskin is a member of the professional staff of Lockheed-California Company, Burbank, California. She received her B.A. from the University of California at Riverside in 1966. She is Editorial Assistant for *General Semantics Bulletin,* and is active as an operations research analyst and technical writer.

9

A SEMANTIC EXPERIMENT: SEARCHING FOR UNDEFINED TERMS *

D. DAVID BOURLAND, JR., CHARLES H. MORGAN, and KAREN L. RUSKIN

KORZYBSKI asserted that "all linguistic schemes, if analyzed far enough, would depend on a set of undefined terms." He described a semantic experiment that illustrates this mechanism: one asks the subject to define some beginning term and then, successively, each term used in that definition. Korzybski stated that the following usually happens: (1) the subject will soon begin to define terms circularly; (2) if pressed for further definitions at this point, signs of affective disturbance will appear, such as restlessness; (3) eventually the subject will indicate that he "knows but cannot tell" the "meaning" of a given word or words.[1]

---

* In scientific literature of the old days, we had a habit of demanding, "define your terms." The new standards of science really should be, "state your undefined terms."

The importance of this semantic experiment seems to lie in two main regards: (1) it provides a technique for investigating the structure of an individual's personal undefined terms; and (2) this experiment can demonstrate to people, however "verbalistic" their orientations, how very close to the silent level we actually live our lives—even our symbolic lives.

In this paper, we describe the initial part of an ongoing research program for the inquiry into sets of undefined terms apparently used by various subjects. The discussion includes results obtained from performing this experiment with individuals having a diversity of educational, etc., backgrounds, plus two small children and one teenager.

THE "FORMAL" IMPORTANCE OF UNDEFINED TERMS

As in so many aspects of his methodology, Korzybski recognized in the formulation of undefined terms,* as used in mathematical logic, an issue of fundamental importance for each of us in our daily lives.

The formal study of the relations between statements has evolved over the past 100 years or so from a somewhat sterile "logic" to the mathematical logic of today. The developments of Boole, Whitehead, Russell, Peano, Gödel, Reichenbach, Quine, and others, have, comparatively recently, seen application in the proliferating field of data processing, particularly in the design of ever-more-sophisticated computer hardware, and also in new approaches to programming languages. A principal preoccupation in mathematical logic concerns the formal manipulation of a minimal number of undefined or "primitive" relations, such as *or* and *not*, to make up more complex relations, such as *implies, if and only if*, etc. These explicitly posited undefined relations show clearly the fine-grain details of the more elaborate structures that we call postulates, and the consequences of those postulates, called theorems.

In physics, one can trace the consequences that follow from structural metaphysics that require different sets of undefined terms. The classical physics of Newton employs "mass" and the separate notions of "space" and "time." In contrast, the non-Newtonian physics of relativity, concerned with systems involving large distances, employs different approaches described as having characteristics of "curvature" and "space-time." Further undefined terms for the non-Newtonian physics of systems involving quite small distances include notions of the "quantum," and such wave-particle phenomena as "photons."

---

* Terms not capable of further verbal elaboration within the given system; labels for first order experiences.

Korzybski based his system upon the explicitly recognized undefined terms *structure, order,* and *relations.*[2] He devoted some 900 pages in *Science and Sanity* to the exploration of the consequences of the interconnections between those undefined terms as basic ways to organize information about ourselves and the worlds we live in. One of the authors some time ago attempted to work through Korzybski's system in postulational form in those undefined terms.[3]

We can easily recognize an analogous mechanism operating in our personal evaluations—once it becomes pointed out, as in the following:

> We see that no statement made by man, whether savage or civilized, is free from some kind of structural metaphysics involving *s.r.* [semantic reactions]. We see also that when we explicitly start with *undefined* words, these undefined words have to be taken on faith. They represent some kind of implicit creed, or metaphysics, or structural assumptions. We meet here with a tremendously beneficial semantic effect of modern methods, in that we deliberately state our undefined terms.[4]

A fellow seminar student recently brought an example of interacting undefined terms to our attention when she somewhat formally defined a "flower child" as a "teeny-bopper trying to become a hippie." This provides a direct analogy in form to Korzybski's definition of "structure" in terms of a "network of relations or multidimensional order." [5]

Wendell Johnson has pointed out that individuals can employ essentially any term as a label for a first order experience and, in that sense, any term can function as an undefined term.[6] We can further remove the "essentially" in the preceding sentence by extending the term *experience* to include an individual's semantic reactions.*

We now turn to Korzybski's suggestion as to how one may ferret out a person's undefined terms, and what we have done in this regard.

KORZYBSKI'S SEMANTIC EXPERIMENT

Early in *Science and Sanity,* while discussing some of the epistemological complexities involved in theories of "meanings," Korzybski described an

---

* We use this term in Korzybski's sense of "the psycho-logical reaction(s) of a given individual to words and language and other symbols and events *in connection with their meanings,* and the psycho-logical reactions, which *become meanings and relational configurations* the moment the given individual begins to analyze them or somebody else does that for him." (*Science and Sanity,* p. 24).

experiment that, to the best of our knowledge, has not previously received the attention it merits:**

> If the objects, as well as words, represent abstractions of different order, an individual, *A,* cannot know what *B* abstracts, unless *B* tells him, and so the 'meaning' of a word *must* be given by a definition. This would lead to the dictionary meanings of words, provided we could define all our words. But this is impossible. If we were to attempt to do so, we should soon find that our vocabulary was exhausted, and we should reach a set of terms which could not be any further defined, from lack of words. We thus see that all linguistic schemes, if analyzed far enough, would depend on a set of undefined terms. If we enquire about the 'meaning' of a word, we find that it depends on the 'meaning' of other words used in defining it, and that the eventual new relations posited between them ultimately depend *on the m.o.* [multiordinal] *meanings of the undefined terms,* which, at a given period, cannot be elucidated any further.
>
> Naturally, any fundamental theory of 'meaning' cannot avoid this issue, which must be crucial. Here a semantic experiment suggests itself. I have performed this experiment repeatedly on myself and others, invariably with similar results. Imagine that we are engaged in a friendly serious discussion with someone, and that we decide to enquire into the meaning of words. For this special experiment, it is not necessary to be very exacting, as this would enormously and unnecessarily complicate the experiment. It is useful to have a piece of paper and a pencil to keep a record of the progress.
>
> We begin by asking the 'meaning' of every word uttered, being satisfied for this purpose with the roughest definitions; then we ask the 'meaning' of the words used in the definitions, and this process is continued usually for no more than ten to fifteen minutes, until the victim begins to speak in circles—as, for instance, defining 'space' by 'length' and 'length' by 'space.' When this stage is reached, we have come usually to the *undefined* terms of a given individual. If we still press, no matter how gently, for definitions, a most interesting fact occurs. Sooner or later, signs of *affective disturbances* appear. Often the face reddens; there is a bodily restlessness; sweat appears —symptoms quite similar to those seen in a schoolboy who has forgotten his lesson, which he "knows but cannot tell." If the partner in the experiment is capable of self-observation, he invariably finds that he feels an internal *affective pressure,* connected, perhaps with the rush of blood to the brain and probably best expressed in some such words as "what he 'knows' but cannot tell," or the like. Here we have reached the bottom and the foundation of all *non-elementalistic meanings*—the meanings of *undefined terms,* which we 'know' somehow, but cannot tell. In fact, we have reached the unspeakable level.[7]

This experiment suggested by Korzybski contains a variety of assertions and conditions that do not readily match the "intuitive" understanding of

---

** In addition to reviewing the literature, we have asked personnel at the Institute of General Semantics and the Speech Department of the University of Denver about related studies by others. They knew of no such endeavors.

many people. Due to the importance of the issues involved, it seems worth further inquiry. This we have begun.

SOME PRELIMINARY FINDINGS

As simple as the semantic experiment sketched above may sound, most people feel surprisingly reluctant to perform it. Even dedicated students of the discipline have gone over the quoted passage on several different occasions without taking the trouble to try it on themselves. Our current small sample of records (fifteen surveys on eleven individuals) actually represents a nontrivial beginning.*

In most instances we "briefed" our subjects by having them read the part of the quotation given in the immediately preceding section that describes this "semantic experiment." The exceptions consisted of the three children whose responses we recorded. On the whole, we do not currently regard this practice as establishing a favorable "psychological set," in that it seemed to lay the foundation for hostile reactions. Hostile reactions to the procedure, when projected onto the questioner, became so extreme in one case that the questioner broke off the session.

We found it necessary to adopt the following two conditions as functional, operational definitions for the point at which we had reached an "undefined term":

1) A "loop" occurred, in Korzybski's sense of defining "length" by "space," and then "space" by "length."
2) A subject's inability to go further in verbal explication of a term became manifest, usually with some marked affective reaction (e.g., raised voice, general fidgeting).

In some instances, a review of the record showed the frequent use of a term in the definitions, suggesting that it may serve the given individual as an undefined term. These tended to consist of such general labels as "something."

Our conduct of these surveys had the following purposes:

1) to explore some of the hypotheses implicit in Korzybski's description of this semantic experiment
2) to accumulate enough information on the interactions between pairs of questioners and subjects to gain some insight into how better to structure such data-gathering sessions

---

* We recognize that these fifteen surveys comprise a tiny sample, and accordingly we remind critical readers once again that this paper only seeks to provide a progress report with some tentative findings.

3) to obtain at least a preliminary appreciation for the kinds of terms individuals use as undefined.

We believe we have accomplished something useful on the first and third purposes. It still appears too early to have produced very much on the second.

Table 1 gives a listing of the undefined terms employed by the individuals we surveyed. Please keep in view the constraint that in no single survey did we attempt to delve deeply enough or long enough to supply a "complete" set of an individual's undefined terms.

TABLE 1
OBSERVED SETS OF UNDEFINED TERMS

Survey Number	Date	Undefined Terms	Remarks
1	2 Jan.	Scheme	Self-administered
2	2 Jan.	Human, Boundaries, Mankind	Same Subject as in #1
3	2 Jan.	Alter	Self-administered
4	2 Jan.	Something, Mental, Anticipate, Consider	Same Subject as in #3
5	3 Jan.	Between, Space, Points, Collection	Written on blackboard by Subject (Not Rec.)
6	4 Jan.	(Fragment . . . excessive hostility)	
7	4 Jan.	Thing, Something, Symbol	Same Subject as in #1
8	19 Jan.	Activity, Energy, Part, Whole	
9	26 Jan.	Experience, Awareness, Event, Connection, Element, Sensory	
10	1 Feb.	Time, Separation, Structure, Order, Relation, Characteristic, Collection	Self-administered
11	19 Feb.	Something, Object, Mind, Being	Age 14
12	27 Mar.	Something, Know, Do, Means, Is, Look	Age 6
13	27 Mar.	Something, Know, Do, Means, Is, Find	Age 7
14	10 Jul.	Idea, Remove, Isolate	
15	22 Jul.	Facts, Neatly	Same Subject as in #1

Wendell Johnson asserted that when confronted with the problem of defining a term, an individual could either go to a relatively higher or lower order of abstraction.[8] We found in our records a third possibility: one may also go to a completely different chain of labels relative to another structural differential. We observed this happening in three distinct ways: (1) shifting to a homonym (e.g., *no* rather than *know*); (2) changing to follow a different usage of a given term (e.g., *know* in the sense of understand, and *know* in the sense of acquaintance); and (3) introducing additional sets of comparatively high order abstractions (e.g., see Table 2). In our opinion, the questioner should not allow the first two evasions; however, the third requires exploration in the interview.

TABLE 2
EXCERPT FROM A SURVEY
(Illustrating Divergence)

Question	Response
Sequence	That which follows in an orderly fashion
Orderly	Anything which, within context, is structured
Structured	A logical expansion or continuation of an idea
Idea	A mental picture
Mental	Pertaining to the mind

DISCUSSION

We found that people do indeed define terms circularly (what we have called "looping"), as Korzybski asserted we would. Under the conditions of this experiment, those questioned invariably showed signs of affective disturbance, as Korzybski suggested they would. The forms of the disturbances varied with the individual and the circumstances (e.g., questioner, technique, relations between questioner and subject).

The different subjects displayed different (partial) sets of undefined terms in general. However, an age effect may have appeared already in our data. Two young children and a 14-year-old showed interesting similarities in their undefined terms. Since we have data on only three such youngsters, however, we do not wish to seem to make this conclusion unduly general.

The comparatively unstructured nature of this undefined term survey would seem to make it a potentially useful psychological test—somewhere between a Rohrschach * and the Haney Uncritical Inference Test.[9] Our personal interest in the undefined-term survey focuses upon the general semantics aspects. Accordingly, we encourage "professional" psychologicians, psychotherapists, etc., to join us in these investigations.

---

* We have half-jokingly referred to these surveys among ourselves as comprising "Word Blot Tests."

Our future intentions include the following:

1) continue to build a firmer base by testing more "normal" individuals
2) study trends, if any, by retesting
3) with the assistance of clinical personnel, gather data on hospitalized "mentally ill"
4) investigate individuals from so-called culturally deprived areas.

REFERENCES

1. Korzybski, Alfred. *Science and Sanity: An Introduction to Non-Aristotelian Systems and General Semantics.* Lakeville, Conn.: International Non-Aristotelian Library Publishing Co., 4th ed., 1958. Distributed by the Institute of General Semantics.
2. *Ibid.,* p. 93 ff.
3. Bourland, D. David, Jr. "Introduction to a Structural Calculus: A Postulational Statement of Alfred Korzybski's Non-Aristotelian Linguistic System," *General Semantics Bulletin,* Nos. 8, 9, 1952.
4. Korzybski, *op. cit.,* p. 153.
5. Korzybski, Alfred. "A Non-Aristotelian System and Its Necessity for Rigour in Mathematics and Physics." Presented before the American Mathematical Society at the New Orleans Meeting of the A.A.A.S., December 28, 1931. Reprinted as Supplement III to *Science and Sanity;* and *Science and Sanity,* p. 20, 58 ff. For an additional example of the current discursive use of an undefined term, see the recent article on the employment of "soul" by the black community by Ulf Hannerz, "What Negroes Mean by 'Soul'," *Trans-Action* (July–August), 1968.
6. Johnson, Wendell. *People in Quandaries.* New York: Harper & Row, 1946, pp. 129 ff.
7. Korzybski, *Science and Sanity,* pp. 20–21.
8. Johnson, *op. cit.*
9. Haney, William V. "The Uncritical Inference Test: Applications," *General Semantics Bulletin,* Nos. 28, 29, 1962.

APPENDIX 1

RECORD OF SURVEY NUMBER 12

Survey #12, taken 27 March, 1968; comments by Questioner and Subject in parentheses. (Subject: six-year-old-girl)

Query	Response
Play	I have fun.
Fun	It . . . I like it.
Like	Something . . . or someone that I love.
Love	I like someone.
Someone	It's a person.
Person	I thought you were going to say go or to or is or it. (We'll come to them later.) (Shrug) (Prod) A child.
Child	I don't know . . . (Prod) (Shrug) a little girl.
Girl	(Diversion) Something with long, long hair.
Something	(Stall) (Play with rubber band) (Prod) You see something.
See	You look at it . . . (I know you're going to say look.)
Look	You see something. (You're not going to use see again.)
See	I look at something.
Is	It is. (Prod) (Silence) I don't know . . . I don't know what it means.
Means	It means "means." (Prod) (Scratching) It doesn't mean scratch your head. You're doing something. (Walking around, evasive activity) (Prod) I don't know.
Know	You may not. (Know?) I'm not sure. I don't quite have anything for it. (Prod) (Shrug) I don't know. (Prod)
Do	You do something.

APPENDIX 2

RECORD OF SURVEY NUMBER 13

Survey #13, taken 27 March, 1968 comments by Questioner and Subject in parentheses. (Subject: seven-year-old boy)

Query	Response
Play	You do something that is fun.
Fun	Something that you like.
Like	You . . . someone . . . you are very fond of.
Fond	You like to be with it . . . many times.
Something	Like . . . something means a thing.
Thing	Thing means some kind of figure.
Figure	A shape.
Shape	Shape means like something is round . . . .
Something	Already did that.
Round	Something (Is that ink?) (Laughter, looking at notes) (Drawing circle) It's a shape.
Is	It is something. (Prodding for more) (Questioning about notes) (Statement of interest) Already told you.
Do	Means like you *do* something . . . (Prod) Well . . . you do something like make your bed . . . .
Make	You make something, and you try to make it better.
Better	Like . . . you should do something. (Question about what doing with "this.")
Should	You better do something before it gets too late.
Gets	Like you go to the store and get some bread and two gallons of milk.
Go	Go someplace and you sometimes come back.
Two	That there is two rubber bands on the table. (There are in fact two rubber bands on the table.) (Prod) There is two people and two is two things that sometimes are together and sometimes aren't. Are you going to ask Meda (the subject of Survey #12)?
Is	Means like "where is my bat?" and it means you can't find something and you want to know where it is.
It	Let me think. . . . You have something that you wanted to find.
Found	You were looking for something and you found it.
Looking	You want to find something.
Something	(Silence) What was that word? There is something on the table. Is that all? What else? (Playing with rubber band) (Read back) Also means where is something? I found something.
Word	That . . . word is something that you say.
Say	You open your mouth and you can hear a word.
Talk	You say some words to someone.
Mean	I don't know. What does it mean to you? . . . Is that what you wrote down? (Prod) I don't know. (Prod) Oh now I know. Mean means like there's two means. You say something to someone and you don't know what a person is talking about, and the other mean means you don't like something.

Cecil J. Coleman (Mrs. Merrill Coleman) is Professor of
Speech at State University College of Arts and Sciences at
Geneseo, New York. She is a member of the Advisory Board
of the General Semantics Foundation, and of the Editorial
Board of the *General Semantics Bulletin.* She was selected for
membership in Delta Kappa Gamma, an honorary international
sorority for distinguished women teachers, and won an Irving
J. Lee award for outstanding research in general semantics.

10

RELEVANCE: GENERAL SEMANTICS AND A TRUE BELIEVER

CECIL J. COLEMAN

THE United States is now a nation in deep and growing trouble. General
unrest and discontent crept surreptitiously upon a complacent people,
until smothered tensions flamed into disorders and violence that now have
been accepted, by many, as a way of life. Some believe the ever mounting
violence can destroy not only our society but also our nation, while others
adhere to the belief that it has been exaggerated and glorified. Because of
disorders, peaceful coexistence of peoples within our nation seems no
longer possible. "The True Believer is everywhere on the march, and both
by converting and antagonizing he is shaping the world in his own image."
Everywhere people are wondering what causes the concomitant mass movements so disruptive to our culture, and what kinds of persons answer their
appeal. Many viewpoints have been voiced, written and orally, in thousands of words, but one of the most interesting to me was one I came
across in a book entitled *The True Believer,* which seemed to me to discuss
historically mass movements from a fresh viewpoint—one which is relevant
to general semantics.

Eric Hoffer's *The True Believer*[1] was published in 1951. Timeless in its
perceptive analysis, it presaged today's social, political, academic, and financial restlessness. His philosophical treatment of the appeal of mass movement, and those who are attracted to it (whom he designates the "True Believer") will, because of its relevance today, constitute the prevailing idea
of this paper. It is not my purpose here to present a book review, but this
paper will draw heavily from Mr. Hoffer's penetrating study.

It will be my purpose to discuss from Mr. Hoffer's viewpoint the appeal of mass movements, the potential convert (called the "True Believer"), his characteristics before joining a mass movement, and their alleviation after identification with a cause. This paper will focus on the relevance of Hoffer's writings to general semantics, specifically that a True Believer with his disoriented semantic reactions is ruled by signal behavior, and that a "True Seeker" (the term my students gave to those not attracted by mass movement) displays a greater degree of sane semantic reactions, and is governed by symbol behavior. It will be the basic assumption that the behavior of one guided by the general semantics of Alfred Korzybski, and the behavior of those caught up in movements as described by Eric Hoffer, are mutually exclusive—at opposing ends of a continuum.

Therefore, the thesis of this paper might read: A True Believer, as described by Eric Hoffer, resembles one with semantic reaction disorientation.

The structure of this paper necessitates an explanation of terms as used by Mr. Hoffer. He does not see all mass movements as identical, but maintains they share certain essential characteristics:

> All mass movements generate in their adherents a readiness to die and a proclivity for united action; all of them, irrespective of the doctrine they preach and the program they project, breed fanaticism, enthusiasm, fervent hope, hatred and intolerance; all of them are capable of releasing a powerful flow of activity in certain departments of life; all of them demand blind faith and single-hearted allegiance.
>
> All movements, however different in doctrine and aspiration, draw their early adherents from the same types of humanity; they all appeal to the same types of man.[2]

The True Believer is a "man of fanatical faith who is ready to sacrifice his life for a holy cause." Frustration generates most of his characteristics. Mr. Hoffer uses the word "frustration" not as a clinical term, but the frustrated are herein considered as being those who feel their lives are spoiled or wasted.

A "holy cause" is a fanatical belief or system of beliefs erupting in a cause that consumes individuality, and the evaluative ability of those supporting it.

SOME CHARACTERISTICS OF A TRUE BELIEVER

Now, let us look at a True Believer who searches for a haven in mass movement. His deep unconquerable frustration is an integrative ingredient, fusing his other negative qualities according to his perception. The heaviest burden that he carries is an impaired, even hated, self, from which he feels irrevocably estranged. To lose this self, and the revulsion from it, to begin a new life with a new identity, to "belong," becomes a passionate desire. And it is this desire that compels him to accomplish these purposes through individual anonimity, new pride, confidence, and a sense of worth offered by mass movement after identifying with a holy cause. For the frustrated, the urge to escape a hated self is also the urge to escape the rational. He is impelled to deceive himself, to weave a false map for an unwanted territory. And is it not true that one who easily deceives himself is easily deceived by others, and recklessly follows where he is led? A man who does not respect himself cannot respect others; a man who does not trust himself cannot trust others. Self-respect must come first, but when it is lacking the need to be like associates, to imitate, cannot be suppressed. When the frustrated cannot experience satisfaction with himself, his need to imitate fertilizes his ability to lose awareness of his hated self. While rejection of the self stimulates imitation, it also promotes group unification through contempt for the outside world.

Frustration, then, produces a longing to be unified with a cause, and a readiness to sacrifice self for its achievement; but it also creates mental processes exemplified by selfishness, boredom, hatred, recklessness. Such emotions simulate reality when unconsciously projected onto one's environment. Frustration creeps upon the selfish, who may become fanatics when they lose faith in themselves. The bored are primarily bored with themselves, and to give meaning and excitement to their lives they join a holy cause. Hitler was supported and financed by bored wives early in his career. Perhaps today's protesting college students are in truth bored. The insecurity of a meaningless existence is relieved by passionately identifying with and supporting a cause.

Fanatics who are leaders protest established order and call for freedom of speech and freedom to shatter accepted modes of conduct. But they do not seem to realize that the masses who follow them do not crave *all* freedoms, but seek freedom from the burden of free choice and the responsibility of their ineffectual selves. "They sweep away the old order, not to create a society for free and independent men, but to establish uniformity, individual anonymity and a new structure of perfect unity." [3]

The sharing of a common, unreasonable hatred is the most infectious of all unifying processes. Self-contempt changes to a hatred more vicious when feelings of inadequacy, apprehensiveness, and helplessness are present. Hatred is a strange and puzzling emotion. It is not always directed against one's wrongdoers, but is sometimes aimed at an innocent person or group. The German Nazis, angered by the Versailles treaty, exterminated the innocent Jews. Radical Black Power advocates vent their hatred by burning and looting businesses of unoffending owners. Robert Kennedy fell before an assassin's bullet, a target of nationalistic hatred.

Even more baffling is the theory that when one feels superior to his offenders, he may despise them, and certainly pity them, but he cannot hate them. One cannot hate those he despises. For example, in World War II many Japanese respected the Americans more than most Americans reciprocated that esteem; therefore the Japanese hatred was more vicious. Those Americans who have a sense of superiority over all other nations cannot hate ruthlessly. Ruthless hatred stems from weakness, and a mass movement offers a haven from it as well as a place to pamper a fanatical grievance. Yet we find that mass movement itself often imitates those it desires to resist. For instance, one may join a civil rights movement because of a dislike for intolerance, and then become intolerant of those outside the movement. Campus protest movements demanding freedom of speech and certain privileges often deny others the rights they are seeking.

Kindled within the True Believer is an extravagant hope for an unblemished future. He cares not for what he has, but is ready to die for that which he doesn't have. The future holds infinitely more attractions than the present. His dreams and wild hopes are, to him, realistic tools with which he fights for his future. The weakedness of the True Believer create his diaphanous source of strength. Through his intensional orientation, he molds an unrealistic map for his world, a map that includes no process analysis for its achievement.

In a column in the *Democrat and Chronicle* of Rochester, New York, on Sunday March 3, 1968, Mr. Hoffer was reported as saying:

> It has been often said that power corrupts. But it is perhaps equally important to realize that weakness, too, corrupts. Power corrupts the few, while weakness corrupts the many. Hatred, malice, rudeness, intolerance, and suspicion are the fruits of weakness. The resentment of the weak does not spring from any injustice done to them but from the sense of their inadequacy and impotence. We cannot win the weak by sharing our wealth with them. They feel our generosity as oppression. St. Vincent de Paul cautioned his disciples to deport themselves so that the poor "will forgive you the bread you give them."

The True Believer who is fully engrossed in a unified movement for a holy cause is then no longer frustrated. He feels a new group identity. He has achieved his purposes. He has a new power, faith in the future; he belongs, yet he cannot feel secure. He has no choice of behavior, for his deliverance from his hated self is dependent upon the will of the unified movement. "He must cling to the collective body or like a fallen leaf wither and fade." So his struggle for utmost unity may be more agonizing than the trials of frustration. "The True Believer is eternally incomplete, eternally insecure." [4]

In brief, frustration is alleviated when a True Believer joins a mass movement. Self-hatred is forgotten as a holy cause is substituted for the whole self, and therein faith in a holy cause becomes a substitute for faith in oneself. No longer does one need to depend on himself; there is no need to think, only to do—to act. There is no need for evaluation, for decision-making; there is no need for personal philosophy. Some would say that the True Believer is no longer semantically disoriented, because he is, to an extent, unaware of his environment. He is no longer capable of exercising evaluative processes; he is submerged and without identity as an individual. Complete dependence is like a hypnotic drug; he is lost in his own fantasy of life.

APPEALS OF MASS MOVEMENT

The appeal of mass movement for the potential True Believer can be channeled loosely into three areas: 1) the desire of the convert for change, 2) a strong desire for substitutes for inadequacies inside-his-skin, and 3) the ease with which mass movement can change in focus.

DESIRE FOR CHANGE

Mass movement demands drastic, catastrophic, immediate change. Campus revolutionaries, civil rights and protest marchers seek instant success. Such bold insistence is the mode of the juvenile who grossly misinterprets the territory. The analytical thinker knows that most desired change comes through growth. In his syndicated newspaper column, Mr. Hoffer recently wrote: "To the juvenile mentality, continuity and gradualness are synonymous with stagnation, while drastic change is a mark of dynamism, vigor, and freedom."

Countries that experience succeeding revolutions are led by those demanding immediate change in a way of life. But when the accomplished change fails in shaping the territory so that it satisfactorily represents the map of the revolutionaries, a further revolution must begin. History is replete with examples of nations whose leaders fail or succeed in their causes in direct proportion to their ability to fail or succeed in arousing the fervor of the people toward their cause. Some years ago the Labor Party in Britain met with difficulty in changing the economy of the country, partially because it failed to set in motion reckless hope and enthusiasm for its advocated program. On the other hand, Japan was modernized into an impressive nation with extraordinary rapidity concomitant with nationalistic enthusiasm. Perhaps a contributing factor to the apparent hopeless stalemate in our present undeclared war in Asia is that it has failed to become a holy cause. Soul-stirring demand for victory has not come from the people. War songs have not been written and sung to cheering throngs; our servicemen have not marched in our streets.

Unbridled excitement, kept at a high pitch by leaders, generates a reckless daring and extravagant hope. Means to this end are symbols, such as the Nazi swastika, and the communal chanting of phrases like "Black Power," "We shall overcome," and "Hell no, we won't go." Unison singing binds together like cement those who share it. Leaders know that marching as a unifying activity stifles certain men's thoughts and individualties. They know that frustration often is nourished by a wanting to act but not knowing how; the opportunity for action through marching therefore elicits an eager response from the frustrated. Marching is a basic ingredient for stimulation of reckless excitement, as Hitler knew and practiced. And when marching, symbols, chanting, and singing are combined, excitement is rampant. Even in war, uniforms, flags, emblems, marching, and music can kindle an enthusiasm and daring obliterating the otherwise overwhelming reality of life and death. Leaders hasten to capitalize on this proclivity.

One's conscious awareness of environment, his rational relating to his environment should make clear to him that time gently enfolds important changes. While the electrochemical changes in the nervous system necessary for the transmission of stimuli to the brain are instantaneous, the processes involved in evaluation take place at a much slower pace. There is an interval between initial understanding of what one reads or hears, and getting it inside-his-skin. Thus a wise individual delays somewhat in assimilating new ideas, and concordantly changing his way of life.

DESIRE FOR SUBSTITUTES

We have seen that a major appeal of mass movement for potential converts is the desire for swift, sudden change. A second appeal is an overpowering desire for substitutes for weaknesses inside-the-skin. People with self-esteem are not attracted to mass movements. A mass movement attracts and holds a following not because it can satisfy the desire for self-advancement, but because it can satisfy the passion for self-effacement. Those who are filled with self-effacement crave the loss of identity possible in a mass movement. The hopelessness of their sense of failure arouses a longing for a new life. Able to abstract on one level only, the potential True Believer seeks rebirth, confidence, and hope through identification with the search for a holy cause. Prone to two-valued thinking, his failure, to him, becomes success as his faith in the holy cause substitutes for the lost faith in himself. His frustration is relieved, his life is bearable, as he cherishes the inference that the power sought from his alliance with the mass movement will be transferred to him. Unable to affirm purpose and achievement for his own self, he can now claim it for his holy cause. Emotion transferred to the adopted substitute, because it enriches a futile, spoiled life, will necessarily be passionate and extreme, devoid of rational evaluation. The kinds of things one abstracts concerning himself are of vital importance!

INTERCHANGEABILITY OF FOCUS

A third appeal of mass movement is the interchangeability of their holy cause. When one is emotionally ready for a mass movement, the particular cause seems to be unimportant. Even after a zealous True Believer has become a convert to a movement, he may shift his fidelity in a manifestation of one form of casuistry. "In pre-Hitlerian Germany, it was often a toss-up whether a restless youth would join the Communists or the Nazi's movement." [5] The civil rights movement involving the Poor Peoples March to Washington deteriorated in Resurrection City into a welfare plea. A Hippie movement with its cause of love and peace culminated in a religious assemblage atop a Rocky mountain near Boulder, Colorado, to await the end of the world.

Dr. Alex Platt, Associate Dean of Columbia University, declares that campus protest demonstrations represent, in part, a religious phenomenon. He believes revolutionary students are in truth searching for a purified community, and that sometimes through violence they feel purged and purified. Thus their original protest causes become the means to an end, which is purification of their souls.

Last year, a small band of students at the State University of New York at Geneseo initiated a movement to protest what they chose to call an *in loco parentis* position, which they believed the college demonstrated by enforcing hours for women students. Successful in abolishing women's hours, they then shouted *in loco parentis* concerning a ban on the use of liquor on the campus. Through newspaper headlines, they announced their freedom from any abridgement of their liberty and their ability to handle themselves as adults. Succeeding demands were gratified until even the most liberal could no longer accuse the college of *in loco parentis.* But my experience in the classroom with these same students convinces me that the territory has little relationship to their verbal map. Actually, most students in an academic environment expect and want leadership in at least two areas—knowledge and values; and a teacher who dispenses only knowledge dismays them. It is my opinion that despite some verbal student rebellion against *in loco parentis,* they long for guidance and direction that will permit them to discover and implement lasting values. And they want the teacher to exemplify them in his professional and social ethics.

GROUPS INVOLVED IN MASS MOVEMENTS

No strata of society is immune to the appeals of mass movement. The wealthy may become as frustrated as the poor. Mr. Hoffer discusses the poor on interesting lower levels of abstraction, yet, in his discussions, fails to reach the individual level. He tells us that mass movement holds infinitely more charm for the new poor and the free poor than for the abjectly poor, 'the creative poor, and the unified poor, all of whom are relatively free from frustration.

The *new poor* "throb with the ferment of frustration. The memory of better things is as fire in their veins." [6] In the seventeenth century, the new poor joined the successful Puritan Revolution in England. In Germany and Italy, the new poor were the strength of the Nazi and Fascist revolutions. On the other hand, the *abjectly poor* have no time for revolutions. Their desperate struggle for food and shelter occupies all their time and strength. Success to them is a full stomach. Theirs is a world of low-level abstraction, and mass movement on a high-level abstraction has no appeal for them. "When people toil from sunrise to sunset for a bare living, they nurse no grievances and dream no dreams." For most people, frustration is greater "when we have much, and want more, than when we have nothing and want some—we are less dissatisfied when we lack many things than when we seem to lack but one thing" [7]

The *free poor* are more frustrated than those to whom slavery is a way of life. Free from competition and individual prominence, the equality fostered by slavery discourages frustration. To the free poor, freedom is a burden that only intensifies frustration by giving them the responsibility for decision-making. So, "to be free from freedom," to gain anonymity, they may seek the eddy of a cause. "It was not sheer hypocrisy when the rank-and-file Nazis declared themselves not guilty of all the enormities they had committed. They considered themselves cheated and maligned when made to shoulder responsibility for obeying orders. Had they not joined the Nazi movement in order to be free from responsibility?" Those who cry the loudest for freedom are very often least likely to find happiness in a free society. James Oppenheim expresses this sentiment in a poem called *The Slave:**

> They set the slave free . . .
> Then he was as much of a slave as ever.
>
> He was still chained to servility,
> He was still manacled to indolence and sloth,
> He was still bound by fear and superstition,
> By ignorance, suspicion, and savagery . . .
> His slavery was not in the chains,
> But in himself . . .
>
> They can only set free men free . . .
> And there is no need of that:
> Free men set themselves free.

The *creative poor* are seldom frustrated. Those who work with their hands usually find contentment, therefore mass movement holds little or no appeal for them.

The *unified poor,* such as a Chinese family with strong family ties, or an intensely religious group such as the Quakers, Mormons, or Mennonites are relatively free from frustration; families who love and work together seldom heed the call of a mass movement. But "where a mass movement finds the corporate pattern of family, tribe, or country in a state of disruption and decay, it moves in and gathers the harvest." [9]

SOME CHARACTERISTICS OF A TRUE SEEKER

A semantically disoriented individual—a True Believer—who seeks a promise of fulfillment through mass movement, engages in a flight from his reality.

What can we say about the semantically oriented person whom my students have labeled a "True Seeker?"

He is the person Korzybski might call an "organism-as-a-whole-in-an-environment," Rogers might say a "fully functioning personality," Maslow would call him a "self-actualizing individual," and Bess Sondel might say "one who is feeling + thinking + doing."

It seems to me the referent of these descriptive labels would viably epitomize a high degree of human achievement. His respect and love and trust of others would be commensurate with his respect and love and trust of

---

* From *Songs for the New Age.* New York: Alfred A. Knopf, 1914.

himself. These qualities would infuse him with enthusiasm for life and his unique place in it. His faith in the future integratively both enhances and is evidenced by his personal philosophy, his code of ethics, his devotion to his work, and his caring for his fellowman. He would know his values and understand his prejudices; he would be teachable since he abstracts on all levels and is aware of a process world.

Moreover, frustration in a True Seeker acts as a stimulus for exploration, and insecurity as an impetus for inquiry. His actions are not impetuous; he is guided by symbol behavior.

RELEVANCE TO GENERAL SEMANTICS

This brief sketch of the True Seeker delineates some of the characteristics of one who employs the tools of general semantics as a highly rational approach to human evaluation and ethical behavior.

An intensionally oriented True Believer draws his impelling forces from an inadequate map of the territory, but for strength and serenity the general semanticist maintains internal stages in harmony with continuously changing external states. He can astutely change his level of abstraction in problem situations. He checks his verbal map with the territory because it is constantly changing in his process world. He is aware of the difference between belief and bigotry, between selflessness and selfishness; he recognizes a situation as it is and not as what he wants it to be. He indexes intellectually as well as emotionally; he discriminates intelligently. He is viable, beautifully and fully alive, and continues to grow and achieve as an effective time-binder.

Korzybski's general semantics is concerned with human welfare—with advancing its values, ethics, and capacities to the highest good. Therefore, it doesn't work for people involved in such mass movements. Korzybski gave people a way to develop as a whole individual, and at the same time function as an effective member of a democratic society. Strong individuals don't wantonly rebel against or break the laws of the society in which they live.

In 1968 candidates for the office of President of the United States declared the problem of social unrest today to be the primary one facing our country, and many sociologists agree. The relevance of general semantics to the solution of these problems is not to be denied, for the characteristics of a True Believer, as described by Eric Hoffer, are incompatible with those of a general semanticist.

We all have weaknesses; most of us recognize them. We also recognize our strengths. And we know these may change from day to day and from moment to moment. We are comfortable with this change. We are careful of our abstractions about ourselves. We know that we must have a feeling of belonging, whether it be to a family or a group, but we know that for inner strength we cannot depend completely on a sense of security flowing from other people.

I do not speak of general semantics as a panacea, but as an exceedingly effective system through which man can deal with his semantic reactions to his internal and external environment. We all need to believe in something, to believe sincerely, devotedly, enthusiastically. But when we polarize as a True Believer does, when we totter on the end of a continuum, we are in danger. We need process thinking—a recognition of the difference between reckless abandonment of reason, in order to get what we want, and advancing our beliefs with a caring consideration for others. And if a True Believer, as described by Eric Hoffer, is to be helped in finding himself through general semantics, it must become a vital part of his resocialization.

General semantics, by its very structure, prevents the fruition of frustration and fanaticism.

Harry L. Weinberg, in *Levels of Knowing and Existence,* says, "The deliberate and constant use of semantic devices helps to provoke and maintain the vitally important awareness of the dangers of oversimplification, dogmatism, and static-mindedness, and aids in the development of that sophisticated innocence which enables us to look with a fresh and inquiring eye upon the world around us." [10]

The True Believer, as described by Eric Hoffer, could not flourish in such an environment.

REFERENCES

1. Hoffer, Eric. *The True Believer.* New York: Harper & Row, 1951, p. 160.
2. *Ibid.,* p. 9.
3. *Ibid.,* p. 129.
4: *Ibid.,* p. 117.
5. *Ibid.,* p. 25.
6. *Ibid.,* p. 31.
7. *Ibid.,* pp. 33–34.
8. *Ibid.,* p. 36.
9. *Ibid.,* p. 39.
10. Weinberg, Harry L. *Levels of Knowing and Existence.* New York: Harper & Row, 1959, p. 47.

S. I. Hayakawa is currently President of San Francisco State College where he was formerly Professor of English. Canadian born, he studied at Manitoba and McGill Universities, and received his Ph.D. from the University of Wisconsin. He is editor of *ETC: A Review of General Semantics,* author of *Language in Thought and Action,* and a number of other books and articles.

11

A SEARCH FOR RELEVANCE [1968] *

S. I. HAYAKAWA

I DON'T need to tell you that general semantics is relevant in our times. But there is one particular aspect of this relevance that presses on my mind very much. I want to share it with you.

Like Marshall McLuhan, I'm much concerned with television and its impact on the world. And like Marshall McLuhan, I agree that no medium of mass communication is as powerful in its effect on people.

In 1963, at the International Conference on General Semantics, I argued that the Negro revolution was triggered by television. Before the advent of radio and television, to be a nonreader was to be cut off from the world. But today, the illiterate and poorly educated can hear about and see events and people he formerly could know nothing about. Electronic communication has brought the whole big startling world into the lives and imaginations of millions who otherwise would not have been aware of it.

Furthermore, American television is commercially sponsored. It finds its economic support and justification in pushing consumer goods. Therefore, television is always friendly and cajoling and persuasive. It tells everybody, "No matter how miserable your present condition, you too can be attractive. You can be as good as anybody else. You can enjoy all the satisfactions of living in this lush and abundant consumer economy."

---

* It was subsequent to the conference on which this volume is based that Professor Hayakawa assumed the post of Acting President [now President] of San Francisco State College—a task that has absorbed most of his time in recent months. This paper is not, therefore, the paper that he might have preferred to prepare for this volume, but is based upon an edited tape-script of one of the talks that he made at the conference.—EDITOR.

As I said in 1963, imagine that you are a young Negro to whom the television set with such messages has been his constant baby-sitter and companion. All your life the friendly television set has been saying to you, "You are an American. You are entitled to eat, drink, and wear what other Americans eat, drink, and wear. You are a member of our national community." Then imagine you are this young Negro, deprived by social custom and by lack of education and lack of training from sharing all these things. Would you not be frustrated and angry?

There are a lot of things about this message which create what Alfred Korzybski called our semantic environment. Our semantic environment is the whole environment of messages in which we live. Television is a powerful contributor to that semantic environment.

The basic message of commercial television is "Want this product. Want this convenience. Want this luxury. Buy. Buy. Buy. If you have enough things, all your problems will be solved. This hairdressing, this headache remedy, this broiler, this luxurious carpeting, this new automobile will bring you charm, popularity, sexual fulfillment, domestic bliss, and the envy and respect of your neighbors." All happiness and all significance and all values that human beings might strive for are transformed by advertising into purchasable commodities.

Such, then, are the messages of television. For the culturally unsophisticated, there are few messages from other sources. In many lower-class homes, white and Negro, the television set is never turned off from morning till night. Into these homes, a multibillion-dollar industry beams daily and nightly messages—messages skillfully devised to create demand, to stimulate desire, to nurture the spirit of envy. "Man, I wish I had one of them," they say as they stare into that color television.

Can anyone doubt the enormous greed for consumer goods that has actuated every outbreak of looting and burning since Watts? This greed is by no means confined to Negroes. For example, what characterized the disorders in Detroit, according to all accounts, was the apparent lack of racist motivation among many of the looters. Whites helped Negroes, Negroes helped whites load into their cars and carry off television sets, furniture, tape recorders, end tables and luggage, all in a spirit of interracial brotherhood. We read that a gay carnival spirit attended much of the looting. One Detroit police sergeant was quoted as saying, "This isn't a race riot. It's a riot of thieves."

At the heart of all this, the central fact is that the message of television is: "Don't wait. Buy today. Don't postpone gratification."

This message comes at a most inopportune time, right on top of the Civil

Rights movement. One of the real problems of the lower-class Negro, still retaining one hundred years later some of the horrid and tragic inheritance of slavery, is the inability to postpone gratification. Under slavery, postponement of gratification made no sense. If you saved your money or improved your land, it all belonged to your master anyway, so slaves had too much sense to work all that hard for somebody else. Many underprivileged Negroes, as we all know, have inherited from slavery days the habits of irresponsibility and living from moment to moment.

The tragedy is that, at the very moment when the postponement of gratification begins to make sense for the American Negro (as for all the other poor, because of the great increase in educational opportunities and openings in trades and professions), lower-class Negroes are bombarded by television with messages *not* to save their money, *not* to practice self-denial, but to hurry, hurry, hurry to the nearest furniture store or automobile showroom and brighten their lives with the latest models now on display, for only a tiny down payment and 36 months to pay.

In other words, television discourses with fantastic skill, with fantastic persuasive talents, on the rewards that our economy can offer to those who prosper. But television says nothing about the long years of self-denial, the long years of study and practice, the patient discipline of daily work (and getting to work on time despite the fact that you don't feel like it) for year after year after year in order to earn seniority and promotion and better salaries.

TV is creating, in many of us, the mentality of certain happy South Sea Islanders who lived for the day and did not worry about tomorrow, because all they had to do was to reach out their hands for an abundance of coconuts, bananas, or fish. At the very moment, then, when it becomes worthwhile for the underprivileged Negro to postpone gratification, he is urged not to do so.

So the ordinary frustrations of ignorance and poverty are sharpened for Negroes and for everybody who is poor today. It is by no means limited to the American Negro. The ordinary frustrations of poverty have been sharpened to an unprecedented extent by the impact of television. No wonder there is anger and frustration in the Negro community, and no wonder there are such angry manifestations as, for example, the Black Panther movement.

Since that is a good example, I'd like to comment further on the Black Panther movement. As Wendell Johnson said, "Every speaker is his own most interested and affected listener."

The word *black* has evil connotations in our culture. For a long, long time we avoided saying "black people." We said "Negroes," because the word black had connotations of dark, black, evil, Satanic, sinister, and so on. White had connotations of purity, loveliness, elegance, truth, brightness, clarity, and so on. When people call themselves Black Nationalists, Black Panthers, they, like everybody else, are victims of the English language. So they wear black berets, black sweaters, black trousers, black shoes, and black sunglasses, and they role-play being black, suggesting dark, evil, sinister, Satanic.

The policemen of Oakland, California also speak the English language, and they have a semantic reaction to all this Black Panther business. They act as if there were evil, Satanic, ferocious, predatory black forces at loose in the world. The Oakland Police Department arms itself, and prepares for all kinds of trouble. So the black people and the white policemen are all role-playing around the words *black-white, black-white*—both of them trapped by the English language.

What would happen if the Black Panthers had called themselves, instead, the Soul Brothers Mutual Assistance Society? It's a beautiful name. Soul Brothers. That's fine. Mutual Assistance. That's fine. And the cops wouldn't· have to organize themselves in this ferocious way against the Panthers.

This groping around for improvement of self-concept is tragic, kind of mixed-up. Certainly, the semantic analysis of the factors that go into creating such social situations is a tremendously important one.

So I would call upon students of general semantics to study the mechanisms of semantic reaction, and also to study the content and nature of what Alfred Korzybski called the semantic environment, now made so much richer and more complex by the advent of television.

Knowing more about semantic reactions to semantic environments, educators, government, and the broadcasting industry itself might have better facts and better knowledge with which to govern future policies in the interests of more wise use of the greatest instrument of time-binding ever invented—television.

Dwight R. Kauppi is currently Research Fellow, Work Adjustment Project, University of Minnesota. Formerly, he was a visiting lecturer in Counseling and Behavioral Studies at the University of Wisconsin; Coordinator of the Counselor Education Program of the American Rehabilitation Foundation, and Vocational Counselor at the Minneapolis Rehabilitation Center. He is a candiate for the Ph.D. in Psychology at the University of Minnesota.

12

THE APPLICATION OF GENERAL SEMANTICS TO THE CLASSIFICATION OF MENTALLY RETARDED [1]

DWIGHT R. KAUPPI

IN applying general semantics to the classification, "mentally retarded," we can first specify some of the characteristics of a classification system based on the principles of general semantics. Primarily, we might suppose that such a system would work, producing some scientifically and technically desirable results. The system should allow better communication by summarizing large amounts of information about individuals in neat, easy to handle packets. We would expect that there would be great agreement among users of the terms as to how the system should be applied. This would permit discourse to begin at a level deeper than whether a specific set of symptoms should or should not be given a particular name. We would expect that in some cases the system should have extensional definitions. One may not be able to point to "a mental retardation," but one should be able to point to specific attributes of people who bear the label. If the system is to have any usefulness beyond a nominal one, it might also be expected that individuals within a class be like one another in more characteristics than what was measured to put them in that class, and furthermore that these characteristics have some important predictable results. Placing a person within a class should increase the probability that he will possess a particular set of traits, or that he will benefit from certain treatments and suffer from others, or that a particular outcome is likely. If the process of classification is especially expensive in comparison to the alter-

89

native methods of deciding treatment or predicting outcomes, then the implications of that classification must be more vital or more certain. If important characterisitcs of what is to be classified are multivalued, the classification system used should be multivalued so that the system does not obscure when it should illuminate.

Does the professional and scientific usage of classification systems follow these reflections of general semantics principles? There is much evidence that it does not, and that ignorance of general semantics principles costs a great deal in money, wasted effort, and actual harm to people.

First, there is evidence that agreement on the use of the words and labels is not great, especially when the importance of the system and the time spent in its development is considered. In a recent survey of the systems in use, Gelof[2] found 23 major classificatory systems proposed and used by the various professional, institutional, and governmental groups, and individuals interested in the field of mental retardation. These systems differed not only in the words used as labels for similarly described phenomena, but also in the phenomena referred to by the same words. Thus, the same person could be given one of eight or ten labels, depending upon which system was used by the person diagnosing him.

Second, persons classified as mentally retarded are not necessarily similar. Although most persons so classified have a "low IQ," most classification systems insist on the use of some kinds of judgments in addition to a low score on the intelligence test. One of the ultimate results of such a multiply-determined, multiply-based classification is a reduced consistency in the people who are labeled the same. One may have a relatively high IQ but also have trouble in getting along with one's peers. Another may bear the same label because of a lower IQ and difficulties in school work. Still a third may be included in the same group because of low IQ, poor school work, slow development, and social retardation, all due to what might more accurately be diagnosed as an emotional problem.

With such a diversity of subjects included within the same categories, it is not surprising that predictions based upon this classification system are sometimes inaccurate. Research on the results of special class education for students classified as mentally retarded is equivocal.[3] This may be because the tools of special-class teaching are not yet well enough developed. It may also be that mentally retarded persons are so unlike one another that any special system of teaching does not result in uniform benefits, any more than the regular system does. In predicting outcomes beyond school, the classification system has even less success. When persons labeled mentally retarded during their childhood and adolescent years are followed up as

adults, their rankings on a variety of social, personal, and economic variables are scarcely different from a similar group not called mentally
retarded.[4]

The use of the term seems to have been reified. Although many researchers pay at least lip service to the merit of using "mental retardation"
as an arbitrary designation for the lower end of a continuum of a specific
kind of ability, much of the research done is devoted to specifying the "es-
sense" of the term. Such research seems to presume that since we can name
the classes and put people in them, then the people in the classes must have
something that people outside the classifications don't have. What began as
a category of convenience is now guiding much research—research that
yields inconsistent and equivocal results. With such a variety of ways for
putting persons into the "mentally retarded" classification, it is not surprising that they tend to be heterogeneous, with a variety of "essences."

There are many reasons why such a semantically muddled classification
system developed despite the scientific training and ability of the professionals involved. One reason seems to be the involvement of the medical
profession, necessary through the association of many kinds of diseases, ill-
nesses, and physical defects with mental retardation. Medical handling
stresses the importance of diagnostic classification based on etiology with
specific treatment then implied by the "cause" of the problem. Another reason is that there are self-fulfilling prophesies inherent in the system. A person is first labeled "mentally retarded" on the basis of a suspected status,
which has implications for certain predicted outcomes. He is then treated in
a particular way, deprived of the usual educational, social, and vocational
experiences and opportunities. The accuracy of the earlier classification is
then "proven" by his eventual atypical status on these dimensions. Third,
researchers seeking the "essence" of mental retardation sometimes compare
the characteristics of retardates who have spent much of their lives in special classes or institutions with age and sex matched normals, and then attribute the differences found to the "mental retardation" of their experimental group. With such factors as institutionalization, experimenter bias,
halo effect, and criterion contamination at work, a person once called mentally retarded is almost certain to show the characteristics we attribute to
mental retardation. Fourth, our ability measurement tests are usually designed for use in educational settings, for use in making educational decisions. They utilize similar formats, and measure various aspects of motivation, test taking skill, and verbal facility in addition to the ability that the
test is being used to measure. As a result, persons who are similar in performance on the measure used to classify them as mentally retarded (e.g.,

an individual intelligence test) will also be similar on measures of a wide variety of other abilities. This seems to validate the practice of such classi- fication, but may be based on no more than the similarity of like-classed subjects' test-taking abilities. Sometimes surveys of groups of "retardates" are taken to find their status on some nonintellectual characteristic such as speech problems. Since many of the persons in such a group will suffer from physical and central nervous system damage of one kind or another, the incidence of speech and articulation problems will be greater than it is in a "normal" group. This difference from normal incidence is then re- ported and noted as though it were a part of mental retardation rather than as being related to a state of affairs that is sometimes also associated with what is called mental retardation.

Another aspect of the system that perpetuates its use is the easy explana- tion offered for problems noted within the individual or within the educa- tional system. Once a person is labeled as mentally retarded, it is easy enough to use this label as the explanation for all sorts of social and per- sonal deficiencies, many of which might be better diagnosed and remedied were it not for the easily applied "explanation." Similarly, failures of our classrooms to provide the retarded with needed skills are often blamed not on the teacher nor on the educational system, but on the inability of the "retardate" to learn.

There is one powerful argument often given in favor of categorizing some people as "mentally retarded." Even if they are alike only in sharing a lack of certain verbal abilities related to academic success, verbal abilities are so important in our culture that is is worthwhile to classify on that ba- sis. It would be difficult for anyone versed in general semantics to deny the importance of verbal symbols in mastering our environments. But it seems wasteful to include so many other kinds of abilities and characteristics in the classification. We should classify and treat people who have trouble with book learning on the basis of their trouble with book learning, and not call it something else with even broader implications.

How could the teachings of general semantics be better applied to the la- beling and classifying of the "mentally retarded?" One relatively simple but far-reaching step would be to stop the reification of the concept. If we rec- ognize that in classifying, the best we can do is simply to seek a useful or- dering to an underlying continuum of a particular set of abilities, then we can stop wasting time looking for the "essential nature" of the people we choose to place there. We might also recognize the result of our labeling. If some way could be found to give needed educational and other attention to needful individual students without calling them retarded, their needs might be served without causing additional problems, and without assuming that because they all have trouble, they are all alike. Further, the time honored semantic device of indexing might serve to achieve some of the desired results. If we could remember that retardate $_1$ is not the same as retardate $_2$ or even that Educable Mental Retard with a Stanford-Binet IQ of 65_1 is not the same as Educable Mental Retard with a Stanford-Binet IQ of 65_2, many of the dangers and problems associated with our classification system would be reduced. In addition, we should index abilities in order to remember that ability$_1$ is not ability$_2$, and that measuring a person's ability to define words on a multiple choice test does not tell us how well he will do in an art class.

This multivalued orientation should not be difficult for the scientists and professionals working with the mentally retarded. The desired individualizing could be better maintained if the end result of the diagnostic "work-up" were not assignment of the subject to a particular cell in a classification system but rather an evaluation of the person's many abilities and the many facets of his personality. Such a system requires that the same tools of measurement be developed for the mentally retarded as are available for the normal. We do not, after all, suppose that we know all that is relevant about a young person seeking vocational guidance when we say that he is in the normal range of intelligence. We need to know much more: How well does he work with numbers? Is he quick with simple motor acts? How much can he lift? Does he like to work alone? Does he need to make a lot of money? There is no reason why we should not ask these questions about the individual called "mentally retarded."

The ultimate question that might be asked of any mental retardation classification system is: Is it effective? Unquestionably, most of the people included in the mental retardation category share in lacking a set of abilities that are important in many of today's activities. But has the process of abstraction for classification hidden more than it has revealed? Are individuals who are alike on these attributes really alike on many others, or do we create alikenesses through our perception and handling of them because of the label? Are they as a group really unable to learn and function usefully, or is part of the problem our inability or unwillingness to teach in ways that they can profit from? The evidence seems clear. Recurrent problems in devising a classification system that will be satisfactory will not be solved by changing the names or shifting the criteria for categories. The problems that recur seem ample evidence of the results of ignoring the importance and relevance of general semantics principles in devising a classification system.

REFERENCES

1. This paper was supported, in part, by Research Grant RD–2568–P from the Social and Rehabilitation Service, U.S. Department of Health, Education, and Welfare.
2. Gelof, Malvin. "Comparison of Systems of Classification Relating Degree of Retardation to Measured Intelligence," *American Journal of Mental Deficiency,* 1963, *68,* pp. 297–317.
3. Sparks, H. L., and Blackman, L. S. "What is Special about Special Education Revisited: The Mentally Retarded," *Exceptional Children,* 1965, *31,* pp. 242–247.
4. Goldstein, Herbert. "Social and Occupational Adjustment," *Mental Retardation,* eds. H. A. Stevens and R. Heber. Chicago: University of Chicago Press, 1964.

Stanley Krippner is Director of the William C. Menninger Dream Laboratory, Maimonides Medical Center, Brooklyn, New York. He also serves as a Consultant in Special Education, Staten Island Mental Health Clinic, is Director of Research for the New York Institute for the Achievement of Human Potential, teaches courses in child development in the graduate school of Wagner College, and is the author of over 80 articles in educational, psychological, and psychiatric journals. He is a Fellow of the American Society of Clinical Hypnosis, a member of the Institute for the Study of Drug Addiction, and on the Advisory Board of the Student Association for the Study of Hallucinogens. He is Vice President of the National Association for Gifted Children, and received, in 1959, the YMCA's Service to Youth Award. He received his Ph.D. from Northwestern University in 1961.

13

PSYCHEDELIC EXPERIENCE AND THE LANGUAGE PROCESSES *

STANLEY KRIPPNER

AYER once claimed that "we are unable, in our everyday language to describe the properties of sense-contents with any great precision, for lack of the requisite symbols. . . ." [1] Ayer's statement about normal, everyday perception has even greater application when chemically-altered perception is considered. The difficulties subjects have in describing their experiences are compounded by the difficulties experimenters often have in interpreting these reports in terms of some organizational structure.

One of the more successful attempts to categorize subjective reports of psychedelic ("mind-manifesting") experience has been made by Masters and Houston. [2] Having guided 206 subjects through a large number of LSD and peyote sessions, Masters and Houston proposed the existence of four levels of mental functioning in the psychedelic state: sensory, recollective-analytic, symbolic, and integral.

At the first or sensory level, the subject may report a changed awareness

* The author expresses his appreciation to Arthur Melzer and Gordon Goodman for their assistance in the preparation of this paper, which was supported by a grant from the Erickson Educational Foundation.

of the body, unusual ways of experiencing space and time, heightened sense impressions, synesthesia ("feeling sounds," "hearing color"), and—with the eyes closed—vivid visual imagery. Experiences at the sensory level tend to "decondition" a subject, to loosen his habitual conceptions, and to ease the rigidity of his past imprinting.

At the second or recollective-analytic level, the subject's reactions become more emotionally intense. He may relive periods of his life. He may formulate insights into himself, his work, and his personal relationships.

Only 40 percent of Masters' and Houston's subjects reached the third or symbolic level. At this level, visual imagery generally involves history and legend, or the subject may recapitulate the evolutionary process, developing from primordial protoplasm to man. He may also embark upon a "ritual of passage," and imagine himself participating in a baptismal ceremony or puberty rite.

Eleven percent of Masters' and Houston's subjects reached the fourth or integral level at which religious or mystical experiences occur. Masters and Houston have described the religious experience as a confrontation with the "Ground of Being"; they contrast mystical experience as a dissolution, as a merging of the individual with the energy field of the universe. One woman related, "All around and passing through me was the light, a trillion atomized crystals shimmering in the blinding incandescence."

Masters and Houston have stated that without a properly trained guide, subjects generally fluctuate between the first and second levels because they are unable to send themselves more deeply into the experience. Another advantage of a professional guide is the avoidance of unpleasant consequences; none of the subjects in the Masters-Houston study had untoward reactions.

Masters and Houston have defined psychedelic experience as the experiencing of states of awareness profoundly different from the usual waking state, from dreams, from intoxication states, and from most pathological states. "Sensory experience, thought, emotions—awareness of self and of world—all undergo remarkable changes. Consciousness expands to take in the contents of deep, ordinarily inaccessible regions of the psyche." [3]

THE EVOLUTION OF LANGUAGE

Like psychedelic experience, human language processes may be studied in four different manifestations. The development of social language begins at the approximate age of nine months with the acquisition of a simple listening vocabulary.[4] By one year, most children have spoken their first word. In the American culture, two other forms of language—reading and writing—are usually introduced when the child enters school, although some children acquire these abilities before formal education begins. Speaking and writing are expressive skills and involve encoding one's experiences. Listening and reading are receptive skills and require decoding of another person's attempts to communicate. Speaking and listening, both aural in nature, have developmental priority over the visual activities of writing and reading.

Language may be defined as a structured system of arbitrary vocal sounds and sound sequences, or a system of written or printed symbols that represent vocal sounds. A language system is used in social, interpersonal communication, and rather exhaustively catalogues the objects, events, and processes in the human environment.

A limited number of attempts have been made to investigate the effects of psychedelic experience on either receptive language (listening and reading) or expressive language (speaking and writing). The four levels of psychedelic experience (sensory, recollective-analytic, symbolic, and integral) provide an organizational structure in which these investigations may be explored and discussed.

RECEPTIVE LANGUAGE: LISTENING

Trouton and Eysenck have pointed out that psychedelic experience is influenced not only by factors related to drug administration, but by personality, physiology, set, and setting. In their account, they also mention "suggestion" and "reinforcement of responses by the experimenter," which takes into consideration the importance of language in determining how a subject reacts.[5]

A ritual developed by the Native American Church illustrates the use of language to produce a positive set and setting for the ingestion of peyote. A ceremonial leader, the head chief, initiates the singing of songs, and coordinates requests by individuals for special prayers. The ritual is so arranged and so coordinated to the needs of the communicants that the maximum possible likelihood of a positive spiritual experience is enhanced.[6]

Language, however, may also be used to develop a negative set and setting. Houston has described one of her initial observations of LSD administration. The subject was told by the psychiatrist that he would have "a terrible, terrible experience" filled with "strong anxiety and delusions." The drug was administered in an antiseptic hospital room with several observers in white coats watching him. As the effects came on, the psychiatrist asked such questions as, "Is your anxiety increasing?" At the end of the experiment, the subject was in a state of panic. The psychiatrist announced to the group that LSD was, indeed, a "psychotomimetic" substance that induced psychotic-like behavior.[7]

Listening is the receptive process by which aural language assumes meaning. As listening involves attending to a stimulus, the act often includes a commitment to respond in some way to the messages that are received. The Native American Church communicants commit themselves to a positive experience, and the unfortunate subjects of poorly handled LSD experiments commit themselves to a negative experience. In both cases, language plays a key role in determining which way the commitment will turn.

A vivid description of a psychedelic session has been given by Watts which demonstrates how the quality of what is listened to may change as the listener shifts from the sensory to the recollective-analytic, symbolic, and integral levels. Initially, Watts describes listening to the music of an organ that "seems quite literally to speak . . . every sound seems to issue from a vast human throat, moist with saliva." [8] This is the sensory level of psychedelic experience; perceptual changes have transformed the organ music into a human voice.

At the recollective-analytic level, Watts speaks of listening to a recording of the Roman Catholic mass and suddenly perceiving a pompous quality to the priest's tones; "I can hear the priest 'putting on' his voice, hear the . . . studiedly unctuous tones of a master deceptionist who has the poor little nuns, kneeling in their stalls, completely cowed." Going deeper into the analysis of what he hears, Watts discovers that the nuns "are not cowed at all." To Watts, "the limp gesture of bowing nuns turns into the gesture of the closing claw." The nuns are shrewdly playing the game of survival; "With too few men to go around the nuns know what is good for them: How to bend and survive."

At the symbolic stage of the psychedelic session, Watts hears, in the priest's voice, "the primordial howl of the beast in the jungle," and, in the nuns' reply, "the feminine stratagem of stooping to conquer . . . and the meek inheriting the earth." The priest's voice seems to recapitulate the evolutionary process while the nuns' response echoes female archetypes.

Finally, Watts reaches the integral level of psychedelic experience, hearing himself in the voice of the priest and in all the precursors of that voice. He notes, "I can hear in that one voice the simultaneous presence of all the levels of man's history, as of all the stages of life before man." At that point, Watts comes into contact with the very center of his being; "I feel, with a peace so deep that it sings to be shared with all the world . . . that I have returned to the home beyond home." Watts concludes, "The sure foundation upon which I had sought to stand has turned out to be the center from which I seek." [9]

RECEPTIVE LANGUAGE: READING

Reading, the assigning of meaning to perceived printed symbols, also plays a key role in some psychedelic sessions. In one experiment conducted by Jarvik and others, subjects ingested 100 micrograms of LSD and demonstrated an increase in their ability to quickly cancel out words on a page of standardized material, but a decreased inability to cancel out individual letters. The drug seemed to facilitate the perception of meaningful language units while it interfered with the visual perception of nonmeaningful ones.[10] Corroborative experimental data are lacking, but a number of clinical cases suggest that if the meaning of printed symbols happens to dovetail with the ongoing psychedelic experience, the symbols will be perceived quickly. If their meaning does not happen to tie in with the experience, the words might not be perceived at all.

One subject became interested in studying famous paintings after ingesting 30 milligrams of psilocybin, and assertedly lost his reading ability entirely: *

> In college, I had studied central nervous system disfunction, and knew that psycholexia is a condition in which a person has difficulty attaching meaning to printed symbols. I experienced a similar condition after the psilocybin began to take effect. I glanced at my watch, but could make no sense out of the numerical symbols. I looked at an art magazine. The pictures were beautiful, almost three dimensional. However, the script was a jumble of meaningless shapes.

The same subject, near the end of his "psilocybin high," reported still another alteration in the reading process:

> Earlier, I had tasted an orange and found it the most intense, delightful taste sensation I had ever experienced. I tried reading a magazine as I was "coming down," and felt the same sensual delight in moving my eye over the printed page as I had experienced when eating the orange. The words stood out in three dimensions. Reading had never been such a sheer delight and such a complete joy. My comprehension was excellent. I quickly grasped the intent of the author and felt that I knew exactly what meaning he had tried to convey.

---

* Except in those cases where a reference is cited, all first-person reports are from the files of the author.

In the former instance, motivation for reading was low, as the subject was interested in studying art prints. In the latter episode, the pleasure of eating an orange permeated the act of reading a magazine, which then became a delightful experience.

The cases cited above both involved the sensory level of psychedelic experience. At the recollective-analytic level occur the examples of purported spiritual inspiration from reading sacred literature. Biblical passages or religious terms formerly meaningless sometimes acquire vivid meanings for many readers. Like the individual who through conversion experience suddenly finds himself in possession of the meaning of the term "salvation," so the LSD subject may find similar terms illuminated for him.[11] An example can be cited of an individual who found significant meaning in a Biblical passage during a session with morning glory seeds:

> I found a new interpretation for the twelfth chapter of Ezekiel. The prophet spoke of a "rebellious house," and of people—perhaps in need of psychedelic substances—who have "ears to hear and hear not." The injunction of Ezek. 12:13 is to "eat your bread with quaking, and drink water with trembling," an appropriate description of the consumption of psychedelics. Ezekiel 12:23–24 states that "the days are at hand and the fulfillment of every vision." Everything I read under the spell of the morning glory seeds became directed toward the psychedelic experience.

Once again, in this instance, there was an integration of the act of reading into the ongoing psychedelic experience. As a result, a number of "connections" were discovered that would have eluded the subject had he not ingested morning glory seeds. This phenomenon is surprisingly common among frequent LSD users; their belief in direct interrelations among most of the events of their lives may well influence their behavior and their view of the universe.

The reading process is rarely associated with the third or fourth levels of psychedelic experience, but some individuals have been catapulted into a deeply moving symbolic or integral episode following a chance glimpse of a line of Hebrew script or an Egyptian hieroglyphic. In other cases, a line of print has occurred at the end of a segment of the experience, and has seemed to summarize it. One subject reported such an episode at the symbolic level during a mescaline session:

> I was propelled back into time, back into the primeval jungle. I saw two savages stalking each other in the underbrush. Each savage carried a bow and arrow. Each was prepared to kill the other upon sight. Blood was on their minds; murder was in their hearts.

Suddenly, each saw the other. Each gasped in surprise. Each dropped his bow. The two bows fell together on the ground, forming a mandala. The arrows fell upon the mandala dividing it into four sections.

The savages fell upon each other—but in an embrace rather than in an assault. As they strolled into the jungle to enjoy their newly discovered companionship, the mandala turned into a white button. Upon the button, in red and blue, appeared the words, "Make love, not war."

During my own psilocybin experience, I had an unusual visualization. I pictured a whirlwind carrying away all of the words, letters, numbers, and verbal symbols that had acculturated and conditioned me through the years. One might say that my session was a form of nonverbal training, a dramatic confrontation with naked events that reminded me not only of the awareness encountered among preliterate tribes, but also of Korzybski's writings in the field of general semantics.

Korzybski considered man's consciousness of the abstraction process to be the most effective safeguard against semantic problems (such as confusing words with objects), and the key to further human evolution. Consciousness of abstraction was defined by Korzybski as an "awareness that in our process of abstracting we have *left out* characteristics." [12] An individual apprehends himself and his world fully and accurately to the degree that he continually translates higher-order abstractions back to the level of concrete experience. An individual is "sane" to the extent that he becomes experientially aware of the discrepancy between conceptualization and sense impressions. Developmentally, man (both as a species and as an individual) progresses from the preliterate stage, in which he is enmeshed in concrete experience, to the early literate stage, in which he confuses words with things and becomes split off from nonverbal reality, to a fully developed literate stage, in which he uses the printed word, but does not confuse it with the object for which it stands.

Mogar has stated that, at its best, the psychedelic state can permit the individual to evaluate with some detachment both the structure of his semantic framework (i.e., its similarity to reality) and his semantic reactions. [13] These two kinds of learning were strongly recommended by Korzybski as the most effective means of increasing one's consciousness of the abstracting process.

Marsh has described how, under LSD, "we seem to come up against that part of our inner world where meanings are made, where the patterning process operates in its pure form." [14] He has further noted that, semantically, the condition of being absolutely present to the outer and the inner reality has at least two advantages. First, it allows a person to tune in on that feedback, both external and internal, which enables him to correct his own errors in encoding. He is able to reduce the noise level in the various communication systems in which he is involved by re-encoding his message streams until they convey the meanings that he intends them to convey. Secondly, it allows a person to inhabit the world of the actual, the world of fact, instead of the unreal and empty world of the prefabricated abstraction. It allows him to experience the world instead of merely thinking about it and, perhaps, to begin to live in it at last.

The psychedelic session as nonverbal training represents a method by which an individual can attain a higher level of linguistic maturity and sophistication. On the other hand, some psychedelic episodes have been reported in which an opposite phenomenon took place, in which language was concretized—the letters becoming transformed into images and objects. One subject, while smoking marijuana, looked at a magazine cover and reported a concretization experience:

> The magazine featured a picture story about Mexico and the cover featured large letters spelling out the name of that country. As I looked at the letters, they turned into Aztec men and women. They retained their shape as letters, but subtle shades and shadows became eyes, heads, arms, and legs. That part wasn't so bad, but when Aztecs began to move across the page, I quickly turned the magazine over!

The concretization of letters has been put to artistic use by illustrators throughout the centuries. For example, Ferdinand Kriwet designed a mandala composed of nothing but several hundred capital letters. Joshua Reichert produced another mandala that consisted of several types of script. A number of contemporary poster artists have publicized "acid rock" musical performances by producing advertisements that fuse the letters with the pictures, making the names of such groups as "The Grateful Dead" and "The Byrds" an integral part of the overall design, thus combining the "medium" and the "message." The "psychedelic poster" has, within a few years, become an original art form.[15]

The variety of effects that psychedelics have upon receptive language functioning have at least one factor in common: they point up the role that language as a "connecting system" plays in verbal memory.[16] Electric brain stimulation and hypnosis have been able to retrieve long forgotten memories; psychedelic drugs often produce similar effects, especially at those periods of time when subjects are at the recollective-analytic level.

Physical shock and psychic trauma often lead to the forgetting of verbal material or a regression in verbal functioning. In these cases, the "connecting system" breaks down, just as it does in certain episodes with psychedelics. Michaux has stated, "After an average dose of hashish one is unfit for reading." [17] Other artists and writers, however, say that they appreciate receptive language (e.g., listening to poetry, reading novels) even more when they are "high." A great deal of research is needed to explore the variables that determine what effects psychedelics have upon language as it connects one's past memory with his present experience.

EXPRESSIVE LANGUAGE: SPEECH

A number of investigators have reported a reduction or even an absence of speech among LSD subjects. Some writers have suggested that these drugs suppress activity in the cortical levels of the brain where the speech centers are located. Von Felsinger and his associates, for example, noted that there was a "slowing down of speech and expression" with their LSD subjects, none of whom were psychiatric patients.[18] On the other hand, Hertz, a Danish physician, described a patient whose long-standing stuttering condition disappeared following LSD treatment.[19] An American team of researchers found that schizophrenic children became more communicative following LSD treatment.[20] As with other types of language, the alteration of expressive language under LSD can take a variety of forms depending on how it happens to mesh with other aspects of the psychedelic experience.

One research team studied the effects of LSD on group communication using both an experimental group of subjects and a control group. The subjects in the control group increased their verbal output during the observation period, while among those who had taken LSD there was a reduction in word output. In addition, the subjects who took LSD asked more questions and made more statements pertaining to orientation (e.g., "What's happening?" "Where am I?") than those in the control group.[21] These findings are consistent with the typical reactions of subjects at the sensory level when traditional time-space orientation is lost.

Another reason for reduced verbalization during psychedelic sessions may be the presence of visual imagery.[22] When an individual becomes involved in "the retinal circus," he often loses interest in speaking. In addition, relaxation and lethargy often mark a subject's first experiences with the psychedelics. In these instances, the speech muscles would be inoperative and verbalization would be reduced still further.

At the sensory level, there is often an increased awareness of bodily feeling that most subjects find difficult to describe verbally. Preliterate tribes paid great attention to these feelings, but the American culture generally ignores them, unless they are unpleasant. Those phrases which most quickly come to mind during periods of acute bodily awareness are "sick to my stomach," "pains in my back," and "nagging headache." Once these words become linked to what may be quite natural (and potentially pleasurable) sensations, an individual may very well get sick, regurgitate, and interpret the rest of his psychedelic session as unpleasant.

It is in this regard that the work of Russell Mason on internal perception assumes importance. Although Mason's experiments did not involve psychedelic drugs, they could serve as models for what can eventually be done with such substances. He asked subjects to specify where various kinds of feelings were located. Love and friendliness, for example, were associated with the central chest area, and sexual feelings with the genital-pubic area. He concluded that "the ability of the individual to permit *immediate awareness* of . . . noncognitive internal perceptions appears to be necessary for healthy psychological adjustment." [23] His data offer a possible physiological explanation for the body changes that take place when drug subjects report feelings of "oceanic love" or "strong sexual responses." They also suggest that persons who are unable to allow this immediate awareness to take place may be poor risks for LSD sessions.

Masters and Houston state that the altered body awareness results from a variety of triggering factors: mood, ideation, perception of various external stimuli, along with inferred unconscious factors.[24] For example, a subject may experience his body as abnormally heavy because he is depressed, because he has begun to think of himself as being too fat, or because he is "thinking weighty thoughts." In this last case, the verbalization "weighty" being applied first to the thoughts and then to the body or, as sometimes happens, only to the head, which "contains" the "weighty thoughts." The heaviness associated with depression is also sometimes the product of a verbalization, as when the subject thinks of himself as "burdened with grief" or "weighted down by sorrows."

Masters and Houston have reported statements from a number of subjects who purportedly "felt" the interior of the body during psychedelic experiments. One subject told about sensing his "interior landscape," describing the "trees, vines, streams, waterfalls, hills, and valleys" of the body. Another described the sensation of blood flowing through his veins, as well as the receiving and transmitting operations of the nervous system.[25] All of these reports reflect awareness at the sensory level of psychedelic experience.

The verbal reports associated with the recollective-analytic and symbolic levels are somewhat different. For example, one subject at the recollective-analytic level reported the insight to Masters and Houston that "I have never been in love with my own body. In fact, I believe that a major emotional problem in my life is that I have always disliked it." At the symbolic level, a number of subjects experience bodily sensations in terms of a mythic dream. One anthropologist reported going through a Haitian transformation rite in which his body began to take on aspects of a tiger.[26]

At the integral level, bodily sensations may also be reported. One of Masters and Houston's subjects had a mystical experience in which he was "overwhelmed by a bombardment of physical sensations, by tangible sound waves both felt and seen" after which he "dissolved." He later stated, "Now I understand what is meant by being a part of everything, what is meant by sensing the body as dissolving."

A great deal of research is needed to correlate the data on bodily sensations with the data on LSD. One important hypothetical formulation that would be helpful in effecting this correlation has been presented by Gardner Murphy and Sidney Cohen. Murphy and Cohen suggested that psychedelic drugs lower the threshold for internal sensations, especially those from the digestive system, the sex organs, and the striped muscles. As a result, body feelings emerge into self-consciousness, and an individual may interpret the experience as one of "cosmic love." Murphy and Cohen also hypothesized that there was a direct relationship between certain physiological concomitants of the experience and the frequently cited statement, by the subject, that his experience has been ineffable, that it cannot be communicated adequately to others.[27] Some subjects assert that no words exist to describe internal events such as those they have felt, and that even if there were such words they would be devoid of significance unless the listener himself had gone through the same experiences.

Richard Blum has described how one learns a language that signifies to other users that one understands and has been through a psychedelic experience. According to Blum, the language is shaped by the culture of the speakers—in this case by the particular subgroup with which the LSD user is socially affiliated, and under whose auspices he has taken the drug. This language is as much a sign of "togetherness" and "belongingness" as it is a device for communicating the content of an experience.[28] It is not unusual that a number of people in drug subcultures become frustrated when talking with nonusers; to the individual who has never undergone psychedelic experience, the user's words are not understood as affirmations that one is a particular kind of person or a fellow member of an important ingroup.

Blum has maintained that learning the LSD language and vocalizing the philosophy of the psychedelic subculture are steps in the commitment of an individual to an identifiable group. Language, in this instance, becomes a device to provide structure and to create a community of experience among persons who have had LSD. Furthermore, whatever one expects from the psychedelics on the basis of prior information and personal predispositions strongly influences the choice of words later used to describe the experience itself.

The experience of being taught linguistic terminology by members of the drug subculture is more than instruction in communication. It is instruction in approved words and approved experiences; it is instruction in a point of view. The terms that are learned can be used to structure the pharmacological response to a drug, giving the experience sense and meaning that it may not otherwise have had. After his first trip, a novice might be told, "Oh yes, from what you say I can tell you really did have a transcendental experience." Such comments are not only instructive, helping the person define and describe his response, but they are also approving and rewarding. As experiments on conditioned behavior have demonstrated, rewarded behavior is generally repeated. In the case of illegal LSD use, the rewards —often linguistic in nature—are frequently great enough to overshadow such potential hazards as psychosis, suicide, and physiological damage.

Regarding legal experimental usage of the psychedelics, it has often been observed that the language used by the guide will influence what the subject says later to describe his session. This observation is borne out by some of the early research studies. It was initially believed that LSD produced psychotic-like reactions, and the drug was termed "psychotomimetic" by psychiatrists and psychologists.[29] LSD subjects were sometimes told by the physician administering the drug, "You probably will go out of your mind for several hours"; many subjects later reported a terrifying experience. One early experimenter took verbatim recordings of an interview with an LSD subject and of an interview with a schizophrenic subject, and outside judges could not distinguish which of the two was suffering from schizophrenia.[30]

As research workers became more knowledgeable, the psychotomimetic label was discarded by many investigators. Pollard, Uhr, and Stern noted that psychotic disorders are characterized "by personality disintegration, and failure to test and evaluate correctly external reality in various spheres." Following the conclusion of their work with LSD, they stated, "In none of the normal experimental subjects to whom we have given these drugs, nor in our own experience, could these criteria be satisfied." [31]

The problem of scientific scrutiny of verbal reports made during psychedelic sessions persists. Two recent investigations, one by Katz, Waskow, and Olsson, and the other by Dahlberg, Feldstein, and Jaffe, have utilized highly sophisticated techniques of linguistic analysis, and may serve as models for future experimentation.

A study involving 69 inmates of a penal institution has been reported by the Katz group. On the basis of self-ratings, the subjects were divided into three groups: those who were euphoric under LSD, those who were dysphoric, and those who were ambivalent. The ambivalent subjects talked a great deal and very rapidly, while dysphoric subjects spoke little and quite slowly. The differences between these two groups were statistically significant, while the euphoric subjects fell in between. These differences characterized the subject's speech both before and during the psychedelic experience, leading to the conclusion that productivity and rate "may reflect a more permanent attribute of the subjects." [32]

Dahlberg, Feldstein, and Jaffe [33] are in the process of making a detailed analysis of verbal reports of psychoneurotic patients gathered during therapy sessions. Before the session, each patient ingested low dosages of LSD. The therapy sessions were spaced over a period of 18 months.

The patient's and the analyst's verbal interactions were transferred to punched cards, and are being submitted to several techniques of linguistic analysis. The Cloze procedure, an index of redundancy, is being used as a measurement of the predictability of interpersonal language in the patient-therapist interchange. The Type-Token Ratio is a measure of vocabulary diversity and, indirectly, an indicator of the informational structure of speech.

One nonverbal technique, the Role Construct Sorting Procedure, is a test to measure changes in the way the patients conceptualize people who are important in their lives. Moreover, these measurements of change are themselves being analyzed for indications of increased and expanded associations on the part of the patients.

The investigators hypothesized that LSD facilitates treatment of early experiences in patients by producing partial regression. It was further hypothesized that LSD would increase the patients' ability to evaluate their problems clearly, and to communicate their insights to the psychotherapist with facility.

The methodology of the study permits both analytic insight into the dynamics of a drug effect, and the pharmacologic augmentation of the psychoanalytic therapy.

EXPRESSIVE LANGUAGE: WRITING

Written language attempts to convey meaning through printed symbols. Although S. W. Mitchell, one of the first to write a description of a psychedelic experience, stated that his session with peyote was "hopeless to describe in language," he wrote an account of "stars, delicate floating films of color, then an abrupt rush of countless points of white light" that "swept across the field of view, as if the unseen millions of the Milky Way were to flow in a sparkling river before my eyes." [34] His account was sufficiently vivid for Trouton and Eysenck to be able to suggest that he substituted primitive thinking in the form of visual images for conceptual thought.[35]

While at the sensory level, during his first LSD experience, a subject attempted to write an account of his subjective reactions, but became fascinated with the very act of writing itself:

> Amazing! Amazing! The fluidity of the panorama of the room. It seems like eons of time pass between each letter when I write it. As I write, I see the loops, the dots, etc., spiral off the page in colors. Off to infinity!

At the recollective-analytic level, imagery persists, but conceptualization is often possible as well. For example, Ling and Buckman have reported the case of a European writer who overcame "writer's block" through LSD therapy. Prior to taking LSD, he was unable to finish a manuscript. After LSD therapy, he went on to become one of the leading authors in Germany. His major work, completed during the time he was in therapy, was translated into twelve languages, and had a wide audience in the Western world.[36]

Material that emerges at the recollective-analytic level does not always lead to the well-being of the subject, especially if the drugs are taken in unsupervised sessions and with an absence of preparation. Following an LSD session, a college student wrote the following account of his experience at the recollective-analytic level:

> Apparently some sort of love-making was going on in the other room because the guide would not let me enter it. As it turned out, this was the wrong thing to do because it started me on the road to paranoia, panic, and "the depths." His refusal to let me enter the room aroused my suspicions of an ulterior motive. I picked one which I have a curious fear of: homosexuality. I was unwilling to submit to what became suggestive words, lewd actions, and a depraved smile. I shudder when I recall it. My fears were not of the act, but that if I submitted I would become "one of them"—and never be able to "return." It reminds me of the movie, "The Pod People," where "people" are grown in pods and substituted for real people. You don't know if your best friend is one of these "people" dedicated to your destruction or conversion until it is too late.

Because of the pathological elements in this written description, the student was advised by several people to do no more drug experimentation.

However, about a year later, the student accepted a friend's invitation to smoke marijuana. The session began with a number of pleasant bodily feelings and unusual perceptual impressions. Suddenly, the student became obsessed with the notion that his friend desired to have sexual relations with him. The student's friend called the police and the student was rushed to a hospital, having entered a serious psychotic episode.* In this tragic instance, the student's written account could have served as a predictor of what would likely happen during future sessions.

An individual attempting to write descriptions of psychedelic experience at the symbolic level has the difficult job of choosing verbal terms that convey some sense of his mythic encounters. This formidable task was well handled by an attorney who stated, following an LSD session, "I saw Rome fall and the Dark Ages begin, and observed as little crossed twigs were tacked up as the only hope in ten thousand wretched hovels. I watched peasants trample it under their feet in some obscene forest rite, while, across the sea in Byzantium, they glorified it in jeweled mosaics and great domed cathedrals." [37]

The attorney's written description is imaginative, yet fairly concrete, just as the mythical world is concrete. The linguistic consciousness of primitive man is nonabstract; its concreteness is marked by a concrescence of name and thing (as exemplified by the various types of name taboos). Cassirer has noted that in some primitive religions the worshipper did not dare to utter the name of his gods; in others, certain words were used for the purpose of hex and voodoo. [38] This concrescence of name and thing is demonstrated by a subject's report of a peyote session:

> The guide asked me how I felt, and I responded, "Good." As I uttered the word "Good," I could see it form visually in the air. It was pink and fluffy like a cloud. The word looked "Good" in its appearance and so it had to be "Good." The word and the thing I was trying to express were one, and "Good" was floating around in the air.

Name and thing are often wedded at the recollective-analytic and the symbolic levels. A subject will say the word *Mother*, and feel that the word itself contains aspects of his own mother—or of his memories of her. A theology student will say the word *Logos*, and imagine that God and Christ

---

* When I interviewed the student, I discovered that no antidote or supportive therapy had been given him once he entered the hospital. Instead, he was interrogated by policemen who insisted on knowing the names of marijuana and LSD users on the campus. This type of treatment, in which the well-being of the patient is relegated to a secondary status by law enforcement personnel, has become commonplace as the general public's anxiety regarding the psychedelics has increased.

are both present within the word. Only after the drug's effects began to wear off can these individuals tear the words apart from the experience.

In some cases, however, the words remain wedded to the context even after the drug's reactions have presumably disappeared. When this happens, the phenomenon resembles a childlike regression in which the individual engages in magical thinking and primitive logic. A college student wrote the following description of an LSD session:

> When my roommate and I were high, we both became imbued with a sense of magical power. We stared at the candle flame, trying to change its color. Nothing happened. My roommate suggested that we utter a magic word. We tried "Abracadabra." The color did not change. We tried "Open Sesame" to no avail. I shouted, "Kalamazoo!" Believe me, we both saw the color of the flame change from orange to blue! It remained blue for five minutes. At that time, my roommate blew out the flame. We were quite shaken by the experience but wanted to try it again. We relit the candle. The flame was orange. We uttered the magic word. It turned blue. This was several days ago. Neither of us has dared to light the candle and utter the magic word. We knew the flame would change from orange to blue as soon as one of us said "Kalamazoo!" And then where would we be?

This experience, and others like it, underline the importance of taking these powerful chemicals in supportive settings, and in the presence of a trained guide. S. I. Hayakawa admits that LSD enables one to transcend habitual ways of thinking and experiencing. However, he wisely notes that "transcending of itself is not enough. What happens afterward? In what ways are perceptions of the self or the environment altered or restructured for the better?" [39]

As with other language processes, psychedelic substances can affect the act of writing by bringing about a regressive-type phenomenon (in which words and experience are united, as they often are with the child and with the primitive tribesman) or improve the process (by removing "writer's block," facilitating verbal expression, etc.). In some instances, both occur, as when a writer engages in concrescence of word and thing at the symbolic or integral level, and later presents a vivid written description of that experience.

To assist the encoding of psychedelic experience an "experimental typewriter" has been invented by Lindsley and Getziner.[40] The typewriter has 20 pens, any of which can be depressed by the subject to describe his ongoing experience. The subject must be trained in the use of the device, and must learn the code which assists him to describe his psychedelic sensations and reactions. For example, the first key is depressed whenever bodily sensations are experienced, while the third key is depressed when feelings about other people are experienced. Although further refinement of this device is needed, the research possibilities seem extensive. A subject could tap out a second-by-second sequence of his experiences, and communicate them, at least in general terms. Experience patterns could be correlated with neurological recordings. A guide could closely observe the subject's reactions should it be felt advisable to modify the experience.

In one first-person report, a subject claimed that he learned how to become a skilled typist by means of psychedelic experience. Instead of emphasizing the more ideational aspects of the writing process, the subject concentrated on sheer motor activity. First, he familiarized himself with the keyboard and learned the proper fingering techniques. To reinforce the matching of fingers and typewriter keys, he took LSD, began to type, and continued for several hours.[41]

The subject's claims regarding a facilitation in motor function are provocative and need to be explored under controlled conditions. P. Laurie has suggested that the act of writing may be feasible under light doses of psychedelic substances but, for most people, impossible under heavy doses.[42] In the case of writing, therefore, one is struck by the same variety of reports as one encounters with other forms of language; certain people under certain conditions claim that their writing functions are enhanced, others assert writing is impaired, and still others report no discernible difference.

Perhaps the varieties of psychedelic experiences reported by different people can be explained, in part, by the users' differences in extensional and intensional outlooks.[43] Korzybski viewed extensionality as the defining of "reality" in terms of specific, concrete instances, by enumeration and classification. Intensionality is the defining of "reality" by verbally ascribing and describing characteristics and properties. Korzybski maintained that intensionality was unhealthy because, among other reasons, it compelled the identification of the word with the object. Extensionality was healthy because it furthered a greater awareness of the abstraction process.[44]

For an extensional-type person, psychedelic experience might illuminate the abstracting process more vividly. For an intensional-type person, however, LSD might increase the seeming "realness" of words, and increase one's tendency to allow verbal symbols to influence one unduly.

This problem is especially acute in the case of LSD-induced perceptual distortions and hallucinations. At the sensory level of psychedelic experience, an individual may distort what he sees, and project other meanings and images into it. A wall might sprout eyes; a flower might grow into a face. Furthermore, the individual might hallucinate and see a dragon, a gargoyle, or a gryphon in the middle of the room. In these instances, the individual would be engaging in what Korzybski has referred to as "a reverse order abstraction process," [45] a very unhealthy phenomenon that involves a high degree of intensionality. Instead of perceiving "reality" directly, the individual projects material from his memory traces into the perceptually received material.

There is no doubt that psychological harm can be done if an ill-prepared person takes LSD illegally and becomes overwhelmed by the intensional aspects of his experience. Even after the experience is over, he may display confusion in the abstracting process. On the other hand, the creative person, whether or not he ingests LSD, often uses intensionality in a positive way. Inventors, artists, and composers would be in a constant state of frustration if they attempted to maintain an extensional outlook at all times.

Nichola Telsa had waking visions that portrayed design principles he later applied to his electrical inventions. James Watt was watching his mother boiling a kettle of water when he visualized a working model for the steam engine. Johannes Kepler's occult experiences were the genesis points for his theories on planetary motion. Peter Tchaikovsky described his mental state while composing as one in which "everything within me starts pulsing and quivering"; he admitted behaving "like a madman" when inspired. Lewis Walkup studied the creative process among scientists and artists, noting that many of them "seemed almost to hallucinate" as they visualized their concepts. William Shakespeare, in *A Midsummer Night's Dream,* (Act V, scene 1, lines 12–17), described the "reverse order abstraction process" often utilized by creative people:

The poet's eye, in a fine frenzy rolling,
Doth glance from heaven to earth, from earth to heaven;
As imagination bodies forth
The forms of things unknown, the poet's pen
Turns them to shapes and gives to airy nothing
A local habitation and a name.

Korzybski contended that human creativity could be "made the rule rather than the exception" if semantic disturbances were eliminated. To Korzybski, the secret of creative work was "freedom from structural bondage, and particularly the structural semantic bondage of words." [46] Contemporary theoreticians in the field of general semantics might well consider whether there might be a role for certain types of intensionality in the creative process. The intensionality accentuating much of psychedelic experience can be a positive value. Intensionality itself is, perhaps, only harmful if one adopts it on a perpetual basis in his everyday life, and allows it to confuse his abstracting ability regarding words and what they represent.

CONCLUSION

Psychedelic substances, when they affect language processes, sometimes appear to assist an individual to observe the difference between the word and the object it represents. In this way, the drugs may serve as catalysts in a nonverbal training program, helping the subject translate verbal abstractions in terms of direct experience.

Psychedelic substances can produce the opposite result as well. The subject may revert to primitive thinking, his ability to conceptualize may decrease, and he may effect a union between the word and its object. This is exemplified by the concretization of letters into pictures and images, by the concrescence of verbalizations with the items they represent, and by the use of words in magical ways on the part of many LSD subjects.

Psychedelic drugs offer an unparalleled opportunity for the investigation of human language processes. The few experimental and clinical reports that exist in the fields of listening, reading, speaking, and writing differ so greatly as to inspire curiosity as to the reasons that the same drugs can produce varied effects at different dosage levels, with different individuals, and under different conditions. An extremely important variable seems to be whether or not language, either receptive or expressive, becomes integrated with the ongoing psychedelic experience. If the integration occurs, an improvement in function will often occur, especially if the session is held with pharmaceutical chemicals,* a trained guide, and a prepared subject. If the connection is not made, language functioning may deteriorate or become blocked altogether.

At the sensory level, words are encoded and decoded in highly unusual ways. At the recollective-analytic level, language often serves as a "connecting system" involving memory and interpretation. At the symbolic level words often become part of a mythic or historical ritual. At the integral level, language rarely becomes a part of the immediate experience. However, several writers and poets have effectively transformed their religious and mystical episodes into prose and poetry.

---

* The importance of chemically pure, pharmaceutical substances for a psychedelic session cannot be emphasized too strongly. Chromosomal abnormalities have been reported among some persons who regularly consume illegal, black-market LSD. However, no healthy subject has been found to suffer chromosomal abnormalities following the ingestion of pharmaceutical LSD, even at fairly high dosage levels (Masters & Houston [3]).

A permanent state of altered consciousness is neither practical nor desirable. However, the individual may return to the world if imprinting, conditioning, acculturation, and verbalization with new insights in his psychedelic session have been properly guided. The research possibilities in the field of language and psychedelics are immense. The data obtained by imaginative and responsible investigators may point the way to methods of enhancing creative functioning, and lead to a better understanding of the human potential.

REFERENCES

1. Ayer, A. J. *Language, Truth and Logic.* New York: Dover, 2d. ed., 1946, p. 65.
2. Masters, R. E. L., and Houston, J. *The Varieties of Psychedelic Experience.* New York: Holt, Rinehart & Winston, 1966.
3. ———, and ———. *Psychedelic Art.* New York: Grove Press, 1968, p. 8.
4. Lewis, M. M. *How Children Learn to Speak.* New York: Basic Books, 1959.
5. Trouton, D., and Eysenck, H. J. "The Effects of Drugs on Behaviour," *Handbook of Abnormal Psychology,* ed. H. J. Eysenck. New York: Basic Books, 1961.
6. Flattery, D. S., and Pierce, J. M. *Peyote.* Berkeley: Berkeley Press, 1965.
7. Houston, J. "A Different Kind of Mysticism." *Jubilee* (June, 1967).
8. Watts, A. W. *The Joyous Cosmology.* New York: Pantheon, 1962.
9. *Ibid.*
10. Jarvik, M. E., Abramson, H. A. Hirsch, H. W., and Ewall, A. T. "Lysergic Acid Diethylamide (LSD–25)," *Journal of Psychology,* 1955, 39, pp. 465–473.
11. Leary, T., and Clark, W. H. "Religious Implications of Consciousness Expanding Drugs," *Religious Education,* 1963, 1, pp. 251–256.
12. Korzybski, Alfred. *Science and Sanity: An Introduction to Non-Aristotelian Systems and General Semantics.* Lakeville, Conn.: International Non-Aristotelian Library Publishing Co., 4th ed., 1958. Distributed by the Institute of General Semantics.
13. Mogar, R. E. "Search and Research with the Psychedelics," *ETC.,* 1965, 22 pp. 393–407.
14. Marsh, R. P. "Meaning and the Mind Drugs," *ETC.,* 1965, 22, pp. 408–430.
15. Masters and Houston, *Psychedelic Art.*
16. Hastings, A. *Language and Memory.* Personal communication (April 18, 1967).
17. Michaux, H. "Light through Darkness," *The Book of Grass,* eds. G. Andrews and S. Vinkenoog. London: Peter Own, 1967.
18. Von Felsinger, H. J.; Lasagna, L.; and Beecher, H. K. "The Response of Normal Men to Lysergic Acid Derivatives (di- and mono-ethyl-amides). Correlation of Personality and Drug Reactions," *Journal of Clinical and Experimental Psychopathology,* 1956, 17, pp. 414–428.
19. Stafford, P. G., and Golightly, B. H. *LSD: The Problem-Solving Psychedelic.* New York: Award Books, 1967, p. 113.
20. Bender, L., Goldschmidt, L., and Siva Sankar, D. V. "Treatment of Autistic Schizophrenic Children with LSD–25 and UML–491. *Recent Advances in Biological Psychiatry,* 1962, 4, pp. 170–177.

21. Lennard, H., Jarvik, M. E., and Abramson, H. A. "Lysergic Acid Diethylamide (LSD–25): XII. A Preliminary Statement of Its Effects upon Interpersonal Communication," *Journal of Psychology,* 1956, 41, pp. 185–198.
22. Tauber, E. S., and Green, M. R. *Prelogical Experience.* New York: Basic Books, 1959.
23. Mason, R. E. *International Perception and Bodily Functioning.* New York: International Universities Press, 1961.
24. Masters and Houston, *The Varieties of Psychedelic Experience,* p. 69.
25. *Ibid.*
26. *Ibid.,* pp. 76–78.
27. Murphy, G. and Cohen, S. "The Search for Person-World Isomorphism," *Main Currents in Modern Thought,* 1965, 22, pp. 31–34.
28. Blum, R., *et. al. Utopiates: The Use and Users of LSD–25.* New York: Atherton, 1964.
29. Rinkel, M. "Experimentally Induced Psychoses in Man," *Transactions of the Second Conference on Neuropharmacology,* ed. H. A. Abramson. New York: Josiah Macy, Jr. Foundation, 1956.
30. Hoffer, A. "Studies with Niacin and LSD," *Lysergic Acid Diethylamide and Mescaline in Experimental Psychiatry,* ed. L. Cholden. New York: Grune & Stratton, 1956.
31. Pollard, J. C.; Uhr, L.; and Stern, E. *Drugs and Phantasy.* Boston: Little, Brown, 1965.
32. Katz, M. M.; Waskow, I. E.; and Olsson, J. "Characterizing the Psychological State Produced by LSD," *Journal of Abnormal Psychology,* 1968, 73, pp. 1–14.
33. Dahlberg, C. C.; Feldstein, S.; and Jaffe, J. Abstract of grant proposal entitled "Effects of LSD–25 on Psychotherapeutic Communication." New York: William Alanson White Institute of Psychiatry, Psychoanalysis and Psychology, 1968. (Mimeographed.)
34. Mitchell, S. W. "Remarks on the Effects of Anhalonium Lewinii (the Mescal Button)," *British Medical Journal,* 1896, 2, 1926–1929.
35. Trouton and Eysenck, *op. cit.*
36. Ling, T. M., and Buckman, J. *Lysergic Acid (LSD–25) & Ritalin in the Treatment of Neurosis.* London: Lambarde, 1963.
37. Masters and Houston. *The Varieties of Psychedelic Experience,* p. 222.
38. Cassirer, E. *Philosophy of Symbolic Form.* New Haven: Yale University Press, 1955.
39. Hayakawa, S. I. "The Quest for Instant Satori," *ETC.,* 1965, 22, pp. 389–392.
40. Leary, T. "The Experiential Typewriter," *Psychedelic Review* (November, 1966).
41. Roseman, B. *LSD: The Age of Mind.* Hollywood: Wilshire, 1966.
42. Laurie, P. *Drugs: Medical, Psychological, and Social Facts.* Middlesex, England: Penguin, 1967.
43. Krippner, S. "Consciousness-expansion and the Extensional World," *ETC.,* 1965, 22, pp. 463–474.
44. Korzybski, *op. cit.*
45. *Ibid.,* p. 169.
46. *Ibid.,* p. 676

Laura L. Lee received her M.A. from Northwestern University in 1938, and is presently Associate Professor of Speech Pathology, Department of Communicative Disorders at Northwestern. She teaches courses in Language Development, and directs language training for handicapped children at the Northwestern University Speech Clinic, Evanston, Illinois.

14

THE RELEVANCE OF GENERAL SEMANTICS TO THE DEVELOPMENT OF SENTENCE STRUCTURE IN CHILDREN'S LANGUAGE

LAURA L. LEE

B ACK in the days when I attended Korzybski's seminars, I vividly recall his saying that the subject-predicate form of a statement made it false-to-fact. I heard him say it many times, and I always dutifully wrote it down in my notebook. I read it in *Science and Sanity:* "The subject-predicate form, the 'is' of identity, and the elementalism of the *A*-system are perhaps the main semantic factors in need of revision."[1] I read it, and I pondered it, but what Korzybski had against the subject-predicate sentence was really a mystery to me. I am not sure I understand all of his objections even now, but I have a somewhat clearer picture of the structure of an English sentence after studying its development in children's language.

Current interest in language acquisition stems from the investigations of psycholinguists. An enormous number of tape recordings have been made of children in the process of language learning, some of them longitudinal studies which run over a period of two years or more. The child's spontaneous utterances form a corpus of linguistic data that can be analyzed in much the same way as an anthropologist would study an exotic language to derive its lexicon and its grammatical structure. A grammar can be written for a particular child's language at any stage of his development. From the corpus of linguistic data, one can determine the precise grammatical rules under which he is operating, and one can predict the next rules that he will generate. The developing grammar of children is not just an immature, ran-

117

dom, partial imitation of the adult model. It is consistent, logical and, to a great extent, uniform among all English-speaking children. It is this uniformity of grammatical development that has led to much psycholinguistic theorizing about a child's "innate capacity" for language learning.*

At the Northwestern University Speech Clinic, we have become increasingly interested in the process of normal language acquisition, for with that as a guide, one can proceed more effectively to teach handicapped children for whom language learning is extremely difficult. We have tape recorded both normal children and clinic children, and we have analyzed their speech samples. A chart of normal language acquisition, entitled "Developmental Sentence Types," has been evolved, and with it one can trace the evolution of sentence formulation.[2]

Between the ages of 1 and 1½, a child speaks in single-word utterances. These early words do not have part-of-speech value to the child, although the adult calls them nouns and verbs and adjectives, the contentives or lexical items of a vocabulary. Words take on part-of-speech value only when combined with other words, when their position or privilege of occurrence in a string of words identifies them as nouns and verbs and adjectives. To the one-year-old child, all words are contentives and merely stand for and call to mind categories of similar events that have veen abstracted cognitively from the flux of sensorimotor experience: *shoe, spoon, car, drink, walk, go, pretty, dirty, all gone.* All words in the beginning vocabulary are on the same level of abstraction; they are labels for the developing categories of experience.

Syntax begins somewhere between eighteen months and two years. Three separate psycholinguistic studies (Braine,[3] Brown and Fraser,[4] Miller and Ervin [5]) all published about the same time, announced the similar finding that a set of rather abstract words, called "pivots," appeared in children's first word combinations, usually in the initial position, with the contentive or open class word following. These pivots included the articles, *a* and *the;* quantity words, such as *some, all, no,* and *more;* designative words, such as *here, there, this, that,* and *it;* and position words in combination with verbs, such as *fall down, stand up, put on,* and *take off.* The pivot-plus-open class combination has now become recognized as a child's first grammatical structure. It allows such typical word combinations as *a doggie, the car, more cookie, no milk, there shoe, here baby, that truck, sit down, turn off,* etc. Occasionally two open class words are combined. Two nouns make an immature possessive, *Daddy hat;* an adjective and a noun make an imma-

---

* See the paper by S. A. Pace, Chapter 17.—EDITOR.

ture noun phrase, *big car;* a verb and noun make a short verb phrase, *see horse, turn wheel, read book.* While these are not subject-predicate sentences by adult grammatical standards, they are complete sentences in child grammar. They express an entire, unified bit of information, and the child seems to consider them complete statements.

The next step in syntactic development is the recognition of the noun phrase as an independent grammatical unit. There is a cohesiveness about the noun and its modifiers that allows them to be moved about in a string of words, preserving their grammatical integrity. The former pivot combinations are now expanded into constructions of three words or more by including the noun modifiers in their proper sequence. *That doggie* becomes *that a doggie* or *that a big doggie; car dirty* becomes *the car dirty* or *Daddy car dirty; read book* becomes *read a book* or *read more book.*

At this point, three distinct types of statements are apparent. With considerable uniformity, normally developing children seem to have three different kinds of things to say, three varieties of verbal observations. The first of these we have called the "designative construction," which merely points out and names an item of attention: *here a horsie, that a big car, it a funny hat.* These designative words, *here, there, this, that,* and *it,* which were pivot words at an earlier stage, seem now to serve as verbal replacements for a pointing gesture, which formerly accompanied the naming of objects. Designative statements are extremely common in the speech of two-and-a-half-year-old children.

A second type of statement we have called the "predicative construction." Here the noun phrase comes first in the string, and is followed by an adjective, prepositional phrase, or other noun. Typical examples are: *the milk all gone, the car in garage, Bambi a little deer,* or *Billy a good boy.* These constructions are noun phrase expansions of their earlier two-word counterparts.

The third type of statement contains a verb, but it is a verb phrase only; the subject is missing. The child who says *have a cookie* is not inviting you to take one; rather, he is announcing that he himself has a cookie. He accompanies his play with predicates describing his own activities: *see a big car, put it here, take another cookie.* These constructions are expansions of the two-word, verb-object combinations.

It is easy to see what the next step in grammatical structure is going to be. The "designative" and "predicative" constructions require the addition of an *is.* The "verb phrase" construction merely requires the subject to be added to form a subject-predicate, actor-action sentence. These steps are normally accomplished well before the age of three. Typical three-year-old child sentences are: designative—*there's a car, it is a house, that's a doggie;* predicative—*the light is on, the dress is pretty, Spot is a good dog;* actor-action—*the boy sit down, me put on a hat, the doggie run away.* Students of general semantics will quickly recognize both the "*is* of identity" and the "*is* of predication," as well as the complete subject-predicate form in these three-year-old child's sentences. If these language structures are to be called "false-to-fact," then the best one can say is that children certainly get an early start in the wrong semantic direction.

To what extent this sequence of sentence formulation is a universal of language development, and to what extent it differs from one language to another, remains to be seen by extensive cross-cultural studies. A Japanese-speaking graduate student at Northwestern tape recorded four Japanese two-year-old children who had moved into the Chicago area from Tokyo, and we had an opportunity to study Developmental Sentence Types in Japanese.[6] These same three sentence types were clearly evident in all four Japanese children. The designative words, *kore* (this), *koko* (here), and *achi* (that direction), combined with open class words were common pivot constructions: *kore uchi* (this house), *koko kuruma* (here car), and *mama achi* (mama that direction). Predicative statements included *me omoi* (eyes heavy) and *tsume itai* (fingernails hurting). Verb-noun combinations were present also, but here the two languages differed to some extent. The subject of a Japanese sentence is often unspoken, merely understood, so that the child's *mizu dasu* (turn on the water) was grammatically complete in Japanese, although it was only a verb phrase in English. But the essential constituents of these developmental sentences were very similar. The Japanese children, like the English children, had three kinds of things to say: *this is a house, the eyes are heavy,* and *mama turn on the water.* From this data, it would appear that the subject-predicate form and the "*is*'es" are also developmental steps in the acquisition of Japanese.

Children's language development does not stop here with the formation of basic subject-predicate sentences. The three-year-old child has already embarked upon another stage of language growth—the transformational level of syntax[7]. Here his basic kernel sentences are transformed into other types through the use of negatives, interrogatives, passives, etc. He learns to conjoin two sentences, to subordinate some sentences to others, or to include one sentence within another by means of infinitives, participles, and gerunds. He learns the elaborate English verb tenses, and modifies the "*is* of identity" and the "*is* of predication" from *it is* into *it was, it should be, it could have been.* But always, as the substrate of any transformational structure, lies the kernel sentence, a basic linguistic unit, a bit of verbal information, which we all learned as children between the ages of two and three. All adult sentences can be reduced from their transformational complexity into one or more of these three underlying kernel sentence types. This classification of Developmental Sentence Types closely parallels the kinds of sentences about which Korzybski wrote: *"is* of identity," *this is a knife;* "*is* of predication," *the knife is sharp;* "subject-predicate," *the knife cuts.*

Watching language-delayed children struggle through syntactic development has given me a healthy respect for the sentence, and for the three-year-old nervous system that can accomplish it. The subject-predicate sentence forms the basis for further language development; it is the basic unit of information, and a substrate for verbal thinking. I cannot believe that Korzybski intended to "revise" the subject-predicate form out of existence, or to replace it with some agrammatical, formless string of words. Clinic children and some adult aphasics compose such nonsyntactic strings, and they communicate poorly. *Big light buy mommy me no* and *me too go mommy my school* are not only poor subject-predicate forms, but they reflect the unstructured cognitive level of the child who composed them. Language learning is a stage in child's growth that must be accomplished if further development is to proceed in a normal pattern. Syntactic structures, including subject-predicate formulation and the copular *is,* are essential steps in linguistic growth.

What kind of "revision," then, did Korzybski suggest? I offer this explanation: just as one must learn to abstract before becoming conscious of abstracting; just as one must learn to make inferences before distinguishing between facts and inferences; just as one must learn to categorize before doubting the validity of categories; so one must learn to compose subjects and predicates before coming to realize their implicit limitations. It is not the sentence itself that is false-to-fact, but one's assumptions about it. The "main semantic factors in need of revision," to which Korzybski referred, are one's attitudes and beliefs about the role of language and its adequacy for symbolizing experience. The semantically sophisticated speaker recognizes that no sentence or set of sentences "tells all" about a topic, that there always remains an unspoken "etc." which the sentence omits, that the *"is* of identity" confuses the levels of abstraction, and that the *"is* of predication" often tells more about the speaker than about the object it describes. These are areas of semantic enlightenment that hopefully come with maturity. But the sentence itself remains an indispensible linguistic unit, learned by all of us before the age of three.

REFERENCES

1. Korzybski, Alfred. *Science and Sanity: An Introduction to Non-Aristotelian Systems and General Semantics.* Lakeville, Conn.: The International Non-Aristotelian Library Publishing Co., 2nd ed., 1941, p. 371. Distributed by the Institute of General Semantics.
2. Lee, L. "Developmental Sentence Types: A Method for Comparing Normal and Deviant Syntactic Development," *Journal of Speech and Hearing Disorders,* 31, 1966, pp. 311–330.
3. Braine, M. D. S. "The Ontogeny of English Phrase Structure: The First Phrase," *Language,* 39, 1963, pp. 1–13.
4. Brown, R., and Fraser, C. "The Acquisition of Syntax," *Child Development Monographs,* 29, 1964, pp. 43–79.
5. Miller, W., and Ervin, S. "The Development of Grammar in Child Language," *Child Development Monographs,* 29, 1964, pp. 9–34.
6. Ando, Kyoko. Unpublished study, Northwestern University, 1966.
7. Chomsky, N. *Syntactic Structures.* The Hague: Mouton, 1957.

Howard F. Livingston is assistant professor of English at
Pace College, Westchester, New York. He has published articles on English education, literary criticism, and communication theory in various journals, and is a communications consultant in industry and education.

15

THE EFFECTS OF INSTRUCTION IN GENERAL SEMANTICS ON THE READING OF POETRY

HOWARD F. LIVINGSTON

OVER the past few years, there have been several investigations concerned with the effects of instruction in general semantics on students'
reading and writing ability.

Berger, in his study, "Improving Composition Through Emphasis in
General Semantics,"[1] reported improvement in writing skills as a result of
instruction in general semantics. A study I conducted revealed that critical
reading ability improved as a result of instruction in general semantics.[2]
While these studies—*restricted to the reading and writing of expository
material*—have indicated the salutary effect of instruction in general semantics, several educators in the language arts field have suggested that instruction in general semantics may have a deleterious effect on a student's
ability to respond appropriately to fictional literature in general, and to poetry in particular.

The reasoning behind this hypothesis, which, simply stated, is that instruction in general semantics would limit appropriate responses to literature and to poetry, proceeds along these lines:

From the standpoint of general semantics, they argue, the closer words
or statements are to the event, process, thing (the extensional referent), the
more meaningful or comprehensible is the language and, consequently, the
more accurately is the information transmitted from speaker or writer to
listener or reader. In other words, communication is most efficacious at the
descriptive level.

General semantics, they say, instills the habit of referring statements to
lower orders of abstraction. They cite Hayakawa, Lee, and Johnson that
high level abstractions and generalizations should be viewed with distrust if

123

they cannot be referred to a referent on a lower level. This is not to malign the habit of seeking referents on lower levels, but to show a particular gestalt that general semantics attempts to inculcate with respect to a person's language habits.

Doesn't general semantics demonstrate quite forcefully and accurately, they add, that the descriptive language of reports is more to be trusted than the language of inferences, judgments, and generalizations? Doesn't the language of reports and description give a more accurate picture of the territory? Doesn't general semantics encourage responding at the descriptive level rather than higher inferential levels? This orientation or language habit, these educators insist, while appropriate for expository purposes, will prevent the semantically trained person from meeting the demands made by poetry.

THE PRESENT STUDY

The purpose of this investigation was to test that hypothesis—that instruction in general semantics will prevent an appropriate reading of poetry. The investigation compared the responses, to a poem, of a group of college students who had had instruction in general semantics with a group of college students who had not.

The investigation was conducted during 1965 and 1966 at nine colleges in the United States. Geographically, the colleges were dispersed across the country, ranging from New York and New Jersey in the East to California and Washington in the West.

Eighteen classes—two from each school, one experimental, one control —comprised the sample for this study. All students participating in this study had completed courses in freshman literature or the equivalent. Also, this study assumed that all participants had studied literature in elementary, junior and senior high school. The experimental group consisted of nine classes in the final week of a course in general semantics. The control group consisted of nine classes in the final week of a literature course.

At the beginning of a class in the final week of the semester, members of both groups were given the following poem, and were told by the regular instructor of the course: "You have fifteen minutes to write your responses to this poem." (There was no discussion until after the responses were collected.)

The play seems out for an almost infinite run.
Don't mind a little thing like the actors fighting.
The only thing I worry about is the sun.
We'll be all right if nothing goes wrong with the lighting.

Anonymity was assured—no names were required on the students' responses. The title of the poem, "It Bids Pretty Fair," and the name of the poet, Robert Frost, were purposely omitted in order to avoid influencing the responses of the participants.

The evaluation of the responses was based on a single criterion derived from a universally accepted assumption about the nature of poetry, and best summed up in the words of J. V. Cunningham (in *Poetry: Form and Structure,* ed. Francis Murphy) "Poetry is with what its terms suggest rather than what they state." Therefore, for purposes of evaluation, an adequate or appropriate response to Frost's poem would entail looking beyond the specific referents of such words in the poem as *play, actors,* and *run.* An adequate or appropriate response would look for another level of meaning suggested by these words, that is, beyond the objective, referential level of experience to which the words point, to a more abstract, symbolic level.

The students' responses were evaluated on the basis of their awareness that the ultimate intention (purpose, meaning) of the poem resides on the symbolic level. Therefore, responses were classified as "appropriate" if they gave *any* indication of the respondent's awareness of the level of meaning embodied in the poem's underlying metaphor, *viz.,* "All the world's a stage." In other words, a response was considered "appropriate" if the respondent moved from the denotative referents that point to the drama, Broadway, producers, directors, etc., to the metaphysical considerations that "inhere" in the poem. A response was characterized as "appropriate" if this symbolic jump occurred for only one word. A valid interpretation integrating all the elements of the poem was not necessary.

In the experimental group (the group just finishing the course in general semantics), there were 68 "appropriate" responses out of 219. In the control group, there were 76 "appropriate" responses out of 226. The standard error of the difference between two percentages showed that there was no significant difference between the responses of the experimental group and the responses of the control group. Therefore, it seems reasonable to conclude that instruction in general semantics did not, in this limited test, adversely affect students' ability to respond appropriately in the reading of poetry.

In other words, the hypothesis of the educators who believed general semantics to be inimical to the appropriate reading of fiction was, in this limited investigation, not supported.

When one considers that a "valid" interpretation of Frost's poem (one that integrates all the elements of the poem into an organic whole) was *not* a factor in the evaluation of the college students' responses, serious questions can be raised as to the general ability of all students to understand poetry. It would seem that the findings in this study suggest other areas in which research is greatly needed.

REFERENCES

1. Paper presented at the International Conference on General Semantics, August, 1968.
2. "Instruction in General Semantics on Critical Reading Ability," *California Journal of Educational Research,* March, 1964.

COMMENTS ON DR. LIVINGSTON'S PAPER

Neil Postman is currently Professor of English Education in the Division of English Education, Speech, and Educational Theatre at New York University.

NEIL POSTMAN

I WELCOME the opportunity to add a brief commentary to Dr. Livingston's paper. In addition to my natural interest in a former student, I am attracted by Livingston's programmatic approach to general semantics research; that is, he actually follows through on questions that are opened by his own research.

Frankly, I am surprised at his results. As everyone knows, Korzybski, Hayakawa, and other writers on general semantics are rather unconvincing in their treatment of the literary experience. The best their works suggest is that one must develop a sort of controlled schizophrenia: in one context *not* responding to symbols as if they were things; in another context (e.g. a play) responding to symbols as if they *were* things. Hayakawa is somewhat vague on this point. On the one hand, he ridicules the sort of response that impels someone to send a telegram of condolence to a soap opera character who has lost her fictional husband. On the other hand, he obviously acknowledges the therapeutic value of an intense aesthetic experience. (For example, someone's identifying almost totally with a character in a movie or play.) What I am saying is that general semantics theory does not treat adequately the role that symbols play in what might be called the aesthetic experience. Dr. Livingston's findings were surprising because I would have expected that people who have had general semantics training would in fact be *less likely* than others to "suspend disbelief" or to enter fully into a poet's symbolic world. I am pleased that his very tentative experiment indicates that this was not so. But he does not give any explanation of why it was not so, and there is nothing in general semantics theory that would help him very much in providing an adequate explanation.

Perhaps the work of I. A. Richards would be more helpful here than the work of general semantics scholars. In one place, Richards defines a good reader as "a person whose mind is behaving itself." Much of Richards' work amounts to an explanation of that definition. In brief, Richards asserts that a good reader uses a text as a kind of blueprint, and then builds a unique structure from it. Of course, Richards specifies what the rules are for building a structure that will stand. For example, one of those rules is that the reader must account in his interpretation for everything that is to be found in the blueprint. But this is not the forum for a lengthy discussion of Richards' theories of meaning. I want only to suggest that Richards' work may be more helpful than anyone else's in accounting for what Livingston has found. For instance, does general semantics training make one more sensitive to "levels of meaning"; to an author's tone and intention; to the nature of his own responses to language?

We don't know the answer to these questions, but I'm glad Livingston's study opens them up.

KENNETH G. JOHNSON*

IN his paper, Dr. Livingston says, ". . . several educators in the language arts field have suggested that instruction in general semantics may have a deleterious effect on a student's ability to respond appropriately to fictional literature in general, and to poetry in particular." He then goes on to give the reasoning behind their hypothesis.

Just as reasonable an argument can be made that general semantics would *help* students to respond appropriately to fictional literature and poetry. If the aims of general semantics could be summarized in a word, that word, I believe, would be "conditionality"—that is, the response to words, or events, should be appropriate to the conditions. A fully developed course in general semantics would not emphasize lower orders of abstraction *at the expense* of higher orders, nor the scientific use of language at the expense of the poetic, although *a brief* exposure to the field might have the effects that the language arts teachers fear.

What Dr. Livingston's findings suggest to me is that *both* general seman-

---

* See previous biographical sketch, Chapter 4.—EDITOR.

tics students and the literature students could use more "consciousness of abstracting."

CHARLOTTE S. READ *

I AM not surprised at the results, as training in general semantics ought, it seems to me, to bring about a greater flexibility in interpreting what we read. No doubt there are other important factors besides. I would regard the interpretation of general semantics by the language arts educators referred to as erroneous—disregarding the necessity of high order abstractions and inferences (the point being that we must be aware of them). Dr. Livingston does not indicate whether or not he agrees with their interpretation.

This study raises questions about the teaching of literature and poetry, or perhaps more important, fostering attitudes toward it. It also raises questions about the teaching of general semantics. I might add ironically that the language arts educators, if they wanted to stick to their position, could suggest that what general semantics was taught was not taught effectively enough.

---

* See previous biographical sketch, Chapter 8.—EDITOR.

16

GENERAL SEMANTICS AND TODAY'S WORLD

HARRY E. MAYNARD

NO human activity that involves two or more people occurs without cooperation. No collaborative effort that involves two or more people
occurs without communication. No communication occurs without the use
of symbols and language. And, no large-scale human cooperation takes
place without management. How we manage and fashion our various associations and organizations will determine our futures.

Our essential task as educators and managers of education, as so many
observers of our current scene have pointed out, is "to deal with change."
As Max Ways has pointed out in *Fortune* (July 1, 1966): "What indus-
trialization was to the nineteenth century, management is to the twentieth.
Almost unrecognized in 1900, management has become the central activity
of our civilization."

I happen to believe that to the educator belongs the most important formal role and responsibility for the management of change.

Outside the family, it is the educator's main responsibility to prepare our
young for the explosive changes of today. His job is to help the young with
this opportunity (for the first time in history) to deliberately organize our
civilization around the processes of social change.

All of us have communication problems. Let's take an absurd example
from our own culture. In a *New York World Telegram* column, Norton
Mockridge reported:

> A gentleman I know named Douglas went into a Midtown restaurant one
> lunchtime recently and ordered a hamburger sandwich with lettuce and to-
> mato.

"Sorry, sir," said the waitress, who didn't seem to be sorry at all, "but we don't serve 'em that way."

"You mean you don't have any lettuce in the kitchen, and not even a teensy tomato?" asked Douglas, pleasantly, although he wasn't feeling pleasant.

"Yeah, we got 'em," said the girl, flatly (although she herself wasn't very flat).

"Well, then, can't you just put a piece of lettuce and a slice of tomato on my hamburger, please, pretty please?" asked Douglas angrily because he was, indeed, angry.

"Sir!" said the waitress, "I already *tole* you, we don't serve 'em that way!"

"All right," said Douglas, giving up. "Just put some lettuce and tomato on a plate and I'll fix up the hamburger myself."

"Well, then," said the waitress, "I'll have to charge you for a salad."

"Okay, charge me for a salad," said Douglas. "Give me a salad and, I myself, will put the lettuce and tomato on. Is that all right, all right, all right?"

"Yes, sir," said the waitress. "Now what kind of dressing do you want on your salad?"

The improvement of human communication via symbols—usually with words—is the number one task of educators today. However, we have a language gap.

I believe that the greatest roadblock to any form of human communication is what the social scientist refers to as ethnocentricism. The most observable differences between cultures are speech, dress, living habits, politics, and religions. But each culture is like a gigantic iceberg, carrying along beneath the surface of its observable differences its own assumptions, premises, and biases.

Our everyday language is the most pervasive, ubiquitous, and ethnocentric factor in our cultures. One can liken language to air—colorless, odorless, necessary for survival; but language can also be like carbon monoxide, also a colorless, odorless gas, but very poisonous.

Language acts as the cultural carrier of both the good and the bad of much of our human predicament today. Language and symbols have given us the means for accumulating knowledge and the tools to transmit it. Language has given expression to our finest ethical, philosophical, political, and legal insights. Language, in short, has given us civilization and turned us into human beings.

But too many people (and this includes some linguistic scholars) have examined language primarily as an artifact. In so doing, they remain prisoners of their ethnocentricity. Here is one writer's defense of the study of Greek and Latin as a necessity for anyone aspiring to write English: [1]

I believe that the conventional defense of them is valid; that only by them can a boy fully understand that a sentence is a logical construction and that words *have basic inalienable meanings,* departure from which is either conscious metaphor or inexcusable vulgarity. Those who have not been so taught—most Americans and most women—unless they are guided by some rare genius, betray their deprivation. The old-fashioned test of an English sentence—will it translate?—still stands after we have lost the trick of translation.

Why does he think this way? I think it is because during the eighteenth century the rise of the middle and upper middle classes took place in England. Their desire, like most middle class types, was to do the right thing. They had, like most middle class types, deep concern and apprehension about their language and saw in it a criterion of social prestige.

The semantic Emily Posts of that day naturally turned to classical Latin in order to frame a grammatical reverence for English. Many books on verbal etiquette appeared at the time, such as Bishop Lowth's *Short Introduction to English Grammar,* published in 1762. Thirty-three years later, in the United States, Lindley Murray wrote a grammar which sold a million copies between 1795 and 1850.

These are only a few of the many writers at the time who Latinized English, and attempted to prescribe what was acceptable in speech and writing and what was not.

As a result, certain impressions sprang up that were both false and unfortunate:

1) Language is a divine institution, originally perfect, but debased by man. (No serious study of language history supports this idea; as a matter of fact, it demonstrates just the opposite point.)

2) English is a corrupt and degenerate offspring of Greek and Latin. This canard is equally absurd. Yet, a distinguished writer like Dryden did not credit English with having a grammar. He went so far as to carefully translate his words into Latin so that he could make corrections in his English. Supposedly, we still can't split infinitives in English, or end a sentence with a preposition, because it can't be done in Latin or gracefully translated into elegant Latin. Johnathan Swift felt so strongly about establishing the ground rules for "correct English" that he became one of the leading advocates for establishing an academy similar to the Spanish and French academies. He did this because he felt it was the only way English could be protected from further corruption. Samuel Johnson, too, wrote on verbal etiquette with this aim in mind.

Recently, modern thinkers like Otto Jesperson, Bloomfield, and Sapir have clearly demolished this antiquated point of view. We see today that language changes constantly, and that change is inevitable and normal. Our spoken language is our language. Correctness rests on usage and usage is relative.

Every man in every culture is immersed in an ocean of language. Like amphibians, we are part both of the world of words and of non-words. This means we have all the accumulated wisdom and nonsense wrapped up together in our individual psyches and personalities that language has put there.

Our only hope of improving our culture and seeing through its accumulated nonsense as well as preserving its wisdom is to see through the verbal game—or we will suffer not only from a tyranny of words, but from the tyranny of nonsense assumptions and premises imbedded in the words and symbols of our culture.

Alfred Korzybski put it well:

> We do not realize what tremendous power the structure of a habitual language has. It is not an exaggeration to say that it enslaves us through the mechanism of semantic reactions. These structural assumptions and implications are inside our skins.—If unravelled, they become conscious; if not, they remain unconscious.[2]

How do we dig our way out of this predicament so that we can begin to communicate across our cultural barriers?

Aldous Huxley suggests:

> A culture cannot be discriminatingly accepted, much less be modified, except by persons who have seen through it—by persons who have cut holes in the confining stockade of verbalized symbols and so are able to look at the world and, by reflection, at themselves in a new and relatively unprejudiced way. Such persons are not merely born; they must also be made. But how?
>
> In the field of formal education, what the would-be hole cutter needs is knowledge. Knowledge of the past and present history of cultures in all their fantastic variety, and knowledge about the nature and limitations, the uses and abuses of language. A man who knows that there have been many cultures, and that each culture claims to be the best and truest of all, will find it hard to take too seriously the boastings and dogmatizings of his own tradition. Similarly, a man who knows how symbols are related to experience, and who practices the kind of linguistic self-control taught by the exponents of general semantics, is unlikely to take too seriously the absurd or dangerous nonsense that, within every culture, passes for philosophy, practical wisdom and political argument.[3]

Note that Huxley writes of general semantics. How does this discipline differ from semantics? Historically, "semantics" has usually been associated with the narrow study of word meanings and the history of verbal etiquette. A semanticist of the classical variety can tell you that the largest French-speaking city in the world during the thirteenth century . . . was London. He can tell you that the word *giddy* once was used to describe a very bright and knowing young lady. He can trace the contraction *ain't* through increasingly less pejorative descriptions in successive editions of Webster's dictionary.

The general semanticist, however, is interested in the broader spectrum of human responses to, and uses of, various symbols, including words. We humans also communicate by pictures, gestures, tone of voice, the clothes we wear, the automobiles we drive, and by many other devices with which we encode information and semaphore each other's nervous systems.

Scholars have classified over twenty different human senses. They are variations on the so-called "five windows of the soul." Research in perception shows that from two-thirds to 85 percent of all the information the human nervous system takes in enters through the eye. Once we have taken in this information, we internalize it. We feed it back to ourselves. It becomes our human reality, and eventually determines how we think, feel, and behave. This information becomes our assumptive knowledge.

The general semanticist is concerned with this process of talking to ourselves, the formation of assumptions that we continously apply to newly internalized information.

The general semanticist recognizes that our languages contain our philosophies, that each of our languages contains an implied theory of man and the universe. He urges us ever to be alert to the power of our assumptions.

The general semanticist tries to delimit our cultural biases and prejudices by inventing all sorts of specialized languages, but even these get caught up in the grasp of assumptions.

Our assumptive knowledge is so subtly acquired and internalized that it takes a great deal of special education and training to escape it or, as Huxley says, "cut through it."

The force of semantic rigidities, of unconscious and erroneous assumptions, is so great that our most creative and painstaking scientists are affected.

For many years, they labored under the false premise that it was beyond their reach to split the atom. Enrico Fermi first did split the atom in 1934, at the University of Rome; he did not know what he had done.

When one of our greatest scientists is trapped by his assumptions—consider the predicament of us lesser mortals!

Somewhere the biologist J. H. Woodger once phrased it well: "Man makes metaphysics just as he breathes, without willing it, and above all without doubting it most of the time."

What are the implications of the tyranny of our assumptions and our ethnocentric predicament for international communication today? Our ethnocentric premises are bumping into each other at speeds unknown in the previous history of man. This goes a long way in explaining the rather turbulent state of the world today. Previously, most human beings could sit on the sidelines when various individuals and groups quarreled over their short-term economic, political, and religious differences. No longer.

What light can the students of semantics, general semantics, and linguistics throw on our human predicament? I believe general semantics can help us, as Wittgenstein once said, "fight the bewitchment of our intellect by means of language." For only those who know what they deal with are free to deal with it. Language is one of our best tools to analyze language. We have few others.

We must bring our assumed premises out in the open—up to the surface —where they can be examined by ourselves and the world. Each of us has a perpetual self-inventorying job to do in this area of premise evaluation. Each of us must also try to analyze the assumptions which underlie words and symbols in other cultures.

Our culture trains us and reinforces us to view the world through semantically colored glasses. Language is our greatest habit. One of the notions of general semantics, which is pretty well confirmed by modern psychology, is that we all see the world, taste the world, smell the world, touch the world, hear the world—differently. Out of necessity, we all start with a different point of view.

Our Western culture has begun to pay considerable attention to the specialized languages of science. However, we have strangely neglected the everyday language, our colloquial language, the language in which we do most of our thinking and perceiving—the language with which we try to solve our moral problems, political problems, our religious problems, and our psychological problems. We dismiss these as a mere "matter of semantics." We handle these problems as if they were below the attention of any deeply concerned person.

The limits of our world are determined by the limits of our language and symbol systems. Necessity may be the mother of invention, but definition is its father. We must recognize that the problems of man's inhumanity to man—problems of poverty, nutrition, living space and disease—are before *language*. To state the problem properly is not the solution to the problem. But it may be a major step in solving it. And recognizing the assumptive differences built into our everyday languages may be one of the first steps in adjudicating our differences.

The scientifically oriented men in our society looking at our everyday language are in a unique historical position. We do not have to accept our culture nor our language as fate, just as we soon won't have to accept the weather. We can rise above our own vernaculars; we can transcend our own languages and, as Marshall McLuhan has pointed out, "the limitations of our own assumptions by a critique of them."

We need to adopt this attitude towards both our cultures and our languages if we intend to begin to settle our differences.

REFERENCES

1. Orville Prescott, on Evelyn Waugh in the *New York Times,* November 4, 1964.
2. Korzybski, Alfred. *Science and Sanity: An Introduction to Non-Aristotelian Systems and General Semantics,* Lakeville, Conn.: Non-Aristotelian Library Publishing Co., 4th ed., 1958. Distributed by the Institute of General Semantics.
3. Huxley, Aldous. "A Philosopher's Visionary Prediction," *Playboy* Magazine, November, 1963.

Sue Ann Pace received her Ph.D. from Northwestern University in 1966. She is currently Assistant Professor in the Department of Speech Pathology and Audiology, Southern Illinois University.

17

GENETIC TRANSFER OF VERBAL LEARNING DISABILITIES

SUE ANN PACE

FOR some time general semanticists, behavior theorists, psycholinguists, and others have been interested in man's use of symbols, the relationship of the symbols to the cultural milieu, the way in which these symbols are learned, and those factors that alter the verbal learning processes. As speech and language pathologists, we are continuing to look at those perceptual and cognitive disabilities that alter one's abilities to learn symbols. Of particular interest to some of us are verbal learning disabilities, which appear to be expressed repeatedly within family constellations. The literature suggests that although the familial transmission of speech and language disorders has not been explained, inherited determinants have an influence upon speech and language learning abilities. Familial syndromes have frequently been reported in cases of delayed speech development, specific dyslexia, developmental aphasia, and articulation disorders.[1,2]

We know that there are cultural and environmental factors that influence the character of the verbal symbols children acquire. There are cultural determiners of the aspects of the world that require codification into the semantics and grammar of that culture.[3] Further, there are environmental factors that accelerate and shape a child's learning of his language in order to communicate.[4] A child's language learning appears to be accomplished by a process of his "inducting" the constructional rules from his linguistic environment, generalizing these rules, thus constructing for himself a generative grammar.[5] In her paper in this volume, Mrs. Lee has demonstrated that most normal children construct essentially equal grammars of some complexity with remarkable rapidity at an early age, and in a consistent developmental pattern.* Such a highly complex abstracting and conceptualiz-

---

* See Chapter 14.—EDITOR.

ing process as verbal learning must require a highly elaborated and integrated nervous system.

Of current interest is the tentative hypothesis that there are biological factors, apart from general intellectual capacity, beyond the cultural and environmental aspects that may in some instances affect the child's ability to manipulate symbols. This genetic structure may be the invariant which is transformed by the verbal behaviors acquired through the environment and the culture.

In 1966, I undertook to study the psycholinguistic abilities of 14 families, each of which included a child that had been clinically diagnosed as displaying a perceptual or symbolic learning disability which interfered with verbal learning and thus academic achievement.[5] The purpose of this study was to determine whether a genetic etiologic hypothesis, in regard to the origin of verbal learning disabilities, was tenable. These children's syndromes were designated as having nonspecific etiologies. Psychometrics indicated normal or better overall intellectual abilities, neurological examination indicated no organic brain damage, nor did birth histories, as reported by the hospital records, indicate the possiblity of perinatal brain damage. Ophthalmological and audiological reports indicated normal visual and auditory acuity, and psychologists reported no emotional disorders except universal disapproval of school. Peer and family relationships were good.

A method commonly employed by researchers in genetics studying the transmission of similar disorders involves measuring the performances of parents and siblings of affected individuals. If the trait under study is not genetically transmitted, its frequency of occurrence in the pooled group of parents and of siblings should not be greater than that found in the population as a whole. An expression of the disability in the parents as well as a proportion of the siblings would suggest a genetic transmission. This method was then employed to study the verbal abilities of these families.

In order to study the psycholinguistic abilities of the family members, a battery of tests was compiled. The standardized tests were reported to have reliability and validity in measuring basic verbal skills, which I thought might reflect genetic endowment and might be, at least partially, resistant to the effects of training, and to home and school environments. Some of these tests included the *Frostig Developmental Perceptual Test,* the *Bender Visual Motor Gestalt Test,* the *Illinois Test of Psycholinguistic Abilities,* and the *Wechsler Intelligence Scales,* Verbal and Performance. I hoped to discover some residuals of disability in the parents even though considerable training in verbal skills had intervened.

The results of the administration of the test battery was most revealing. While no parent or sibling was intellectually deficient, *all* of the parents and 47.8 percent (11 out of 23) of the siblings displayed a learning disability, while the remainder of the siblings displayed normal learning abilities. The learning disorder in the affected sibling often centered on a deficit in perception or recall through visual or auditory channels. The histories of these parents and siblings often indicated that they had previously experienced difficulties in verbal skills such as delayed speech, stuttering, and reading disabilities, but had overcome the disability.

Criteria for evidence of a disability in this study was performance poorer than the fifth percentile on one or more tests. The test battery included well standardized instruments; therefore, it is difficult to explain such observations as chance deviations from normalcy. The discrepancies in abilities were highly significant in some cases, e.g., 30–40 I.Q. points difference between verbal and performance I.Q. scores.

It is most difficult to interpret the percentages of affected parents and siblings in terms of expected Mendelian ratios because of the limited sample, but the percentages are observed to be at least supportive of the possibility that a genetic etiological hypothesis is tenable in the expression of verbal learning disabilities. Another genetic study is being completed in Florida at this time. The study is reported to be yielding similar results.[6]

Three areas of verbal disability were particularly obvious in the familial study I have described. The experimental subjects frequently displayed (1) visual and auditory perceptual problems, (2) word retrieval latency, and (3) memory disabilities for serially produced symbols. These areas of difficulty appear particularly important in understanding many of the subjects' difficulties with verbal learning.

The relationship between visual and auditory decoding processes and linguistic behavior is not thoroughly understood. However, mediation of meaningful symbols in speaking, reading, and writing appears to require decoding of visual and auditory stimuli.

Consider single word recall. Certain subjects had considerable difficulty retrieving the appropriate word, most particularly when the word served as a label. Descriptive and designative modifiers were generally easily retrieved. Retrieval difficulty is often referred to as dysnomia, an inability to call forth the name of a familiar object while recalling its modifiers. Certain family members in the genetic study discussed were most capable in verbal areas of information and comprehension, but had difficulty with single specific word retrieval tasks.

The third area of verbal difficulty displayed by the experimental population appeared to be sequential storage of symbols. Research has indicated that much of our linguistic information is stored on the basis of temporal sequences. Learned phoneme combinations in words are sequenced automatically. The young child has particular difficulty with phoneme sequencing, substituting *p asg hetti* for *spaghetti, aminal* for *animal, mitts* for *mist,* and *axe* for *ask*.

Temporal ordering is particularly important for the learning of syntax in languages with limited inflectional markers, such as English, in contrast to an inflected language such as Russian. Research suggests that we are first able to order and retrieve the order of phrases and later phrase combinations. Braine has suggested that a child determines word classes by observing the ordinal position of words in sentences. Information about the previous ordering of the word is then transferred to novel sentences. The child is then able to place this segment in the same position in other contexts. His assimilation of syntax is in part a matter of learning the proper location of words in sentences. Children learn the order of words in phrases quite early. The child learns the linguistic rule: (quantifier) + (qualifier) + N, e.g., "Two red Ball (s)," and he seldom, if ever, permutes them incorrectly after he has learned to combine them. While it is doubtful that syntactic relations develop solely from serial order in the sentence, it is probable that in some languages the serial order of elements within phrases and within sentences is an important information bearer.

A preliminary report from the Florida researchers suggests also that the familial syndromes observed in their study can best be described as manifesting inconstancy of spatial and temporal relations. This inconstancy results in inadequate association and integration of symbols with attendant language disabilities.

In studies of family constellations, it is impossible to separate out environmental and genetic influences upon verbal abilities. However, the consistency with which parents were found to be affected along with a proportion of the siblings appears to suggest that there are factors of a biological nature, genetically determined, which affect the perception and recall of verbal symbols.

We might postulate that we possess, in our nervous systems, unique symbol storage-retrieval mechanisms and serial analyzers, which upon occasion are defective. As clinicians, we frequently observe such disabilities in the presence of organic brain damage, which insults the integrity of the nervous system. These mechanisms may be genetically, as well as environmentally, alterable, thus producing verbal learning disabilities in the absence of neurological insult, mental subnormality, or emotional disturbance.

It is likely that the ability of man to acquire a complex symbol system is determined by a neural network which is uniquely endowed with visual and auditory systems capable of perceiving and retaining images of a complex nature. Another great advantage of the human nervous system over infrahuman organisms is in the area of symbolic retrieval and storage, both short term and long term memory. This function is requisite to the development of verbal behaviors.

It is suggested by this research that the facility with which the nervous system can acquire verbal behaviors may be related to the genotype of the individual. The biological determinants, genetic in origin, precipitate an inability to perceive, and thus select and abstract properly from silent nonverbal levels to verbal levels. This may cause a confusion of the levels of abstraction. Data supportive of such a hypothesis is incomplete, but challenges the researcher to explore the relationship between verbal learning and genetic mechanisms.

REFERENCES

1. Hermann, K. *Reading Disability: A Medical Study of Word-Blindness and Related Handicaps.* Copenhagen, Denmark: Munksgaard, 1959.
2. Ingram, T.T.S. "The Association of Speech Retardation and Educational Difficulties," *Proceedings of the Royal Society of Medicine,* 56, 1963.
3. Hoijer, Harry. *Language and Culture.* Chicago: The University of Chicago Press, 1954.
4. Skinner, B. F. *Verbal Behavior.* New York: Appleton-Century-Crofts, Inc. 1957.
5. Pace, Sue A. "A Genetic and Clinical Study of a Group of Children With Psycholinguistic Learning Disorders." Unpublished Doctoral Dissertation, Northwestern University, 1966.
6. McGlannan, F. K. "Familial Characteristics of Genetic Dyslexia: Preliminary Report from a Pilot Study," *Journal of Learning Disabilities,* 1, (3), 1968.
7. Jakobovits, L. A., and Miron, M. S. *Readings in the Psychology of Language.* Englewood Cliffs, New Jersey: Prentice-Hall, Inc., 1967. (See article by Braine.)

Walter Probert received his B.S. and J.D. from the University of Oregon, and his J.S.D. from Yale University. He has taught at Western Reserve University, Northwestern University, the University of Denver, and is currently Professor in the College of Law at the University of Florida. In 1969, he was a Research Visitor at Oxford University, studying Law-Communication, and soon plans to publish his book: *Law, Language, and Communication*.

18

SOME REFLECTIONS ON LAW-LANGUAGE *

WALTER PROBERT

TO a large extent, the proper study of law involves a study of language, and more generally of communicative behavior, if nothing else, to see the interconnections. For instance, while it is true that law can be legislated for the masses, language use cannot be. Yet there are linguistic restraints on the extent to which legislation can work. The evolutionary development of law is dependent upon language phenomena too. I refer to the common law whose rules change slowly, not only in a way similar to the way word uses change, but *because* laws are necessarily linguistic and must have key terms that are open-ended. Yesterday's word forms take on today's values, culture, and changing social relationships because that is the way they are used. Law is nothing if it is not dependent upon human language and communication—as they actually work, not as they are idealized.

Law has continuously been the subject of philosophic inquiry, both as an idealized human institution, and as a pragmatic mechanism of individual and social adjustment. We know how much language has been a subject of philosophic inquiry; and indeed today as an object of study and speculation its interest value seems to surpass that of law. Naturally enough, the tangled web of law and language has provided much food not only for philosophic thought, but for all the branching-off disciplines that swirl around our efforts to understand human endeavors. There are many lines of inquiry

* Prepared at Oxford University while under a grant from the National Foundation for the Humanities.

that are relevant to anyone who is interested in any branch of linguistic or communicative study. One in particular continues to baffle even those whose customary dogma camouflage many such problems from their own view. I refer to ambiguity, the inescapable ambiguity that pervades the very fibre of law. That, despite law's image as knowable, predictable, and generally stable.

Take that slice of years beginning with this century. In those days, law was described and viewed as a body of fixed rules, fit for stowing in even primitive computers. Were law really that way, there would be no need for judges, except maybe as ministers to juries whose findings could have been programmed and fed on tapes to machines whose output would have barely equalled the sterile rhetoric of those earlier courts. But as the century moved into the iconoclastic days of the twenties and thirties, that view of law was laid to rest, hopefully forever.

Communication students of almost every stripe would be interested to follow the attack of the legal realists as the subversives were styled. It was not general semantics theory they used, but a combination of logical positivism, psychology, anthropology, and scientific philosophy that added up to a carbon copy of the skeptical component of Korzybski's kind of analysis. While they attacked law's entire conceptualism, what I particularly wish to note is the upshot of their views about legal rules.

What is remembered today is that they seemed to say that legal rules simply did not operate the way traditionalists pronounced them. Indeed, they wondered if they existed at all. They proved in the experts' faces that no specific case or problem was determinable or logically controlled by any rule that could be proclaimed. That should be a familiar argument to a general semanticist who realizes that on the nonverbal level, every situation is unique. Words and generalized utterances—such as rules—are only abstractly related to situations. The fit of words to situations is by fiat or a matter of expedience.

Such a view may leave us just the same with an uneasy feeling. It may help to realize that a kind of rhetoric was being used to counter the dogma of numerous obstructionist judges and other traditionalist influential fixtures in the legal profession. The upshot of the view was that with respect to specific cases, the bare body of rules of law were indeterminate. Whether a particular rule and case fitted each other constituted a kind of ambiguity or indefiniteness that could not be resolved by the rules themselves.

As one might guess, such a view could not last, although its impact has been lasting. The responses have been many and still continue. Of particular interest is a counterview that has been influenced by the linguistic philosophies of Wittgenstein and J. L. Austin.[2,3] So far, their philosophies have been modestly, perhaps conservatively, applied. But it is in the broad ground still unoccupied between the extremes that much work of value might still be done, ought to be done. Today's threat to law is not from such critics as the legal realists so much as it is from dissatisfied people whose skepticism about law and its rules stems from different causes. Their view is something other than theoretical. Even so, midrange theory might be helpful to shore up so much of the fortress as deserves to be saved.

Korzybski was well aware that words in the stock of language were a scarce commodity compared to the situations to which they had to be applied.[4] He must have been aware, therefore, that words do not adhere to things or situations. They are *applied* or *acted out* in acts of human judgment. In this view, rules are not just reasons or guides; they may be the very act of decision. Still, even he did not seem to believe that application was helter-skelter or chaotic, as relativistic as his therapeutic side necessarily was or tended to appear. His quasi-mathematical formulations pretty clearly applied the brake. The notion of multiordinality was one such brake. This notion, incidentally, significantly anticipated related analyses of Wittgenstein and Austin.

While the latter two remarkable men were "philosophers," their views were in some ways anti-philosophical in much the same way as Korzybski's "philosophy." They were all opposed to the tendency of many philosophers to take terms out of their situational contexts of use and project them into space, so to speak, as independent entities. The Good, the True, and the Beautiful, are favorite even though extreme examples. But it has never been just philosophy in which this abuse of not just conventions of word usage but the foundations of linguistic understandings occurred. Korzybski and his popularizers have well established the range of the abuse. Wittgenstein and Austin tended to limit their criticisms to philosophers, but their analyses can be used with as sweeping effect as Korzybski's.

It was mainly the legal realists who decried the conceptualistic tendencies among lawyers. But remember that I have said the popularizers of Wittgenstein and Austin used their methods against the legal realists. It is no doubt because the later methods are less skeptical and more saving of conventional usages that they are more acceptable, more saving of many large and important faces.

All these views share in skepticism of the word *meaning*. As we know, Korzybski turned to "semantic reaction," the notion that meanings were not in words but in people who were using and reacting to words. But as I have said, his notion of multiordinality suggests that people were not completely free to use words as they wished. Rather certain words were seen as incomplete, as symbols, taking part of their meaning or value from previous uses, and part from the moment of use—in a way that is strikingly similar to lawyers' *stare decisis* doctrine, the view that a given case decides for the future, establishes a rule. Wittgenstein's notion of language games is much like Korzybski's. In that notion, a given word is used in a number of ways that are related, but there is no one, overriding or essential meaning of the abstract family term. The very word *game* is an example. No overriding definition can be given that covers all situations called *games,* but there are interrelationships from usage to usage.

While Austin's efforts are said to be independent of Wittgensteinian influence, his actual analysis also showed that a given abstract word was used in ways that did not justify any overriding meaning being given to that word. But in both of their works, there is the implicit faith that analyses of conventional usages in depth often resolve riddles that philosophers produced. For Austin, such hard, probing analysis was actually an empirical route to new conscious insight of the kind previously buried in surface convention. It is a matter of understanding how language is in fact used as it evolves in man's progressions. The legal realists were onto something of that sort, but they created a riddle in the process.

Take that word *rule.* We might ask, "What is a rule?" The question is seductive, but it seeks a definition at too abstract a level. Even so, there can be found numerous examples of rhetoric in and out of law where similar seductions prevail. The very idea, now so impressive in Chomsky's work, that "language" is an independent entity may be one such. Much of the rhetoric subsumed under the "law and order" banner is of that kind. It suggests that all legal rules are of one variety, to be followed blindly, and enforced equally blindly.

But the legal realists committed the same blunder in believing that if rules were not what they were said to be at the abstract level, then they were nothing at all. What they failed to do was to look to see the way in which the word *rule,* and the utterances called *rules* actually were used in various parts of society—not just in the official parts such as courts, but in lawyers' offices and the mass media, for instance. Even as to courts, the necessary analysis has progressed only a little way. It is not, please, that we should know what rules "are," but that we should *see,* not a chaos of words called *rules,* but some functional structure of conventions. A multiordinal utterance called a rule branches out into sub–utterances that get used in a number of interrelated but still not identical ways. Of course, no matter how far we go in analysis, we should not expect everything really to fit neatly together into neat bundles, but at best only into loose assortments.

Even the "rule" prohibiting murder is multiordinal (*K*), is a counter in many language games (*W*), is subject to differing conventions of usage (*A*). Even if we define murder as intentional homicide, we find that the word *intentional* ranges over notions of malice, purpose, foresight, and foreseeability, depending on the kind of situation. The key words in a rule, say "intent" in the murder rule, are themselves multiordinal at the abstract level of a general rule statement. The "rule" against murder does not get used only in prosecutions, but also in sermons, lectures, counseling, plays, and so on. These uses too are significant in any thoroughgoing analysis. There are other "rules" that are not prohibitory in the way of the murder "rule," like those regarding the payment of compensation for committing negligent acts that cause damage, or requiring payment of taxes, and so on. Some "rules" are not addressed to the general populace, but to judges or policemen, for instance. Lawyers use "rules" sometimes therapeutically, sometimes morally, and of course often in some form of legal persuasion. There is much more that even now could be said, but even more that has not yet been probed or analyzed. We may seem to be getting back only to Korzybski's caveats against elementalism, but such a caveat is only the beginning of a host of arduous tasks that often we might wish to avoid.

Thus, the great variety of "rules" vary in appearance and significance, and in their pragmatics. If any rules are applied automatically outside the law, only a few are within. And as I have said, words often amount to an evaluation rather than just the mere description they seem, or as a reason. The legal realists were still right, however, in insisting that rules ought not usually to be accepted as their own justifications.

Even this midground approach, which I have only lightly sketched, is bothersome to many whose conceptions and images of law are somehow different or even opposite. To the extent that some cultural conditioning is involved, then something like Korzybski's therapeutic awakening (guided awareness) is still very much relevant and necessary to prepare us all to see how law really operates. If we are prepared, then we will not simply lie down on the floor and cry, or throw rules against the wall, or take to guns. It is at least of passing interest to note that English linguistic philosophy has also been referred to, maybe scornfully, as therapeutic.

If I seem to have brought English philosophy through the back door, let me justify it. I believe that it would be possible to make a good case that Korzybski's original theory in *Science and Sanity* is relevant to law—1968. However, I believe the case can be better made for a neo-Korzybskian approach. It seems to me that general semantics should be looked at as open-ended, if any subject should, not frozen as of 1933. I have mentioned one related view, and one way in which "linguistic philosophy" coalesces or blends with Korzybski's formulations and interpretations. There are also McLuhan, Chomsky, group dynamics, sensitivity training, and so on. All this is the stuff of general semantics. Certainly it will be for the next genius.* Even so, I remain convinced that lawyers could be better trained for court, for human relationships with clients, for interpretation, for writing and drafting, and generally for being better public servants, if they were only confronted with Korzybski, 1933–1968.

REFERENCES

1. Wittgenstein, L. *Philosophical Investigations.* Translated by G. E. M. Anscombe. New York: Macmillan, 1953.
2. Austin, J. L. *Philosophical Papers,* eds. J. O. Urmson and G. J. Warnock. Oxford: Clarendon Press, 1961.
3. Austin, J. L. *How to Do Things With Words,* ed. J. O. Urmson. Cambridge, Mass.: Harvard University Press, 1962.
4. Korzybski, Alfred. *Science and Sanity: An Introduction to Non-Aristotelian Systems and General Semantics;* Lakeville, Conn.: International Non-Aristotelian Library Publishing Co., 4th ed. 1958. Distributed by the Institute of General Semantics.

* Cf. Hardt's conclusion, Chapter 3.—EDITOR

Thaddeus J. Pula received his B.S.E.E. from Villanova University in 1947, his M. S. Eng. from Johns Hopkins University in 1950, and his Dr. Eng. from Johns Hopkins University in 1957. He serves in a management advisory capacity for Electrical Design Engineering at the Westinghouse Aerospace Division of the Westinghouse Electric Corporation. He was Instructor of E.E. at Johns Hopkins, and Associate Professor of E.E. at the U.S. Naval Postgraduate School at Annapolis, Maryland. He is coauthor of the book *Self-Saturating Magnetic Amplifiers*.

19

GENERAL SEMANTICS AS AN EDUCATIVE TOOL IN THE ELECTRICAL CURRICULUM *

THADDEUS J. PULA

INTRODUCTION

IF there is any doubt that considerable ferment exists in electrical engineering education today, we need only refer to a few recent events that come readily to mind:

1) changing the name of a School of Engineering to School of Engineering Science
2) accepting a large foundation grant to study the pros and cons of abolishing electrical engineering at the undergraduate level, and structuring it to be exclusively a graduate discipline
3) after a curriculum review, deciding that electrical engineering requirements were becoming too heavy and "solving" the problem by establishing a five year B.S. Eng. program
4) the proliferation in various schools of engineering-physics majors.

Add to these signs the increasing attention being paid to the problem of engineering obsolescence by industrial and government activities, in addition to academic institutions, and it is clear that curriculum changes in engineering education are here to stay—and that their rate of change is increasing.

* This paper was originally published in the *IEEE TRANSACTIONS ON EDUCATION,* Vol. E-11. No. 2, June, 1968. Reprinted with Permission.

Every "practicing electrical engineer" has been molded by electrical engineering education and has observed some of its trends since the completion of his formal training. In addition, I have lived and worked for most of my adult years with many electrical engineers—especially those in the industrial research and development environment. Therefore, my motivation in writing this paper from the "vantage" or "disadvantage" point of an electrical engineer in industry is, hopefully, to stimulate discussion in the academic community regarding some of the *positive* ingredients that should be added to the electrical engineering curriculum to keep it distinctive from, e.g., a physics major, and that might stimulate the earlier formation of that most valuable attribute of our topflight professional men, "sound engineering judgment."

My theme will revolve around three central concepts:

1) *levels of abstraction* as an attitude for all math, physics, and engineering subjects, with some related discussion of the obsolescence problem
2) *multiordinality* as of central importance in preparing to deal with people from manufacturing, purchasing, marketing, product reliability, subcontracting, etc., as well as with "engineering and science" types
3) *semantic reactions* in ourselves as well as others as important cues in regulating our professional and interpersonal lives.

These concepts are neither mine nor recent. They were first systematized in a fascinating book by Korzybski [1] in 1933, and have evolved into an active field of study called "general semantics." [2] The object of this paper will be to discuss, in a preliminary way, how these few concepts taken from the general semantics discipline might be used to advantage in the admittedly dynamic electrical engineering curriculum. The body of the paper will, therefore, be organized as follows:

1) a brief exposition of the main thrust of Korzybski's general semantics, placing the above concepts in context
2) discussion of levels of abstraction awareness in scientific courses
3) discussion of multiordinality awareness in preparing students for dealing with various types of people during their professional careers
4) discussion of semantic reactions as related to our own learning process and that of others.

A NOTE ON GENERAL SEMANTICS

The principal thrust that led Korzybski to formulate the system that now is known as general semantics was the awareness which he gradually developed that so many of his professional colleagues (incidentally, he was an engineer by formal education) and intellectual circle of associates judged situations in general in right–wrong, yes–no, true–false, or what he called an "Aristotelian" way—a phrase that he coined from the system of deductive logical reasoning originating with Aristotle. Korzybski, on the other hand, became convinced that many situations, phenomena, etc., did *not* lend themselves to such a "binary–digital" formulation, and that, in fact, such non-Aristotelian situations included many of the most important areas of scientific and cosmological investigation. He came to feel, for example, that the separation of human illness into *either* physical *or* mental was becoming an impediment to progress in psychiatry, and that the dichotomy represented by use of *either* the expression waves *or* particles in physics was behind much of the confusion in quantum theory.

Most fundamentally, he diagnosed this limiting thought process as resulting from what he termed "the *is* of identity." Indeed, Korzybski's entire non-Aristotelian formulation revolved around attempts to eliminate the *is* of identity. Thus, he attempted to bring home forcefully to the student (i.e., any inquiring human being—I almost said "mind") that *all theories are abstractions* in the sense that they leave out certain known and unknown attributes of reality, either intentionally or unintentionally, in the process of formulating the structure of their particular theory. Furthermore, he stressed that as a theory becomes more and more refined, sophisticated, and general, it leaves out more and more particular attributes of the real, and therefore becomes more and more abstract (e.g., he would have said that the question "*Is* the electron *really* a wave-packet?" adds up to an accumulation of noise syllables, and can have no sensible answer). In general, he held that all theories, by nature, involve some abstraction, that various theories differ in their levels of abstraction, and that even though theory is a very important ingredient in scientific progress, we must realize that we can never fully formulate what reality "really is," and that all of our theories are, to some extent, provisional and "in the mind." Korzybski cryptically denied the identity of theory and reality by saying, "Whatever you *say* a thing is, it is not."

The second most fundamental contribution of Korzybski was to insist that a human being is more than just "intellect-logically-reasoning," and that the reactions of the "whole person" must be taken into account (viz., such very important areas as how we learn and remember and what we understand when we read, listen, talk, etc.). This thrust led to an awareness of the different reactions to the same words by different people depending on their previous education, home environment, etc., and the different reaction of various types of people to the same oral versus written information. This total response of human beings he called their "semantic reactions." It involves such abstractions as mental understanding, temperament, memory, etc., but is more than their sum because it refers to the response of the whole person on what he called the "silent level": all we can theorize about involves these various abstractions already involved in our interpersonal communications—even this one.

An offshoot of studying differing semantic reactions leads to the recognition of our third central concept, which Korzybski called "multiordinality." This involves the realization that the same words often have very different meanings depending on the context, manner of expression, etc., for various people, and that, furthermore, these words include some of the most important concepts in language. Therefore, the recognition of this problem of multiple meaning (multiordinality), in scientific as well as professional and daily exchange of ideas, constitutes another important awareness which humans should develop for their professional growth and mental health. Korzybski especially stressed that a term whose meaning depends on context (i.e., may have *many* meanings) does not have any general meaning, but must be visualized as a series of connotations. This realization actually contains the most important insight into the multiordinality concept.

This much explanation should serve to give some introduction to the terminology. The interested reader is referred to Korzybski for a weighty and involving experience, but Bois might be better for a more linear exposition. (As we will note later, creativity and inventiveness are seldom "logical" in the pedestrian sense.)

LEVELS OF ABSTRACTION IN SCIENCE COURSES

The *explicit awareness* of the various levels of abstraction employed in all science courses should be stressed to the electrical engineering student beginning with his very first course. Projecting myself back to my first electrical engineering course, and to the course in "Elements of Electrical Engineering" for which I was a graduate student laboratory instructor, I think it would have been very helpful if the professor had, on the very first day, written across the board in bold letters:

LINEARITY IS AN ABSTRACTION
LUMPED CONSTANT CIRCUIT ELEMENTS ARE ABSTRACTIONS
MAXWELL'S EQUATIONS ARE ABSTRACTIONS
. . . etc.

He could then have proceeded to explain the usefulness of the *idealization* called "linearity" for beginning circuit theory, while making the students aware of the necessity of establishing that approximate linearity exists in a network *before* employing linear analysis.

Two examples come to mind from my own early experience with electromechanical servomechanism design. First, I can remember that two models of our device, one in the laboratory and the second across the country undergoing flight test, were giving quite different frequency response records. We proceeded to "get correlation" between them by setting up fixed maximum amplitudes for the signal generator inputs we were using to obtain the frequency responses, without ever taking time to investigate the importance of the fact that a finite input was needed before any output was obtained. Second, I recall quite clearly studying frequency response records, and observing that they were dramatically different when taken with decreasing frequency through their peaking frequency than when taken in the normal, to us, increasing frequency manner through resonance. Our solution was to standardize a procedure requiring that all runs be made with increasing frequency so that similar runs between different equipment would be reproducible. So much effort had been expended in applying linear servomechanism theory that this possibly crucially important nonlinearity was completely ignored—except in devising test methods which would suppress it!

Similarly, regarding lumped–constants, it would be helpful to warn even the neophyte that the circuit elements must appear electrically short, and stress all the restrictions on physical size versus frequency which are required to make this abstraction useful before voluminous calculations or computer runs are made using any particular set of approximating abstractions. Appropriate qualifying comments could be provided for other abstractions listed.

Another help to the student in his first electrical engineering course would be an explicit discussion (preferably with the help of diagrams so that there could be visual–auditory reinforcement plus an opportunity for referral during the undergraduate curriculum) of the *structure* of the entire range of course offerings. Although there is no uniquely best way to present such a diagram, what I envision, in general, is first a list and general classification of some of the major physical phenomena that form the basis of operation of electrical engineering devices and systems. Second, there would be a general listing and classification of the principal mathematical techniques that are used in electrical engineering analysis and design. Third, I would dive into the *sine qua non* of engineering: the art of useful approximation. This could be done in several phases, the following being only illustrative examples..

1) Areas in which circuit lengths are electrically short and where radiation can be safely neglected could be approximately identified, and several course offerings which use these assumptions centrally could be tagged by name or number. Even an occasional warning that "by the time you're a senior we may not be giving that as a separate course" would seem helpful in alerting the beginning student to the fact that the electrical engineering curriculum is and will remain dynamic, although to be dynamic must not mean that at any cut through time there is not a relatively definite *structure* (since structure is such an important ingredient of systematized knowledge).

2) Areas could be identified in which an analytical approach is definitely inadequate with present methods and which, therefore, must rely heavily on measurements and empirical design techniques using physics and math only as a guide and a "reasonableness check" for various limiting cases.

3) Areas could be mentioned in which the course offerings are only in the discussion stage among faculty members—presently being at the graduate level, being taught in the physics or math department, or just in the graduate seminar stage. This part of the discussion could also weave in the continuing physics and math courses which the student will get during his course work.

No diagram has been presented to illustrate the structure of course offerings, not merely because there is no "best" diagram but, more tellingly, because it is very difficult to make such a diagram without discussing its shortcomings and, therefore, without letting it evolve through professor--student discussion. This merely emphasizes the student's confusion as he begins his curriculum. I feel very strongly that the sooner the student realizes that "there are packages, but the lids don't seem to fit exactly, and they never will, because the size of the packages keeps changing," the better the start he will be getting in the "awareness" portion of his education. Another benefit of such a thought exercise between professor and student is that the student may realize much sooner, and even less painfully, that there are vast areas of "the potentially knowable" which are not included in any course offerings and that, in addition, certain courses may atrophy. This will get him to appreciate, right from the start, that *education is an open system,* and that he should continue it at some rate after graduation. What better time to implant his own antiobsolescence campaign in his subconscious mind!

In general, it would seem helpful for the mental health and earlier maturation of the electrical engineer for the professor to admit, from the outset of the first course, that all theories are abstractions, and as such cannot provide a complete representation or basis of prediction regarding reality. This realization is of the utmost importance, and should pervade our attitude of alertness and criticism as we study theory in any scientific discipline. This very attitude, however, should not sour us on theory; it is better to understand and foresee incompletely than not to attempt these systematizations at all. A corollary to this attitude regarding the inherent incompleteness of theory, however, seems equally important, and is often overlooked in scientific teaching methods. It is this: if we are alert to the limitations of a theory (often stated in early works on a subject but at times glossed over in reviews and textbook treatments), we will then not fall as readily into the trap of trying to understand something which the particular theory does not set out to make understandable! We will then be freed from the intellectually fatiguing and wasteful position of continuing to look to a particular theory for clarification of problems that it cannot possibly provide. In this way, our energies can be more quickly diverted to studying different theoretical formulations, attempting to extend the insufficient ones, or concentrating on more detailed empirical procedures for accomplishing our designs.

At an advanced undergraduate level (e.g., when beginning the senior thesis, if such is included in the undergraduate curriculum) or during the first semester of graduate school, a more sophisticated use might be made of the notion of abstraction in leading the student into the proper mental set for reading advanced and current literature, and in preventing the authoritarian encrustations of the theoretical establishment from dulling his youthful vision and enthusiasm for the unknown. He could be made to realize that since an original investigator proceeds by observation and then abstraction from "the world" of his investigation, our purpose as educators is to help him approach the educative process as much as possible from the disadvantage point of the *learner* as an original investigator. We would plan to guide him to catalogue and contemplate the phenomena, which were studied by the original people who developed a theory, then help him to visualize himself in such an intellectual position attempting to formulate a particular theory. It would be especially valuable if we could draw him on to make a few of his own attempts at abstractions from the phenomena, and of trying to systematize this set of abstractions. After he has spent some effort at such attempts, he would, when exposed to the actual new (to him) theory, be much more alert to those phenomena that the theory omits in forming its set of abstractions. His mind would also be receptive to grasping the interrelationships presented (i.e., the state of curious confusion rather than one of ignorance or, possibly, disinterest).

This type of "learner oriented" approach should also improve the rate of preparation of students for their own possible research work, since their whole mental habit will be molded toward the type of thought sequence that research investigators from time immemorial have necessarily employed. The phenomena are prior to and independent of the theories that men concoct to systematize their interrelations. In this sense, a theory may be regarded as somewhat like a catalyst—it is not part of any of the phenomena known at the beginning of the investigation, nor is it part of any new phenomena discovered, yet it serves as a vehicle for guiding the search by the investigator. It is often a useful vehicle, but never the only vehicle, and at times even a hindrance to further discoveries.

The entire role of theory and modeling can thus be grasped in its true perspective as *provisional* and *in-the-mind*. This structure erected by man is then seen as the systematized "abstract art" of scientific methodology. Also, in this way the neophyte investigator who leans toward the laboratory "take-a-lot-of-measurements" approach will be freed from the feeling that to really be a topnotch research man he must first learn all there is to know about all of the existing theories. Similarly, students who lean toward studying the interrelationships among phenomena will see that broadening a synthesis by being able to reduce the severity of the abstractions can, in itself, constitute worthwhile research, even if they themselves discover not one new phenomenon.

MULTIORDINALITY AWARENESS IN INTERPERSONAL RELATIONSHIPS AFTER GRADUATION

In my electrical engineering curriculum, graduate or undergraduate, I hardly remember ever discussing *people*—after all, weren't we becoming professionals, learning to be objective and scientific? As students of the scientific method, what need had we, what place was there, for worrying about people's subjective reactions? If some particular guy had a hidden bent for sales, let him take a Dale Carnegie course on the side; we were preparing ourselves to "design things."

What I am suggesting now is that in my week-by-week professional life, hardly a day goes by where my associates and I don't discuss people and their partly subjective, partly impulsive, partly idealistic, partly intuitive, partly careless, partly dedicated, partly expert evaluations, decisions, and electrical designs.

Of course, it might be argued that when an electrical engineering student grows up among his group of fellow students, he gradually gets a pretty good feel for "the engineering breed of cat," and that since his interpersonal dealings will be light at first, after graduation he has some years of on the job experience to get a further feel for people. At this point, I am not even inclined to attack this possible argument, although I would not admit that it is unassailable. I am much more interested in discussing the dealings that engineers often have in the very first years after graduation with personnel from several other departments, e.g., manufacturing, testing, purchasing, subcontracting, and marketing. Here they certainly meet disparate types—and fast. I will admit that my point here may be too general and approaching the "so cultural factors are important too—how can we possibly fit this type of material into an electrical engineering curriculum?" reaction. Perhaps I can be a bit more constructive if I discuss several small examples of things which could possibly be woven into the present course structure.

1) *Report writing:* First, I am not suggesting that the English courses be transferred into the Engineering Department. What I would suggest is that since the most important aspect of a report (written or oral) is to assess the type of intended audience, wouldn't it be interesting and informative to the student if from time to time he were asked to write one of his assigned reports as if it were addressed to a foreman in manufacturing? Or even to write three or four different versions of the same material—one to manufacturing, one to marketing, and one to purchasing? Believe me, the content *should* be different, and not simply because of an innate desire "to win friends and influence people." My experience with quite a few engineers is that most of them hate to write; it is my opinion that at least part of the reason is that they visualize it as more

dull "fact putting" following extensive fact finding. If they could learn to visualize reporting as an extension of their powers of persuasion during which someone would hear them out without interruption (*if* the material is well organized and tailored to the intended *reader*), it is my opinion that they might even consider writing as an occasional challenge.

2) *Use of words:* Let me illustrate this point by citing an example from my own work experience. The engineering manager from one of our major programs was holding an oral design review with the leader of a specialist group that had performed the electrical design for a significant portion of his developmental equipment. One of the performance values was testing below specification. The program had been initiated only a few months earlier on a crash basis, and many of the ground rules for design had been transmitted orally. Now, here was an indisputable fact—one of the performance values was testing below specification. The engineering manager for the program, in reviewing earlier meetings, which had set the guide lines, stated that it had always been inferred at these meetings that the particular ground rule was thus-and-so. Unfortunately, this very talented engineering manager considered "infer" and "imply" to be synonymous. He was merely referring to what he had meant to convey at earlier meetings. The design leader, however, well aware of the clear distinction that should exist between an implication and an inference took this as an affront to his integrity. He, in effect, was being accused of having made the proper inference on the ground rules at an earlier meeting and, with such knowledge, not redirecting the design effort. The most interesting point of the story is that the engineering program manager couldn't figure out why the design leader had "suddenly gotten so huffy"; it never occurred to the design leader that perhaps not everyone understood the English language as well as he.

My principal point regarding multiordinality (I admit that I have few detailed constructive suggestions here.) is that it provides another example of an area of appreciation that the electrical engineer would find valuable in his professional life, since he is, or should be, preparing to work with various types of people, to a considerably greater extent than the student of phsyical science. Perhaps even to graduate with this general awareness would be a valuable career cue.

SEMANTIC REACTIONS AND THE LEARNING PROCESS

The last area of my paper, and perhaps the most difficult to discuss constructively, involves the recommendation that as part of the engineering curriculum professors discuss the learning process itself with their students despite the fact that there is, and probably always will be, much that is mysterious in this process for each of us. My own knowledge in this area is quite rudimentary, so I will conclude by merely suggesting a few fragments that I have found to be helpful on a limited scale of personal experience, and that might merit further consideration by those in academic circles.

First of all, I have found it helpful to the morale and method-of-attack of certain junior staff members to explain that the process by which humans obtain new knowledge seems to be categorizable into five largely sequential but partially overlapping phases:

1) ignorance
2) confusion
3) understanding
4) facility
5) expertise.

It can then be pointed out that it is to be expected that there *should* be a feeling of confusion during the early stages of a new investigation—that, in fact, this shows that the mind is working. Often, new ideas will spring up by allowing time to mull over areas of confusion. Further, the observation can be made that the dichotomy in roles between engineering management and the engineering specialist only arises after phase 3. Finally, it is very important for engineering managers to stay with the learning process this far in any particular specialty area in order to retain the base knowledge for decision making, and in order to appreciate, as well as retain, the ability to supervise their engineering specialist staff.

An additional related point regarding planning meetings can sometimes be made. Once an individual is familiar with this "five phases of learning" theory, and realizes that the phases are largely sequential, he can often be made to appreciate that in some instances it is foolish to attempt to convince someone (potential customer, superior, interdepartmental associate, etc.) of a major concept at one meeting. In such cases, our advance planning should dictate a strategy where we attempt to break off an initial discussion before any decision point is reached, to allow time for mulling over, checking into, etc., on the part of our hoped-for "convincee."

The next point I would like to touch on involves inventiveness. The principal observation that I would like to make is that in my personal experience inventiveness is *not* included in these five phases of acquiring knowledge. Here some mysterious element predominates; I would say that these five phases form a necessary but not sufficient base for inventiveness. On this subject, however, especially since inventiveness is such an important attribute for an engineer, it might be worth considering the discussion of a book such as the provocative one by Gordon, perhaps as part of some senior undergraduate or first-year graduate seminar.[3]

Finally, I have seen some engineers who seem to have a very constructive attitude and a zest for new assignments, while others are dour and want all the ground rules carefully outlined before they proceed. No, I don't expect the limited time for electrical engineering education to include psychoanalysis, motivation study, or smiling exercises, but I can't conclude without mentioning how valuable I feel it would have been to my mental and emotional development if I had been made aware of such very important career cues as the general adaptation syndrome so brilliantly discussed by Selye.[4] He makes us aware that our energies *are* limited, our attention span *is* finite, our batteries *do* need recharging by hobbies, exercise, and idle time, and, above all, that the content of life exceeds the content of work—engineering or otherwise.

REFERENCES

1. Korzybski, Alfred. *Science and Sanity: An Introduction to Non-Aristotelian Systems and General Semantics.* 4th ed. Lakeville, Conn.: International Non-Aristotelian Library Publishing Co., 1958. Distributed by the Institute of General Semantics.
2. Bois, J. A. *Art of Awareness.* Dubuque, Ia.: W. C. Brown & Co., 1967.
3. Gordon, W. J. J. *Synectics, the Development of Creative Capacity.* New York: Harper & Row, 1961.
4. Selye, H. *The Stress of Life.* New York: McGraw-Hill, 1956.

Anatol Rapoport is Professor of Mathematical Biology and
Senior Research Mathematician in the Mental Health Research
Institute, University of Michigan. He taught at Technical Uni-
versity of Denmark in Lyngby, Denmark during 1968–69. In
1941, he received his Ph.D. from the University of Chicago,
where he later was a member of the Committee on Mathematical Biophysics. He was also a Fellow at the Center for
Advanced Studies in Behavorial Science at Stanford. He is
Coeditor, since 1956, of *General Systems;* Associate Editor of
Behavioral Science, Journal of Conflict Resolution, and *ETC.:
A Review of General Semantics;* and a member of the Advisory Boards of several European scientific publications. His
writings—six books and several monographs—include: *Strategy
and Conscience; Operational Philosophy; Science and the
Goals of Man; Fights, Games and Debates;* and *Two-Person
Game Theory: the Essential Ideas.*

20

THE QUESTION OF RELEVANCE *

ANATOL RAPOPORT

WORLD War I, and the rise of totalitarianism following it, demolished
the Victorian faith in progress as the inevitable result of growing science and widening political democracy. It turned out that the development
of science was lopsided; it conferred power without wisdom, and political democracy created mass societies and pseudo-participation of populations in public affairs. Mass literacy and the mass media, instead of lib-
erating the populations from passive submission to tyranny, made them
vulnerable to manipulation by charlatans and demagogues who defrauded
them and recruited them as participators in crimes against humanity.

In the early 1920's, Alfred Korzybski and John Dewey (whose outlooks
overlap in many respects) proposed a reevaluation of the cognition process. Dewey's emphasis was on a thorough overhaul of educational methods,
Korzybski's was on the construction of a science of man based on a far-
reaching empirical investigation of the way man's perception of "reality" is
distorted by the screen of language interposed between him and his world.

---

* "Relevance[1968]"

As on previous such occasions, now is the time to take stock once again of what has and what has not been accomplished. The title theme of this conference emphasizes the task. We ask to what extent is general semantics relevant to the problems and dilemmas of our day?

One way of answering this question is to reiterate the eternal verities of general semantics. In so doing, we would be enhancing our self-esteem. Another way is to examine what general semanticists are doing in 1968.

Before 1965, it seemed to me that our concerns were fundamentally relevant to the concerns of humanity. Today it seems to me that they are not. If the program of the 1968 conference is a reflection of what we are doing, it does not seem to me that we are doing anything different from what we were doing in 1958, 1948, or 1938.

Recall the fundamental epistemological premise of general semantics: reality is made up not of things and categories, but of structural relations. To know something, it is not sufficient to examine it in isolation. It is necessary to examine it in a web of relations to other things. This is the principle of nonelementalism known to all of you. An acorn *is* not a "future oak tree." It *becomes* an oak tree only if placed in proper soil in a proper climate. The personality of a person is not something inside his skin (where the soul was once supposed to be). Personality manifests itself only in relations between one person and others. A disease is not an inevitable result of the presence of pathogenic organisms in the body. A disease results from biochemical interactions between the invaders and the body tissues.

It is especially important to bear in mind, when evaluating philosophies, that a philosophy in itself is nothing. It becomes something or other depending on the cultural soil from which it receives nourishment. Thus the Christianity of fourth-century Egypt bears no resemblance to the Christianity of seventeenth-century Spain. The history of nationalism in Switzerland bears no resemblance to the history of nationalism in Germany.

It is not enough to assert that nationalism$_1$ is not nationalism$_2$. Nascent German nationalism did resemble Swiss nationalism. Both were born as movements of national liberation. It was the *subsequent* development of German nationalism, nurtured by easy military victories and delusions of invincibility, that turned the Germans into savages a century and a quarter later.

Now, general semantics (I am here speaking of the activities of people who profess to be general semanticists) has become what it is in the process of growing up in "White Middle Class America," where pragmatism is the dominant ideology. Strains of pragmatism pervade also the so-called scientific outlook and the school of thought called logical positivism, from both of which stem many of the basic notions of general semantics.

The person with adequate semantic reactions, according to Korzybski, thinks more like a scientist than like a metaphysician, a theologian, a lawyer, or a philosopher. Thirty or forty years ago, the logical positivists declared all the problems of philosophy, except those pertaining to logical and syntactic analysis, to be meaningless. The ideologues of logical positivism at that time seemed to prophesy the end of philosophy in much the same way as the ideologues of American pragmatism proclaim the end of ideology.

Underlying the entire outlook of pragmatism is a profound distrust of theoretical constructs springing from mental images, the sort that has always pervaded speculative philosophy. The watchdog questions, "What do you mean?" and "How do you know?" are the pragmatist's defense against a challenge to look beyond the observable and the immediately verifiable. These questions are also inscribed on the escutcheon of general semantics.

There is no doubt that this insistence on clarity and evidence is indispensable in science and of great value in daily life. The pragmatist's attitude reflects the problem-solving mode of thought, which both John Dewey and Korzybski insisted is the proper *human* orientation toward the world. The ideologues of nonideology have carried this orientation into politics. Sane politics, they declare, is problem-solving politics, apparently the antithesis of the politics of ideological struggle.

When I embraced the cause of general semantics, I embraced also this view. In my first book, I expressed myself through the protagonist character Dr. *N* as follows:

> Here is one group shouting that taking a profit on the exchange of goods and services is utterly immoral. Another group shouts equally loudly that everything people hold dear—human character, scientific advancement, the sanctity of religion and the home—depends on the preservation of the profit system. Freed from moralistic shackles, [we] can study possible ways of organizing economy and *try* them! While the champions of "ideologies" engage in lofty and self-righteous arguments about the superiority of capitalism to socialism or vice versa, the self-studying society would examine under what conditions what degree of control over what industries is required for optimal efficiency and adequate insurance both against scarcity of commodities and against the excessive concentration of economic might in irresponsible hands.

For many years afterwards, I held conflict resolution to be the central task of politics. The key to conflict resolution seemed to me to be in the possibility of establishing three conditions: first, an area of common interest or concern; second, a thorough understanding by each party of the *actual* (not just verbally defined) goals and commitments of the order; third, the perception of similarity between the parties.

In some contexts, the establishment of the first condition may already open the way to conflict resolution. This was dramatically demonstrated by an experiment with two groups of boys.[1] The two groups were kept separate in a summer camp and imbued with a strong sense of group identification through adroit use of group designations, flags, etc. Upon contact between the two groups, the expected ingroup loyalty and outgroup hostility were immediately observed. They persisted, aggravating, until circumstances (imposed by the experimenters) demanded that the two groups cooperate to achieve a common goal. Thereafter hostility sharply declined.

I remember also an illuminating paper by Herbert Thelen,[2] where the argument was made that racial tolerance in neighborhoods can be achieved only by deemphasizing the emotional and moral issues of race relations. The way to help Negroes and whites accept each other as neighbors is not, Thelen insisted, by discussing racial prejudice or the brotherhood of man, but by enlisting the residents of both races in common tasks, such as improving garbage disposal.

On the international scale, Roger Fisher argued for "fractionating conflict"; that is, approaching the problem of conflict resolution piecemeal instead of globally.[3] Specifically, in Fisher's opinion, a reduction of tensions between, say, the United States and the Soviet Union can be better achieved by attacking one problem at a time (at that time it was Cuba and Berlin), rather than by summit conferences aimed at achieving far-reaching settlements.

In my own discussion of the East–West struggle, I did not bypass the ideological issues (as Fisher recommends), but on the contrary attempted to meet them head on. However, I, too, saw conflict primarily as a "problem" to be attacked cooperatively by the opponents. On several occasions, I outlined the so-called ethical debate between liberalism and communism, to be conducted according to the rules of role reversal, along lines proposed earlier by Carl Rogers.[4] The aim of ethical debate is to bring out the common ground of the two positions, to increase the effectiveness of communication between the opponents, and to induce a perception of similarity.

I trust that what I am about to say will in no way be understood as a disavowal of conflict resolution and of the problem-solving approach to it. The point I wish to make is one already made in the philosophy of science and, in particular, in general semantics. Just as every proposition has a circumscribed region of validity, so does every method. Extrapolating a proposition beyond its region of validity induces a false map of reality. Pushing a method beyond its range of applicability is a first symptom of ossification.

Let us extrapolate the observations of Dr. *N,* cited above, to another situation. Recently the Swedes were debating whether to hang on to left-handed traffic, like Britain, or to switch to right-handed traffic, and be like everybody else. Imagine my Dr. *N* proposing a "pragmatic" solution:

> Let us not succumb to either-or thinking. Let some fraction of all the vehicles drive on the right, and let the remainder continue to drive on the left. By varying the mixture, we shall eventually arrive at the optimum solution of the traffic problem.

Let not the absurdity of the example obscure the point: conflict resolution by compromise has a circumscribed range of applicability.

The so-called extensional orientation, which demands that each concept and each assertion be immediately redeemed by the legal tender of observable referents and corroborated observation, also has its drawbacks. If Galileo had remained "extensional," he would never have discovered his law of falling bodies (the rate of fall independent of weight). Aside from cannon balls dropped from leaning towers, the vast majority of falling objects (leaves and raindrops) do *not* obey Gallileo's law. They obey rather Aristotle's law (which Galileo *refuted*): like war waging states, the bigger they are the faster they fall. If physicians remained extensional, they would forever try to cure the symptoms instead of the disease, let alone the patient, because, for the naive empiricist, the symtoms *are* the disease. In the philosophy of law, the extensional–positivist orientation leads to the bizarre dictum of Oliver Wendell Holmes, Jr., repeatedly cited with approval by general semanticists: "The prophesies of what the courts will do in fact, and nothing more pretentious, are what I mean by law."

At least Holmes mentioned the courts in his definition of law. Edward McWhinney,[5] starting with this text, in effect defines international law as anything that the *litigants* may choose to do. Here we get a caricature of the Anglo–Saxon pragmatic conception of law as emerging from practice rather than from principles. But a theory of law cannot be strictly descriptive (as the positivist linguists regard grammar to be). By the nature of the subject of its concern, a theory of law must have a prescriptive component, whether or not its proponents recognize it, because how people think about law is a factor in determining the evolution of law. (The same remark can probably be made about grammar). By insisting that the limits of international law are set by the willingness of the great powers to abide by it and nothing else, McWhinney takes an apparently unassailable "realistic" position); but in doing so he also contributes (to the degree of his influence) to the perpetuation of international anarchy.

Let me now return to my main point. General semantics grew on American pragmatic soil, in a climate hostile to abstract thought. Along with the healthy skepticism toward abstraction, the general semanticist has acquired the myopic orientation of "barefoot empiricism." Awareness, he often implies, is what comes through the five senses. Society appears to him as an aggregate of individuals. Good social relations are identified in his thinking with good human relations. Knowledge is skill. Law is what the courts decide. Politics is what politicians do.

Against the background of the dogmas of yesterday, of pompous speculation, of intoxication with verbiage, these "no-nonsense" attitudes appeared salutary. But against the background of what is happening on this planet now, especially beyond the habitat of White Middle Class America, these attitudes are crippling. The most crippling attitude of all stems from the dogged insistence that conflict is typically a "problem" to be solved by improving semantic reactions and communication among people. This view of conflict rests on the assumption that humanity is composed of human individuals (the old nominalist dogma). If humanity were indeed primarily an aggregate of individuals, the general semanticist's concept of conflict would have considerable validity. Communication between individual human beings is always possible in principle. Common values can indeed be found which most human individuals call their own. On that level, that is, wherever people come in contact with people, it may very well be true that most conflicts are resolvable; in other words, courses of action can be found which all parties to the conflict prefer to the continuation of conflict.

But the main actors in the drama of large human conflicts are not human individuals. They are *systems,* "super-organisms," that no more resemble their human components than the latter resemble their constituent cells. These super-organisms do not understand human language. One can speak to the human *components* of such a system and perhaps even affect them; but such communications typically have no discernible effect on the *system.* The system has receptors of its own. It can receive only those signals to which these receptors are sensitive. It has data processing centers, but it can process only the data admitted to the centers, and only according to the rules by which the centers have been programmed. It has effectors, but they can perform only acts included in the repertoire of the system (not of the human beings that compose it).

These super-organisms are institutions and organizations. They come in many sizes and types. Of particular concern to man is the species *status belligerans,* the war-waging state; and of these, of most concern is the giant variety. Only five specimens of this variety exist today, but two of them could annihilate the entire product of time-binding in a few hours. Of these two, one is presently systematically destroying a sector of humanity and terrorizing a great portion of the remainder.

As this is written (February, 1968), what is going on in Vietnam is seen by the White Middle Class American as an acute phase in the chronic struggle between the communist and the "free" worlds. A dwindling but still considerable number of those who so interpret the war wholeheartedly support the United States administration.

Let us see what mental images one must cherish in order to support the administration and its war. If one completely accepts the official doctrine, one must believe that the Geneva Accord of 1954 set up two independent states in Vietnam; that one became totalitarian, while the other chose the road to democracy; that the communists of the North attacked or, at least, "infiltrated" the South to "take it over"; that the freedom loving southerners called upon the United States, champion of democracy, to help them; and that the United States is honor bound to keep its commitment to preserve the freedom of South Vietnam.

This mental image is contradicted by facts, which can be checked by anyone who will take the trouble. No partition of Vietnam was effected or intended by the signers of the Geneva Accord. On the contrary, the demarcation line (drawn for the purpose of allowing an orderly withdrawal of the defeated French troops) was specifically declared *not* to constitute a political boundary. The government established in Saigon was from the beginning a protectorate of the United States. (Ngo Dinh Diem was imported from New Jersey.) It was not committed to democracy. On the contrary, Diem established a combination of police state mandarinate and a huge racket. (Recently, his widow bought the second largest bank in Paris for cash.) Resistance against the police state developed in the South among the indigenous population, and among the savagely persecuted religious *majority* (the Buddhists). Diem, backed by the United States, refused to allow the general election provided for by the Geneva Accord. As former President Eisenhower wrote, had the election been held, Ho Chi Minh would easily have received 80% of the vote. In short, in order to hold onto the officially induced map, one must disregard the territory. Therefore, anyone who professes to be a general semanticist cannot hold on to the official interpretation of the origins and nature of the war in Vietnam.

For those who cannot accept this interpretation, there is another. This is the "Yellow (or Blue) Peril Theory," the image of a billion yellow Chinese in blue pajamas preparing to overrun white Christian civilization. In this version, defense of democracy is not the issue. We are fighting for our very existence, not for the Vietnamese. To hold onto this image, one must ignore not only the territory, but even the map (the geographical one, that is). For a glance at the map shows clearly who is threatening whom. If we were to practice role reversal, and so put ourselves in the position of the Chinese, we would have to imagine Mexico partially occupied, and systematically devastated by an enemy in possession of unlimited destructive power; enemy bases on Staten and Catalina Islands; regular enemy reconnaissance flights over the United States; and assertions to the effect that the Washington government is not American. (In 1949 Dean Rusk, the most recent discoverer of the Yellow Peril, asserted that the Peiping government was not Chinese. He has never forgiven the Chinese since for having made a fool of him.) One cannot profess to be a general semanticist and continue to believe that China is a mortal danger to the United States, ·and that China's fear of the United States is a paranoid delusion.

Among White Middle Class Americans, there are many who are sick of the war, of reading about villages put to the torch, about napalmed children, poisoned rice fields, daily kill scores; sick of seeing on TV how G.I.'s cut ears off corpses for souvenirs, and how corpses are removed by steam shovels. By and large, however, White Middle Class Americans (in whose ranks the general semanticist most often finds himself) hold on to the conviction that these horrors are the results of errors of judgment. Since we live in a democracy, these people feel, the proper way of setting things right is to induce our rulers to choose a wiser course. Since the United States is governed by chosen representatives of the people (it says so in the Constitution), the will of the people will be done. When enough people feel that the war is wrong, the chosen representatives will put a stop to it. If they don't, the people will choose representatives who will. If, on the other hand, most of the people continue to support the war or fail to elect representatives who will change the present policy, then that's that. The will of the people will be done.

This attitude rests on two assumptions: first, that we are governed by democratically elected representatives responsible to the electorate; second, that the decision makers, in their political role, are human beings with whom one can communicate in human language.

I submit that neither of these assumptions is justified. As a political entity, the United States resembles a corporation rather than a consumers cooperative. You understand the difference. In the cooperative, decisions are made on the principle of one member, one vote. In a stock corporation, decisions are made on the principle of one share, one vote. In a cooperative, people vote; in a corporation (as in the "free market"), dollars vote. Now, the dollars (or shares) held by an owner or a bloc of owners cannot vote independently. They must vote as blocs, the way their owners direct them to vote. If you examine closely the political procedures in the United States (the territory, not the map), you will see a similar situation. Popular vote is organized by political parties who mobilize tens of thousands of precinct workers, ward heelers, etc. These workers obey orders. Their job is to *deliver* the votes that put or keep their party in power. In legislatures, too, votes are welded into blocs, each bloc representing a set of "interests." Not the least of these interests is the retention of influence with patronage-dispensing authorities and of bargaining power in forming coalitions with other blocs.

The ideologues of "nonideology" (among whom many who profess to be general semanticists are found) are wont to proclaim this horse-trading process to be the very essence of democracy. I shall not argue about definitions; but I submit that democracy so defined has little to do with democracy as it is defined in our sacred texts, and even less with democracy to which people aspire who have not yet attained it.

I have already discussed the fallacy of the second assumption, namely that decision-makers are human beings in their political roles. The United States is ruled not by human beings, but by a vast "program" of decision rules built into the nervous system of a super-organism that I have called the war-waging state. To be sure, the "cells" of this organism are human beings; but in their roles as the cells of the super-organism, they do not behave as normal human beings are expected to behave in normal human contexts. In those roles, they are insulated (often physically) from normal human contacts. Messages about human needs, human aspirations, human suffering, human despair addressed to the cells of the war-waging state cannot change its behavior because they cannot change its decision rules.

Let us, as befits general semanticists, come down to the extensional level. Assume the role of the extensionally oriented observer cleared of all preconceived notions about democracy, communism, the Yellow Peril, national interests, and national honor. Imagine yourself a woman of age 35 in a village in Southeast Asia. You have lived in this village all your life. Your world has been your family and neighbors, the fields and the animals that feed you and your family. Since you are a human being, you have imbued your life with meaning, as human beings do everywhere. Your way, the way of your people, has been to derive a sense of continuity of life (a sort of immortality) by revering the graves of your ancestors. You would no more think of leaving those graves than you would of leaving your children.

This is most of your world, but not quite all of it. For over twenty years you have been dimly aware that you have bonds not only to your family and neighbors, but also to something called Vietnam. People talk about "the war." So far it hasn't come to your village, but young men went off to fight against the French, who, they said, were trying to reconquer the country after the Japanese were driven away. You remember the Japanese and the French before them, arrogant, rude strangers who gave orders and meted out punishment; and while you are afraid of war, and think it is terrible to kill people, you somehow see the justice of not letting the French come back to rule your land.

After eight years of fighting the French, some of the young men came back, some did not. Those that came back said that the French were defeated. Thereafter life went on as before, except that the landlord was gone. The young men who came back from the war told you that your land was now your own. There was no more rent to pay. You felt good about it. To be sure, new "authorities" appeared in the villages to whom you soon began to pay taxes and who made changes in the life of the village. Some changes were good. A school was built, and a medical aid station. Some were not so good. The young men in authority were aggressively emphatic "explaining" the new life, and sometimes said scandalous things. There was much "organization," and you were saddled with new, unusual duties. But the authorities were not arrogant. They talked to you as to an equal, and seemed genuinely interested in your welfare and in the welfare of your children. They loved to talk about a better life to come. And indeed life seemed to improve from year to year. Above all, they were your own people, not like the landlord or the French who seemed like beings from another world, and to whom you never could talk at all.

As the years went by, you started to hear of strange and terrible events. A dictator appeared in Saigon, backed by foreigners (no, not the French this time; other foreigners called "Americans"). The dictator proclaimed himself master of the whole land. He arrested the locally elected village chiefs and appointed strangers in their stead. He was said to put thousands of people in jail who had done no wrong, and was especially harsh to the Buddhists (that is, your people). He brought the landlords back, protected by soldiers who, although Vietnamese, had fought on the side of the French against your people. The most terrible unbelievable rumor of all was that the dictator built compounds surrounded by barbed wire, and put whole villages of people into the compounds where they languished in idleness and disease, often separated from their families.

You were not sure whether to believe those things. So far, none of this has touched your village. But the young men went off to fight once more. They now called themselves the National Liberation Front. They said they were fighting to keep the dictator's army and police away from your village. Sometimes the young men came back for a while and resumed their normal chores. Then they went away again. Eventually, all the young men in your village became such part-time fighters. Aside from that, life went on as before.

Then you were told another terrible thing. The Americans sent their planes over the rice fields, spraying them with a powder that made the crops wither and die. They did this, you were told, so that the people would starve. If the people starved, the Americans were saying, they would have to abandon their villages and go into the compounds.

And one day a plane did come flying over the fields, spraying the poisonous powder. Several villagers were working in the fields, and one of them, your husband, stood up and shook his fist at the plane. The plane made a wide arc and came back swooping down, spewing bullets as it came. The people threw themselves on the ground. Your husband and four others were killed and fourteen were wounded, of whom six later died. The rice, too, died.

National Liberation Front people brought in some rice and rationed it. Life became much harder. But no one thought of going to live in the compounds. You would no more think of leaving the graves of your ancestors than of abandoning your five children.

One night you were awakened by the blare of loud speakers. The disembodied voices told you that the village was surrounded by the soldiers of the Republic of Vietnam, and that every one would be "resettled." You already knew what this meant. Soldiers went from house to house and ordered people to gather in the village square. They said that anyone trying to escape would be shot. Your eldest son, aged 17, ran out of the house before the soldiers came. You heard shots, and you knew that the soldiers were shooting at your son and the other young men who ran for the fields, but you did not know whether your son escaped or died or was lying wounded in a rice field.

You grabbed the baby, and your 13-year-old daughter grabbed the toddler. You were going to obey the soldiers' commands. But your 75-year-old father hid in the bomb cellar (one had been dug by every householder at the direction of the NLF). Your 8-year-old son went with him. (Since your husband's death, he clung to his grandfather.) Suddenly a giant appeared in the doorway. He was eight feet tall. (This is the way an American soldier would look to you if you were a Vietnamese woman of average height.) Then he opened the trap door and shouted in Vietnamese, "Come out!" There was only silence. The giant tossed a grenade into the cellar. You screamed and got slapped in the face. Then you and your children were pushed out of the house. You stood in the square with your neighbors and watched the soldiers going from house to house, dousing each with gasoline and setting it on fire. Later, when you were already in the compound, you heard that the Americans rode bulldozers over the charred ruins, leveling everything to the ground. They rode bulldozers over your ancestors' graves and over the altar, and over the cellar where your father and your son died.

Now, the question I put to you is with whom was this woman supposed to have communicated in human language? With the giant? With the driver of the truck who was taking her and her neighbors to the "New Life" hamlet, as the Americans called their concentration camps? With the guard who manned the machine gun tower of the camp? With Marshall Ky? With General Westmoreland? With the President of the United States?

The situation is not much different with us who are "free to speak" and to "influence" American policy. The story I have just told you is essentially a true story. But, to make sense, the story must be told in a language that contains terms and concepts entirely foreign to the language in which "policy" is formulated. Therefore, the fact that those who formulate and execute policy are "human beings" in their daily lives has not the slightest bearing on the possibility of communicating to them whatever compassion you may feel for the Vietnamese, or whatever indignation arises in you at what we are doing to them. Perhaps it is this sense of futility that induces people to suppress whatever compassion or indignation they may feel.

Ironically, it is often impossible to communicate with the present administration even in their *own* language, the language of megabucks, megatons, and megadeaths. Military strategists have pointed out that the strategic importance of Vietnam is not worth the "investments." Political scientists of the "realist" school have pointed out, to no avail, that Vietnam was the worst possible choice as a battlefield on which to "fight communism." The *status belligerans,* once it is activated, has a will of its own. It is governed by its own appetite and its own reflexes.

Is what I am saying relevant to the principles of general semantics and their application to present day problems? A general semanticist could have a field day with the falsehoods and the bla-blah disseminated by the administration in the attempt to bolster crumbling delusions about the war in Vietnam. The strategic community has sunk to new depths in the manufacure of gobbledygook euphemisms in order to dull the sensitivities of its own research personnel. The language of our bureaucracy is now indistinguishable from the macabre jargon of the gestapo and the SS. When Norman Morrison immolated himself in front of the Pentagon, the incident was reported to security officials as "a small fire of undetermined origin." [6] Here is indeed a job for a general semanticist. What has been done? Next to nothing.

You might ask why I have not done the job, if I feel so strongly about it. My answer is that the job is no longer worth doing. A semantic analysis of the present depravity would hardly serve any purpose now except the edification of semanticists.

What is now developing in the United States, the home of "nonideology," is a conflict that cannot be resolved by traditional semantic analysis, because the parties to the conflict belong to different species. This is no longer a conflict between people with two contrasting views of life and of society, as I had previously imagined the ideological conflict between East and West to be. *That* phase of the conflict (if it ever existed) was indeed largely a communication problem, one that could be attacked by "men of good will" on both sides. But that is not the conflict I am now speaking about. I am speaking about the conflict between human beings and the beast, *status belligerans.* The Vietnamese peasant talked to the beast. By shaking his fist he was saying, "Curse you! This is the rice that feeds my children. I hate you for bringing starvation to our village!"

The beast killed him.

Now what will you say? That the peasant should have sent another message, like dropping to his knees as if to say; "Please don't do this to me. We are poor. You are rich. Go back to your own bountiful land and leave us alone"?

Would this have saved his crop? And how is it with us? What have the tens of thousands of American clergymen accomplished by their prayers, their appeals, their cries of anguish? They may have reached some *people*, but they did not reach the beast. The beast cannot be reached, because he does not understand human language. The beast must be subdued. How to do it is the problem relevant to 1968.

I see nothing in the program of this International Conference on General Semantics to indicate that the problem will even be posed, let alone attacked. If it is not, then the efforts of general semanticists are irrelevant to the world of 1968.

REFERENCES

1. Sherif, Muzafer, and Sherif, Carolyn W. "Research on Intergroup Relations," *Perspectives in Social Psychology,* eds. O. Klinberg, and R. Christie. New York: Holt, Rinehart & Winston, 1965, pp. 153–177.
2. Thelen, Herbert. "Shall We Sit Idly By?" *ETC.,* 11, 1 (Autumn, 1953), pp. 3–15.
3. Fisher, Roger. *International Conflict and Behavioral Science.* New York: Basic Books, 1964, pp. 91–109.
4. Roger, Carl. "Communication: Its Blocking and Facilitation," *ETC.,* 9, 1952, pp. 83–88.
5. McWhinney, Edward. "Soviet and Western International Law and the Cold War in the Era of Bipolarity," *The Canadian Yearbook of International Law,* Vol. 1. Vancouver: University of British Columbia, 1963, pp. 75–81.
6. Woode, Allen. "How the Pentagon Stopped Worrying and Learned to Love the Peace Marchers," *Ramparts* (February, 1968), p. 47.

COMMENTS ON DR. RAPOPORT'S PAPER

Allen Walker Read is Professor of English at Columbia University. He has taught at Columbia University since 1945, with special interest in the areas of semantics, lexicography, and the relation of language to cultural developments. He is now President of the American Name Society, and has in the past been President of the American Dialect Society, and a Member of the Executive Committee of the Linguistic Society of America.

ALLEN WALKER READ

Critical Evaluation

M Y reaction to Rapoport's paper is primarily one of deep sadness that a person of his talent can fall into such utter despair. His paper is a cry of anguish about the present state of the world. I, for one, share his feelings about the despicable war in Vietnam; and also I do not know any easy solution. He expresses his feelings passionately, and that is justifiable and laudable. However, he couches his despair in terms of a failure of general semantics, and from this I am obliged to dissent. Theoretical issues should be discussed in a mode of clear, calm reasoning, and here Rapoport has shown himself sadly deficient.

Rapoport's paper has many shortcomings, and it would take a reply of equal length to deal with them. I shall here take up only a few.

His paper includes many of the tired clichés of disillusionment. Some of his points are no more than the false negativisms by which disgruntled people attempt to justify their unhappy spirit. He claims that "political democracy" has created "pseudo-participation of populations"; but it has also created some genuine participation. And does "political democracy" have any better alternative? Again, he says that "mass literacy" has not liberated populations but has "made them vulnerable to manipulation." Would he prefer "mass illiteracy?" Surely the tendency toward mass literacy is one to be approved.

As a second shortcoming, the paper exhibits a peculiar stereotyping of human beings. Rapoport apparently has considerable hostility to a type that he calls, in capital letters, "White Middle Class Americans." In that rank, he says, "the general semanticist most often finds himself." Those of us who are white cannot help being white, and most of us can hardly help being middle class. Does Rapoport have to be told that the members of the "white middle class" are individuals, and that there is great diversity, especially among those who can be called "general semanticists"? I would hazard the opinion that thinking for oneself is much more common among general semanticists than among the general run of the white middle class.

As a third shortcoming, the paper is full of a loose use of labels for theoretical or philosophical positions. In talking about "pragmatism," "logical positivism," etc., it is important to discriminate the positions carefully, but Rapoport throws the terms about like loaded epithets. There are important differences between the outlooks of John Dewey and Alfred Korzybski.

Most revealing is Rapoport's yearning for what he calls "ideology." This usually refers to an a priori doctrine, dogmatically held; and it does not fit into the framework of general semantics. The term *ideology* was discussed as follows by Professor Robert E. Lane, of Yale University, in the *American Sociological Review,* October, 1966, 31, p. 652:

> If we employ the term "ideology" to mean a comprehensive, passionately believed, self-activating view of society, usually organized as a social movement . . . it makes sense to think of a domain of knowledge distinguishable from a domain of ideology, despite the extent to which they may overlap. Since knowledge and ideology serve somewhat as functional equivalents in orienting a person toward the problems he must face and the policies he

must select, the growth of the domain of knowledge causes it to impinge on the domain of ideology.

General semantics has its "theories," based on deliberate assumptions, but they are not frozen into an "ideology." Rapoport also makes scornful remarks about "the ideologues of nonideology," among whom, by implication, he classes the students of general semantics.

As a fourth shortcoming, Rapoport asks that the application of general semantics provide direct solutions to the great problems of the day. I agree that the great problems should concern us deeply as responsible citizens, but general semantics, as a general theory, should not be expected to provide specific solutions. As human beings, we must restructure ourselves for making adequate evaluations, and our particular choices will depend upon our skill and judgment.

In the fifth place, the paper contains shocking distortions of general semantics. Take, for instance, the following sentence: "Along with the healthy skepticism toward abstraction, the general semanticist has acquired the myopic orientation of 'barefoot empiricism.' " Who would suppose from this that "consciousness of abstracting" is one of the most fundamental formulations of general semantics? As for "barefoot empiricism," this would apply only to an incompetent student of general semantics. Of course science needs an empirical basis before generalizations can be made, but then the generalizations are necessary. Korzybski devoted several chapters of *Science and Sanity* to the importance of the theory of abstraction (pp. 371–451), and he stated forcefully (p. 483) that a principal aim of education is to develop the ability of passing to higher and higher abstractions. One wonders, in fact, whether Rapoport is talking about general semantics at all. Toward the end of his paper he says that our present troubles "cannot be resolved by traditional semantic analysis." This is very true, but general semantics cannot be equated with "traditional semantic analysis."

In the sixth place, Rapoport presents a tortured argument which supposedly proves the inadequacy of general semantics but which will not stand careful scrutiny. As this is his main point, it must be faced squarely. He claims that the large human conflicts, such as the Vietnam war, are no longer between human beings, but are between systems or "super-organisms" that cannot be reached by human communication. He then, by what is basically a rhetorical device, personifies such a "super-organism." The United States becomes a *status belligerans* (a pseudo-Latinism), and in his last pages it even becomes "the beast." The system, he says, has receptors of its own and can act only according to the rules by which it has been programmed. But who, I should like to know, does the programming? Human beings are still in charge. Rapoport has come close to the silly fallacy that computers can "think" independently.

In dealing with such problems, general semantics draws upon the best findings of the social sciences. Sociologists have long known that when individuals gather into groups, special patterns of behavior develop. Gangs and mobs have their own dynamics, and the literature about them is enormous. The role of a powerful establishment is constantly being explored by social scientists, and they will give us guidance even for dealing with the *status belligerans*. Students of general semantics, as "generalists," will look to the expertise of the sociologists for advice on controlling "the beast"; and Rapoport's melodramatic personifications are not likely to prove helpful.

In dealing with the super-organism, there is another solution, another way out, that Rapoport does not consider. This is the right of revolution. I regret that I may appear subversive, but I do believe that in an extremity, when conventional means have failed, beyond so-called "law and order," we have a right to activist rebellion. That is a very unhappy situation, as I well know from the disorders at Columbia University in the spring of 1968; but still human beings can undermine entrenched authority. The super-organism, even the "military-industrial complex," would have to give way before the onslaught of an enlightened populace that has become aroused. Forward to the barricades!

I have left to the end a matter from which we may gain a constructive lesson out of Rapoport's paper. It is important that every student of Korzybski's work should continually examine and reexamine himself about his attitude toward general semantics. When Rapoport speaks of the "eternal verities" of general semantics, he exhibits an attitude wholly out of harmony with the discipline. Worse still, he speaks of the time when he "embraced the cause of general semantics." General semantics is not a "cause," but a discipline drawing upon the best scientific method for the deep restructuring of human beings to make optimal use of their potentialities. In his reply following this, David Bourland will explore the unfortunate implications of regarding general semantics as a "cause."

It would appear that Rapoport adopted general semantics as a shallow verbal veneer. Apparently, it never got deeply into his nervous system, and he sloughed it off readily when he came face to face with a serious social issue. He reveals an inadequate grasp of a deeply embedded general semantics. Thereby he challenges us to redouble our efforts to show that he is wrong in discarding general semantics. I reject his posture of despair. In the beginning of his article, he asks the question, "To what extent is general semantics relevant to the problems and dilemmas of our day?" My own answer is a resounding affirmation of relevance.

D. DAVID BOURLAND, JR.*

Relevance₁, Relevance₂ . . .

THIS paper contains a discussion of some of the broader questions raised by Dr. Rapoport. I have attempted to correct some technical misunderstandings unfortunately held by Dr. Rapoport in connection with the Korzybskian methodology called "general semantics" in another paper.[1]

The density of gloom and dissatisfaction purveyed by Rapoport may appeal so strongly to some people that this effort will not reach them. While I regret such a circumstance, I can detect one ray of hope: a great number of previously overly idealistic people (usually but not uniformly young and/or members of the academic community) currently display and demonstrate their inevitable frustration and demoralization† with developments on the national and international scene. This current situation may constitute the second state of a dynamic dialectic that could eventually produce a more mature and extensional basis for participation in human affairs of great moment. In my opinion, the potentiality just described provides an analogue to what some see in the current social upheavals as typified by the "Hippie Movement," long-haired boys, social unrest among minority groups, bizarre dress, the alleged "new sexual morality," etc. My friend and colleague Harry Holtzman interprets those activities as exuberant expressions by elements of a sick society that could never improve without, as a first step, recognizing that conditions exist that require basic and drastic revision. But let us return to the Rapoport paper.

---

* See previous biographical sketch, Chapter 9.—EDITOR.

† See the "IFD disease" as discussed by Wendell Johnson.[2] Johnson described the progression from idealism to frustration to demoralization as having predominated in the specific difficulties and semantic ailments he had treated: "In my experience, no other ailment is so common among university students. . . . The IFD disease . . . is not so much affliction of individuals as it is a reflection of strong semantic forces that play upon and through individuals.

THE MATTER OF A "CAUSE"

Rapoport, after giving a slice of history, stated that at some past time he "embraced the *cause* of general semantics" (and I emphasize *cause*). I single this statement out for comment, since we have seen it, or the same orientation, before.* I hope the readers of this paper will join with me in assisting others to correct any lingering aura of "cause" that may surround the work of Alfred Korzybski and others in the field of general semantics. Korzybski originated—single-handedly—a methodology for individuals to use in relating better to themselves and the human and nonhuman aspects of their environments, including their neurolinguistic environments. Whatever else we may properly say about Korzybski's methodology, it simply does not consist of some kind of "cause" that one should "believe in." You would probably (and correctly, in my opinion) chuckle at the gaucheness of a person who said he "believed" in biology, for example. If someone told you that they embraced the principles of physics, say, you might wonder about their "model of the real world." Please respond similarly to those who take a mystical approach to general semantics!

PROBLEMS WITH "STATUS BELLIGERANS"

In an earlier exchange with me,[3] Dr. Rapoport himself stated that, "Great ideas are degraded not by their critics but by their orthodox champions. So it was with the ideas of Freud, of Marx, and of Jesus. So it may be with Korzybski, if the verdict of history puts him among the foremost thinkers." In my opinion, he tends to support his own point when he states: "If humanity were indeed primarily an aggregate of individuals, the general semanticist's concept of conflict would have considerable validity." He claims that one cannot take an extensional approach to large scale human affairs due to a high-order abstraction he calls the "status belligerans" (war-waging state). He defines this high-order abstraction as a kind of super-organism (institutions and organizations) composed of humans who function feebly as mere cells. He despairs at reaching the super-organism through dealing with the loosely coupled human cells. Now this is a classic illustration of semantic confusion that the Korzybskian system supposedly guards against. Yet we find it purveyed by one who supports "the cause of general semantics." The path to such super-organisms clearly lies through dealing with their human members in an *appropriate* extensional fashion. But what did Rapoport do? He advanced a gruesomely realistic, but fanciful and individualistic example to illustrate his concern. His example comes

---

* As in his paper,[3] a response to an earlier critique of mine.[4]

to us in terms of the highly complex war in Vietnam, but he could just as well have drawn it in terms of the highly unpopular (in some circles) American Revolution, Civil War, World War I, World War II, or Korean Conflict.

A MECHANISM FOR CHANGING FUNCTIONAL SYSTEMS

People have frequently expressed their concern over the discrepancies between stated ideals and various "factual" aspects of organizational behaviors. We have seen exhortations cast against City Hall, "the system," the Establishment, etc. Occasionally critics, by somehow mobilizing an adequate measure of popular support, have brought about highly beneficial changes. The key to useful and effective criticism seems to lie in finding a mechanism for initiating and carrying through the following steps:

1) obtaining reasonably correct data
2) performing appropriate analyses
3) developing sound results
4) making the results available to the key individuals responsible for the functions of the system or organization
5) insuring that adequate popular support for the proposed changes exists.

Rapoport sounds pessimistic about such a "rationalistic" procedure, and what does he propose? The only thing I can understand, as his answer to the "So What?" one must ask of his paper, consists of (1) despairing of the eventual utility of the field of conflict resolution, and (2) disembracing a nonrelevant general semantics.

We cannot reach a high order abstraction such as "status belligerans," but we certainly can deal with the denumerable set which consists of the world's political leaders. I would estimate this set as having of the order of 1,000 elements. If the pace of beneficial change seems too slow to you, then proceed to work on the elements of that set!

Korzybski has provided explicit suggestions for beneficially changing "human nature," and that appears to constitute our focus here. For example:

> As it is impossible to eliminate the influence of the higher order abstractions, we should investigate whether or not we can control these processes and the related *s.r.* [semantic reactions]. We can learn to regulate these processes, which otherwise may become pathological, and to redirect the currents into constructive survival channels. I can state definitely that this is possible. We can control physiologically the *s.r.* through the elimination of identification, by training in order, in consciousness of abstracting, and simi-

lar disciplines, and thus eliminate the pathological semantic disturbances of confusion of orders of abstractions.

Once again, more explicitly, Korzybski stated:

The consciousness of abstracting, which involves, among others, the full instinctive semantic realization of non-identity, and the stratification of human knowledge, and so the multiordinality of the most important terms we use, solves these weighty and complex problems because it gives us structural methods for semantic evaluation, for orientation, and for handling them. By passing to higher orders these states which involve inhibition or negative excitation become reversed. Some of them on higher levels become culturally important; and some of them become morbid. Now consciousness of abstracting in all cases gives us the semantic *freedom* of all levels, and so helps *evaluation* and selection, thus removing the possibility of remaining animalistically fixed or blocked on any one level. Here we find the mechanism of the 'change of human nature.'[5]

Dr. Rapoport's theory of "general semantics" may indeed have no relevance for the world of 1968. However, Korzybski's methodology, on the other hand, embedded in a semantic context of time-binding, offers explicit relevance for attacking human problems by changing so-called human nature. Now I grant you one cannot immediately solve the Vietnam war, air pollution, urban blight, water resource limitations, etc., by applying the Korzybskian methodology. However, this system does provide a technique for training humans so that they may more effectively deal with such problems. Which humans? The humans who now occupy the key decision-making positions, and who in the future will occupy such positions.

That, to me, constitutes the relevance of Korzybski's general semantics for 1968, 1978, 1988, etc.

REFERENCES

1. Bourland, D. D., Jr. "On the Varieties of Non-Research in General Semantics," presented at the Tenth International Conference on General Semantics, Denver, August, 1968.
2. Johnson, Wendell. *People in Quandaries.* New York: Harper & Row, 1946, pp. 14 ff., 18.
3. Rapoport, Anatol. "Reply by Rapoport," *ETC.: A Review of General Semantics,* Vol. 23, No. 1 (March, 1966).
4. Bourland, D. D., Jr. "Critique of a Review by Rapoport," *Etc.: A Review of General Semantics,* Vol. 23, No. 1 (March, 1966).
5. Korzybski, Alfred. *Science and Sanity: An Introduction to Non-Aristotelian Systems and General Semantics,* Lakeville, Conn.: International Non-Aristotelian Library Publishing Co., 4th ed., 1958, pp. 297, 441. Distributed by the Institute of General Semantics.

Reply by Anatol Rapoport

IT is difficult in a brief rejoinder to do justice to all the issues raised by Bourland's and Read's comments. I hope, however, that further discussion will be stimulated, perhaps in the pages of *ETC*.

With regard to the question of whether general semantics is a "cause," my choice of words may be open to criticism. But Mr. Bourland himself implies that general semantics has a normative aspect when he defines it as "a methodology for individuals to use in relating better to themselves and the . . . environment." The term *better* implies a value judgment. By "embracing the cause of general semantics," I meant simply that I subscribed to the values I believed to be inherent in the methodology. Specifically, in cultural milieus where images imposed by language are mistaken for reality, general semantics seemed to me to offer an antidote in the so-called extensional orientation.

However, as I pointed out in my paper, an oversimplified view of the extensional orientation can also lead to a sterile outlook embodied in what I called "barefoot empiricism," that is, declaring bankrupt all theoretical constructs that do not pay off in immediate sense referents on demand. Especially ill-conceived is the identification of "the scientific method" with a schematized procedure that invariably starts with the recording of sense impressions. Had science confined itself to this procedure, it would have dried out at the time of Francis Bacon, who recommended it.

The greatest advances in science were consequences not of routine applications of "the method" but, on the contrary, of drastic reorganizations of entire frameworks of thought. The gathering, interpretation, or reinterpretation of data played its part only *after* a new conceptual framework was established, often on a very high level of abstraction. For example, the apparently trivial discrepancy in the precession of Mercury's orbit (40 seconds of an arc per century) became of crucial significance only in the light of the General Theory of Relativity. But the theory itself was formulated in terms that defy any attempts to relate it to sense referents.

Whatever merit the notion of the war-waging state conceived as an organism may have, it is not refuted by being labeled a "high order abstraction" (of course it is), or by insisting that political leaders are distinct human beings (of course they are), or by pointing out the obvious differences between organisms so far known and this alleged "organism." Certain properties of organisms are shared by all organized entities, including states. To perceive and to study these common properties, one must necessarily rise to higher orders of abstraction. Indeed, elementalism is the tacit assumption that the properties of wholes are simple summations of the properties of the constituent parts. Similarly, on the level of action, it is evidence of elementalism, in my opinion, to believe that to change the behavior of states, one does best by influencing its political leaders. I do not believe this is possible in the case of the great powers (the war-waging states). First, the political leaders of the powers are psychologically and even, as a rule, physically all but inaccessible except to their own coteries. Second, whatever may be their personal values, the values that political leaders *act* upon in their political roles are those of the super-organisms they serve; and they would be denying their roles as political leaders if they acted otherwise.

The situation is not new. The social critics of the eighteenth century put their hopes on "enlightened monarchs" like Catherine II of Russia and Frederick II of Prussia, and derived encouragement from being listened to with amused interest. It was not clear to the apostles of rationalism that the rationality and the good intentions of even absolute rulers were powerless against the massive inertia of the "system" they represented. (There is another "high level abstraction"; but to deny its reality is to deny the possibility of understanding social phenomena.) The abolition of serfdom, the realization of primitive freedoms, and the unleashing of the vast productive forces in Western societies were not results of influencing princes, but of the collapse of the social structures supported by the power of absolute monarchs; in other words, of revolutions.

I believe that the present crises portend another wave of revolutions. They will break out when the tide of indignation and disgust with the absurdities imposed by the war-waging state passes a certain threshold. In the light of at least the immediate outcomes of past revolutions, I am not overly optimistic about the immediate outcome of the impending ones. Nevertheless, I believe they must be encouraged and supported, if only because they offer the only hope of destroying the monstrous parasite feeding on our species—the war-waging state.

Dr. Read seems to share my view when he says that, "in an extremity, when conventional means have failed, beyond so-called 'law and order,' we have a right to activist rebellion." I would, however, take exception to his call "Forward to the barricades!" A successful revolution (whether scientific or social) presupposes a recognition that the old methods won't work, and this goes for the old methods of revolution as well as those of conventional politics. I doubt whether the current versions of the *anciens régimes* can be overthrown by street fighting any more than by "working on" the 1,000 or so political leaders of the world.

I do not know how a successful revolution can be "made," but I think I know how it can be prepared, namely by undermining the ideology that keeps that *ancien régime* in power. Since Dr. Read has misunderstood the context in which I used the term *ideology,* I must elucidate it. I could not have given evidence of "yearning for an ideology," because the point I was making was that, contrary to the assertions of some sociologists to the effect that American pragmatism has sounded the death knell of ideology, there *is* a powerful dominant ideology in the United States. In fact, no culture is without one. To prepare a revolution means to undermine the dominant ideology. This is what the men of the Enlightenment were doing to the ideology based on the Divine Right of Kings. This is what the young intelligentsia is doing to orthodoxy in countries ruled by communist bureaucracies. And this is what American revolutionary youth and intelligentsia are doing to the myth that the war machine protects America, that America protects freedom, and that the cornerstone of freedom is the freedom to make money.

General semanticists could have played an important role in this historical mission. They had been debunking myths all along, but always from standpoints compatible with the ideology of White Middle Class (liberal) America. It has been comfortable to demolish the myths of pre-New Deal economics, of dogmatic religion, of doctrinaire Marxism, or of racism. But when 20th-century revolutions caught up with *us,* general semanticists for the most part have either remained silent or have defended the dicta of conventional wisdom.

I realize that a searching reexamination of one's own ideology is an almost impossibly difficult job. Nor can a reexamination be constantly demanded. Normally, one needs an anchorage in an ideology to be able to think at all. But a reexamination becomes imperative when the absurdities of an ideology become apparent. The absurdities that justify continued spending of 80% of the national budget on the wholesale murder industry ought to have become apparent to general semanticists, but the program of the conference gave no evidence that it did. The content did not change appreciably from what it was ten, twenty, and thirty years ago. It was centered, as usual, on self-improvement, whether in one's personal or professional life, or in one's awareness of sensual stimuli. I did not mean to disparage the importance of these topics, which is, after all, a matter of individual values. I was merely pointing out the irrelevance of these topics to what I thought were the critical problems of 1968.

Concerning stereotyping of which Dr. Read accuses me, the charge could be substantiated if I dismissed the views of a specific individual by attaching a class label to him. However, I was speaking on another level of abstraction, the cultural one. The epistemological lesson to be drawn from general semantics is not that only one level of abstraction (that of the individual and his sense impressions) represents "reality," but that reality can be perceived and represented on several levels of abstraction, and that one must distinguish clearly among them.

I had hoped that distinguishing levels of abstraction would help general semanticists recognize more clearly the limitations as well as the potentials of effective communication in conflict situations. Resolution of conflicts between individuals is often facilitated by improving communication, because the clearing away of semantic confusion may disclose a common area of agreement, or a common set of values previously obscured by verbiage. The resolution of conflicts among social groups, nations, or cultures is more difficult, because the very existence of these groups depends in part on the perpetuation of loyalties induced by verbiage. Still, as long as we are dealing with conflicts among entities of comparable level (person *vs.* person, nation *vs.* nation), improvement of communication may play a more or less important part in the problem of conflict resolution. It is doubtful whether the problem of communication is relevant where the conflicting parties belong to incomparable categories. Nor can one speak of conflict resolution in such cases. To take an extreme example, there is no basis for resolving the "conflict" between the human race and assorted plagues that threaten it, e.g., cholera, malaria, etc. I believe that the present military establishments of the great powers present no lesser threats. The fact that human beings are involved in the "decisions" made by these establishments is no more relevant than the fact that cholera, malaria, etc. also involve human carriers.

Once the incidental role of the human individual in the operation of the systems is realized, the futility of individual terrorism as a revolutionary method becomes apparent. I do not think many general semanticists would take me to task for having arrived at that conclusion. I have done no more than point out the obverse side of the same conclusion, namely that individual persuasion, improvement of communication with decision makers, etc., are no more relevant than individual terrorism to the task of effecting the sort of changes that can insure the survival of civilization based on time-binding.

Persuasion and education are, of course, of vital importance in preparing the impending revolutions. But the targets of persuasion and education ought not to be the establishments. They should rather be the victims of the establishments, the threatened, the demoralized, the deprived. The primary object of such persuasion and education ought to be, in my opinion, one that establishments East and West—military, corporate, and bureaucratic —with perfect justification call "subversive": the cutting of the bonds that have hitherto insured the acceptance of the paranoid delusions perpetuated by those establishments, and compliance with their psychopathic decisions.

Bent Stidsen, born in Denmark, and a Canadian citizen, is currently Lecturer at the Wharton School of Finance and Commerce, University of Pennsylvania. He holds an M.D.A. from the University of Western Ontario, and was formerly Research Associate with the Marketing Science Institute. He is a candidate for the Ph.D. in Applied Economics at the University of Pennsylvania.

21

GENERAL SEMANTICS AND ECONOMICS: SOME SPECULATIONS

BENT STIDSEN

The "symbol-using animal," yes, obviously. But can we bring ourselves to realize just what that formula implies, just how overwhelmingly much of what we mean by "reality" has been built up for us through nothing but our symbol systems? [1]

When the result we predict becomes the cause, or one of the causes of the result, we have what is called a self-fulfilling prophecy.[2]

THIS paper is intended entirely as a speculative venture. It seems to me that a reconsideration and perhaps a reevaluation of the body and tradition of economic theory in the light of some formulations of general semantics might produce some interesting and perhaps useful insights and implications. I do not, in this paper, presume to present a systematic reconsideration of economics. Indeed, since I am neither a general semanticist nor an economic theorist, I feel free to follow my speculative impulses.

Actually, economics comprises a formidable body of theory and a deeply rooted tradition of scholarship. It is undoubtedly one of the most highly developed and thoroughly explored "sciences" of human and social behavior. And it would be unreasonable to accuse economists of taking their work lightly. Most generally accepted statements of economic theory have earned this acceptance by withstanding thorough critical review by some of the best and most exacting minds in the social sciences.

Yet, when economists discuss the relation between their theories (maps) and the real world (territory), they frequently reveal Newtonian

189

orientations.[3] Note, for example, the following statement by a well-known economic historian:

> And so, has there been progress in economic theory? Clearly, the answer is yes: analytical tools have been continuously improved and augmented; empirical data have been increasingly marshaled to verify economic hypotheses; meta-economic biases have been repeatedly exposed and separated from the core of testable propositions which they unmesh; and the workings of the economic system are better understood than ever before.[4]

This quotation summarizes very well the economist's philosophy of science.[5] The ideas of the map and the territory are clearly there, and so is the concern with the relationship between the two. But the concept of relativity is lacking. The map is taken to be derived from the territory, and progress in economic theory is measured by the degree to which the map has been shown to actually represent the territory. But this, of course, is an insufficient criterion for the measurement of progress if we realize that economic theory both derives from and creates the world of economic phenomena.[6]

Let me emphasize that economists are aware of, and indeed pride themselves upon, the fact that their theories and teachings have influenced the course of history.[7] For example, Adam Smith (1776) developed the logic of labor specialization,[8] and David Ricardo (1817) argued forcefully for the repeal of the legislative remnants of mercantilism to make way for the industrial revolution.[9] Karl Marx (1867) influenced our views of the social implications of capitalism so extensively that we are now quite incapable of contemplating economic reality as dispassionately as nineteenth-century economists were wont to do.[10]

And there are many other examples. Alfred Marshall (1890) popularized the view that consumers determine value, thus creating an alternative to the labor theory of value on which Marx had built his theoretical edifice.[11] Thorstein Veblen (1899) gave expression to a dislike for conspicuous consumption—a dislike which has since permeated the American scene.[12] John Meynard Keynes (1936) greatly influenced our attitudes toward central management of national economies by providing what seemed a plausible economic rationale for government intervention.[13]

But even though economists seem aware of their impact on economic history and attitudes, a peculiar naiveté still pervades their theoretical discussions.[14] Many economists know that their theories are abstractions, but they nevertheless see their theoretical task as one of "discovering truth." In short, economists, on the whole, operate as if their maps derive entirely from the territory.

For example, economists will generally argue that Karl Marx was "wrong" when he predicted that the capitalistic, free enterprise economic system would ultimately collapse. But is it not possible that Marx, by making this prediction, prevented the collapse he was predicting?

Or consider the depression during the 1930's. Widespread unemployment and a drastic fall in prices constituted the evidence. To some economists the "problem" was wages while to others "it" was investment.[15] The so-called "classical" economists tended to see a reality governed by the reluctance of workers to obey the laws of supply and demand, thus preventing the economy from reaching its "natural" (full employment) equilibrium.[16] Others, taking their cue from Keynes, tended to see a reality governed by the reluctance of businessmen to invest in the face of relatively high interest rates.[17]

One of the theoretical postulates on which economists have relied heavily is that the "real" economy is a closed system. That is, the more there is of yours, the less there is of mine.[18] Without some such postulate it would, of course, have been difficult to build a coherent economic theory or map. But consider the impact this analytical "shortcut" has had on our everyday activities. Since the total value of economic benefits is taken to be fixed (e.g., fixed with respect to size of population,[19] investment opportunities,[20] the supply of money,[21] or some such "external" factor), it follows, of course, that one can get more only by taking something away from someone else Economists call this latter phenomenon "competition."

The idea of competition is to an economist what "life" is to the biologist, or what "mind" is to the psychologist, or what "culture" is to the sociologist. It is that indeterminate "something" that lets us explain "why" by definition.

Competition, to the economist, is both a driving force and a moral value generator. Business enterprises are said to keep expanding and improving their product lines "because" of competition. And under conditions of "perfect competition," everyone is said to receive his "just and fair" share of the economic pie. Indeed, the basic assumption is that if one can maintain a condition of "perfect competition" then there is no need to decide what we are to mean by "just" and "fair." Everything will automatically work out for the best.[22]

Quite apart from the intellectual inadequacies of the mythology of competition, one wonders what the world might have looked like without the assumption that human potential in the economic sphere is limited by "natural" factors. Would we perhaps be more concerned with questions pertaining to values and broad strategic issues, and less with questions pertaining to techniques and narrow tactical issues? Would we be more concerned with the encouragement of human competence and creativity in the economic sphere and less concerned with the "problem" of income distribution? If we postulated that the more there is of yours, the *more* there is of mine, could some of the energy and resources now devoted to the resolution of "pressing" economic problems or to the negotiation of "fair" shares be turned to more constructive ends?

It is not my intention to attempt to answer those questions here, but to suggest that *many of our current social and economic "problems" derive from the way economists have named and explained economic phenomena in the past.* By being almost exclusively concerned with the "discovery" of economic "truths," economists have failed to see that *any* theory will "explain" complex phenomena. But in economics, as in any other "science," the task is not just to explain, it is to explain advantageously.[23] It is in this context that general semantics seems relevant to economics.

WHAT IS IN A NAME?

Economists seem quite aware of the potential consequences of naming certain things in certain ways. That is, there seems to be no concern in economics with the influence of labels upon understanding of economic phenomena. Though it may seem self-evident to a semanticist that people attribute both factual and value connotations to names or labels,[24] economists have exhibited little interest in the implications of this fact with respect to the impact of their theories on economic behavior.

Thus, general semantics can contribute more to economics than merely reveal that economic theory is an operationalization of prevailing values and not simply an "objective" interpretation of "facts." Not that this is unimportant. There is an element of intellectual irresponsibility involved in proclaiming theories as essentially value free when in fact they cannot be. And economists are fond of saying that theirs is a pure "science" involving no value preferences and, indeed, no policy recommendations.[25] Such scientistic hubris is potentially dangerous.

Economists, among themselves and in their roles as "scientists," undoubtedly do seek to remove the value implications of their terminology. For example, the preference for mathematics exhibited by many modern economists could be interpreted as an attempt to avoid the value implications of everyday language. But economic theories must necessarily be understood by noneconomists before they can be acted upon or implemented as policies.[26] Thus, even though the economist may "intend" the statement, "a monopolist will tend to make excess profits," to have only factual

and no value connotations, few laymen would read it in this neutral fashion. Consequently, laymen will enact laws to prevent the monopolist from
making "excess" profits, being unaware of the possibility that the characteristic he is seeking to eliminate inheres not in the "territory" but in the verbal "map."

Since several maps might fit the territory of economic phenomena, the
quality of some particular map must be judged both with respect to the degree to which it fits the territory and in relation to the quality of alternative maps. And that, it seems to me, is the fundamental function of any science—to enrich our collection of maps rather than to seek the one "true"
map, and then use this collection as a basis for "solving" or "fixing" those
phenomena we have come to label as "problems" or "ills."

WAGES: COST OR INVESTMENT?

Problems of "semantics" are not new in economics. As early as 1827,
Robert Malthus devoted a book to definitional issues.[27] Of more recent
date is a collection of essays authored by Fritz Machlup in which he takes
economists to task for failing to define their terms and concepts
consistently.[28]

But attempts by economists to discuss "problems" of semantics are, on
the whole, superficial. Definitional confusions may, indeed, be annoying
and detrimental to the discipline as such, but they have also been known to
contribute to the evolution of knowledge. In any case, they become a serious problem only in the context of a closed system of concepts such as that
of quantum mechanics or relativity theory.[29] In a discipline as immature
as that of economics, it is often difficult to decide what is a definitional in-
accuracy and what is merely a different way of thinking about similar phenomena.

But the principles of general semantics have deeper and more important
implications for the field of economics than that of helping resolve squab-
bles about definitional accuracy. These implications pertain to the *relation*
between the manner in which economists label economic phenomena and
the institutional structure of the world of economic behavior.

Consider, for example, the term "wages":

> In the price of corn, for example, one part pays the rent of the landlord,
> another pays the wages or maintenance of the labourers and labouring cat-
> tle employed in producing it, and the third pays the profit of the farmer.[30]

At first glance this quote from Adam Smith may seem to indicate a mere logical division of the proceeds from the production and sale of corn. But note that wages are thought of as "maintenance," quite unlike profits:

> The profits of stock, it may perhaps be thought, are only a different name for the wages of a particular sort of labour, the labour of inspection and direction. They are, however, altogether different, are regulated by quite different principles, and bear no proportion to the quantity, the hardships, or the ingenuity of this supposed labour of inspection and direction.[31]

One of the standing controversies of early economic theory was the problem of defining a concept of *value* that could be used to close the conceptual scheme of economics.[32] That is, as the early economists saw it, any theory of economics had to be self-sufficient and self-supporting. There had to be some way of deciding in economic terms (i.e., in terms of the economic map) what the relative prices (shares of income) should be—given the following factors of production and their associated return:

Factors	*Returns*
capital stock	interest
land	rent
labor	wages
entrepreneurial talent	profit

To Adam Smith, the relative shares were largely determined by "an invisible hand." There were, as he expressed it, "natural rates of wages, profit, and rent."[33] David Ricardo faced the problem more squarely:

> We have seen that the price of corn is regulated by the quantity of labour necessary to produce it with that portion of capital which pays no rent.[34]

This is the basic statement of the labor theory of value, which was later to form the cornerstone of Marx's theoretical edifice. But note how Ricardo attained closure on his theoretical "reality":

> The natural price of labour is that price which is necessary to enable the labourers, one with another, to subsist and to perpetuate their race, without either increase or diminution.[35]

The rest follows from these two statements. Since the price of corn is determined by the amount of labor and the (fixed) amount of capital required to produce it, and since the wages of labor [36] are determined by what today is called the "price level," then profits, rent, interest, and wages all must come out of the same *fixed* fund of revenues.[37] Rent and interest were thought to be determined by the degree of competition for land and capital respectively, and profits were taken to be a residual.[38] In sum, we have the following determinants of relative shares:

Factor Shares	*Size Determined by*
interest	profits
rent	productivity of land
wages	subsistence [39]
profit	residual

In the hands of later economists, it became customary to think of these relative shares as being payment *for* something.[40] Thus, Alfred Marshall suggests the following terminology: [41]

Factor Shares	*Payment for*
interest	waiting
rent	payment necessary to keep land in present use
wages	disutility of work
profits	entrepreneurial talent

Marshall also rejected the labor theory of value, and theorized that the basic measure of value was consumer utility for the goods produced.[42] But for our purposes here, the labor theory and the utility theory of value come to the same thing: *the total returns to factors of production comprise a fixed amount (from the producer's point of view), production determines rents, and profits determine interest. Thus, the level of profits depends entirely on the level of wages. Economic "reality" had thus been construed as a conflict situation.*[43]

Note that the manager–entrepreneur has been neatly separated from "labor," the latter being remunerated for "disutility of work." In other words, "wages," from the point of view of the manager–entrepreneur are a cost. But from the point of view of workers, "wages" are, of course, *income* received in return for the sale of energy, competence, time, and the like.[44] Thus, we have the interesting conceptual paradox that products buy from workers what they do not sell, and workers sell what producers do not buy.[45]

But more importantly, by defining "wages" as a *cost* to the producer, the economist *automatically* put them in the category of payments to be *mini-*

mized. Profits, on the other hand, being defined as entrepreneurial *income,* fell into the category of payments to be *maximized.* Thus, the stage was set for management–worker conflicts for years to come.[46]

Thus, what economists have divided, managers, unions, and lawmakers have had to unite by negotiation or legislation. And such is the basis for much of our economic legislation and many of our economic "problems." The idea of labor being different from entrepreneurship and management is older than the industrial revolution, and was not "invented" by economists. Yet, the perpetuation of this distinctly feudal notion in the structure and operation of modern industrial economics nevertheless suggests that at least some parts of economic theory derive from and describe the phenomena of a bygone era.

With respect to the economic theory of wages, what difference would it have made had economists conceived of payments to workers as an *investment* rather than as a *cost?* From a theoretical standpoint, it is as simple to think of the economic enterprise as a "stock" of human competence as it is to think of it as a stock of capital goods.

Briefly, if we did think of wages as an investment, then we might construe the objective of the enterprise vis-à-vis its members as one of *maximizing* the return to its "stock" of human competence. The entrepreneurial or managerial task would thus emerge as one of creating opportunities to fit the aggregate competencies of the enterprise, or modifying the aggregate competence of the enterprise to fit available opportunities, or both.

In addition, if we conceive of wages as an investment, we automatically remove labor from the realm of short term variables and place it squarely at the center of the economic system. In other words, the objective of the economic system then would emerge as one of maximizing the utilization of human potential, rather than as one of maximizing that arbitrary residual we now call "profit."

Furthermore, the wages-as-cost doctrine may be at the root of a number of social and economic issues. For example, the idea of labor and management *opposing* each other in the pursuit of what might be conceived as their common interest seems preposterous. Labor no more earns its "share" of the wealth created by economic enterprises from management than management earns its "share" from labor.

And much of what we call the "need" for social legislation might be traced to the fact that we tend to think of the return to labor as a cost rather than as an accruing benefit or an investment. In thus conceiving of labor as a means and production as an end, we have indeed created a requirement for government or social intervention in the form of social welfare legislation. One might plausibly hypothesize that if we conceived of people (labor *and* management) as the end, and production as a means of an economic system, the "need" for welfare legislation would be greatly diminished.

Perhaps the point has been made. The basic function of a social science, such as economics, must be that of creating, through symbolic representation, a "map" advantageous to the pursuit and attainment of human potential. Some economists, and some other social scientists as well, may occasionally see the function of their science as one of "fixing" the world by policy recommendation. They do occasionally lose track of the fact that most of what we call economic "reality" resides only in abstractions.

These are some of the reasons that the ideas of general semantics seem highly relevant to economics and economists.

I shall let this issue stand as a challenge to general semantics. Certainly, for anyone interested in examples of the "isomorphism" of maps and territories, economics offers a rich challenge.

IN CONCLUSION

Perhaps economists, in their eagerness to be "scientific," have leaned too far in the direction of "the scientific method." Perhaps they have ignored the fact that social science theories have a tendency to be self-validating if only because people listen and act *as if* the theories were true. Perhaps economists, in seeking to maintain innocence of value judgments, have merely succeeded in introducing values indirectly through their careless use of abstractions. Perhaps economists, in their adoption of the concept of a "natural wage rate," had a great deal to do with the later history of union and government efforts to secure a share of the economic pie for labor.

Nineteenth-century economists were fond of arguing that whatever happened was "in the nature of things." Thus, to them, the suggestion that their theories had anything to do with later institutional developments would have been largely incomprehensible. Our faith in the power of science to change the world has increased greatly since then.

But economists and politicians are still kept busy "solving" the problems of an economic "reality" created in the nineteenth century.[47] We know now that there is nothing inevitable about the economy—that we can conceptualize economic behavior in practically any manner we wish. But traditional concepts do not die easily—particularly not in a discipline as well developed and as conscious of its standards of "scholarship" as economics.

Thus, instead of seeking to reconceptualize the structure and function of economic activity to fit the phenomena of an economy of abundance, economists have preferred to argue about and "prove" the "truth" of their theories in the incredibly obscure but "neutral" language of econometrics. And except for variations on old theories, little that is new has been added to economic theory since Keynes published his *General Theory* in 1936.

In the midst of all this scientific complacency, we have witnessed the incongruous spectacle of the world's entrepreneurs bending their not inconsiderable mental powers to the minimization of the wages of labor. And unless one views this particular direction of economic self-interest as being an inevitable element of human nature,[48] one must ask why economists maintain such a narrow view of the entrepreneurial function in an age where machines are increasingly taking over the menial tasks formerly performed by labor. Also, in an age where "work" is increasingly that which man does to improve himself, it seems incongruous to treat labor as a variable cost to the enterprise.[49] The important question is: if the sources of these incongruities are the abstractions economists have become accustomed to using, then what would be the implications of using different concepts, different words? And if, as it seems, the ideas of general semantics are relevant to economics and economists, how might these two disciplines be brought to bear on each other?

REFERENCES

1. Burke, Kenneth. *Language as Symbolic Action: Essays on Life, Literature and Method*. Berkeley, Calif.: University of California Press, 1966, p. 5.
2. Johnson, Kenneth G. *General Semantics: An Outline Survey*. Madison, Wisc.: University of Wisconsin Extension Division, 1960, p. 14.
3. Actually, this may be unfair to Newton. He did believe that he was discovering natural order (like modern-day economists), but at least he kept his theology straight (unlike modern-day economists and, perhaps, social scientists in general).
4. Blaug, Mark. *Economic Theory in Retrospect,* rev. ed. Homewood, Ill.: Richard D. Irwin, Inc., 1968, p. 8.
5. There are some notable exceptions. See for example, Kenneth E. Boulding. *A Reconstruction of Economics*. New York: Science Editions, Inc., 1962.
6. I think this issue of relativity is what we, as intellectuals, have to come to grips with. And I doubt that a return to empirical realism will help us here. The "tyranny of words" is not removed by doing away with highly abstract concepts. On the contrary, it is by enriching conceptual frameworks that the social sciences can best contribute to the realization of human potential. See Stuart Chase, *The Tyranny of Words*. New York: Harcourt, Brace & World, Inc., 1938.
7. Heilbroner, Robert L. *The Worldly Philosophers*. New York: Simon and Schuster, 1961.
8. Smith, Adam. *An Inquiry into the Nature and Causes of the Wealth of Nations*. New York: The Modern Library, 1937.

9. Ricardo, David. *The Principles of Political Economy and Taxation.* London: J. M. Dent & Sons, Ltd., 1911.
10. Marx, Karl. *Capital: A Critique of Political Economy.* New York: The Modern Library, 1906.
11. Marshall, Alfred. *Principles of Economics.* New York: The Macmillan Company, 1948.
12. Veblen, Thorstein. *The Theory of the Leisure Class.* New York: The Modern Library, 1934.
13. Keynes, John Maynard. *The General Theory of Employment, Interest and Money.* London: Macmillan & Co., Ltd., 1961.
14. See also, Joan Robinson. *Economic Philosophy: An Essay on the Progress of Economic Thought.* New York: Doubleday & Company, Inc., 1962.
15. Hicks, J. R. "Mr. Keynes and the Classics: A Suggested Interpretation," *Econometrica,* Vol. 5 (April, 1937), pp. 147–59.
16. Hagen, Everett E. "The Classical Theory of the Level of Output and Employment," *Readings in Macroeconomics,* ed. M. G. Mueller. New York: Holt, Rinehart and Winston, Inc., 1966, pp. 3–17.
17. See also, Lawrence R. Klein. *The Keynesian Revolution,* 2d ed. New York: The Macmillan Company, 1966.

   It is interesting to note that Keynes, in suggesting that it was possible to save too much (thus decreasing effective demand and precipitating a recession), was reviewing an idea suggested by Robert Malthus (1820). But the idea that saving, like eating, might be overdone was, of course, unacceptable to a nineteenth-century economic "scientist."
18. Robinson, Joan. *op. cit.*
19. Malthus, Robert. "A Summary View of the Principle of Population," reprinted in *On Population: Three Essays.* New York: The New American Library, 1960, pp. 13–62.
20. Keynes, John Maynard. *op. cit.*
21. This is, of course, a generally accepted "limit" to economic expansion and the main element of control available to the federal government.
22. Perfect competition is not only a sufficient condition for optimum social welfare but, it seems, also a necessary condition. Without the postulate of perfect competition (which, of course, is as "unrealistic" as a perfect vacuum), economic theory has little to say about the conditions for optimum social welfare. See also R. G. Lipsey and K. Lancaster, "The General Theory of Second Best," *Review of Economic Studies,* Vol. xxiv, No. 1, 1956, pp. 11–32.
23. And the relative usefulness of various theories or maps cannot be determined from the territory—it is necessarily a matter of judgment, though not necessarily by scientists. See also, T. C. Chamberlin, "The Method of Multiple Working Hypotheses," *Science,* Vol. 148 (May 7, 1965), pp. 754–59.
24. See also, Anatol Rapoport, "What is Semantics," *The Use and Misuse of Language,* ed. S. I. Hayakawa. Greenwich, Conn.: Fawcett Publications, Inc., 1962.
25. See also, Milton Friedman, *Essays in Positive Economics.* Chicago, Ill.: University of Chicago Press, 1953.
26. Bakan, David. *On Method: Toward a Reconstruction of Psychological Investigation.* San Francisco, Cal.: Jossey-Bass, Inc., 1968.
27. Malthus, T. R. *Definitions in Political Economy.* London, 1827.

28. Machlup, Fritz. *Essays in Economic Semantics,* ed. Merton H. Miller. New York: W. W. Norton & Company, Inc., 1967.

29. See also, Werner Heisenberg, *Physics and Philosophy: The Revolution in Modern Science.* New York: Harper & Row, 1958.

30. Smith, Adam. *op. cit.,* p. 50.

31. *Ibid.,* p. 48.

32. Blaug, Mark. *op. cit.*

33. Smith, Adam. *op. cit.,* p. 55.

34. Ricardo, David. *op. cit.,* p. 64.

35. *Ibid.,* p. 52.

36. Actually Ricardo differentiated carefully between the *amount* and the *cost* of labor. Thus the *value* of corn would be determined by the amount of labor required for its production, not by its price. But since labor value, as such, is difficult to measure, real wages (monetary wages corrected for changes in the value of money) became the *de facto* measure.

37. This notion was further developed by John Stuart Mill into the "wages fund doctrine." John Stuart Mill, *Principles of Political Economy.* New York: Longmans, Green & Co., 1909.

38. That is, interest was determined in the capital market, and rent was determined by the relative productivity of land parcels. Ricardo's theory of rent is still quite widely accepted and taught.

39. Actually, wages were taken to be determined by the supply relative to the demand for labor. But since it was assumed that the population would increase in numbers with the wage rate, the long run equilibrium wage rate in effect became that subsistence wage rate at which the size of the population just equalled the demand for labor.

40. The reason for this, particularly in the labor market, was the necessity of "explaining" the tendency of labor supply to diminish with increasing wages above a certain wage rate. One could, of course, have sought to "explain" this phenomenon in terms of alternative uses of time (as was done in the case of rent and alternative uses of land), but that would have necessitated a theory of labor rather than a theory of *employment, and* a better notion of decision making than was available at that time.

41. Marshall, Alfred. *op. cit.*

42. Marshall thus precipitated much of the more recent controversy centering on cardinal measures of utility. But much of this framework has now been replaced by indifference analysis. See J. R. Hicks and R. G. D. Allen, "A Reconsideration of the Theory of Value," *Economica* (1934), p. 56.

43. This differentiation of factor payments is not as clearcut as it might at first glance appear. Economists have never really agreed on a good definition of profits. See T. Scitovsky, "A Note on Profit Maximization and its Implications," *Readings in Price Theory,* selected by a Committee of the American Economic Association. Homewood, Ill.: Richard D. Irwin, Inc., 1952, pp. 352–58.

44. Economists apparently did not see it this way even though Adam Smith among others argued that one of the benefits of specialization was the possibility of a general improvement of labor skills.

45. One reason for this paradox may have been that economists were working with a theory of *employment* rather than a theory of *labor*. Thus, though capital theory

was divided into *stocks* and *flows,* the theory of employment and wages was concerned with *flows* only. The firm was taken to be the locus of a production function, and *even today economic theory cannot accommodate a concept of the firm as a stock of human competence* in addition to a stock of capital goods.

46. One reason for these disparate definitions, perhaps, was that the economist found it necessary to "explain" why entrepreneurs invested in capital goods, and the notion of subsistence level wages would not really do in the case of the capitalist.

47. Note, for example, that Mr. Nixon still talks about "balancing the budget"—a notion deriving from early theories of saving and the idea of prudence. But, of course, if the government is to balance anything it is the *total economy,* and not just that arbitrary part we call "the budget."

48. Which, to be sure, some do. But it would seem that even economic man is necessarily limited in the pursuit of his self-interest by his *theories* of what serves his purposes and what does not.

49. See also, Sidney Weintraub, *Employment, Growth and Income Distribution.* Philadelphia, Pa.: Chilton Books, 1966.

Mel Thistle was born in Newfoundland, graduated (B.Sc., M.A.) from Mount Allison University, and has been employed since 1938 at the National Research Council of Canada as a Biochemist, Editor, Public Relations Officer, and Historian. His books include: *Peter the Sea Trout, The Inner Ring,* and *Time Touch Me Gently,* which won a prize for English poetry in 1967.

22

THE NATURE OF PARADOX *

MEL THISTLE

ONE use for the WIGO—WIMTH† dichotomy is to sort our paradoxes into two piles: those that have a root in the first level of reality, and those that are pure talk about talk. The paradoxes of Zeno, such as the famous one about a man who is never able to catch up with a tortoise, clearly belong to the second group and can be dismissed from the WIGO grouping. They are like the two statements:

1) "This sentence contains seven words."
2) "This sentence does not contain seven words."

Both are false. We are supposed to wonder how this can be, when one is the converse of the other. Of course, the subject, "this sentence," is not the same in the two examples, so that one sentence is not the converse of the other; both belong to the WIMTH alone, and as such can be left out of the category with content in space–time. Just that: leave it to one side, as a purely verbal set of noises, as talk about talk. Some purely verbal paradoxes are *otherwise* not so easy to dispose of, such as the celebrated Cretan liar paradox consisting of the single statement, "I am lying." True or false?

I do not wish to suggest that second-order paradoxes invariably have something "mere" about them, or that they "should" be abolished. They can be quite a lot of fun if that is the kind of fun you wish to have at a given time.

---

* This is the eighth in a series of fifteen lectures on "Language and Human Communication," presented by the author in a course at Carleton University, 1968–1969.
† WIGO = "What is going on"; WIMTH = "What it means to humans."

But here I wish to stick mainly to first-order affairs, and to give the WIGO the right of way. Therefore I will deal mainly with paradoxes that refer to ongoing events, and I will neglect those that consist of statements about statements in most of what follows—except for one or two minor bits that I cannot resist.

The Arabic genius for mathematics had one curious result—the Wall of Al Araf. It is described in the Al Araf chapter of the Koran: forever on this wall stand those whose good works exactly balance their evil deeds—people who therefore deserve neither Paradise nor Gehenna. If I believed in that kind of afterlife, I feel certain that I would end up on the wall. However, I happen to believe, as Lancelot Law Whyte says in *The Next Development in Man,* that, "So long as man is fully part of the whole, no demand for permanence can arise."

I have often been dazzled by the fact that for every action there is an equal and opposite reaction. This is a strangely beautiful and entirely elegant facet of physics. But, as a rainbow will sometimes show traces of a second and wider arc standing at some distance, so does the basic structure of the universe find its faint echo in the affairs of men. Echoing action and reaction, a convincing case can often be made for the opposing side of almost any question that engages us.

Occasionally the abundance of paradox will fascinate a man; G. K. Chesterton had a lot of fun. But for the most part, humans have a strange ability to find their way through the forest of paradox that surrounds them from birth. It is only now and then that we give it a thought, when a curiously colored paradox is squarely in our path; we gaze at it admiringly while we are in the process of going around it to our intended goal. It is very rare—but it does happen—that a paradox will actually trap us, like the wait-a-bit. Then we must perforce pick at the paradox until we are free, and carry some few prickles with us for a time.

Sometimes the resolution of a paradox can be quite simple, by placing the opposing sides in the obviously different orders of abstraction to which they belong. One example, chosen from everyday proverbs, is:

1) Many hands make light work.
2) Too many cooks spoil the broth.

This is clearly a function of scale, depending on a great many circumstances which, according to a third proverb, alter cases. Ten men could mow a small meadow more easily than one man could; but a thousand men, if they were silly enough to try it, would get in each other's way, trample the crop, wound each other with scythes, and end in a first-class mess. The original job is the same—mow that little meadow—but the outcome will be different depending on the order of magnitude.

3) Circumstances alter cases. This is a proverb at a higher order of abstraction than,
4) Look before you leap.
5) He who hesitates is lost.

The situation might be diagrammed as in Fig. 1, in which the conflict between 4 and 5 is annulled by the higher-order 3, which contains them both as special cases.

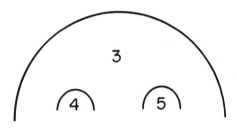

Figure 1

These quite trivial examples may serve as a model to examine more serious paradoxes, such as:

6) Important phenomena have fuzzy edges.
7) Important phenomena are all-or-none.

This paradox is often puzzling to people who have recently (and about time!) overcome the educational efforts of parents and teachers, and have just begun the novel and painful process of thinking for themselves. To elaborate a little:

Proverb (6), the really "important phenomena have fuzzy edges." Nothing is either black or white; everything is various shades of gray. Thus no man is either all "bad" or all "good"—nor for that matter is he entirely male; there are various degrees of femininity in completely normal "males." It is quite impossible to say with any great accuracy just where the water ends and the shore begins, or exactly how many miles above the earth the atmosphere ends and space begins, or indeed where anything ends, from a piece of cloth to the edge of a razor. Use fine measurements and look through a microscope, consider molecules, atoms, electrons, and you are in serious trouble. Notes on a piano are entirely arbitrary, and we could put another X notes, just as valid, between any two of the "standard" notes: hence the various scales used by different cultures. Light intensity varies as the square of the distance from the source. Gravity and growth and many other phenomena are accelerative functions. Gradation is everywhere. Change is everywhere. Impressions of certainty are misleading; it is quite impossible to be certain about anything; one must not be guilty of unconscious projection; in a fuzzy universe, one must compromise.

Proverb (7), the really "important phenomena are [of the] all-or-none" type. Nerve cells fire or they do not; electricity is either off or on. We defy any woman to be just a little bit pregnant; this is an all-or-none event, and it is not accident that it is important to the people concerned. So is death. All electrical equipments, from television to the electronic computer, operate on all-or-none phenomena; in television, the cells are either black or white. Newspapers employ the same contrast; businesses operate either in the black or in the red; binary is the basic language of the universe. We can always find out, ultimately, which of two ends is up; certainty is inevitable; compromise is impossible.

Or (3), the explanation, of course, is the same as for the proverbs: "circumstances alter cases." Philosophies based entirely on one or the other of these attitudes may be useful, so long as you don't believe them. Both are "real"; both are "true." The universe has no trouble being "opposite" things at the same time. The difficulty is a human one only; we have to face the possibility that we may never be able to decide whether light is continuous or discontinuous, a "particle" or a "wave." It may indeed be truly both. Perhaps all that is needed is practice in not boggling. Scientists who are concerned with such problems in their own flesh-and-blood work have no trouble in shifting gears according to need. The rest of us might follow their lead—but over the whole scale of paradox, which seems to me to be extensive.

A further example, (8), of basic paradox is that, "to succeed, we must fail." This seems to be considerably affected by *time,* which grades our victories into at least the following three classes: trivial, great, and ultimate.

Trivial: It is possible to claim an undoubted success by putting a time limit on it, very close to us. All physical contests and all games make use of this device, which produces champions—for the time being. Eventually all champions are beaten, of course. If a success is of this sort—where you do not acknowledge your eventual defeat, and, in fact, do your best not to be aware of your inevitable defeat—it is trivial. But trivial victories are of-ten necessary. A hole-in-one is valued by men who cannot be described as small-minded, and who know very well how little it really means.

Great: Great victories are those that have in them an ultimate defeat, known and acknowledged. For instance, the Dutch have made themselves a great nation by their quite uneconomic damming back of that great ocean, the Atlantic, which is certain to overwhelm them in the end. No one is more aware of this outcome than the Dutch themselves. The counterpart, in Canada, is a railway system that will probably never operate in the black, but that nevertheless turned a territory into a nation.

Gardeners fall into this class, since all of their enemies—weeds, insects, plant diseases, weather—are certain to overcome them in the end. In spite of 2-4-*D*, the dandelion will grow in triumph on our graves. All gardens are only a tiny island in time; some gardeners know this, and go ahead anyway. It is no accident that so many philosophers are prone to garden-ing. A good garden, at a given moment in time, is not a trivial achievement; it involves photosynthesis, the carbon cycle, genetics; it is in fact a great victory of the human spirit—*if* the ultimate defeat is kept clearly in mind.

Ultimate: Ultimate victories are those that have their origin in defeat, which is *not* acknowledged, but denied, and used as a springboard. The victory is impossible without that initial defeat.

One obvious example is the death of Jesus, which was the beginning of Christianity. His whole life was aimed at his death, and his teaching abounds in paradox, curiously neglected by some of his most ardent follow-ers.

In ordinary life situations, the fact that "to succeed we must fail" is per-haps best exemplified in our attitude toward our children. We honestly do our best to teach them to obey us, to conform to the cultural taboos, to be of little trouble to us, and so forth. Yet, if they actually do these things, they become quite useless, and we are genuinely disappointed. A first-class human must be able to survive his teaching, to defy it, to overturn it. Un-less we fail in our efforts to teach, and in our efforts to obey, we will never succeed. On the home front, also, a relaxed woman who acknowledges that her mate is not her possession, and that her children will eventually grow away from her, is loved with an intensity unknown to the woman who tightly asserts possession. Freedom will bind a grown man or a grown child more firmly than any assertion of rigid possessiveness.

Now it is true that the passage of time renders all activity useless, but nevertheless, activity is valuable—and not only for its momentary success. The main justification for activity is that it is fun. In fact, a pretty good

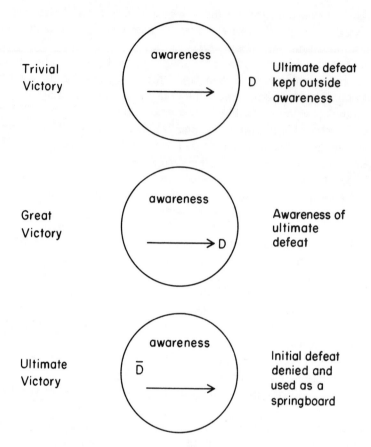

Figure 2. Awareness is important. The migration of defeat can change a great victory into a trivial achievement, i.e., a garden built *without awareness* of defeat. The reverse is also true; in *The Old Man and The Sea,* the man *became aware* of his defeat —and so this trivial incident of the fish was converted into a great victory of the human spirit.

case can be made for the proposition: "Life is a positive force, and every normal function of it holds some delight." If you are not having fun, you are wasting your time. I regard it as a moral duty to have fun, to enjoy yourself. If you do not, you cheat your employer as well as yourself.

If time renders all activity useless, and it does, then it follows that all conquests ultimately peter out and, of course, all defenses ultimately fail.

To dally with the conquests for a moment: a Chinese, when taxed with the historical fact that every wave of barbarian attack on his country from the north seemed to succeed, replied, "If you add a drop of blood to a bucket of water, you still have a bucket of water." Now this is entirely true. In India, for thousands of years, the strong barbarian in the hills looked down upon the plains and said, "These people are fat and lazy and rich and very weak; I will conquer them." So he did. And a few generations later it was his descendants who were fat and rich and defeated. Time ultimately defeats us all, including conquerors.

But I am much more interested in negative aspects, which always seem to have more vitamins. What about the defenses that ultimately fail? It seems to me that everyone who stops to apologize, or to defend his actions, is already defeated. Defense, in this sense, is about the silliest activity that a human can engage in. In the military field, every defensive measure of the physical-structure type has invariably failed—the Great Wall of China, the Wall of Hadrian, the Maginot Line, the Siegfried Line and, to anticipate a bit, the DEW Line, the Mid-Canada Line, the McGill Fence, and so forth. All military defenses are obsolete *before* they leave the drawing board. They are useless because they *are* a defense. Another peculiar property of these pernicious activities is that all of them, without exception, are not only useless, but crushingly expensive. It is for this reason that some men sigh over their income tax—knowing that somewhere between a third and a half of it is being expended by extremely well-meaning people in the name of "defense." An intelligent man hates to have a large portion of his income wrested away from him in order to ensure his own defeat.

Of course, the economy of this continent would collapse overnight unless we had something absorbent to engage it. One idea that is in the air is to use our embarrassing surplus over the next fifty years in aiding the older peoples to come up to our own level of technology, instead of wasting it on military defenses that cannot possibly be of use for defense.

This notion of "helping" the older civilizations has much to recommend it—the chief one being that it isn't anything of the sort at all: we stand to gain a great deal more in cultural exchanges than we can possibly give. While money—representing human time saved by machines—is by no means to be despised, it isn't really very important compared with what we stand to gain by a genuine exchange with the East. Let us not forget that the religions, which so many of us value, were not originated either in the Americas or in Europe. The East is older than we are and, I think, it has more to give than we have, of the things that matter. What we have to give them is *science* of a particular kind—one that induces a love of freedom for the individual human spirit—and if we can really do that, free time will also be added to them. As a matter of fact, it may be easier to export this attitude, now held by some of our best scientists, than it will ever be to spread this attitude abroad in our own culture.

What the East has to give us, I suspect, is at least as valuable. You see, even the things we have to give them had many of its roots in the East: the notion that a single individual is valuable came out of Judea; and much that is good came from Greece via Rome; much of our mathematics came from India via Arab culture—our numerals, the concept of the zero, and algebra. Some of us have already forgotten that *zero* and *algebra* are Arabic words, and that our numerals are a form of Arabic script.

But to return to the ultimate uselessness of activity, which progresses to this goal by many thorny and difficult paths. Another path is this: anything really worth doing is theoretically impossible.

This is easy to establish. First, a couple of trivial examples:

1) You can get your *first* book published easily and quickly, if you *already* have a well established literary reputation for excellent books.
2) The only way to borrow money from a Canadian bank is to prove to the manager that you do not *need* the money.

An example that is not trivial is this: the only way to bring up children properly is to catch the parents and teachers when they are young and bring *them* up properly.

The problem of breaking this closed circle is crucial for humans. The only way I know is long and slow and painful and difficult, and is called "adult education."

This whole process of adult education is rendered extremely difficult by one more paradox, and that is: the only things that we can learn are those we already know. We see what we are set to see.

It would seem that the learning center is not in the conscious mind at all, but in the unconscious. It fires when ready. Then we have a revelation. And we can learn consciously only what has already been revealed to us.

Ever watch a scientist at work? He spends weeks in the library, reading everything that everyone else knows about and around his problem. What's he doing? Feeding his subconscious. His own personal revelation comes, not when he is at work, but when he has one foot in his pajamas. The conscious mind is a parasite and a thief of credit: honest poets will tell you about the muse; honest scientists will talk about the hunch. This is the way new things are learned, and the effect is: that we learn only what we know already.

Much of this learning consists of denying what your teachers have taught you.

A statement must be made before it can be denied. Denial, then, is later in time and, if agreement is secured, the denial becomes mature. Nonsystems are wider and greater than the systems they contain and replace, e.g., non-Euclidian, non-Newtonian, non-Aristotelian.

But the nonsystem is in a sense a parasite, and attains its stature by standing on the shoulders of a previous system. The nonsystem is the wiser of the two; however, it cannot really afford to be scornful of its progenitor and teacher. When a nonsystem enters the mind of a man, it is very likely to be stated first in rather ungentlemanly terms, since the unconscious mind, from whence it comes, is not a gentleman. It is only later, when the new system is surely and firmly based in wide agreement, that the conversational terms used are couched in becoming language. When this happens, the definitive books of the nonsystems are dedicated to the originators of the old original systems. The debt is acknowledged at last by a man who can afford to be humble. But only because he no longer has to fight for his brainchild, which has become mature enough to take its chances.

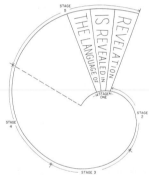

Figure 3. The highest sophistication has strong links to the lowest stage, with which it is in assonance. Therefore the language of revelation is primitive: the way to the future is through the past.

Paradox hits us almost from the moment of birth. Parents are the source of love and punishment, pleasure and pain.

When we ourselves mature and become parents, we find ourselves dishing out both love and punishment, too. We must punish, if only to keep the children from killing themselves. If we really love them, we really must punish them.

Later on, we generalize these experiences in attitudes toward society. Which freedom do we want more: the freedom to bash the first man we meet with our umbrella, or the freedom to walk down the street without being battered over the head by somebody's umbrella?

The changes in our attitude toward others are amusing. We begin by being annoyed at the restrictions. For instance, we worry about the dandelions in our garden, and we dig them out. But the neighbors on all four sides don't give a damn about their gardens, and the seeds from their dandelions blow into our garden. So we wish for a campaign of adult education that will teach the neighbors the proper way of life. A few years later, we engage in a program of adult education, but is isn't aimed at the neighbors. It's for ourselves. The object is to learn enough respect for human differences so that we will understand our neighbor, and respect his right to do whatever it is he does instead of looking after his garden.

This program of self-education is also aimed at finding out exactly what we want to do with our own life. If what we really want to do is to garden, then we must give it enough of our time and our substance to put up a greenhouse, and become independent of the environment. And if it appeals to us more as a way of life than as a hobby, then we should quit what we are doing for a living, and become a florist or a horticulturist or a farmer.

> Twinkle, Twinkle, little star—
> How *we* wonder what *we* are.

If we want to know what we are, watch closely what we do. Because we *are* what we *do*. And it is here, if anywhere, that we will find a clue to what we really are.

The paradox with which we begin our lives—pleasure and pain coming from the same source—confuses a great many of us in a basic way, so that we don't know what we want to do with our lives. Some never find out, and drift. Some are not really confused for very long, and assert their own pattern early in life. Most of us are lucky if we really find out about ourselves by the time we are thirty.

We see much talent wasted because of this confusion—people who want to play on the team or lead an orchestra, and who never notice that they have a genius for organizing teams or orchestras. Maybe you're a teacher instead of a doer. Some of the greatest violin teachers and science teachers were no great shakes on the violin or in the laboratory. That's why I say, examine what we do, closely. A little off the center of our ambition, we may be great. Look at the edges of what we do. Our hobby may be more important for us than our present profession.

The inescapable paradox that takes up so much of our early life beclouds the two main issues: first, finding out what you really want to do with your life, based on your own differences from all the others; second, having found out what you *want* to do, find someone who will *pay you* for doing what *you want to do*.

Another generalization of this early experience of paradox is reflected in our attitude toward the universe. Intellectually we tend to regard life as a series of happenings in an unimportant corner of the universe. We had a reducing atmosphere when the earth was cooling; the earth was small enough to let most of the hydrogen escape; the atmosphere then became an oxydizing atmosphere, and we had oceans full of organic compounds in which it was possible for life to begin. Water is one of the very few substances that is denser as a liquid than as a solid; the liquid state itself is very rare—almost everything in the universe is either a gas or a solid; in the long history of evolution, just about everything that could happen, did. The diplodocus is the largest cold-blooded animal that could exist, at the time. The elephant is the largest warm-blooded land animal that could possibly exist, right now. The whale is the largest possible animal that can exist as an entity in the support of salt water. Every niche is filled in time and space with the biosphere, using the earth's supply of carbon over and over again with the aid of the double-edged device of love and death. This biosphere has now endured much longer than the mountains. At exactly the right time, our animal ancestors were driven up into the trees, where they developed an opposable thumb, acute vision, and a tendency to chatter. Also something was taken away—the terrible importance of smell, which restricts the lives of our grounded and still animal cousins. In humans, 40% of the nerves entering the brain come from our eyes, largely at the expense of smell. Our sojourn in the trees did that for us. Again, we were driven back to the ground at exactly the right time in history, so that we learned to walk and assume an upright posture. Those who came down too late became baboons, and some are still up there. Our present lives depend on the balance of several thousands of knife-edges in physics and chemistry and biology and geophysics and what-have-you.

When we try to walk away from a knife-edge, difficulties begin, and the difficulties increase exponentially with distance from the norm. Just a few hundred miles north of here, with a mean temperature not very much meaner than this, we must expend ten times as much energy to operate.

It is very easy to illustrate with everyday trivia: Come to work early, and there is no one around to notice your virtue; come to work late, and everyone raises his head and says, "Aha! Today you are coming to work late." The dice are loaded against us, and inconvenience tends to a maximum. We are pressed upon, in big and little, by the weight of many laws.

But while we can understand this very clearly, and adjust our views as new discoveries are made, we can't let it go at that. The story of life is beautiful and clear and simple in outline, intricate and clever and enticing in detail, mysterious and beckoning and enthralling in its shadowy parts— but this paradox into which we are born will not let us go. The mere fact that we are born means that we are creatures of love and death, and our parents shape us with pain and love. We cannot help looking at the universe from the ground on which we stand. The pattern of the bars on our cradle is still showing in our view of the universe. We see it in terms of love and death, of pain and pleasure.

We see that we are part of the universe, sentient carbon compounds, with a capacity for awareness. We speculate that all of the universe must be a little bit aware, or we could not specialize in it as we do, just as the electric eel could not specialize in electricity if electricity did not exist in a great many places outside the eel—in us, for example, every time we will a finger to move.

Similarly, since we find ourselves immersed in paradox, we cannot help but impute paradoxity to the universe at large. We eventually find ourselves at home with the notion that light may very well be both a wave and a particle, at the same time.

In a tree, the sap rises against the force of gravity—water running uphill. The law is still there and still valid, but we also have laws of biochemistry, such as osmosis, which have *their* sway. Circumstances do alter cases.

But when we get through exploring some of the reaches of paradox— enough to catch the flavor—we come back to what we started with: that either horn of the dilemma is merely a point of view, and that this point of view is appropriate and useful under certain circumstances only.

Occasionally we are aware of paradox because some of the materials of thought are lacking. A few years ago, from the then current theories of aerodynamics, it was totally impossible for a bumblebee to fly. The bee didn't know that he was aerodynamically unsound, so—he flew.

If we are aware of a paradox—comfortably aware—then all is well. A playful awareness of paradox is, I think, healthy. Then we can keep things in balance.

But an uncomfortable awareness of paradox is a sign of danger. This happens when we are rigidly committed to a viewpoint, but are aware that the opposite view has some aspects that rather appeal to us—and moreover, some of the people we admire most seem to believe this pernicious thing. This makes us uncomfortable.

The thing to do then, it seems to me, is to swap sides on the debating team: to propel ourselves across from 1 to 2, and live the opposite view with all the enthusiasm we can muster. For a time, we should act as though we believed 2.

Then, with a foot in both camps, we can rise to the higher order of 3, in which both 1 and 2 are true under certain conditions. Then we will not be trapped into thinking that if 50 men can build a house in 10 days, it follows that 50,000 men can build a house in 10 minutes. And while it is quite legitimate to have trouble about the precise location of the terminal electron in a razor blade, Heinsenburg's Uncertainty Principle, there could be circumstances in which that blade is being held against your throat by an unfriendly hand, and you *know where the end of the blade is* for all practical purposes.

It seems to me that paradox supplies us with a chance to live (and therefore to learn) one of the simplest elements in Korzybski's system—multiordinality. Multiordinality is taken from the alphabet of general semantics. It looks like Fig. 4 below.

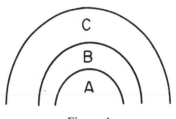

Figure 4

When we have dealt successfully with a paradox, then we have also lived an example of multiordinality. Then we know what it feels like to be consciously multiordinal about something; we are aware of many orders; we know that most of our words have a different meaning depending on the order of abstraction—and then we are a little bit more at home in this kind of universe.

Donald E. Washburn, Ph.D., is Professor of Humanities and Communication Studies at Edinboro State College. A graduate of Yale University and the University of Denver, he has been interested in general semantics since 1952, when he attended his first IGS Seminar. His publications have appeared in the *General Semantics Bulletin,* and *The Journal of Communication.*

23

THE EXTENSIONAL WORLD OF FRANÇOIS RABELAIS

DONALD E. WASHBURN

THE lessons of general semantics are encountered in the most unlikely places. But nowhere, I think, more delightfully than in the imaginative worlds of art and fiction.

Consider this episode from one of the great classics of French literature —François Rabelais' *Gargantua and Pantagruel.* It begins like this:

Or, en ceste propre saison, estoit un proces pendent en la court entre deux gros seigneurs desquels l'un estoit Monsieur de Baysecul, demandeur, d'une part, l'autre Monsieur de Humeresne, defendeur, de l'autre, desquelz la controverse estoit si haulte et difficile en droit que la court de Parlement n'y entendoit que le hault alemant.

Now at this time there was a lawsuit pending in court between two mighty lords: on the one hand, Mr. Bumkisser, plaintiff, and on the other, Mr. Souse, defendant. They might just as well have spoken in Old High German, for, so difficult and legally involved was their quarrel that the court was unable to understand a word of the story.

The author goes on to tell us that the most learned men in the land were baffled by the problem. Finally, in desperation they decide to call in Pantagruel, the hero of the tale, who was known far and wide as a great debater and settler of disputes. Pantagruel insisted that the two contestants appear face to face and state their case without the usual mountains of documents

217

and opinions. But the joke is that what follows is some of the most incomprehensible word-salad ever written. Language seems to have become totally divorced from reality. Neither party, in short, makes any sense. It is an outrageous lampoon of legal mumbo jumbo and verbal obfuscation. And since the jury understood not one word, it falls on Pantagruel to make the judgment.

Resourceful fellow that he is, he comes up with the perfect pronouncement—four minutes of double-talk, which although perfectly meaningless, leaves, strange to say, all parties satisfied. It would be hard to find a more devastating account of man's tendency to become a dupe of language. But then, it is important to remember that the issue of how men should speak is at the very heart of Rabelais' book.

Korzybski, who was fond of quoting Jonathan Swift, might well have plucked a pungent text or two from *Gargantua and Pantagruel*. Historically, the shift from a word-centered, intensional orientation to an emphasis on a language geared to experience took hold during the Renaissance. A shift so fundamental, of course, created all kinds of intellectual and social dislocations. It formed for a time a kind of "semantic interface"—an area of collision between psychological worlds, each with its interdependent doctrines, methods, and institutions. Truly contemporary people were caught between two incompatible and competing versions of reality. They were, in effect, living at the interface; and it was difficult for them *not* to be aware of the various ironic perspectives created by the changes taking place.

Rabelais, for example, was educated in the church. As a young man he was a member of the Franciscan order of monks, and technically he remained a priest until the year of his death. But he was also a humanist—an admirer, that is to say, of the new learning based on the pre-Christian culture of Greece and Rome. And he was a physician, sensitive to the importance of empirical investigation. He wrote treatises on anatomy and dissected cadavers. He knew the many viewpoints or vocabularies of his day—the speech of the old world that was dying, and the speech of the new world that was emerging. It was out of this clash of tongues that he fashioned his book, the implicit purpose of which was to discredit through laughter the rigid orthodoxies and verbal flim-flammery of the medieval establishment.

Keep in mind that the writer, who is usually among those most sensitive to the semantic environment, plays an important role in preparing the way for change. In providing the community with new symbols, he makes possible the emergence of new institutions. It seems that a semantic revolution is necessary before a social revolution can take place.

But Rabelais is more than just a saboteur of language out to discredit the opposition—although there is plenty of that. His book is also a probe, in the McLuhan sense, investigating the whole question of what symbols do to people. Gargantua and Pantagruel are giants, with enormous appetites and enormous curiosity. They represent a new attitude toward man and the universe. Their size is a kind of redefinition of man, who is no longer the frightened, dogma-ridden sinner of the Dark Ages, painfully aware of his limitations. Instead we have figures bigger than life, committed to experience, contemptuous of the word-shuffling and woolgathering of the theologians.

A large part of Book One is devoted to a description of the way in which the new man is to be educated. In place of the bookish traditionalism of the pedagogues, we find a method based on something very close to Korzybski's notion of the natural order of abstracting. Although book learning is still important, especially in the areas of mathematics and physical sciences, the principle emphasis is on active experience and, wherever possible, direct observation. Man is invited to assimilate his world with a kind of zest, usually reserved for food and drink. Indeed, this book fairly bursts with descriptions of people eating and drinking. There is a whole chapter devoted to a drinking party and the heady conversation that results. Wine and alcoholic spirits can be identified with the spirit of release and the explosion of psychological energy that results when a more limiting version of reality gives way to a multivalue, pluralistic conception of man's nature and purpose.

This sense of expansiveness, this feeling of being in a large frame of reference, extends even to Rabelais' compositional style. His tale is told with a minimum of attention to narrative consistency and logic, and an almost surrealistic fascination with detail, with double meanings, with bumptious wordplay. He seems to be reasserting the freedom and fluidity of language, its richness, its capacity for multiple meanings and startling incongruities. This is the reverse of dogmatism, which strains to make words have a single static meaning. By fixing language, the totalitarian mentality aspires to fix people. But Rabelais plays up and down the ladder of abstraction as though it were a xylophone. He is a mimic, a ventriloquist, a prestidigitator, a compiler of catalogues. And he exploits the possibilities of the interface, making us aware of the ironic discrepancy between the assumptions of the older order and those of the new.

In the chapters on the Abbey of Thélème, for example, he turned the medieval institution of monasticism inside out. Every value and practice of the typical monastery gives way to its opposite. In place of the ideal of discipline is the motto, "Do As You Like." Whereas medieval monasteries were gloomy and forbidding, this one is light, airy, cheerful, and full of color. The membership, instead of being composed of the rejects of society, is made up of the most beautiful and intelligent people that can be found, male and female. The dress is gay, the curriculum lively, the arts abundant, the learning liberal, and the atmosphere conducive to virtue and moderation. In this image, where the two worlds intersect, there is no question about where Rabelais' allegiances lie—with the new learning and the new man.

Like any good satirist, he also dwells on the problem of reality and illusion. And the role of language in promoting the latter is made inescapably obvious.

We chuckle to read how King Picrochole's advisors—the Duke of Riffraff, Count Chipshoulder, and Captain Krapp—embark on a verbal conquest of the world. They describe to the King how his armies will proceed, occupying town after town, nation after nation, until all of the known world is won, from Greenland to Mesopotamia. The Kingdoms topple like cards. It seems so easy, as the three lords describe it. Paper armies are supported by paper navies. And as the verbal conquests swell, Picrochole's ambition seems to swell with them. At the end of the scene he calls out enthusiastically, "Forward, let's make haste with all due preparations, and let he who loves me follow after."

Needless to say, he discovers later that the map is not the territory. After being routed by Gargantua's forces, Picrochole is last seen stripped of his clothing. Rumor has it that he subsequently became a lowly dock worker.

Book Two ends with a piece of advice: "Do not trust people who peep through holes, especially through monks' cowls." This jest provides an apt metaphor. It helps us to visualize the shift from the highly circumscribed orientation of asceticism based on denial and restraint, to the more inclusive humanism celebrated by Rabelais. The ascetic assumes that spirit and matter are hostile principles, and that one grows at the expense of the other. Therefore, hooded and sequestered, he shuns any dross or corporeity that might contaminate his single-minded sublimations. He seems almost to be modeling his psychic life on symbols themselves, and striving to attain the same degree of uniformity and abstractness.

The tendency to "peep through holes" has its analogue in language, not only in the limitations implicit in any dogmatic point of view, but also in the verbal taboos that surround well known natural functions and drives. One of the most striking features of Rabelais' style is his obscenity. There is hardly a chapter that does not contain some allusion to excretion, copulation, or the privy parts. But this is in keeping with his attempt to enlarge the symbolic frame through which men are permitted to gaze. The human body, which since classical times had been an anathema, was once again in the Renaissance a fit subject for admiration. As a doctor, Rabelais knew his anatomy and was perfectly willing to enliven his pages with dissecting-room wit. But more than this, he was using the taboos themselves as a way of dramatizing the prevailing hypocrisies, much as today's students bait the Establishment with four-letter words.

As a literary strategy, this has some interesting dimensions. The printing press had given Rabelais two important advantages: a mass audience and relative freedom from the censor. Rabelais' revolutionary message was aimed straight at the disenfranchised classes. Not only is the common man tolerant of coarse humor, but he has a deep distrust of those who have "risen above" vulgarity. He has seldom been comfortable with euphemisms or attempts to gloss over unflattering realities. And he bears an abiding resentment for the overly refined, hypereducated types—lawyers, pedagogues, clerics—who live by juggling words. Perhaps rightly so, since Eric Hoffer argues that, more often than not, he has been exploited by these same symbol manipulators.

The ruling classes, as Korzybski observed, maintain their status through an act of semantic legerdemain. They feel compelled to sustain certain expectations about themselves and about the institutions that they represent. To secure themselves and the system, they foster the illusion that they are hierarchically favored, that they have somehow transcended limitations that trammel people of lesser status. Ribaldry and obscenity remind all men of their common biological dependence, and serve to deny the reality of distinctions based on roles and other social conventions. Rabelais' vulgarity is therefore functional. It approves him to his audience, and it is a powerful satirical weapon against the lofty powers that he wishes to unseat. They are, forgive the pun, brought back down to earthiness.

Laughter itself is another leveler. It is rooted in a double awareness and the discrepancies that become apparent when two versions of reality are held in unexpected contrast. Laughter is a threat to the composure of dignitaries, who lose face when they can no longer maintain the illusion of absolute congruity with the expectations that sustain them. And, also, by exploiting multiple perspectives, laughter makes it more difficult to entertain dogmatic, single-valued interpretations of reality. The "allness bugs" that general semanticists know to be so pernicious cannot flourish in such an impure medium. Rabelais was himself aware of the health-giving properties of comedy. He regarded it as a kind of medicine. And, like a conscientious physician, he applied it to a society still stiff from the long chill of medievalism.

There are countless examples in *Gargantua and Pantagruel* that show that Rabelais had a highly sophisticated awareness of the ways in which men make fools of themselves over words. In Book Four, there is a description of the Island of Ruach, whose people lived entirely on wind, eating and drinking nothing but air. Rabelais adds, "Ils n'ont maisons que de gyrouettes." (All they possess in the way of houses are weather vanes.) What better way to describe people who make words more important than things?

Word magic is also the target in the episode of the Chitterlings, a delectible but warlike race, who threaten to attack Pantagruel and his men. A familiar superstition comes to light as our heroes discuss their chances for victory. It seems that the names of the opposing generals are each suggestive of some act of violence done to edible entrails. Since a Chitterling is a food prepared from the intestines of a hog, the omen is not difficult to interpret in a favorable way. There follows a long discussion about predicting the future on the basis of names. The premise is clear: a name somehow indicates the character or fate of the one who bears it. This prescientific intuition is one of the mainstays of the intensional orientation. Rabelais' subtle mockery, however, is more than a match for obfuscation and mumbo jumbo.

Another group of islanders, the Papimaniacs, worship words in the shape of a sacred book, and fear to come into contact with what Rabelais describes as a rather inferior sculpture of the Pope. It is not difficult to find in this account a non-Aristotelian impatience with people who are unable to distinguish between symbols and things.

Perhaps the tendency for symbols to be reified and to take on a spurious objectivity can best be seen in the strange account of the frozen words. It seems that while at sea, the travelers discover that in frigid climates words can freeze and not thaw out until the following spring. Only when they melt can people actually hear what was said. On board ship, Pantagruel and his friends listen, intrigued by the sounds of a battle long since finished. But they decline to save any frozen words, since it makes no sense to hoard a commodity "so easy to come by." Marshall McLuhan proposes that the frozen words are an allusion to written language. Perhaps this cryogenic time-binding can be equated with man's ability to "freeze" his symbols technologically.

But it does no good to abandon words and rely on sign language. One of the funniest episodes in the book describes the debate between Panurge, a disreputable student who becomes a crony of Pantagruel, and an English sage named Thaumastes. The debate is conducted before a large audience entirely through the medium of gestures. What the gestures mean is apparently known only to the two contestants, but the audience attends in fascination to a most impressive gush of kinesic gobbledygook. The language of mystification has been reduced to its most elemental form—a set of esoteric signals known only to the initiated. The audience, rather than risking the appearance of ignorance, supposes profundity where there is only conspiracy.

Book Three is an extended exposé of the absurdities that result when language becomes incestuous. Panurge is undecided about whether to marry, and thereby run the risk of being cuckolded. He seeks advice from a host of "authorities," each of whom manages to leave him unsatisfied. Never have so many words been bandied with such meager results. Never have the ambiguities and equivocations inherent in the use of language been so thoroughly explored. Never have the hidden agendas and semantic traps been dramatized with such ebullience. Each answer that Panurge receives is a kind of verbal Rohrschach that he and his friends surround with wordy speculations. They talk and talk and talk in an interminable parody of feudal metaphysics. It is the ultimate *reductio ad absurdum,* the final refutation, the last death gasp of an outworn epistemology based on verbal improvisation.

At the climax of the book, when the adventurers finally put the question to the oracle of the Holy Bottle, the oracle answers with a single word— *Drink!*—a syllable open to many interpretations.

But I submit that one of the possibilities is that people ought to seek wisdom in the world around them, not in the pronouncements of some authority or in the pages of sacred text. Words, which may either clarify or becloud, must be regarded with the kind of detachment that they deserve. They are tools and playthings, not gods. For sanity's sake, man must make the extensional attitude a way of life. Only thus can he hope to avoid the thousand and one symbolic banana peels that wait to make fools of us all.

Irving Lee once described what the ideal semantically sophisticated man was like. Probably he has not yet come of age, but when he does, I am persuaded that he will be able to trace his ancestry back to Rabelais and those irrepressible giants of his imagination.

Part III

VARIATIONS

J. Samuel Bois, Ph.D., lectured at Korzybski's seminars in
1947, 1948, 1949, and replaced him, after his death, at the
1950 summer seminar. He is the author of four books on general semantics: *Explorations in Awareness* (1957), *The Art of
Awareness* (1966), *Communication as Creative Experience*
(1968), and *Breeds of Men* (now in press).

24

A MEDITATION ON WIGO

J. SAMUEL BOIS

In the Viewpoints Institute version of General Semantics, the parabola of
the Structural Differential is taken to represent, not the "scientific object" as
Korzybski intended, but the whole space-time cosmic process, described as
WIGO (*What Is Going On*).

Because of its all-encompassing generality—its high-order-abstraction status
—it has relevance to our participating in any situation, including a conference.

THERE are various ways of describing the ongoing character of the
cosmic process, of which we are both participants and observers.

We are first participants, just as any other happening—long or short,
small or large, slow moving or flashing by—participates in the flow of
space-time ongoings. From the electron to the atom, from the atom to the
molecule, from the molecule to the cell, from the cell to the organism, participation is a common characteristic of whatever exists in the fullness of
the cosmos.

We are observers as well. The first observer was the plant, with its low
degree of awareness. It reacts to direct stimulation by mobilizing the energies of its formative tendencies beyond the intensity of the impact of the
stimulus. It takes into account what impinges upon its functioning and stirs
it to further growth. It is not passively related to the rest of the cosmos; it
relates itself by a display of energetic resources that reside within its organism.

Animals are keener observers. They take into account what lies at a dis-

227

tance in space and in time: they see and hear what happens far from where they stand, they remember, and they foresee, they relate to events that require interpretation of sensory intake, they react to threats and to petting, they perform wooing dances, they build nests, they protect and train their young.

Man's power of observation is greater still. He is conscious of his awareness, expresses this consciousness in the symbols, rituals, laws, and institutions that he creates. These creations in turn react upon their maker, in an ascending spiral of ever widening loops that trace the limits of the world in which he lives. In man, the observer's role brings the participant's role to levels of possibilities that know no limits but those that he himself accepts as the ultimate stages of his own developemnt.

We recognize that the zest, which is living within us, springs from a fundamental urge that pervades the universe, and is identical with the creative force active everywhere in nature. How to describe that form of energy that keeps the cosmic process going?

Depending at what level it was observed, at what period of history it was studied, in what cultural milieu it was taken into account, and for what purpose it was brought to bear upon human activities, it was given different names. Seen under its most general aspects, it was called the "formative tendency" by L. L. Whyte, the "within" of things by Pierre Teilhard de Chardin, the "evolutionary urge" in popular literature. At the level of living forms, including man, Henri Bergson called it "life's momentum" (*élan vital*), and Hermann Keyserling recognized it in the *gana* that is accepted as the hidden determinant of choice and behavior by the people of South America. At the level of psychological functioning, Freud saw it as the *libido* or pleasure principle, Adler described it as the drive for power, Jung called it individuation in the making, and Sylvan Tomkins speaks of it as the dynamic "central assembly" of all drives, affects, values, and conditioning, the integrating power of which Penfield locates in the centrencephalon.

Unspecified and omnipotent, the urge operates in the cosmos as a whole. Specific and limited, it manifests itself in a definitive locus, in a cluster of point-events, in an individual organism, or in a group of organisms in a mutual exchange of vital energies. Man can attune himself to the power of this all-embracing energy by whatever is accepted for this end in his cultural environment; by contemplation at the silent level as suggested by Polanyi and Korzybski, by entering into a mystical trance like the dervishes, by invoking the muses in mythological practice, by praying to the Holy Ghost in the Christian dispensation, or by allowing oneself to commune with the totality of what is going on in a peak experience. It then becomes conscious participation in life's momentum, in the formative tendency, in the evolutionary urge that brings about new emergences. In man, it is being-cognition (Maslow), where observer and the participant roles fuse into a transcending experience. If the flower could be aware of its transformation into a fruit, and if the fruit could be conscious of its growing and ripening, they would have that kind of experience. Man, the self-reflexive form of life, can attune himself to it, contribute to its development, and give it added momentum and direction. This is the source of all creative productions, including scientific advances, artistic masterpieces, and constructive initiatives in human development.

We may picture this urge of creativeness, this dynamic "within" of everything that exists, as a pure activity, sufficient unto itself, self-sustaining and self-propelling. We may see science, works of art, institutions, skills, accumulated experience, etc., as visible, tangible, measurable byproducts of this activity. The activity of being alive, of enjoying life and enhancing it would then be its own justification, as when we say, "It's good to be alive!" The tree does not simply produce fruit; it must "enjoy" being alive and functioning as a system of biochemical exchanges and transformations; its fruit is the by-product of the ongoing activity. Lovers are not planning to "make" a child; they simply enjoy making love, and a child may come out as a by-product of their experience. The artist is not laboriously building a work of art; he is functioning as a participant in the beauty of the cosmic adventure, and he expresses his experience in a painting, a sculpture, a symphony, a poem, or an essay. The leader of an army is not so much "conquering" another country; he is satisfying his own and his nation's appetite for power. The financier is not hoarding millions as a miser; he is expanding himself in values that are widely recognized and negotiable for almost anything he may want.

The process of evolution, in the cosmos as a whole and in each of us when we pursue our individuation—as Jung put it—is not merely a growth in size within a set of unchanging dimensions; it is a transformation to more and more complex orders of dimensionality and existence. It is not simply an enrichment of an established pattern of living; it is a series of successive emergences of new structures, each new one transcending its predecessor, from the atom to the molecule, from the molecule to the cell, from the cell to the organ, from the organ to the organism, and so on through all forms of life, until the growing tip of the cosmos has reached a level of self-reflexiveness, of which man is the most outstanding specimen that we know. This self-reflexiveness is for him a constant invitation to experiment with the forms of life that surround him, and with himself as well, curious as he is to see what happens to the evolutionary process when he puts his hand to it.

Our role as observers becomes a groping kennetic inquiry, a search for richer formulations, a ceaseless creation of new meanings that become, as they materialize, the structural constituents of our world-in-becoming. Bringing substance out of itself and integrating it in firm orders of existence is seen as the central creative function of this self-renewing activity. As the wood of the tree is the by-product of the activity of the sap that it locks in definite channels, so theories and institutions are by-products of man's creative energies, which they channelize and direct to produce the fruits of our culture.

In the light of this scheme of thinking, we evaluate people and events differently. They are "normal" to the extent that they yield to the evolutionary urge and facilitate its implosion to richer and richer orders of existence. Those who seem to slow down this process, or to stop it temporarily, cannot stop it for good, because this procses is the basic reality that makes their very interference possible. They are, in spite of themselves, an expression of what they resist.

We have seen wars between two nations that brought their mutual relation to a clashing climax, and eventually turned it into one of friendship and cooperation. Wars of religion, after centuries of bloodshed and arguments, become ecumenical encounters where formerly estranged parties grow to a better understanding of the oneness of humankind beyond the narrow borders of their own warring field. Each World War of this century was followed by a more keenly felt need to bring the world of humans together, first by the improvised invention of a League of Nations, and later by the creation of the United Nations with a surrounding cluster of quietly effective agencies.

And so, the world goes on. We accept it, trusting that, whatever are the present strains and sufferings, the final outcome will be victory in a metamorphosis that we can only hope for, without being able to picture to ourselves what it will be like when it comes. The beauty and the appropriateness of what was timely yesterday is no indication of its permanence. To keep it in existence may be doing violence to the vital forces; it may be an unwitting attempt to stop the formative tendency in its forward thrust. Destruction of obsolete characteristics becomes a constructive aspect of the ongoing process, a necessary condition of its advance. To accept this way of looking at the world, and to make our behavior conform to it, becomes the self-fulfilling activity of whoever and whatever functions where it belongs and as it should in the space-time WIGO. In such an acceptance we shall find peace of mind and joy in the heart. It goes with the feeling that one's job of the moment is done and new opportunities are opening up in the unknown that keeps welcoming you tomorrow and tomorrow.

This is also a way of envisaging death. Here the term covers both the total death of the self and the partial death of any segment of the self. The practice of this partial death, accepted as a normal condition of living, means detachment or readiness to give up anything that was held in high value for a time. When I go back to the days of my total belief in the Christian version of human experience, I recognize a reference to this mystery of death and rebirth in certain words of Paul the apostle. *Quotidie morior,* "I die every day," he said once. Elsewhere he wrote: *Mihi vivere Christus est, and mori lucrum,* which could be translated, in modern terms: "For me, to live is to act the Christ function—i.e., the function of a conscious and willing participant-observer in the ongoing cosmos—and to die is a gain."

George A. Borden received his B.A. in 1958, his M.A. in 1959 in Mathematics, and an M.A. in 1962 in Communication Methodology from the University of Denver. He received his Ph.D. from Cornell University in 1964 in the field of speech behavior, with minors in mathematical sociology, rhetoric and public address. He coauthored *Speech Behavior and Human Interaction* (1969), and is presently Associate Professor of Speech and Assistant to the Vice-President for Research at the Pennsylvania State University.

25

RELEVANT AREAS OF RESEARCH IN HUMAN COMMUNICATION*

GEORGE A. BORDEN

THE structuring of human-communication research, as detailed in this paper, allows the researcher to orient himself in relation to the whole field of human-communicative behavior. It also indicates that in order to do a thorough job of research in any specific area, he must consider both the individual's communicative system, and how it fits into the larger social discourse system. The researcher may choose any area he desires to study, but he should be aware of its relationship to the other areas of human-communication research.

There are many competent scholars working in the area of human-communication research.[1-11] Yet the state of the art indicates that much still needs to be done to generate a unified effort. In short, we do not have an overall structure to guide us in our research efforts. Thus, most researchers define concepts to suit their own biases and do research in isolated little areas with no thought of how the information they are gathering fits into an overall theory of communication.

If we go back to the beginning of communication research, we find that Warren Weaver introduced two very important concepts into the study of

---

* Although this paper does not deal with general semantics as such, it is relevant in important respects. This and other papers in this volume represent the difficulty that scholars have in writing about the communication process—something very fluid, dynamic, and without precise boundary lines. General semanticists may not recognize the communication process as having the dichotomies and sharp dividing lines Dr. Borden is calling for here.—E. MURRAY

human communication when he called a communique, before it is transmitted, a message,[12] i.e., one has a certain sphere of meaning he would like to evoke in another's mind, and after it is transmitted, a signal, i.e., the symbol "dog" becomes a signal that evokes the image and/or all the connotations you have of the referent to this symbol. The transformations that occur in the process of sending and receiving this signal with its pre- and post-messages can be illustrated using mathematical transformations.[13] The important idea here is the dichotomy between internal and external phases of what we have come to call the human-communication process. The relationships that prevail between the external signal and the internal message are the specific concern of general semantics. Thus, it is felt that an explication of the ramifications of this dichotomy in human-communication theory will be relevant to the student of general semantics.

This dichotomy can be further clarified by saying that man is a system composed of a receiver, a processor, and a transmitter. The two observable components of this system, the receiver and transmitter, are the best understood of the three components. Human communication may then be defined from either side of the system. If one receives information that affects one's processing unit, communication has occurred, though the individual may be the only one who knows about it. On the other hand, if we transmit information that we know is received by another living being, then we know we have "communicated," though we cannot be sure what message we have evoked. Thus there is a signal, consciously or unconsciously transmitted, which is an integral part of every instance of human communication. From this fact we must infer that there is also an internal processing unit that transforms this signal into a meaningful message to the receiver. Two relevant areas of research, then, are (1) analysis of the transmitted signal, and (2) investigation of the internal processing unit.

If we are to understand why one behaves the way one does in a communication situation, we must have some understanding of the system that enables an individual to communicate the way he does. We know that this system has to do with cognitive structures and neurological processes. We may call it the psychoneurological phase of the human-communication process, while the system involving two or more individuals would be more appropriately referred to as the psychosociological phase. These terms indicate that the individual's psyche is the human aspect that forms the bond between the individual and the entire human-communication process. At the same time, the terms neurological and sociological indicate that these are the approaches that seem to be the most relevant in studying these two aspects of the human-communication process. These are not the only approaches, however. We should all be aware of the advances in the biological and physiological studies of the individual, and the advances in anthropological and linguistic studies of the social aspects of this process.

If we turn our attention to the system that enables the individual to communicate, we may glimpse some of the areas that are currently delineated for study by specific disciplines. Perhaps the most profitable approach for this survey is to follow the natural course of events in a normal communicative happening.[14] Of necessity, we are truncating this act of communication, for we recognize that the communication process is a continuous process beginning sometime around birth (depending upon your level of investigation), and ending sometime around death (again depending upon your level of investigation). To make a discrete act out of this continuous function will distort the observable process, but may also lead to some clarifying insights.

We shall take our slice out of the human-communication process so it includes only one individual, begins with his reception of a signal, and ends with his response to the message evoked by this signal. Thus we will be dealing exclusively with the internal phase of the human-communication process. This means that we will look at the individual as a collector, processor, and disseminator of information. Since the study of these three phases of the human-communication process is one way of determining why a person reacts to a signal the way he does, this study becomes immediately relevant to general semantics.

The collection of information is accomplished by our sense organs, which transform the received signal into neurological signals, and sends them to the brain. Of course, each sense organ is a specialist and will register only certain kinds of data. It is also clear that each has a signal detection threshold that may be increased or decreased by one's mental activity or perhaps by processes intrinsic to that organ. There is still some controversy over whether a sense organ picks up and relays to the brain all information impinging upon it.[15] The relation of knowledge about the sensing (reception) process to an understanding of the human-communication process should be obvious.

As the neurological signal leaves the sense organ and travels to the brain, it may be blocked, inhibited, amplified, or modified in some other way by the neurological action emanating from our own central nervous system.[16,17] The possibility that the neurological signal transmitted by the sense organ is not the same as the neurological signal received by the brain has many implications for the human-communication theorist. What we have commonly classified as prejudice, psychological set, and cultural set are all learned, and definitely affect the signals that the brain receives.[18,19] The results of brain damage are all too obvious. Knowledge of the various centers in the brain that direct much of the action in the central nervous system is also necessary for one who is studying the individual's communication system.[20]

When the neurological signal finally reaches the brain, one should know something about how this information is stored and retrieved. Our understanding of this aspect of the individual's communication system is currently going through great turmoil. Psychologists are doing experiments to determine the psychological characteristics of short-term memory, apparently with little concern for the neurological aspects of the phenomena. It is also difficult to ascertain from many of their experiments whether they are working with memory (storage), or memory (recall).[21] Most of the work in long-term memory is being done by learning theorists and physicians, but here, too, one is not always sure what aspect of memory is being dealt with.[22–24]

On the other hand, neurologists are making strides toward understanding how information is stored in the brain. Exciting studies in the behavior of RNA and its effect on protein production have given a possible biochemical basis for short-term and long-term memory (storage). The interference with protein formation prevents one from learning (the development of long-term memory).[25] However, these studies are telling us precious little about the recall mechanisms that allow us to use the information we have stored. This aspect of the individual's communication system is in need of research. Perhaps it will have to wait until we know more about the storage process. At present, we will have to look to the answers given to us by psychological research methods. This may be the most critical area of research at the present time.

Psychological research indicates that our mental processes are in a continuing search for equilibrium—mental balance. We develop mental states such as beliefs, desires, and fears by the accumulation and interrelating of information by our neurological processes. The innate goal of our mental system is to maintain harmony among various aspects of these beliefs, desires, and fears. As new data arrives, and either agrees or disagrees with previously stored data, it will reinforce or disrupt those mental states. A certain degree of cognitive dissonance will be tolerated, but when it exceeds this limit the "mind" must reduce it.[26,27] Rationalizing, finding more information, or refusing to accept the dissonance-arousing information are some of the ways this is done. What information we will or will not accept, as well as our mental states, has a profound influence on our communicative behavior. What we talk about, how we talk about it, and how we accept other's opinions are all determined to some extent by our state of mind. Psychoanalysts and psychiatrists can give us much insight into this aspect of the individual's communication system. Finding out more about attitudinal frames of reference is a very important area of research.

When one tries to understand how these mental states develop, and what is occurring during thought processes in general, one is led to the studies being done on concept and language development in children.[28-32] There is much research being done on how a child internalizes speech, and some on how this develops his thought processes. However, practically nothing is being done to study the effect of nonverbal cues on the development of mental states in a child. Yet it would appear that since a child has learned a great deal about human behavior by the time he develops much language behavior, he must have picked up this knowledge via the nonverbal signals he has received. His ability to communicate anger, pleasure, desire, or dislike are all developed prior to overt linguistic competence. One wonders what effect these nonverbal memories (unrecallable for the most part) have on future personality and, therefore, the communicative behavior of the maturing individual. Thus the ontogenetic aspects of the human-communication process must also be researched.

An individual's ability to speak and write (his verbal behavior), as well as his mannerisms in dress, gestures, and physical bearing (his nonverbal behavior)—in short, how he transmits information—are very important ingredients in the individual's communication system. The way in which these ingredients are integrated into this system is usually studied in conjunction with studies in concept and language development. However, there need to be more studies that look at this phase of the individual's communication system. The study of the relationships that exist between verbal and nonverbal behavior suffered considerable damage by the overzealousness of some elocutionists of the past two centuries. However, these relationships plus the cognitive processes underlying these behavior patterns need to be investigated in greater depth.[33]

There are many ways of organizing studies dealing with the transmission phase of the individual's communication system. One such way is as follows: We may consider whether a signal is conscious or unconscious, intended or unintended, sign or symbol, affective or substantive, vocal or nonvocal, verbal or nonverbal. These dichotomies may be linked together in almost any chain one desires. One such chain is a conscious, intended, affective, vocal, nonverbal sign, e.g., crying.

Perhaps a word should be said about each possible link in this chain.

Given enough time to think, one could come up with an example for each of the many possible chains. Many times the same example will work for more than one chain by simply indicating whether the communicator is conscious of his act, or whether he intended it or not. Many things we do are consciously unintended; others are unconsciously intended, etc. A sign is an integral part of the event that is being transmitted, while a symbol represents something "in" our cognitive structures. Effective signals are transmitted to convey how the communicator feels about a subject, while substantive signals are used to convey objective information about the subject. Vocal and nonvocal have to do with the mode of transmission and, as can be seen, either of these modes may use verbal or nonverbal codes. The verbal code uses words and syntax to evoke meaning, while the nonverbal code, though it may be closely related to words and syntax, e.g., paralinguistics, evokes meaning without the use of words.

Communicative output presupposes the existence of a communicatee and some type of communication environment. In this way, the individual's communication system becomes involved with the larger social discourse system. The various types of environments available could be listed, and social discourse studied by investigating the role each environment plays. However, we would like to concentrate a little more on the overall human-communication process. To do this, we shall consider the three levels of social discourse in which an individual may find himself: interaction, intercourse, and intercontextual.

The first level of social discourse has the least involvement of the individual. It may be characterized by the social greeting we sometimes receive from strangers on a street or the idle chitchat at a cocktail party. You are cognizant of the fact that another human is interacting with you either verbally or nonverbally, but this has little or no meaning to you in your overall view of self and the world around you. It has very little, if any, effect on your total behavior. The dictionary definition of interaction is: "action on each other, reciprocal action or effect." There is no long range meaning evoked at this level.

The operational difficulties we have with the interaction level of social discourse stem largely from the fact that incidental communicative happenings have a way of becoming meaningful happenings without our realizing it. This immediately pushes them up into the next level of social discourse. This level is the level at which we are affected immediately. However, the overall effect may decay rapidly and, in and of itself, has very little long range effect on one's behavior. The majority of one's daily communicative encounters fit into this level. The information we receive and transmit has meaning to us in that there is a conscious feeling of responsibility for the communicative behavior we exhibit. The dictionary term that subsumes these characteristics best is "intercourse," i.e., "dealing between or among people; interchange of products, services, ideas, feelings, etc." This level carries with it a definite feeling of involvement with other beings.

The involvement that the researcher is interested in, on this level, is that of the effect of the signal on the listener. As such, most of the research efforts of the speech discipline over the past two centuries and of rhetoricians for the past 2,500 years falls into this level of social discourse. In fact, we might have called this the "rhetorical" level rather than "intercourse," except that it would be more difficult to dissuade people from their various definitions of rhetoric than it is to get them past the one overriding connotation of intercourse. (And when sexual intercourse is considered in the structure of social discourse given in this paper, it properly falls in the intercourse level.) The main influencing ingredient in this level, then, is the signal sent by the communicator and received by the communicatee.

The final level may be considered as the accumulation of many instances on the intercourse level. On this level, we are interested in the entire phenomenological happening. Thus we look at the entire process of social discourse. This includes the context of past events, the present situation including the physiological, biological, and mental states of the communicants, the cultural and social settings, and the immediate physical situation in which the social discourse takes place. One also considers the short and long range effects this specific episode has on the members involved. Thus, we may designate this the "intercontextual" level since the main concern is with the interrelationships among all the contextual elements of the human-communication process. This type of research is nearly impossible to do with any kind of experimental validity.[34,35] However, its results are often the most interesting of all, and certainly the most meaningful in an historical sense.

Of the three levels, the intercourse level is the most productive of scientific studies. This is probably due to the nature of the ingredients involved. Since the main variable is the signal passing between communicator and cummunicatee, one can construct the chain of signal characteristics that he would like to study, and devise a study that will illuminate these particular aspects. With the advent of the electronic computer into the field of natural language analysis, many new possibilities present themselves to the investigator of this level of social discourse. As the results of well designed studies accumulate, the general semanticist will find he has the relevant data to substantiate or rebuild his theories of human reaction to communicative signals. Thus we may conclude that most studies of the human-communication process are relevant to the field of general semantics.

REFERENCES

1. Andersen, Martin. "A Mid-Century Survey of Books on Communication," *The Journal of Communication* (December, 1964), pp. 203–214.
2. Barker, Larry and Wiseman, Gordon. "A Model of Intrapersonal Communication," *The Journal of Communication* (September, 1966), pp. 172–179.
3. Berlo, David. *The Process of Communication*. New York: Holt, Rinehart and Winston, 1960.
4. Cherry, Colin. *On Human Communication*. New York: John Wiley & Sons, 1957.
5. Dance, Frank (ed.). *Human Communication Theory*. New York: Holt, Rinehart and Winston, 1967.
6. Driessel, A. Berkley. "Communications Theory and Research Strategy: A Metatheoretical Analysis," *The Journal of Communication* (June, 1967), pp. 92–108.
7. Gerbner, George. "On Defining Communication: Still Another View," *The Journal of Communication* (June, 1966), pp. 99–103.
8. Miller, George. *Language and Communication*. New York: McGraw-Hill Book Co., 1963.
9. Miller, Gerald. "On Defining Communication: Another Stab," *The Journal of Communication* (June, 1966), pp. 88–98.
10. Shannon, Claude, and Weaver, Warren. *The Mathematical Theory of Communication*. Urbana, Ill.: The University of Illinois Press, 1962.
11. Thayer, Lee. "On Theory-Building in Communication: I. Some Conceptual Problems," *The Journal of Communication* (December, 1963), pp. 217–235.
12. Weaver, Warren. "The Mathematics of Communication," *Scientific American* (July, 1949), pp. 11–15.
13. Borden, George. "Mathematical Transformations and Communication Theory," *The Journal of Communication* (June, 1963), pp. 87–93.
14. Borden, George, Gregg, Richard, and Grove, Theodore. *Speech Behavior and Human Interaction*. Englewood Cliffs, N.J.: Prentice-Hall, Inc., 1969.
15. Rosenblith, Walter (ed.). *Sensory Communication*. Cambridge, Mass.: The MIT Press, 1961.
16. Eccles, Sir John. "The Synapse," *Scientific American* (January, 1965), pp. 56–66.
17. Melzack, Ronald. "The Perception of Pain," *Scientific American* (February, 1961), pp. 41–49.
18. Rokeach, Milton. *The Open and Closed Mind*. New York: Basic Books, Inc., 1960.
19. Whorf, Benjamin Lee. *Language, Thought and Reality*. New York: John Wiley & Sons, Inc., 1962.
20. French, J. D. "The Reticular Formation," *Scientific American* (May, 1957).
21. Peterson, Lloyd. "Short-Term Memory," *Scientific American* (July, 1966) pp. 90–95.

22. Gagné, Robert. *The Conditions of Learning.* New York: Holt, Rinehart and Winston, Inc., 1965.
23. Nielsen, J. M. *Memory and Amnesia.* Los Angeles: San Lucas Press, 1958.
24. Penfield, Wilder, and Roberts, Lamar. *Speech and Brain-Mechanisms.* Princeton: Princeton University Press, 1959.
25. Kimble, Daniel (ed.). *The Anatomy of Memory.* Palo Alto, Calif.: Science and Behavior Books, Inc., 1966.
26. Festinger, Leon. *A Theory of Cognitive Dissonance.* Stanford, Calif.: Stanford University Press, 1957.
27. Osgood, Charles; Suci, George; and Tannenbaum, Percy. *The Measurement of Meaning.* Urbana, Ill.: University of Illinois Press, 1961.
28. Bellugi, U., and Brown, R. (eds.). *The Acquisition of Language.* Monographs of the Society for Research in Child Development. Yellow Springs, Ohio: Antioch Press, 1964.
29. Piaget, Jean. *The Construction of Reality in the Child.* Translated by Margaret Cook. New York: Basic Books, 1954.
30. Lenneberg, Eric. *The Biological Foundations of Language.* New York: John Wiley & Sons, 1967.
31. Luria, Alexander. *The Role of Speech in the Regulation of Normal and Abnormal Behavior.* New York: Liveright Publishing Corp., 1961.
32. Vygotsky, L. S. *Thought and Language.* Edited and Translated by Eugenia Hanfmann and Gertrude Vakar. New York: John Wiley & Sons, Inc., 1962.
33. Knapp, Peter (ed.). *Expression of the Emotions in Man.* New York: International Universities Press, 1963.
34. Goffman, Erving. *The Presentation of Self in Everyday Life.* Garden City, N.Y.: Doubleday-Anchor, 1959.
35. Hall, Edward. *The Silent Language.* Greenwich, Conn.: Premier Books, 1959.

Deems M. Brooks is currently Assistant Professor, Department of Speech, Florida State University, Tallahassee, and is serving as the Director of Speech Education. He received his Ph.D. from Southern Illinois University in 1968.

Thomas J. Pace, Jr. conducts the work in Interpersonal Communication, Department of Speech at Southern Illinois University. He received his Ph.D. at the University of Denver, did postdoctoral work in Speech and in Philosophy at Northwestern University, and was a member of an Institute of General Semantics Seminar.

26

CREATIVE INTERCHANGE, HENRY NELSON WIEMAN'S CONTRIBUTION*

DEEMS M. BROOKS and THOMAS J. PACE

THE theories of Henry Nelson Wieman and Alfred Korzybski are both based upon a process notion of reality. Where Korzybski was primarily concerned with instrumental meaning—structure, order, relations—Wieman is equally concerned with both qualitative meanings and instrumental meanings. Where Korzybski was concerned with neurolinguistic behaviors which hinder proper evaluation, Wieman is concerned with the creative structure of events. For Weiman, creative interchange combines qualitative and instrumental meanings that are carried by expressive, evaluative, and designative symbols, both verbal and nonverbal. This paper is primarily concerned with Wieman's concept of creative interchange, and its contribution to communication.

What do we ordinarily mean when we use the word "creative" to describe a thought, a person, or an event? Can creativity be forced, planned, or controlled? Or, is there within the interaction of words, thoughts, and

---

* One of our most eminent philosophers, Wieman once told me that, after attending two of Korzybski's seminars, it became necessary for him to drastically revise much of his previous work. "Creative interchange" became the central theme around which he organized his "new" philosophy. In creative interchange, he included much of the general semantics methodology as it bears on interpersonal communication in the exchange of ideas. However, he went further than this; he included the exchange of goods as well as of ideas. His work is especially satisfying to some religionists. This paper reports on several facets of Dr. Wieman's work in language.—E. MURRAY.

events a continuous process beyond direct human control which has positive value? Wieman, an empirical theologian, claims there is such a process. He used the term "creative interchange" to denote the underlying structure within human existence that creates, sustains, and transforms human consciousness in positive directions.

"Nature," for Wieman, is the all-inclusive reality that encompasses all that has been, is, or ever can be. All that has occurred, is occurring, or may ever occur, so far as may be determined, is in the realm of natural events. Knowledge is about natural events. This is why Wieman calls his naturalism a "metaphysics of events." [1] While man can never know all there is to know about the whole of nature, he can inquire into the actual functioning of events as they occur in reality. This view leaves no room for claims to knowledge about ultimate categories, such as Spirit (Plato), Ultimate Being (Aristotle), or Absolute Idea (Hegel), unless they can be shown to have observable consequences in empirical reality.

All of nature is a dynamic, ongoing, unfinished process—a composite of interacting events. [2] The basic unit of nature experienced by the person is an intuited structure of sense and feeling. This basic unit of human awareness, known as quality, is the conjunction of all the strands of nature, including the human mind, necessary to experience an event. Quality is no less objective than subjective since "our own organisms and minds do not have the qualities in themselves any more than do the other strands in the conjunction when taken severally." [3] For example, sunlight streams through the window and a feeling–sense of warmth is experienced. Quality experienced in this way is a convergence of sunlight, window, conditions within the room, a human body, and so on, each maintained in a certain relation to the other. The quality of warmth is everchanging because the sunlight, window, conditions within the room, and the human body are constantly changing with concurrent changes among these relations.

Wieman asserts that "there is nothing in reality [including other minds] accessible to the human mind more basic than events and their qualities and relations. (*Relations* is another word for *structure*.)" [4] The "onward flow of nature," whereby the novel comes into actual existence, exemplifies the process nature of reality. [5] Change in quality is continuous, but by abstraction its structure may be divided into segments for purposes of understanding, explanation, and control.

Structures intuited in immediate awareness, specified by abstract linguistic signs, is a means of taming the flux and flow of events that would otherwise be meaningless to man. Perceiving structure in events is a kind of "cutting-up" of experience. This perceiving, otherwise called "selectivity of attention," is determined by "biological reactions, by the system of linguistic signs, by the physical instruments, and by the cultural demands of time and place." [6]

All events of nature are "happenings in transit, not finished products." [7] For man to be able to experience change (i.e., to experience reality) there must be a "structure, law, or form which does not change." For example, the table that appears relatively unchanging is, in fact, in process— through constant wear and tear, its gradual decomposition, damage, and so on, until the table eventually becomes a different structure. "But each structure, so long as it characterizes the change, is changeless . . . in the sense that it preserves the identity of the something-or-other which is changing." [8]

Knowledge of process events is possible because there is one thing which does not change, and that is the "enduring structure of change," [9] or stated another way, the *purposive continuity* of change. Wieman gives this the name of "creativity" at the organic level, and calls it "creative interchange" at the level of human language. He says: "There is something which retains its identity and its unity through all change in itself and through all changes in other things." While other events come and go, the creative event "has a certain identity and unity throughout all its manifestations, namely, the character of being creative of all the changing orders of the world so far as they are accessible to human life at all." [10]

Creativity is the formative structure within change, making it possible to preserve the identity of events by way of their changing qualities and relations, thus giving value and a sense of continuity to the human level of existence.

The transformational nature of the structure of reality means that abstract linguistic structures, used to represent reality, must be creatively transformed "in adaptation to this continuous flow of nature." [11] Meaning then becomes "any order of events and possibilities which can be brought to conscious awareness by means of some present happening which is a sign representing this order." [12]

Linguistic structures used to represent a network of events and their qualities are man's attempt to quantify quality, to distinguish qualities for instrumental purposes. Quality is a primitive, largely unconscious, valuing activity whereby sense and feeling pertaining to experienced events are intuitively structured by the human organism. When the felt and sensed quality can be represented by a verbal or nonverbal sign, it is qualitative meaning. Instrumental meaning gives more attention to the order, relations, or structure than to the qualitative experience. Qualitative meaning yields intrinsic value in a structure of thought and feeling now intuited, whether it be of past events or future possibilities.

Instrumental value is a result of the individual's felt need to predict and control events. The myriad interconnections of feelings and events, their interminable interrelations both past and future, are ignored for some instrumental end. Instrumental and intrinsic value are usually mixed in actual experience. And they should be mixed, since both are essential to healthy living. But one of the most serious problems of our way of life is the tendency to bifurcate the world into mutually exclusive realms of instrumental and intrinsic value.[13] However, intrinsic value and instrumental value become integrated when "organic attitudes, meanings, and physical conditions" are related to a larger end that is sought so as to produce further values.[14] Wieman says that "specifiable structures (truth) and structures specified (knowledge) can have richness and depth of qualitative meaning only when they keep close to the matrix of structured events as determined by the feeling–reactions of the organism." [15]

The way of progressive impoverishment of human life, until it becomes unendurable, is to give first place to the relatively barren structures uncovered by science and philosophy. Knowledge, then, is a great value when it is used to provide the conditions for men to communicate freely their valuing perspectives. Creative communication cannot be controlled, in that linguistic signs are capable of indefinite expansion of meanings in ways not foreseen by those using them. That men will communicate more creatively and freely under certain conditions can be predicted, "but we cannot predict the specific system of meanings that will emerge from this creative communication." [16]

By restoring the qualitative meaning of events, man is able to communicate in varying degrees his intersubjective value perspectives and feeling–awarenesses about events in community with others. It is just this kind of communication which creates human life, a home with love, and which makes a government based on cooperative effort possible. Creative communication among scientists and scholars is what creates the kind of fellowship, trust, mutual effort, and cooperation that leads to new knowledge and discoveries.[17]

Since man is an outgrowth of nature, his customs and values are subject to descriptive analysis by empirical means just as surely as the amoeba can be analyzed under the microscope. To be sure, there are differences: (1) in the nature of what is observed under the microscope and a value situation, (2) in the finer details of the methods of observation and description of each, and (3) between mere description and correlation of means and ends. The third point needs further clarification.

The valuing activity of the microbiologist who analyzes the destructive nature of cancer cells may be instrumental in the immediate situation. He is certainly intent on discovering structures of possibility that can be put into the form of propositions to be tested for further knowledge. But why inquire into the nature of anything if not to add to the totality of knowledge which increases the creative good of life so that wider ranges of mutual appreciation, understanding, and control are possible despite barriers of diversity. The means used to discover knowledge are inextricably connected with the larger ends of human life regardless of the explicit statements of the researcher who insists that he is only doing "scientific" research where no valuing enters into his project.

Some decision about the larger ends and overall direction of human life has to be made. Not to decide is to be carried along by the processes of life already operant. Decisions regarding the direction of human life cannot be avoided because, "if we refuse to decide, we shall nevertheless be establishing a way of life by drifting into it." [18] Wieman maintains that "the deadly miasma from which to escape is the state of mind that denies any criteria for better and worse that applies to all history and all society." [19]

By utilizing the empirical method for treating questions of good and evil (i.e., correlation of means–ends), value can be analyzed within the contextual situation of natural experience. According to Wieman, there is no subjective appeal to either the human or divine mind, no justification of either a transcendental abstract essence or transcendental concrete reality, not merely a correlation between desiring mind and thing desired. Valuation of the good or evil of an event or course of action is verified in relation to a natural, situational, and observable complex-of-events. Consequently, "no single event . . . is either good or evil when taken by itself." [20] To discover good or evil one must either relate the total event to "other events" or "break the total event down into subevents." Any event when so analyzed can be found to have better and worse relations within it.

Creative communication can be identified by its four subevents. The person himself can reflect on his communication in various situations and determine to some degree whether creativity has occurred. Creative communication includes: (1) emerging of new qualitative meaning in one's mind, (2) integrating of that meaning within one's mind, (3) expanding of the range of one's appreciable world, and (4) a deepening of community with those who shared in this communication. Unless all four occur, it is not "creative." [21] By "community," Wieman means the kind of appreciative understanding which, at best, leads to mutual control.

Creative interchange, according to Wieman, provides a methodology for communication research and practice that correlates the demands of both experience and reason, that will be open to further testing, revisions and clarification, and that will avoid waste of human resources by refusing to rely on principles or theories not accessible to inquiry.

In Summary: All of reality, in Wieman's view, is a dynamic, ongoing, unfinished process. All human experience of reality consists of natural events. Events are known by their qualities and relations. Qualitative meaning is an intuited structure of thought and feeling, which can be represented by a sign, and which yields a heightened awareness of the aesthetic qualities of an event. Instrumental meaning gives more attention to the structure of an event for its utility than for its intrinsic, aesthetic value. Within the qualitative flow of human experience is the underlying formative structure of creativity which is unchanging in its continuous transformation of the human mind when right conditions are present. Creativity emerges at the symbolic level in creative interchange of both qualitative and instrumental meanings. Creativity itself generates new insight in the mind of one or more persons, as a result of the interchange of these meanings in the communicative situation.

REFERENCES

1. Wieman, Henry Nelson. Letter to James L. Adams, January 28, 1961. All unpublished materials are located in the archives of Southern Illinois University.
2: ———. *The Source of Human Good.* Carbondale: Southern Illinois University, 1946, pp. 84–85.
3. ———. *Directive in History.* New York: The Free Press, 1949, pp. 18–19. See also Wieman's, *Now We Must Choose.* New York: The Macmillan Company, 1941, p. 73.
4. ———. *The Source of Human Good,* p. 6.
5. ———. *The Wrestle of Religion with Truth.* New York: The Macmillan Company, 1928, p. 195.
6. ———. *The Source of Human Good,* p. 205.
7. *Ibid.,* p. 68.
8. ———. *Man's Ultimate Commitment.* Carbondale: Southern Illinois University, 1958, pp. 78–80. What is changing are the qualities of the event known as "table," and its relations to other events. The designative symbol does not designate a universal nor an ideal structure in those qualities and relations. But "table" does tell one that the event is harder, more durable than "candy," that the event does not decay at the same rate of speed as "apple," and that the event is much less edible than either. "Table" merely symbolizes a changing structure

that has instrumental and/or qualitative value, depending upon the selectivity of attention of the observer.

9. ———. "The Structure of Divine Creativity: Exchange of Views, II," *Iliff Review*, XIX, No. 1 (Winter, 1962), p. 37.
10. ———. *The Source of Human Good*, p. 298.
11. ———. *The Wrestle of Religion with Truth*, p. 194.
12. ———. "Confessions of a Religious Seeker." Unpublished manuscript, (n.d.), p. 56.
13. ———. *The Issues of Life*. New York: Abingdon Press, 1930, p. 115.
14. *Ibid.*
15. ———. *The Source of Human Good*, p. 172.
16. *Ibid.*, p. 219.
17. ———. Letter to Ralph Burhoe, January 19, 1957.
18. ———. "Science Serving Faith." Unpublished manuscript (n.d.), Chapter 5, p. 6.
19. ———. "Problems of Civilization." Unpublished manuscript (n.d.), Chapter 7, p. 11.
20. ———. *The Source of Human Good*, p. 84.
21. *Ibid.*, p. 58.

Alan Frederickson is an architect with offices located in Evergreen, Colorado. He is leader of the Queen City Jazz Band, which is now fifteen years old, and which has distributed three albums of their selections.

27

JAZZ IMPROVISATION*

ALAN P. FREDERICKSON

"INDIVIDUAL and collective improvisation" is a workable definition of jazz. This paper will stress the latter because of the obvious semantic significance implicit in the creative endeavor of a group, with the attendant communication problems. "Classical" music heard in our concert halls is a reproduction of the improvisation of a composer. His externalized musical intuition is expressed in a framework of reference—the printed score. The only variables available to the performers are interpretation, accuracy, and tonal quality. The conductor is awarded the lion's share of responsibility for interpretation. To the orchestra members falls the onus of managing the rest. Jazz, as I understand it, has afforded each individual musician congress with those parameters of musical production formerly reserved exclusively for the composer and conductor. Individual and collective improvisation in jazz is, idiomatically, "the name of the game."

I believe the relevance of jazz for all of us lies in its demonstrable capacity as a vehicle for self-identity perception through a musical "catharsis of emotion." (Pardon is asked here for the use of the "Aristotelian" phrase.) My experience indicates to me that as musicians we discover our makeup by becoming aware of the emotions we experience in our creative effort. As listeners, we find awareness of self-identity through empathy with the performers, and by evaluating our reactions to their music. Jazz is further capable of shoehorning us into well fitting self-identity evaluations because its performers are closer to our own time and milieu, unencumbered by the

---

* This brief discussion was followed by three demonstrations, designed to enable the audience to observe three levels of intra-band communication. The band first played a tune that they had played several times before. Then they improvised on a tune they had heard, but had not played before. Finally, they demonstrated the level of communication required when improvising on a tune invented on the spot by one of the members.—EDITOR.

greater remoteness in time of many "classical" composers. The back to back self-identity perception of performers and listeners is in turn a function of communication, intra-band and performer–listener. Without such communication, a band will be characterized as forgettable, and its audience unfulfilled.

A jazz band affords its careful listeners insight into some of the mechanics of communication. You all have some degree of awareness of how we in a band inform each other, with and without words. I'm sure you feel that our playing together is predicated on agreements. We willingly play without a printed score, that we may better reap the creative harvest made possible by freedom of expression. Since much of jazz music is in the form of (or rather the lack of form of) empirically derived musical consensus, our band relies on an internalized frame of reference. We collectively evaluate the historical treatments of a given jazz tune by those artists we revere, then decide together how we may best add to what has been done by arranging the sequence of parts (i.e., introduction, verse, chorus, vocal, solos, ending), or by adding unique figures, modulations, or breaks, by determining the key most suitable to our abilities, and by setting that tempo most expressive of our feeling about the work. All this is committed to memory, and comprises our frame of reference. A complication derives from the large number of such agreements. Our band has upward of 200 tunes in our "bag." To play a tune, our cornet player simply calls out the name, sets the tempo by tapping his foot, and we are launched. Each member then discharges his own responsibilities from memory in our collective effort.

We constantly change the tunes we play. This variety keeps our interest, and therefore our creativity alive, and forestalls the cloying nature of mechanical repetition. But to modify existing agreements, communication becomes necessary. For example, we alter the sequence of individual choruses by simply looking at the member who is the intended substitution. If a tune becomes tiresomely long or tedious, individual choruses are prematurely ended when the leader moves the bell of his horn in a circular fashion, indicating, "Let's all play together." If a duet is decided upon, a thumb motion is used by that member inviting another to join him, and if the rest of the band is to be silent, they are individually informed verbally by the more mobile member of the duet. These examples, along with many others, are simple, unsophisticated, and dependable communicative devices.

However, some explanation of the less obvious devices we employ to alter our performance may add to your awareness and understanding of intra-band communication. For example, a member may choose to play his own chorus at twice the rhythmic speed while not changing the melodic speed. He must indicate this musically to the rhythm section in the very short time it takes to play two or three pickup notes at the new tempo. The signal that we are ending the song is found in the cornet player's resolution of the melodic line, the melody being generally his responsibility. If, on the other hand, he feels that the excitement of our rendition warrants it, he does not resolve the melody but rather plays introductory notes that indicate to all of us, "One more time!"—even though we have come to the end of our usual format.

Another variation is that of changing our tradition-oriented assignment of melodic lead, voicing, and contrapuntal or "answering" parts. Although difficult to describe in words, we try to accomplish this by delivering our idea for the change to our fellow musicians by musically changing our own individual parts. It follows that we must be constantly on the alert for a change coming from them, and we do this by keeping an alert "empathy" for our fellow musicians based on an empirically derived understanding of the way each plays. This is the most complicated level of intra-band communication, and the most rewarding when it is effective. From time to time, I have approached the clarinet player to play a background duet figure in support of a soloist, called a "riff." It is rare that previous agreement exists between us as to what to play, in view of our constant search for new and untried expression. It is not often that he and I have the same musical thought at the first attempt, and then one of us joins the other in his idea. However, and this is a remarkable thing, many times we have played the identical figure the same way the first time! I am unwilling to try to explain this. I can only say that when such communication happens, it affords me a joy which ranks with the most exquisite available in this life.

Alfreda S. Galt is Secretary of the Lifwynn Foundation and
Chairman of its Editorial Committee. She took a prominent
part in completing for publication two books edited by her
husband, the late William E. Galt: *A Search for Man's Sanity
—the Selected Letters of Trigant Burrow,* and Burrow's post-
humously published work, *Preconscious Foundations of Human
Experience.* Mrs. Galt participated in an IGS seminar in 1967,
and in the Summer Seminar-Workshop at Geneseo, New York,
later that year.

28

TRIGANT BURROW: AN ALTERED
APPROACH TO UNSANITY

ALFREDA S. GALT

TRIGANT Burrow, who introduced group analysis in the early nineteen
twenties, has at times been compared to Korzybski. Like Korzybski,
Burrow adopted a broadly human approach to ineptitudes of communication, with their corollaries in the conflict and suffering of our species. A review of the parallels and divergences between these two pioneers is not
merely a matter of historical interest; Burrow's observations, like Korzybski's, may be relevant to some of the problems being considered here in
1968.

The first reports of Burrow's group researches were published in 1924
and 1925.[1] They contained a sweeping indictment of what we call "normality" in human relations, and postulated a "social neurosis" of enormous
breadth and severity. These papers came to Korzybski's attention in 1925,
and he reacted at once with an enthusiastic letter to Burrow. " . . . I take at
present *uncritically* all you say as *granted,*" he wrote. And in 1934, he
said, "Your issues are broader, mine are more narrow, but I am convinced
that the works not only do not conflict, but just the opposite, complement
each other." [2]

There were, indeed, many parallels in the interests of the two men: both
questioned the validity of what we call "normality"; both posited a general
maladaptation that involves thinking-feeling-physiology as a whole. Both associated this maladaptation with the development of symbol and language;
both spoke in terms of "verbal conditioning" or "social conditioning," and

its effect on the developing child. Both questioned right–wrong, either–or types of evaluation. Both drew attention to the internal processes of the "observer" as a factor in observation. Burrow, especially, assailed his psychoanalytic colleagues for failing to take into account their own socially sanctioned prejudices in approaching neurotic conditions. Both Burrow and Korzybski implicated habitual neural responses in problems of communication. Both developed nonverbal procedures.

Yet Burrow felt that the methods of phylobiology and general semantics make no essential contact.[3] In reading the long correspondence between Burrow and Korzybski, it is difficult to escape the conclusion that neither man fully grasped the basic concerns of the other. From the vantage point of a later generation of time-binders, perhaps we can do so.

In a description of the structural differential in *Science and Sanity,* Korzybski says, "The number of characteristics [of an object] which we ascribe to the label, by some process of 'knowing,' or 'wanting,' or 'needing,' or 'interest,' does *not* cover the number of characteristics the object has." [4]

Burrow was concerned specifically with this process of "knowing" or "wanting" or "needing" or "interest," that is crucial to what we abstract on the objective as well as on the verbal level. In other words, he was concerned with the process of attention and the factors that direct it. He wanted to understand the motivations that focus the beam of interest, and determine the features of the process world that enter awareness. The principal targets of his group research were the secret incentives and conventional criteria that ordinarily regulate and legislate our interrelational life.

Burrow describes attention as "an essentially . . . ecological process," as the neurophysiological function that "links together organism and environment." [5] His group, or phylo-, analysis developed into an intensive study of factors that influence this process as they are experienced interoceptively and expressed behaviorally. And though there is, as yet, no adequate recognition generally of the function of attention as a central determinant of behavior, it is no news to general semanticists that the set of the organism has a marked effect on the process of abstracting. It is nicely illustrated by three pictures in the "Communications" issue of the *Kaiser Aluminum News* that show the contrasts in a street scene as it might appear to a man who is late for an appointment, to a man wanting to cash a check, and to a young man on the town. Different features would be perceived as "foreground" by each of these "abstractors" with the rest of the scene fading into the "background." Consider, too, the transactional implications in that common expression, "Pay attention." It seems to indicate that if you "buy" one segment of the environment, you do not have attention to "pay" for other parts. The parts you overlook are among the items represented by the hanging strings from the parabola on the structural differential. They do not enter awareness on the objective level.

Many of the exercises in sensory awareness, practiced in the Institute's* seminar-workshops and elsewhere, help to redirect the focus of attention so that more—or at least different—elements of the internal and external environment get "connected" at the nonverbal, objective level. Similarly, Korzybski's extensional device, the "delayed reaction," whatever neurophysiological process may be involved, shifts the focus of attention at a given moment, and permits us to note features of the total situation that may have been overlooked.

Burrow, however, studied attention from a very specific perspective. From 1914 on, he wrote about "the neurosis of man," "the structure of insanity," and "the biology of human conflict," and it is easy to overlook the fact that his basic premise was the solidarity and coordination of our species as a biological unit. For him man's "natural" condition was one of confluence and articulation with his environment, with his kind, and with himself. This phylic cohesion should assure, for the species as a whole, the cumulative beneficial effects of the time-binding process. But something had gone askew. Burrow saw evidence that with the increasing predominance of the symbolic function that has accompanied evolutionary development, attention became diverted from species needs to preponderantly personal concerns.

In group analysis, hostility, "rightness," and partisan "getting together" were not regarded as conditions affecting one so-called side or another. They were examined as *general* conditions, and were related to an unwarranted idea or image of the self that has developed inadvertently along with man's increasing dependence on the symbolic function. Burrow spoke of the "fabricated" 'I'-persona, incorporated in our internal processes as individuals and groups—as families, corporations, nations, etc. He thus implied that what each of us experiences as 'I' does not have a direct counterpart in the process world. In other words, the sense of self involves not only too *narrow* a perception on the objective level, but also a *mis*perception, a *mis*-inference, even though experienced as if real. Burrow described the 'I'-persona as a cluster of effects and prejudices, socially induced and maintained, protected in our institutions—legal, commercial, educational, political, etc. Attention has been deflected to this arbitrary center of interest. The primacy and integrity of phylic process has been disrupted, and

---

* The Institute of General Semantics.

the functional unity of man has been split into discrete, potentially antag-
onistic entities, every group and individual the potential enemy of others.

You probably recall the passage in *Science and Sanity* in which Korzybski describes the "structural unconscious." He speaks of that,

> . . . wider, more general, and impersonal 'unconscious,' which underlies the
> structure of any language, and so is operative in every one who uses a lan-
> guage. . . . It embodies the underlying *structural* assumptions and implica-
> tions which are silently hidden behind our languages and their *structures*
> . . . *totally unknown and unsuspected,* unless uncovered after painful re-
> search.[6]

Burrow's investigations can be described in terms of the structural unconscious, even though the particular postulates of his study do not enter
into general semantics. For in phyloanalysis, a specific hidden structural assumption is challenged—the assumption of a distinctive self-identity divorced from the larger identity of the genus man.

Research that probes the structural unconscious, as Korzybski said, can
be painful. When you come up against the blind assumptions and prejudices that constitute the social mood, and are hidden and corroborated by
language, you are coming up against assumptions and prejudices that are
no less embedded and corroborated in yourself. Not only are they there
and operative, but everything around you declares them to be valid. To
challenge the structural unconscious is to create agitation within and
around you—and so it was in "phyloanalysis," with that small group of ordinary men and women who turned themselves into a living laboratory and
submitted their own secret incentives to immediate and general scrutiny.
Perhaps this research was more painful than Korzybski himself might have
imagined, because the probing of phyloanalysis involved the central identity,
the self-experience, of the participants over a period of years. But eventually, out of the agitation and the severe frustration entailed by the self-
imposed conditions of the experiment, an altered type of attention made
itself felt, and a different way of experiencing events on the process level
made for revaluation of what we call feeling and emotion, including the
feeling of "me" and "mine."

Burrow noticed that at periods of extreme frustration to ordinary incentives—occasioned by the terms of the group experiment—a slight perception of stress or tension, seemingly in the anterior part of the head, made
itself felt. Repeated experimentation confirmed the finding that the sensing
of this stress facilitated abrogation of the self-biased preoccupations that
group analysis had shown to be continuous for normals and neurotics alike.

Feelings to which we give such labels as anger, love, desire, etc., were sensed as far less significant, less pervasive, against the stable background that more and more asserted itself. The unilateral "I"-orientation of ordinary knowing–wanting–needing–interest gave way to a broad, impersonal, affirmative outlook. The organism itself was experienced as a secure, integrated, determining whole, primarily "human" rather than personally "me." "The organism senses its relation to the environment and to others as an integral element within an integral organismic unit . . .," Burrow wrote. "Where this technique has been persisted in by a group of people over a sufficient period of time, the barriers to common interests and activities artificially set up by the socially prevalent 'I'-persona are let down in behalf of the common interests and activities that make for the survival of the individual and the group as a phylic whole." [7]

Slight as it was, the sense of neuromuscular stress in the forepart of the head seemed to signal a general reconstellation of internal tensions. This attentional mode, which Burrow called *cotention,* provided an altered point of reference from which to examine the "structural assumption" of an insular "I." From this internal position, the sickness of man—his division and *un*sanity—can be *felt* as primarily an internal, intraorganismic problem, internal to you and to me—to every you and every me. Our normal interrelational mode—*ditention*—is experienced as a palpable internal distortion of interest and feeling which, though global in scope, is directly accessible to each of us within his own processes as a human being. Thus, through our common internal feelings and sensations, man's *un*sanity may be susceptible to direct observation and perhaps eventually to management. These contrasting attentional patterns were later found to have correlates of physiological change in instrumental recordings involving respiration, eye movements, and EEG.

The biological unity of man is of course a "given" in Korzybski's formulations, and it is implicit in various other disciplines and doctrines. Burrow, however, made explicit a conflict of interest between "my" self and man's self. In doing so, he may have provided a significant link to the empirical world for those concerned with human relational processes and with the factors now crippling the problem-solving powers of our species. For without a clear verbal and experiential distinction between what is man and what is "me," the hidden assumption of a separate "I"-interest is always operative, subverting to personalistic purposes all that belongs to the species—water, food, sex, children, science, etc. Without such a clear distinction, even phylobiology and general semantics are subject to the encroachments and distortions of ditention and the 'I'-persona.

Burrow, then, discriminated between sanity and *un*sanity, in terms of species-oriented motivation as contrasted with the partisan motivations of the 'I'-persona—his own, Korzybski's, yours, mine. He suggested a new map to the territory of self-experience, a map based on the perceptions and experiences of those involved in a unique social experiment. The territory is open for further exploration within the internal processes of our own organisms.

REFERENCES

1. Burrow, Trigant. "Social Images versus Reality," *The Journal of Abnormal Psychology and Social Psychology,* 1924, 19, pp. 230–35; and "A Relative Concept of Consciousness," *The Psychoanalytic Review,* 1925, 12, pp. 1–15.
2. Korzybski, Alfred. Letters to Trigant Burrow (unpublished).
3. Burrow, Trigant. "The Neurodynamics of Behavior—A Phylobiological Foreword," *Philosophy of Science,* 1943, 10, pp. 271–288.
4. Korzybski, Alfred. *Science and Sanity: An Introduction to Non-Aristotelian Systems and General Semantics.* Lakeville, Conn.: International Non-Aristotelian Library Publishing Co., 4th ed., 1958, p. 414. Distributed by the Institute of General Semantics.
5. Burrow, Trigant. *Science and Man's Behavior—The Contribution of Phylobiology.* New York: Philosophical Library, 1953, p. 201.
6. Korzybski. *Science and Sanity,* p. 506.
7. Burrow, Trigant. *Science and Man's Behavior,* p. 388.

29

SPEECH DISORDERS OF THE FLUENT *

WENDELL JOHNSON

AS I become increasingly familiar with the communication problems to be found in industry, in large hospitals and medical centers, in today's proliferating and sprawling universities, and especially in government, I can only conclude that the most serious disorders of speech and language are not those found in clinics. They are not such problems as stuttering or lisping or hoarseness, for example.

The most serious disorders of speech and language are to be found in persons outside clinics—often in positions of awesome influence—who have splendid voices, impeccable diction, and the fluency of faucets, but what they say confuses people, demoralizes and degrades them. Few speakers have been more effective than Hitler in attracting and holding an

---

* Copyright, ©, 1969 by Mrs. Edna B. Johnson. Dr. Johnson included these paragraphs in an early version of the manuscript that he wrote in June, 1961, and then revised through the summer to develop his address, "The Language of Responsibility," for the University of Iowa Commencement that August (see the *Iowa Alumni Review,* August, 1961, and *ETC.,* May, 1962). Their ordering here, and their title are by his associate, Dorothy Moeller, who with him edited the 3d edition of *Speech Handicapped School Children* (Harper & Row, 1967), and who since his death in 1965 has been working on his papers.—EDITOR.

audience. In this sense he was a very good speaker, but the effect of his speech was lethal and millions died of his words.

The contagions of prejudice and hatred, of self-interested bias and motivated rumor, are spread by words as surely and much more effectively than influenza is spread by virus. The standardized errors, as Vilhaljmar Stefansson has called them, to which we have grown accustomed, affect us like epidemics, rendering whole populations allergic to dependable information.

Is there any cure for these folk word-sicknesses? The research and clinical work that I have done makes me at least a little hopeful that there might be. There is some promise, I think, that protection against the ill effects of irresponsible and misleading and confusing speech and language is to be found in the changes that we may be able to achieve in these most distinctively human aspects of our behavior: our reaction to and with language and other symbolic forms.

In order to illuminate the extraordinary importance to us of speech and all other forms of symbolic behavior, let us try for a moment to imagine what would remain if everything symbolic were to be removed from the world around us. There would be, of course, no spoken or written language, no works of art or maps or designs of any sort, no ceremonies or holidays or statues in the park, no motor cars or rockets to the moon, and certainly no commencement addresses or academic degrees! There would be plants and animals, perhaps, sunsets and moonrises, monsoons and tides, but there would be nothing human at all.

Humanity without symbols is unthinkable. And so it seems clear to me that if man survives, his problems will involve directly or indirectly the symbols he creates and uses in interacting with other men and with the world in which all live together.

Consider for a moment a few of the major problems of our own day: (1) the shrinking functional size of the earth through improved transportation and physical means of communication; (2) the increasing mobility and urbanization of our population; (3) the increasing automation of industry, commerce, education, personal services, and homemaking; (4) the rising tide of population and the social and economic changes associated with it; (5) the increasing incidence or significance, or both, of delinquency and crime, personal maladjustment and mental malfunctioning, and family disintegration; (6) the growing implications of our newly achieved enormous advances in the technology of destruction; (7) the growing implications, too, of our unprecedented scientific and political preoccupation with outer space; and (8) the widening gulf between the scientifically educated few and the magically or nonscientifically oriented many.

Not one of these problems, in this very incomplete list, plagues any form of life except man, and if man were not a symbol-creating and symbol-using creature these problems would not concern him either, I think. If we are to deal effectively with such problems—if we are to know them as opportunities rather than catastrophes—it seems to me we need to improve our common languages and other symbol systems, and to cultivate far beyond present standards our individual and cultural capacities for effective communication.

If I were to single out what to me is the most important part of the behavior pattern we call "communication," I would name listening. I regard listening as a rare and precious art, and one of the most neglected—peculiarly neglected. We spend more time teaching writing, reading, and speaking, in that order, than we spend teaching listening. Yet outside the schools, and indeed inside them too, we do more listening than speaking, more speaking than reading, and more reading than writing. A perfect negative correlation between education and life! When we have done enough research to understand this, I think we will understand ourselves and our communicative "fumblitis" much better than we do now. And we will attach much more importance to listening than we have so far, undoubtedly, and do a much more thorough job of training children to listen, of training them, that is, in the art of listening.

My own sense of the fundamental importance of listening has been gained for the most part from the research I have done on the origins of the problem of stuttering. Traditionally, the problem we call stuttering had been assumed to begin with the speaker and, until our data began to accumulate sufficiently to topple that assumption, that tradition held. It had never been supposed that the problem could possibly start with the listener, and that therefore, as we put it, a "stutterer" has four legs.

The gist of our findings is that the problem turns out to be one that exists for the listener before it does for the speaker. The listener, nearly always one of the parents and usually the mother, begins one day to worry as a rule only a little and then more and more, but off and on, about the speaker. The speaker is the listener's child, usually about three years old. What the listener worries about is the child's hesitating and repeating in speaking, but this is something the child had been doing since the birth cry. Once the listener starts to worry about it, however, and to talk about it, if only to herself, as something undesirable and even abnormal, she ceases to remain indifferent to it. She has a word in her eye now: her child is a "stutterer," and it is as a "stutterer" that she sees him. She does something about it, subtle as a rule, gently, but unmistakably. And when she does enough about it, the child begins to respond to what she does. He becomes more hesitant, more repetitious, and eventually tense. In the course of this interaction with the listener, the speaker learns to doubt that he can speak smoothly "enough," and he becomes concerned, even fearful, about what might happen if he doesn't. This is how the problem of stuttering begins, and this is a large part of the reason why I personally consider listening so enormously important.

There is more to listening than that, however. Listening can be done in ways that are very good for people. Freud was one of the first great modern listeners. In his wake, there has come into being a vast and growing company of professional listeners. They have made of listening a great art. And I would hope we would get around eventually to teaching this art and applying it generally in our relationships with one another. Mainly because of my clinical observations, I am quite convinced that teaching your child to listen effectively will go further than any other single thing you could do to insure that he will grow up to become the clear-eyed, kindly, cooperative, alert, constructive adult you would want him to be.

Effective listening may be characterized as Everyman's scientific behavior. It is, fundamentally, a form of competent observation. It is an active rather than a passive process. It involves constant evaluation and disciplined judgment.

It can be understood, first, by being contrasted with the sort of listening most of us do. As listeners we listen considerably less than I think we should, and when we do we make three major mistakes, as I see it. First, we pay too much attention to the speaker, his name, his physical appearance, and particularly his symbols of authority or lack of them, to notice very carefully what he is saying. Second, we listen self-defensively, protecting our accustomed ways of thinking against the threat of new and uncongenial facts and viewpoints. Third, we tend to translate the speaker's unfamiliar words and phrases into those we would have used in saying what we assume he meant to say, and so we end up feeling that he agrees with us far more than he may.

If you would take advantage of the beneficent effects of the art of listening you will, of course, avoid or minimize these common errors, and you will do more than that. You will take a lesson from the more competent listeners among such professional groups, as clinical workers, lawyers, and scientific investigators. Mainly, you will listen much more than most of us do. You will listen calmly and without rebuke, and with an overriding intention, not to refute or impress the speaker, but just to understand him as well as you possibly can. You will listen as though you had read Proverbs

8:13—"He that answereth before he heareth, sheweth himself to be a fool, and worthy of confusion."

In a world that cries out for understanding, and, above all, for a desire to understand strong enough to match the longing to be understood, the universal and intensive cultivation of the art of listening is to be neglected only for reasons that would seem to lie well beyond the bounds of health and informed policy.

In weighing this consideration, it is to be appreciated that in listening well to what others say to us—and especially to what we say to others and ourselves—we are necessarily encouraging the responsible use of language. If we are to build a better world, it is clear to me that we must give our children a dependable sense of responsibility for their own actions and their own words—and about the only way we can do this is by the example of our own conduct. So long as we listen carelessly to phony commercials and to vague political and economic generalizations, so long as we accept without question assertions that are questionable, so long as we continue to honor—and to issue—as statements of fact the verbal equivalents of bad checks, we would not be realistic if we expected our children to learn the language of responsibility. And unless they do, they are ill equipped to communicate in a world where survival and progress depend more heavily with each passing month upon our ability and inclination to say things to each other that are clear, dependable, and worth saying.

It is primarily as listeners that we determine what others say to us, and what we say to others. It is as listeners that we question, or fail to question, the clarity of reference—or lack of reference—of the word to experience and to that which is observable in the world around us. It is as listeners that we ask, or fail to ask, about the adequacy of evidence for stated conclusions. It is as listeners that we keep alert, or fail to keep alert, to the confusion of the world inside our head and the world outside, the confusion of inner and outer space. It is as listeners that we wonder, or neglect to wonder, about the possible effects on both speaker and listener of what is said. It is as listeners that we consider, or forget to consider, the other things there are to say that follow from what has been said. And it is as listeners that we join, or fail to join, words with appropriate action.

Except as we listen well, most especially to our own words, we cannot hope to speak, or to encourage others to speak, the language of responsibility. And it is only by speaking and listening—and by using all other symbolic forms, in the arts and sciences, in the courts and temples, and in all places—with an unfailing sense of responsibility that we may hope ever to make a world in which we shall not be strangers and afraid.

Our greatest hope for a better future lies, indeed, in the changes that we may be able to achieve in the most distinctively human aspects of our behavior, our reactions to and with language and other symbolic forms. The world in which we shall be friends or strangers, stouthearted or afraid, will be, certainly, a world we will have made. It will be, as it always has been for man, a world made and remade unceasingly with symbols of our own creating and our own using and misusing. We have, above all, to select, to fashion, and to use our symbols well, as wisely as we can, and as responsibly as we are able. We all have a stake in communication, just as we do in public health, and control of disease. It is everybody's business if anybody has cholera. We all might get it. It is everybody's business if anybody is a person with whom we cannot communicate. We all may die for it. This is a semantic public health affair.

Ervin Laszlo was born in Budapest, Hungary, in 1932, and won international fame in his youth as a concert pianist. He is currently Professor of Philosophy at the State University of New York, College of Arts and Science at Geneseo, and will be Visiting Professor at Northern Illinois University in 1969–1970. He is Editor of *The Journal of Value Inquiry,* which he co-founded in 1968, Associate Executive Editor of *The Philosophy Forum,* Member of the Editorial Board of *Main Currents in Modern Thought,* and Consulting Editor of *Studies in Soviet Thought.* He is the recipient of an honarary degree from the Sorbonne, and is shortly scheduled to defend his dissertation for its highest degree, the *Doctorat d'Etat.* His books include: *The Structure of Human Experience; Philosophy in the Soviet Union; Beyond Scepticism and Realism; Individualism, Collectivism and Political Power;* and *Essential Society.*

30

MULTILEVEL FEEDBACK THEORY OF MIND

ERVIN LASZLO

Information Flow in a Self-Stabilizing Self-Regulating System

ONE of the basic problems of epistemology is how we can have knowledge of invariant things and principles on the basis of a constantly varying stream of sensory stimulation. It is a problem to which philosophers have addressed themselves through the ages. Plato postulated his immutable Forms in view of it, Aristotle his self-identical substance and general principles, Kant his categories of the a priori, and Whitehead his eternal objects. More recently still, McCulloch and Pitts proposed complex neural loops as the hypothetical answer to the problem.

The solutions have been many, the points of agreement few. Let us reexamine the problem, therefore, and consider the requirements for the simplest possible scheme of relationships that could derive invariant information from variable sources. We shall propose such a scheme, and then show that the various phases and aspects of human experience can be adequately explained in reference to it. Thus the axiomatic proposition will gain empirical application.

Let us outline the scheme in reference to basic concepts in information theory. The problem is to account for the derivation of intelligible "message" from mere "noise." At the minimum, there must be a flow of information between: a noise source E, an input P, and an output R. If there is to be control over the input, there must also be a special correlation between input and output whereby the input could result in an output that acts upon and conditions the noise source. Thus, we include as our fourth term the input–output coupling C.

The extraction of "order" or "message" can then take place in the following way. E provides the noise that contains, in potential, the ordered message. P imposes a limitation in that it admits only certain types of noise to be processed for its information content. In other words, P acts as a filter. The information admitted by P passes to R via the coupling factor, C. That is, the output depends not merely on the filtered information transmitted by P, but on the relevance of that information to C. The output is conditioned by the selective transmission of the information by C. R occurs, therefore, as a specifically coordinated response to P. R then acts upon E, the source of the noise containing the extractable message. So far, then, we have a circular flow of information between four components. (See Fig. 1)

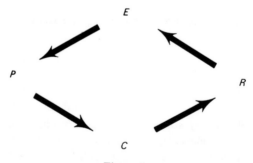

E

P

R

C

Figure 1

By means of this circuit the noise is filtered and specific qualifying responses are injected into it. But no provision has been made yet for deciphering the "message." The latter emerges if the condition of invariance of C with respect to P is observed. Specifically, we shall consider as ordered information an output that satisfies C as the transformation of an invariance.

Consider, then, that C is a built-in code that issues a response on the basis of P satisfying it. That is, C "reads" P and provides for response accordingly. The code that C incorporates is a certain pattern in P. If that pattern is produced, C leads to the specifically coordinated output. The code represents a factor of invariance. It extends over a permissible range of transformations. If P falls within this range, it satisfies the code and response is correspondingly produced. Therefore, the message for the system consists in the reading of P by C. Such "reading" corresponds to the intrinsic standard of the system and, we shall say, represents "intelligibility" for it. The system can produce its coordinated responses whenever P filters information from E that satisfies C. Fig. 2 represents this eventuality.

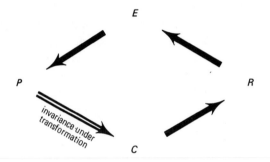

Figure 2

The double-shafted arrow signifies that P is a transformation of an invariance in C. But unless we provide for goal directedness in the system, the satisfaction of this invariance by P is merely a matter of chance. It depends on E providing such noise which, when filtered through P, happens to coincide with the code in C. However, the system can make provisions for the greater probability of this occurrence. Let us not forget that R is a specific response to a given instance of invariance under transformation in the input and in its coding. R, then, can be conceived as a response to this state, which is directed at E, the source of all potential information, in function of producing therein a noise source which, when filtered, satisfies the system's intrinsic code. That is, the output conditions the input to maximize the chances of the input satisfying the code on the basis of which the output was produced. In fact, the code is self-stabilizing: it gives rise to an output that increases the probability of an input that satisfies it. Thus we get Fig. 3.

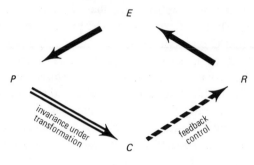

Figure 3

Here we have the concept of feedback control illustrated in our scheme. It is one that presupposes an ongoing flow of information between the components, controlled by an incorporated code or standard that tends to perpetuate itself. The result is that *E* becomes progressively ordered. It becomes more and more conformant to the requirement that, when it is filtered by *P,* the information left over should be a "message" that satisfies the code.

And now we shall complete the axiomatic construction by adding another feature to the system, a most remarkable one—adaptation. We postulate that the code is not fixed, but adaptable to the information transmitted by *P*. That is, the system is not only self-stabilizing, but self-organizing. It adjusts itself to the type of input it tends to receive. It possesses the remarkable property of searching out factors of invariance within the range of its actual input, and evolving the appropriate codes. Inadequate information content in *P* leads to exploratory responses, rather than occasioning the absence of response. The system is such that a given code perpetuates itself through the response only if it is satisfied. Otherwise, it is replaced by alternate codes that, through *R* and *E,* affect the input. If any code produces a response that results in a matching input, it is perpetuated. Full coincidence between input and code issues in the establishment of the successful code in place of the previous unsuccessful one. The self-organizing adaption of the system to its noise source may be represented as in Fig. 4.

The adaptive self-organization of the system is a condition of its persistent functioning if *E* is subject to changes. As a result of changes in *E,* a code that functioned adequately at one time may cease to function at another time. When that happens, the adaptive function is called into play: exploratory responses locate new codes, and the system perpetuates its flow

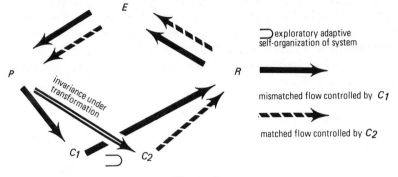

Figure 4

until further changes in E produce a mismatch of input and code, calling for renewed adaptive self-organization.*

The foregoing is, we believe, the simplest possible scheme that could account for the derivation of invariant messages from a fluctuating variable noise source. Its importance is, (1) it applies *in principle* to any control system of the corresponding properties, regardless of the specific nature of the components and materials; (2) it applies *in fact* to biological systems (organisms); and (3) it applies *hypothetically* to the structure and flow of information in human experience. We shall develop each of these contentions in turn.

I

Rather than attempting to devise an artificial regulatory system specifically designed to satisfy the above scheme, we may refer to MacKay's system,[1] which is adequate to satisfy its principle postulates. MacKay develops a theoretic design for a goal-guided artificial system having systems components identified as *receptor, control, effector,* and *field.* The flow of information proceeds from the field, through the receptor, to control, to effector, and back to the field. By using our symbols in MacKay's scheme,† and placing it next to our Fig. 1, the basic logic of relations in the information flow appears isomorphic.

In MacKay's system, the behavior of the effector R is controlled by information received from the field E through the receptors P. The information is in the form of a "mismatch" signal if the programmed "goal" of the

---

* "Adaptive self-organization" satisfies Somerhoff's concept of "directive correlation," and does not imply entelechy or conscious purposiveness. See also, G. Somerhoff, *Analytical Biology,* Oxford, 1950.

† Receptor $= P$, control $= C$, effector $= R$, field $= E$.

system and its actual state do not coincide, e.g., in Fig. 5*a* where the goal is point X on the field E, and the actual state of the system corresponds to point Y. In the event that the goal has been reached, the "mismatch" signal is replaced by a "match" signal. We can extrapolate this state of the system and represent the match signal, consistently with our own notation, by a double shafted arrow.

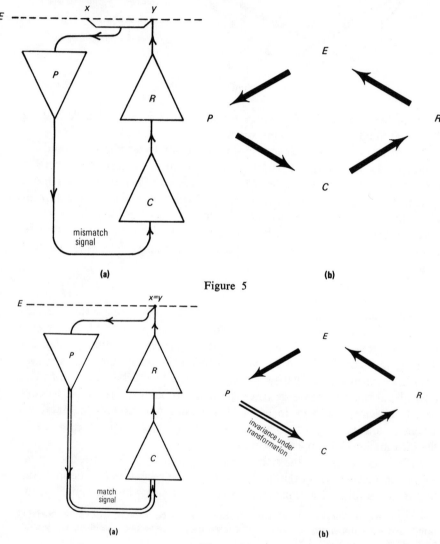

Figure 5

Figure 6

The structure of the information remains isomorphic to our Fig. 2. We can now examine MacKay's model in reference to our postulate, that the system is goal directed, providing for the greater probability that a matching of the received signals and the programmed state occurs. MacKay envisages a self-organizing system in which the mismatch signal automatically adjusts a series of control links governing the effectors, so that successful subroutines of activity become more likely to be tried again, while unsuccessful ones become less frequently essayed. Consequently, the system evolves modes of activity according to their relative success, and diminishes the occurrence of activities that have not been frequently successful. Thus we get negative feedback control in the system, with the output acting on the field to correct the state of the system in reference to a goal programmed in the control element. The feedback operates by means of mismatch-match signals transmitted through the receptors, and increases the probability that the match, rather than the mismatch, signal is obtained. By extrapolating from MacKay's scheme, we can in Fig. 7 represent his chart isomorphically with our previous Fig. 3.

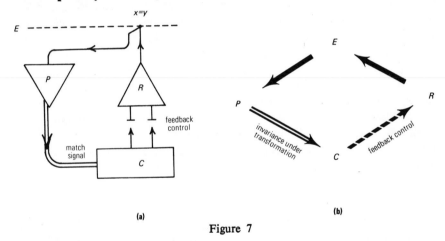

Figure 7

The outcome of the operation of such systems is that its field E becomes progressively ordered in reference to its control codes. The simplest example is the room thermostat, which "orders" the temperature of the air in the room according to its setting. The efficiency of the system in establishing the correspondence of its input to its codes is in direct ratio to the realization in its field of states corresponding to the codes $(X = Y)$. The relationship between the signals and codes may be represented as that between transformations and an invariance. (The relationship between the codes and the manipulatively obtained environmental states corresponds, we shall argue, to the relation between a concept and its objective counterpart.)

To complete the system, we must account for the self-organizing adaptive response of the system to its environment. (This will correspond, in the human mind, to concept formation by means of empirical learning.) Normally, there will be a running representation in the system of those features of the environment to which the system is matching its behavior. To have adaptive behavior, however, the system must produce such code representations of environmental features that are not *de facto* present in the environment, i.e., which are not signalled by the receptors. The system must be capable of "imaginative" or "abstract" operations. MacKay assumes that it is possible and normal for some of the internal organizing mechanisms to "run free" in the absence of excessive stimulation (signal activity).

Merely a flexible inhibitory mechanism is necessary to prevent such free-running activity from affecting the effectors. Internal goal-guided activity can then take place that pursues the goal abstractly, that is, purely in terms of the intrinsic capacities (degrees of freedom) of the system. Hypotheses, MacKay points out, are such free-running subroutines, and refer to features of the environment *if* they are true. Now, to develop these notions further, the testing of the free-running hypothetical codes involves the following: the use of the effectors, the resulting effect produced on the environment, and the use of the receptors to conduce the fresh signals to the control center. The system is so programmed that it automatically reinforces a hypothesized code that results in a match signal. Repeated match signals then establish the code as an operational program: the system "confirms" an environmental counterpart by means of the match signals. We thus get an isomorphism between the extrapolated state of MacKay's system and our Fig. 4, as seen in Fig. 8.

II

The reinterpretation of our "simplest possible scheme for the perception of invariances in a fluctuating variable world," in terms of MacKay's information flow design, emphasizes that our system makes no reference to entelechies or other principles that could not, *in principle,* be reproduced in artificial regulatory systems. The importance of this claim emerges in view of the next contention: that such systems are *de facto* embodied in biological organisms. Thus, if both claims are justified, the regulatory systems embodied in biological organisms can, in principle, be reproduced in artificial systems—no reference to *sui generis* biological and psychological factors or components is required.

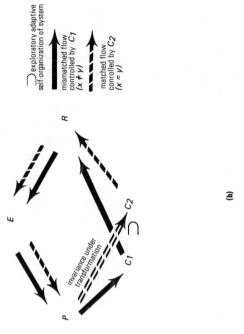

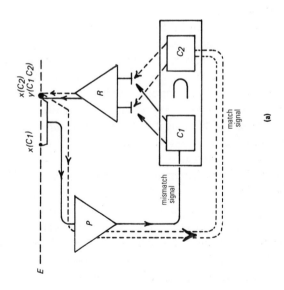

Figure 8

The system is, in virtue of its manipulative and adaptive functions, self-stabilizing and self-organizing. It derives "message" from "noise" by manipulatively matching the environment to its codes and adaptively matching its codes to its environment. Such feedback-stabilized behavior in reference to intrinsic but adaptable codes is the basis of all life phenomena. We need not go into great detail on this score, because the importance of feedback stabilization is thoroughly established in contemporary biology. We can refer to almost any recent work on the self-regulation of living organisms. For example, one biologist points out that "feedback function is not only essential to life as we know it but also . . . this function is the *main* foundation of the life process." [2] He shows that feedback stabilization is already exhibited by the virus, which is "lifelike in its actions only when it is coupling events in the manner that is typical of feedback circuits," and that cells, bacteria, and of course all higher forms of organisms manifest, and essentially depend on, feedback control.

In applying the principles of our postulated control system to biology, we must identify its functions and components with natural entities and events. Thus the sign E stands for "environment"—the source of all information for the organism. The perceptual sensing apparatus of the given organism is P. It is a filtering mechanism that transmits certain energy radiations ("information") from the environment, and excludes others. It ranges from the primitive chemical reactivity of protozoa, limited to a small range of changes occurring in the immediate proximity of their surface, to the sensitivity of vertebrates and other higher forms of life, to a wider range of events occurring at some distance from the organism. C is the full organic (where developed: nervous) conducting network as it transmits, and in transmission transforms, signals received from the environment. R signifies the coordinated environment-directed but self-regulative response of the organic system to its sensed information, in virtue of the latter's channeling through C. The system as a whole represents the organism: no sharp dividing line can be drawn for biological self-regulating *open* systems between the organic boundaries and the relevant environment. Functionally, the latter is a component in the former.

Feedback controlled environment-organism transactions become the province of the nervous system in higher forms of life, where precise coordination and control is a precondition of survival. The nervous system of animals tends to be highly developed since animals, unlike plants, cannot make their own food and must actively search for it. Securing the correct match between their organic norms and the signals that represent the relevant conditions in the environment involves making frequent and rapid adjustments. Satisfying this requirement presupposes a highly evolved control element in the organism; and this is the nervous system (the outer box in Fig. 8a, self-organizingly evolving, if needed, C_1 from C_2).

The manipulative function of the self-stabilizing and self-organizing organic system is exhibited in the conditioning of their environment by most organisms. By building nests, digging burrows, and ultimately working the land and building cities, organisms adapt their environments to themselves. In terms of our scheme, they manipulate E in function of obtaining P's that correspond to their actual C's. But the environment is never entirely constant, and already the manipulative activity of different organisms in one habitat produces changes in it. Hence adaptation is constantly called for. The requirement is satisfied by all adaptable species in seeking out their particular niche and adapting themselves to the conditions there. In addition to such phylogenetic adaptations, we can also note temporary instances, adaptations to short-term changes in the environment. These are plentifully provided by the homeostatic and regenerative processes of organisms. Homeostasis, healing, regeneration, and even reproduction (being but a special case of regeneration) are examples of adaptive self-organization. The adaptability of living organisms is vast: most species, other than certain insects (some of which appear to have stabilized their mode of existence for as much as 25 million years) are, in Julian Huxley's terms, "bundles of adaptation." Their manipulative capacity is often immense: here the most striking example is provided by our own species. The feedback-stabilizing and self-organizing activity pattern of organisms exemplifies the principal features of our basic scheme. By both adaptively and manipulatively matching the signals received from the environment with their intrinsic codes, living organisms extract the relevant "message" from the fluctuating "noise" provided by their environments.

III

We now turn to our third contention, *viz.*, that our basic control scheme applies hypothetically to the flow of information in human experience. In examining this claim, we find that the principal factor to account for is the cognitive basis of our experience. Experience is purposive in regard to known things and events. The cognitive factor is the "plus" in human experience, in distinction to the predominantly homeostatic and instinct-guided self-maintenance of other species. But cognition does not entail the introduction of *sui generis* properties to explain.

First of all, there is no categorical line to be drawn between biochemically and instinctively controlled self-regulation and purposive behavior.

Bergson remarked that, at the end of its growth within the egg, a young chick breaks the shell by a peck of its beak. It performs a purposive behavioral act that represents the culmination of its embryonic processes of growth, This idea can be carried further, Sinnott suggests, by saying that such activities as the building of a bird's nest is simply a continuation, in the form of an instinct, of the processes of development. "There seems no reason to separate the admittedly unknown regulatory activities that go on in the cells of the brain, which underlie behavior, from the equally unknown ones responsible for orderly, goal-directed bodily development and function." [3]

Secondly, there is no categorical divide between noncognitive and cognitive purposive behavior. (We use "cognitive" as the biologist and psychologist, and not as the linguistic analyst and positivist uses it.) The same basic motivation underlies both cognitive and noncognitive behavior. We define this motivation, consistently with neurophysiological information, as an a-specific goal-directedness toward establishing and maintaining the match (relation of transformation and invariance) between the received signals (stimuli) and the organic codes (or norms) of the system.

Animal experiments show that there are established quantities and qualities (patterns) in the signals that correspond to the organic norms of the species. Experiments on human subjects further emphasize the importance, for the entire organism, of respecting the correspondence of the norms and the signals. We refer to the sensory-deprivation experiments and their effects.

The experimental data suggest that the maintenance of a correspondence between the incorporated norms of the system and its interactive relations with the environment represents the precondition of any organic system's normal functioning. It may well constitute the basic motivation of the system. This motivation is a-specific, since it is triggered by any differential between the norms and the input. The motivation is reduced, and may be (temporarily) eliminated by the activity resulting from it. This activity is specific, since it constitutes the purposive searching out of the discrepancy and the manipulative and/or adaptive functions required to reduce and eliminate it.

Thus motivation can trigger either one or both of the conceptually distinct but in fact interpenetrating processes that we denote "manipulation" and "adaptation." Both processes have as their common goal the correspondence of input and norms but, whereas manipulation is directed toward bringing up the input to the level required for the code, adaptation is directed toward evolving the codes that fit the existing input. Hence both purposive environment-directed activity, and the various processes of code (concept) formation, share the basic motivation of input-norm correspondence. The common motivation may be noted as $(P_1 \neq> C)_{t_1} \rightarrow (P_2 => C)_{t_2}$ in the case of *manipulation,* where the activity is directed to produce the kind of P's that will correspond, as a particular transformation to an existent C; while motivation is noted $(P \neq> C_1)_{t_1} \rightarrow (P => C_2)_{t_2}$ in the event of adaptation, where the activity is aimed at producing the C that will correspond, as an invariance, to given P's. The basic schema of motivation is, in either case, $(P \neq> C)_{t_1} \rightarrow (P => C)_{t_2}$.

On the level of physiological homeostasis and instinctive behavior, $(P => C)$ involves not much more than certain basic substances and their sensory correlates. Obtaining these constitutes the normal input, corresponding to the established codes. On the higher level of *cognitive* activity, the requirements imposed on the input by the codes are more stringent. They include, in addition to the substances required for survival, the sensory and perceptual patterns that provide the key to intelligibilty in terms of sensory *gestalten.* In other words, for the complex human organism, the input must not only satisfy organic needs, but also the requirements of perceptual intelligibility.

The patterns of information flow in everyday cognitive activity may be represented in terms of our basic scheme as in Fig. 9.

The evolution of *non*cognitive codes are the result of the slow and laborious processes of phylogenetic evolution: genetic mutations exposed to the test of natural selection. The successful mutants are those that correlate sensing and response by codes that assure the greater probability of match signals. Successful *cognitive* codes, on the other hand, may be developed by the individual in relatively rapid adaptive processes in his nervous system. They too, correlate input (perception) and output (response) in a manner designed to maximize the occurrence of the match signal and therewith the organism's chances of survival. (It is our own introspective experience that such cognitive codes are infused with the remarkable property we call "consciousness." We do not pretend to solve the psychophysical problem of how this could come about; at the most we may point out that a correlation must be supposed to exist between our cognitive codes of self-regulative activity and our introspectively known *gestalten* and concepts.[4])

Cognitive codes assimilate, or reduce, the variable signals of the perceptual field to invariances or standards. There is important empirical evidence in support of this claim. Cognition turns out to be more than the passive reception of sensory information. Neurophysiology tells us that sensory in-

Perceptual Cognition

INFORMATION FLOW

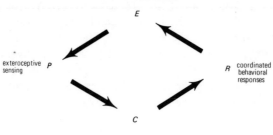

MANIPULATIVE SELF-STABILIZATION

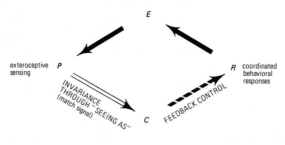

ADAPTIVE SELF-ORGANIZATION

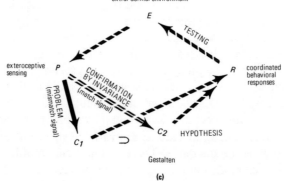

Figure 9

formation is selected, already at the receptors, and then channeled, summated with organic signals, and that the resulting stimuli are conduced to the cortex where they are sharpened and analyzed. If the operation is successful, the outcome is the assimilation of the sensory signals to a familiar *gestalt*. Gestalt psychologists investigate how sensory cognition "improves" the intelligibility of sensory information (the law of *Pragnanz*), and transactionalists show that perceptual cognition is the outcome of a process of adjustment between organism and environment by means of the incorporation of cues and clues into the sensory stimulus pattern, based on past experience and behavior. It is as a result of such an active treatment of the information obtained from the environment that a stable world-pattern emerges from the shifting kaleidoscopic stimulus pattern in the information source. Sensory cognition does not mirror the environment, but reflects, if anything, the relevance of the environment to the transactional requirements of the human organism. As previously noted by others, the perceived world pattern thus mirrors the organized need pattern within.

That our perception of objects is more than the mere "photographing" of items of our experience has been forcibly brought home by Hanson's notation of "seeing as." [5] "There is a sense, then, in which seeing is a 'theory-laden' understanding. Observation of x is shaped by prior knowledge of x." Hanson queries, "How should we regard a man's report that he sees x, if we know him to be ignorant of all x-ish things? Precisely as we would regard a four-year-old child's report that he sees a meson shower." Yet we do not ask, Hanson points out, "What's that?" of every passing bicycle. The fact is that instead of just seeing objects (presumably as they are in themselves), we see them *as* something—something previously experienced and therefore familiar—such as "bicycles." We recognize familiar *gestalten,* to which the variety of our perceptions are reduced, or assimilated to, or, if you prefer, in terms of which they are interpreted. We recognize a dog as a dog even if we have never seen it before, and our child as our own even if he is dressed in a new suit.

This remarkable phenomenon, of "seeing as," may be stated in our scheme in terms of a passage, perfectly spontaneous in the case of ordinary perceptual cognition, from the given P's (the shapes, colors, bumps, and flashes that are the denizens of our sense world) to invariant, familiar, and intelligible C's. These latter we may term "sense codes" or *gestalten.* They are also the "universals" which those philosophers who conceived of all knowledge as knowledge of sensorily perceived objects have spent so much time and effort in discussing.[6]

Our everyday world is populated with things and events that can be readily referred to invariant sense codes. Indeed, we surround ourselves with things that we recognize, and tend to reduce that contingent of our experiential sphere that may be puzzling and unfamiliar. How this "manipulative self-stabilization" of human beings takes place is shown in Fig. 9*b*. Behavioral response *R* affects the environment: this is man's impact as an active and purposive organism on his surroundings. The goal of this directed activity is to bring about perceptually cognizable things and events. (These are the kinds of things which are relevant to human needs, behavior patterns, and projects.) Now, man informs himself of his environment through his exteroceptive senses. The latter give him perceptually cognizable information when the signals are matched (reduced or assimilated) to existent sense-codes or *gestalten*. This relationship (represented by the double-shafted arrow) is the basis for further feedback-controlled behavioral responses, directed at the environment in reference to the actual cognitions. And thus manipulation is an ongoing activity.

Manipulative self-stabilization depends on the presence of invariant *C*'s for the interpretation of the sensory signals. However, the existing *C*'s themselves must have been developed sometime, and still further ones must develop if *P*'s are to be satisfactorily cognized in the various phases and under the diverse conditions of human experience. Thus, we must account for the self-organizing activity involved in learning. The information flow of this activity is represented in Fig. 9*c*.

Learning, psychologists tell us, proceeds by the awareness of a problem, the setting up of hypotheses, and trial and error activities testing the hypotheses. These elements are clearly indicated in our chart. A single arrow connecting *P* to *C* indicates that, although *P* is referred to *C,* no invariance to the latter obtains "mismatch signal". This presents a problem: the sensory signals are not cognized by means of a familiar *gestalt*. In "free-running activities," our nervous system essays various modes of fitting the sensory material to invariant and recognizable forms, i.e., other *C*'s are abstractly envisaged, and these represent the hypothesis. Thus, when C_1 does not function as the standard to which *P* is reduced, C_2 is set up. C_2 is tested by the trial and error process of passing through the feedback circuit by means of a response directed toward the relevant features of the environment, and the sensing of those features. If the resulting *P*'s may be reduced to the standard of C_2, that is, if the puzzling sensory pattern becomes interpretable and testable as the new *gestalt,* the hypothesis is confirmed. Otherwise new hypotheses (C_3, C_4, . . .) are set up and tested, and the process continues until invariance in the sensory field is at last secured—or attention is redirected and the puzzling signals are forgotten or repressed.

Adaptive self-organization represents the processes of learning (*gestalt* formation); manipulative self-stabilization represents the processes of testing the hypothesized *gestalten* and modifying the environment by evolving to them. Learning adapts the organism to the environment by evolving the C's to match the P's, and manipulation adapts the environment to the organism by producing those P's that match the existing C's. The outcome of these joint operations is the constitution of the everyday environment of familiar objects, persons, and events.

We must recognize the fact, however, that the world of human experience extends considerably beyond the world of perceptual cognition. We live in a wider world than that of familiar objects, persons, and events. Although for most persons in primitive societies, and for many even in "high" cultures, the *gestalt* world is satisfactory, for a small minority of people it is not; and they succeeded in enlarging the effective human environment beyond the boundaries of sensory cognition. The principle of sufficient reason suggests that they have done so because, to their mind, the sensory world proved to be deficient in some respect. The principle is vindicated if we consider that, in fact, sense codes prove to be insufficient in at least two principal regards. First, as Hume has shown, they do not include codes for *relations* between perceptually cognized *gestalten*, and the inquiring mind demands that such relations be known. Second, sense codes cannot assure the invariance to a norm of the *emotional connotations* of the *gestalten*. It is suggested here that additional control systems, operating on meta-level circuits, develop meta-level codes that render intelligible the interrelation and/or the emotional connotation of the intuited sensory *gestalten*. The development of the additional circuits and their meta-level codes is motivated, consistently with the lower codes and circuits, by the manipulative and adaptive goal-directed activities, $(P \neq> C)_{t_1} \to (P => C)_{t_2}$. But the a-specific motivation is here forced into specific meta-level channels due to the unsatisfactoriness, to the inquisitive and sensitive civilized mind, of ordinary perceptual cognition. Hence specific varieties of meta-level circuits are caused to evolve, and they establish cognitive activity patterns typical of *science, art,* and *religion*. Each of these vast fields of meta-sensory cognitive activity may be represented in terms of our basic scheme. We take the typical information flow patterns of science first. See Fig. 10.

The contemporary theoretical sciences consist of an increasingly vast superstructure of theoretic constructs, interrelated by "rules of correspondence" ("epistemic correlations" or "operational definitions") with selected specific sensory signals. The rules (correlations, definitions) are theoretically postulated and subsequently validated in crucial experiments. Con-

Science

INFORMATION FLOW

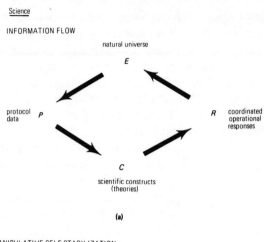

(a)

MANIPULATIVE SELF-STABILIZATION

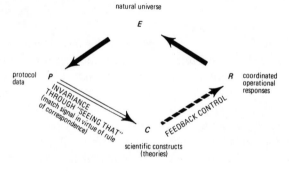

(b)

ADAPTIVE SELF-ORGANIZATION

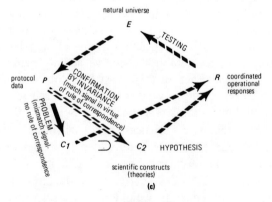

(c)

Figure 10

structs, systematically connected in a theory, generate predictions as to the occurrence of certain sensory signals. The occurrence of the latter represents a "match signal," and entails the validation of the operationally defined construct. The nonoccurrence of the predicted signal constitutes a "mismatch signal" that motivates further hypothesis formulation and testing.

The flow of information in science involves a highly selected environmental field, from which signals are perceived and referred to theoretic constructs. Now, we have quoted Hanson in support of our contention that, even in perceptual cognition, the signals (P's) are not merely inspected, but are always referred to preexisting codes. This is what Hanson meant when he said that, ordinarily, seeing is "seeing *as.*" In science the flow of information is analogous, but with the difference that the preexisting codes are not perceptual *gestalten,* but nonperceived, and perhaps intrinsically nonperceivable, entities (e.g. electrons, fields, etc.). Here the passage from P to C involves more than seeing P "as" C: it involves seeing *that* a given P satisfies the rules of correspondence in a theory for correlation with a given C. That is, in virtue of the logic of scientific theory formulation and confirmation, the appropriate expression in scientific observation is not "seeing *as,*" but "seeing *that.*"

Hanson said, "Observation in physics is not an encounter with unfamiliar and unconnected flashes, sounds, and bumps, but rather a calculated meeting with these flashes, sounds, and bumps of a particular kind—this might figure as an account of what observation is." [7] And this statement applies, naturally, not only to physics but to all empirical sciences. It is precisely by referring the "flashes, sounds, and bumps" to a set of rigorously constructed and connected C's that scientific knowledge becomes possible. The flashes, etc., are meaningless in themselves; what lends them meaning is their epistemic correlation with the C's. For example, in an experiment the physicist's electron counter clicks. He concludes to the passage of an electron through the opening. Metaphorically speaking, the physicist, on hearing the click, "sees *that*" an electron passed through his counter. The invariant construct "electron" is represented by the sensory signal "click" as a transformation appropriate to the experimental situation.

So far, we have considered the information flow in science from P to C. This is the purely cognitive aspect of the scientific endeavor, and treatments of scientific method often end there. But we suggest that we must trace out the full circuit of information if we are to give an adequate account of scientific knowledge and activity. We shall not contend that scientific theories are formulated *in order that* particular responses could be made to them.

That would be to disregard the cognitive aim of pure science and to unduly emphasize one of the components of the circuit. However, we may affirm that, after the purely cognitive phase of referring P's to C's, a passage to R does take place. It does, because the cognitive aim of science can only be accomplished through the process of confirming the hypotheses, which is a feedback circuit involving coordinated responses by the scientists on his test object and his perception of the resulting state of the object. (The operational emphasis can be replaced by successive observations, where the time interval represents the "manipulation" of the test object, and the perceived difference in the state of the object, measured by a temporal scale, indicates confirmation or falsification.) Such theories often prove amenable to application, whereby controlled processes are initiated that restructure some part of the experience of the scientist—and eventually of everyone in his surroundings. The circuit is completed in all these instances.

The rational, empirically coded, feedback circuit typical of contemporary science may be subdivided, similarly to the sensory circuit, into a self-stabilizing manipulative and a self-organizing adaptive phase. Considering the former (Fig 10*b*), we note that the behavioral response (R) of the scientist (technician) affects the state of his test object (E), and this is sensed by him (P). Through feedback control, the response is programmed so to affect the test object that the obtained P's should match the postulated C's. That is, the experiment (or controlled observation or technological application) is designed to confirm the theory by producing the predicted protocol data. The predicted P's are, of course, those that are correlated by rules of correspondence to the system of C's, i.e., which are analyzable as transformations of invariant laws.

The self-stabilizing manipulative phase in the scientific process is constantly corrected and supplemented by the self-organizing adaptive phase. See Fig. 10*c* for the dynamics of theory-formulation—the scientific variant of the process of adaptive self-organization. The single arrow connecting P to C_1 indicates a mismatch signal: the protocol data are not interpretable as transformations of invariant laws (or other constructs). This poses the problem toward the resolution of which various hypotheses are advanced in abstract ("free-running") thought processes ($C_1 \supset C_2$). These require testing, and that means passing through $R \to E \to P$. A successful hypothesis is one which is confirmed by a match signal, accommodating the hitherto puzzling P's as transformations of an invariant construct (C_2). In Margenau's terminology, the thus confirmed C's become "verifact's." They are assigned existential reality, and are viewed, as the sense codes were, as cognitions of states of the test object. The sum total of confirmed scientific constructs extends "reality" considerably beyond the realm of perceptual cognition. It makes up the sum of the scientist's test objects, i.e., the "natural universe."

Our next area of inquiry is the domain of art. We suggested that additional control circuits and their meta-sensory codes are required to account for the interrelation, as well as the emotional connotation, of the sensory *gestalten*. Science accomplishes the task of providing meta-level codes for the theoretical undersanding and empirical testing of the interrelations of the things populating our perceptual world. In doing this, science refurnishes the perceptual world with scientific entities. But the task of elucidating the emotional impact of our experiences still remains to be undertaken, for science does not remove this impact except in the laboratory, and then only for highly specific data. Thus an additional control circuit is called for, to produce meta-level codes in terms of which the emotive factors associated with the signals could become intelligible. This, we suggest, is the function of *art*.

The patterns of information and control in art are represented in Fig. 11.

Sir Herbert Read describes the process of artistic activity in three stages. First, there is a perception of material qualities (colors, sounds, gestures, etc.); second, there is the arrangement of such perceptions into pleasing shapes and patterns. Third, there comes a stage when such an arrangement is made to correspond with a previously existing state of emotion or feeling. "Then we say that the emotion or feeling is given *expression*." [8] Artistic activity, in the above sense, is a feedback controlled process, conformant to our basic scheme. The various sensory signals that represent the artist's materials are correlated with purposive environment-directed responses resulting in an arrangement of perceptions that matches the artist's aesthetic ideals. Thus the artist embodies his ideals in an environmental "control object": the work of art.

The flow of information in the artistic process approximates the sensory cognitive process in that the perceptual signals are not matched with postulated nonperceived entities, but with sensory *gestalten*. The artistic process *differs* from the ordinary perceptual one, however, in that the perceptual signals are not cognitive "hard" data but emotive "soft" ones. The signals are assessed in terms of their emotively felt import, and not their cognitive significance. Immediate experience is emotional in character. (We agree with Whitehead, who said that "the separation of the emotional experience from the primitive presentational intuition is a high abstraction of thought.") The emotively connotative signals of immediate sensory experience are matched, as Read suggested, with previously existing states of

Art

INFORMATION FLOW

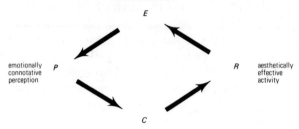

(a)

MANIPULATIVE SELF-STABILIZATION

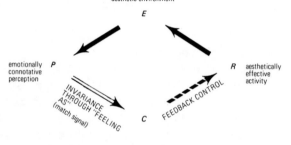

(b)

ADAPTIVE SELF-ORGANIZATION

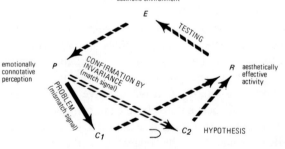

(c)

Figure 11

feeling. Hence the appropriate description of the aesthetic perception of art works is "feeling *as*." The "as" refers to the aesthetic work of art that has gained emotive import through the perception.

Sensory signals gain their meaning through the codes to which they are assimilated. For example, the perceived color *red* may occur in the context of variously coded circuits of cognition and behavior. It may be a patch of tulips in a garden, a red light on the electronic apparatus of the experimental physicist, or a splash of color in an impressionistic painting. In the first instance, we see it *as* an environmental entity matching our *gestalt* for "tulip"; in the second we see *that* a certain wavelength of radiation is obtained in the experiment, and in the third, we *feel* it *as* an element in a harmoniously balanced, emotively moving visual whole.

The function of art is to enable one to have the last named kind of experience, in terms of which the perceptual world of everyday objects and events takes on an emotively disclosed significance. A host of writers on art and aesthetics would subscribe to this basic proposition. We interpret it in terms of our scheme as the feedback controlled, self-stabilizing activity whereby the artist manipulates his environment, producing therein the artistic "control objects," which, when perceived, match his intrinsically meaningful aesthetic visions (Fig. 11*b*). But this manipulating activity presupposes that aesthetic "visions" or "intuitions" should preexist in the artist's and his public's mind. In order to account for the development and constant evolution of these visions, and thereby for the genesis of art and the dynamics of stylistic change, we must turn to the self-organizing adaptive scheme (Fig. 11*c*).

The presence of a "problem" (mismatch signal) means that the arrangement of perceptions actually beheld by a subject does not match up with his aesthetic "visions" or "intuitions." The perceptions are not "felt *as*" meaningful and significant. Free-running, self-organizing processes are initiated then, consisting of the imaginative envisagement of new types and sequences of feeling. The "hypotheses" are empirically (and perhaps also behaviorally) tested, by means of the repeated perception (perhaps under varying conditions) of the work. A hypothesis is confirmed as a proper aesthetic ideal of the given perceptions when the subject succeeds in feeling the work *as* significant and meaningful. Then he has organized his sensibilities to match the perceived significance of the given work of art. The work now occasions a match signal in reference to his new emotive codes.

Such adaptive processes play an important role in artistic creativity, permitting the artist to evolve his aesthetic ideals in the very process of creating his work. Thereafter, the new ideals occasion more passive adaptive responses in his audience. By means of these joint processes of self-organization and manipulation, by artist as well as by public, the environing world and man's appreciation of it become mutually matched. In ages where aesthetic ideals dominated behavior, as in classical Greece man's world became a harmonious projection of his taste. But in times when further considerations supervene as motivating forces of behavior, as in our own, the aesthetic harmonization of man and environment is disadvantaged by industrial, technological, economic, and other goal-directed activities.

A last domain of meta-sensory cognition and coordinated behavior needs to be noted to complete this brief sketch of human experience in terms of our basic information-flow scheme. The presence of this domain is justified by the consideration that the feelings evoked by our perceptual cognition of the environing world are not always capable of being adequately referred to the immanent codes of artistic vision and sensibility. Some feelings cannot be properly assessed *as* clear and satisfying emotions—they require the introduction of what we may term "transcendental" codes. The relationship between such feelings and their codes is similar to that occurring between scientific protocol data and scientific constructs; by means of postulated correspondence rules, the signals are referred beyond themselves to codes that stand for nonperceived events and entities. The roots of *religion,* we submit, lie in a primitive *feeling* that refers beyond itself, and proves to be understandable in terms of constructs with which it is correlated by the rules of correspondence postulated by its theology. The flow of information in our basic scheme can be represented as the religious circuit of cognitive activity. See Fig. 12.

The world of religion is a world of reason based on particular emotions and purposes. As Whitehead said, it is "an ultimate craving to infuse into the insistent particularity of emotion that nontemporal generality which primarily belongs to conceptual thought alone." [9] The naturalistic interpretation of religion, which is the one that is congruent with our systems-analytical approach to human experience, suggests that religion has its roots in feeling and its superstructure in general ideas. After reviewing many reports of religious experiences, James concludes that

> it is as if there were in the human consciousness a *sense of reality, a feeling of objective presence, a perception* of what we may call "something there," more deep and more general than any of the special and particular "senses" by which current psychology supposes existent realities to be originally revealed.[10]

Religion

INFORMATION FLOW

world of religion

E

emotionally
significant
perception   P   R   religious
                                                           activity

C

religious constructs
(theologies)

(a)

MANIPULATIVE SELF-STABILIZATION

world of religion

E

emotionally
signicant
perception   P   R   religious
                                                           activity

INVARIANCE BY
"FEELING THAT"
(match signal in virtue
of rule of correspondence)   FEEDBACK CONTROL

C

religious constructs
(theologies)

(b)

ADAPTIVE SELF-ORGANIZATION

world of religion

E

TESTING

CONFIRMATION BY
INVARIANCE
(match signal in virtue of
rule of correspondence)

emotionally
significant
perception   P   R   religious
                                                           activity

PROBLEM
(mismatch signal:
no rule of correspondence)

C₁   ⊃ C₂   HYPOTHESIS

religious constructs
(theologies)

(c)

Figure 12

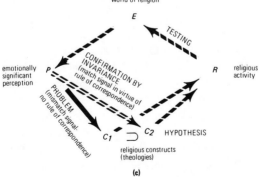

This phenomenon James subsequently called "sense of presence." He explicitly names it a religious *feeling*. He would agree, we believe, with our view that it is essentially a "feeling *that*." The transcendental nature of the feeling makes it possible to postulate "rules of correspondence" to pass from the feeling itself (the "sense of presence") to a religious concept (nonperceived divine being or supernatural event). Once in the realm of concepts, the rational mind takes over and derives further concepts from those implied by the feeling and provides systematic connection between them. Thus there are systematic sets of "religious constructs" that make up particular theologies. Some of these constructs are "operationally defined" (by means of rules of correspondence with religious feelings), and others are "constitutively defined" (through rules of logical inference to other religious constructs, some of which have been operationally defined). Hence the theoretical edifice of theology is not radically different from that of science, *beyond the nature of the original datum*. That datum, however, is very different. It is an element of feeling infusing a perception in religion, and a "hard" sense datum in science. It may be summed up in the contrast between "*feeling* that" and "*seeing* that." Were it not for observation, science could hardly be said to be capable of existing. Similarly, had religious feelings not existed, theology and religious philosophy could not have developed. James tells us that:

> . . . feeling is the deeper source of religion, and . . . philosophic and theological formulas are secondary products, like translations of a text into another tongue . . . I mean that in a world in which no religious feeling had ever existed, I doubt whether any philosophic theology could ever have been framed.

Theological speculations, James holds, must be "classed as over-beliefs, buildings-out performed by the intellect into directions of which feeling originally supplied the hint."[11] This discussion shows that religion is based on an element discovered in the stream of human experience, and that this element is correlated with a concept or idea, which represents our assessment of its transcendental significance. The element in experience belongs to $P,$ and it is by nature a feeling. The concept or idea belongs to $C,$ and it is what we call a "religious construct." P and C are correlated by means of "match signals" validated by theological rules of correspondence. Since most religious constructs are part of an interconnected theological system, any response to a religious feeling is not merely the response to the religious construct with which it is immediately matched, but to the system of constructs in which the given construct is a component (this is much the same in the case of other systems of constructs). For example, the "sense of presence," whether occurring in a religious ceremony or more randomly in the context of everyday life, calls forth a response not merely to a given construct, like the presence of a supernatural being, but to the entire system of religion that identifies the being and places it within the context of its system. Thus at Lourdes, Bernadette responded to the Holy Virgin of Christian theology, and not to an unknown supernatural woman; at communion the devout Catholic responds to the flesh and blood of Christ, and not to an unidentified feeling of transcendental significance.

Religion is institutionalized in all civilized societies, and religious experiences usually occur at designated times and places, namely *in* the places and *on* the days of worship. Experiences of a religious kind, such as having a "sense of presence" even in a mild form (e.g. as a sense of awe or transcendent beauty) occur relatively rarely outside these occasions. When they do, our responses to them tend to be nondeliberate and undirected. We may stand dumbfounded, or exclaim in delight. But these are the exceptional cases. Most religious experiences are had in the context of religious ceremonial, and here our responses are highly deliberate and clearly directed: they maintain, or modify, the cult or ceremonial. In fact, the ceremonial itself is a collective response to the religious experiences generated by it. If this implies a circularity it is well—for this is where we encounter feedback controlled, purposive manipulation in religious activity. We can analyze it in terms of the manipulative self-stabilization scheme (Fig. 12*b*). Here R stands for a purposive response to religious experience, which increases the probability that such experience occurs in the future. Religious activity obtains in response to religious experience, and is designed to bring about such experience. It accomplishes this by the building of shrines, altars, and buildings as places of worship and location of ceremony; by devising and performing the ceremony; and by using such ritual accessories that strengthen the religious experience. The tolling of bells, burning of incense, the robes, the chants, and the many other correlates of a cult create a total experiential pattern that is dedicated to one thing: the production of P's matching the "operationally defined" C's of the theological system.

In terms consistent with other facets of experience, we can say that religious response acts on the environment in function of producing experiences analyzable as transformations of invariant religious constructs. The ordered religious experience consists in a feeling, triggered by carefully coordinated sights, sounds, smells, and movements, which is matched as a particular transformation with an invariant religious construct. The latter may be a key concept denoting a supernatural being, or merely a subsidiary one, such as the notion of purification of sins by the confessional. When individual experience conforms to any such invariant theological concept, it has established the invariance of the given religion in the individual's experience. The thus reinforced C's, systematically correlated with others in the theological system, serve as the ground for new responses, having further impact on the environment, and tending to produce further confirmations of the religious system in experience. Thus, by means of R, religious experience is self-stabilizing, precisely as are the other circuits of human activity.

The adaptive self-organization of religious activity (Fig. 12*c*), provides for "learning" and flexibility under changing patterns of religious experience. It permits the development of C's whereby religious experiences that do not fit the established constructs can be accounted for. If a religious feeling lacks a correlated theological construct (i.e., if it is mismatched with the existing constructs), a problem arises. To resolve it, abstract thought processes (free-running activities) explore the intellectual horizons (the system's "degrees of freedom") in search of a hypothesis. The hypothesis is tested both in regard to its cogency to match the experience and its consistency with the existing constructs of the theology. Depending on factors thoroughly explored in the philosophy of science, the existing construct system—in this case the theology—is either modified or replaced. The history of religion provides ample examples of both the modification and the replacement of religious systems. Whether by revolution, reformation, or evolution, theological movements self-organizingly evolve a set of C's related by match signals to the prevalent types of religious feelings. The behavioral responses based on them prove suitable for optimizing the probability of the occurrence of the corresponding kind of feelings. Thus, the flow of information in religion, precisely as that in ordinary perceptual cognition, science, and art, turns out to be self-stabilizing through manipulation and self-organizing through adaptation.

Science, art, and religion are by far not the only types of circuits of cognitive activity of the civilized man. But together with perceptual cognition, they may be the only *pure* types, in the sense that all further activity and cognition patterns may represent specific combinations of them. (For example, much of economics is based on perceptual cognition with a significant degree of scientific theory, a measure of aesthetic vision, and even a degree of religious conviction thrown in,* and so on.) No man is exclusively an artist, a man of religion, or a scientist. Some men are all of these

---

* Compare with the paper by Bent Stidsen, Chapter 21.—EDITOR.

things, and all men are, whatever else they may also be, commonsensical, perceptually cognizing beings. Thus, although our analyses refer to idealizations, isolated for the sake of conceptual clarity, they may account for actualities through proper combinations.

CONCLUSIONS

We have asked how we can have knowledge of invariant things and principles on the basis of a constantly varying stream of sensory stimulation. In essaying an answer, we explored how far we can go toward designing a basic information flow in a self-organizing and self-stabilizing system that could be adequate to the task. Having outlined a basic design, we explored it in relation to the better known patterns of biological, neurological, and cognitive activities. The complex design called for to fully satisfy the requirements of these activities may never be perfected and rendered operational. But, on the basis of this preliminary sketch, we see no reason to believe that, *in principle,* such a design could not be produced.

The self-stabilizing and self-organizing regulatory system embodied in the human mind (more exactly in the brain and nervous system) is an order-extracting and imposing circuit, interacting with its environment. It is an invariant control system in itself, designed to manipulatively and adaptively extract invariances from its environment. The multilevel transformations of mind range from ordinary perceptual cognition and relevant behavior to scientific theory formulation and confirmation, the production and enjoyment of works of art, and the postulation and celebration of religious events and entities. The invariances extracted by these multiple circuits from the environment include the sensory *gestalten* that populate our everyday world, the invariant entities and laws of science, and the visions of artists and men of religious temper. The invariant flow of information embodied in the mind elicits the invariances disclosed in human experience; the invariance that is the *subject* of experience extracts the invariance that is its *object.*

If, as Margenau holds, reality is associated with invariance, then the reality of the objects of experience lies in the invariant codes in terms of which they are known. And likewise, the reality of mind lies in the invariant structure of its manifold operations. This assessment of reality does not lead to dualism. The invariance constituting the reality of mind constitutes the reality of a multilevel feedback-controlled self-stabilizing and self-organizing system. Such systems were thought, until recently, to be unique to living things. At present, thanks to the pioneering work of cyberneticians, information theorists, general semanticists, general systems theorists, and systems analysts, we come to the insight that the properties of the systems are independent of the origin, material, and individual identity of their components. The same regulatory system, expressed in a diagram or an information flow chart, may be realized as a system of transistors and capacitors, as a hydrodynamic system, or as a system of nervous pathways and synapses. The exploratory hypotheses of this study suggest that, underlying the complex phenomena of the human mind, there is a basic regulatory structure that permits one to conceive of the reality of the mind as the reality of the self-stabilizing and self-organizing system embodied in the nervous system. If this assessment can be upheld, investigation could be directed to the elucidation of the manifold cognitive processes that represent so many subroutines of the mind's invariance–extracting activity, untroubled by intimations of bodily and mental, physical and biological, dualism.

The reality of the subject of experience is also the reality of its objects —both are associated with the invariant structures that underlie all knowable phenomena. And if this conclusion is a fallacy entailed by the bias of the invariance-seeking human mind, then it is an incurable one; there are no "other" minds with which to inspect our own.

REFERENCES

1. MacKay, Donald M. "Towards an Information-Flow Model of Human Behaviour," *British Journal of Psychology,* 47, 1956.
2. Thornton, R. "Integrative Principles in Biology," *Integrative Principles in Modern Thought,* ed. Margenau, to be published.
   Similar statements are found in Miller, "The Organization of Life"; Cannon, *The Wisdom of the Body,* and Wiener, *The Human Use of Human Beings, et al.*
3. Sinnott, Edmund W. *The Biology of the Spirit.* New York, 1955.
4. Compare with the author's *The Structure of Human Experience,* to be published.
5. Hanson, N. R. *Patterns of Discovery.* London: Cambridge University Press, 1958.
6. Compare with Walter Pitts and Warren S. McCulloch, "How We Know Universals: The Perception of Auditory and Visual Forms," *Bulletin of Mathematical Biophysics,* 9, 1947.
7. Hanson, *op. cit.*
8. See Sir Herbert Read's work, *The Meaning of Art,* published in 1931 in London.
9. Whitehead, A. N. *Process and Reality.* New York: Social Science Books, 1929, p. 23.
10. James, William. *The Varieties of Religious Experience.* New York: Random House, 1904.
11. *Ibid.*

Patrick Meredith, M.Sc., M.Ed., Ph.D., F.B.Ps.S., is presently Chairman of the Department of Psychology at the University of Leeds, England. Trained as a psychophysicist, he is now completing a four-year operational research on the treatment of dyslexia with the aid of a grant from the British Department of Education and Science. He has recently published *Instruments of Communication,* and plans to publish a mathematical treatment of Epistemic Communication in a work on "The Modular Calculus."

31

THE STRUCTURE OF COMMUNICATION

PATRICK MEREDITH

INTRODUCTION

THE editor has asked me to expand the paper I preparde for the International Conference on General Semantics in order to bring out its relevance to general semantics. Korzybski, who gave the name "general semantics" in order, presumably, to distinguish his particular approach from semantics in general, covored such a wide field that it is difficult to thnik of any topic that is totally irrelevant to general semantics. Communication has an obvious relevance, but the title I was given was "The Structure of Communication," and the word *structure* raises problems that Korzybski certainly recognized, but I think it may be said that he did not see the necessity for the kind of solution that is now required. But in his concept of "time-binding," he did contribute an essential ingredient toward what I would regard as the kind of solution we most need.

I speak of a "kind of solution" because communication is like a Diophantine equation, having many solutions—possibly an infinity of solutions. But if we can just find a few solutions that actually work here on Earth, and between here and the Moon, we may later extend them to the problems that will arise, possibly in the '80's, when men may land on Mars. These problems are relevant not only to astronautics, but to our interpretation of history, and, indeed, to any problems in which there is both a time gap and an experience gap between sender and receiver. The most concrete and urgent instances of these communication problems are to be found in our educational systems, and especially in remedial education. And it is as editor of the *International Journal of the Educational Sciences* that I take this opportunity of pressing for much more precise thinking about how the educational system works. Although there are all kinds of gaps between intentions and fulfillments, it is the time gap and the experience gap that provide the most serious problems.

If we ask why we need the word *structure* when we already have words such as *shape, form, distribution, space, pattern,* etc., we could give various answers, but for our present purpose we might say that the noun *structure* is clearly related to the verb *to construct.* A structure is something that *has been constructed.** It therefore embodies time as well as space. It includes a dimension different from any space dimension, and yet, if we write equations or draw diagrams on flat paper, we are losing not merely one dimension of space but, because the result is static, we also lose the whole dimensionality of time (which, incidentally, I take to be not merely a "fourth dimension," but an infinity of dimensions). So we have a very tough problem in communicating what we mean by "structure" (even if our own thinking about it is clear, which is by no means always the case).

Neither spoken language, which is unidimensional, nor visual communication, which is primarily two dimensional (though it can create stereoscopic impressions, moving into a third dimension), can adequately express the structure of a process in time, in which changes are going on in 3-*D* space. Our difficulty in *representing* structure inevitably affects our conceptualization of structure, and that is what this paper explores.

The word *representation* nearly always suggests some type of "visual" form. This is because our visual sense, being by far the most precise and informative of our senses, has come to dominate all our other sensory capacities. It is enormously difficult for sighted persons to imagine a representation devoid of all visual components. Yet the inner world of the congenitally blind person is made up entirely of nonvisual components, and he can think and find his way around in such a world with remarkable facility. Indeed, in a sense, his is a more fundamental world than ours. And this is *our* "experience gap."

What is being explored, in the Epistemic Communication Research Unit at Leeds, is the problem of constructing an intersensory structural language equally meaningful in *any* sensory modality. With this research it is hoped to establish a common semantic field in which the blind and the sighted, the deaf and the hearing, the dumb and the articulate, the paralyzed and the "hapticals," the babe and the adult, the Earthman and the Martian, can reach one another across their experience gaps and time gaps. The basis of

---

* Compare with the paper by James M. Broadus, Chapter 1.—EDITOR.

this language is time itself. For the pulsation of time is common to all the senses, and a language of drumbeats can be translated into every sensory form. Every experience is a *timing of space*. The "binding" of these time patterns in a sensory representation is a *spacing of time*. It freezes the information and enables the "reader" to apprehend it at his own tempo. Thus, our study of the structure of communication may be described as the first step in a new science—the science of "the generalized intersensory and interpersonal document." This is a science of what Warren McCulloch calls "experimental epistemology" in studying its neurophysiological basis in the brain, and what I call "epistemics" in studying the output and input messages *between* brains. These brains belong to people, and a science of intersensory representation is essential for interpersonal communication in a community of individually differing sensitivities.

STRUCTURAL FEATURES

Structure is the way we describe space. It is the language of space differences. Empirical space presents us with various kinds of phenomenal objects—shoes and ships and sealing wax, and cabbages and kings. A shoe is a hollow cell for holding a foot, and it is either a left foot or a right foot. A ship is a complex structure of volumes, surfaces, and lines having a certain bias toward forward movement. A stick of sealing wax is a linear structure, diminishing in length as it is used. A cabbage grows by absorbing light and gases through its surfaces, and fluids through its roots, and its substance feeds us. A king has a head and feet, a front and back, a left and right side. These bodies all display the features of which structure is composed, such as shape, size, orientation, degrees of symmetry, dimensionality, solidity or hollowness, bias and sidedness.

ABSTRACT AND CONCRETE STRUCTURES

Mathematical space is, of course, a much cleaner, tidier affair. It is so clean that it can't be seen, for even the graphite of a pencil mark is so much dirt. Nor can it be touched or in any way demonstrated, for it is purely abstract. It can be described only by words that must be taken on trust, without even knowing what or whom we are trusting. When expressed in symbols, these are acts of faith. The axioms are not arguable, and the primitive terms are undefined. In short, it is a religious doctrine of the ineffable. Indeed this religion, which started in the mysticism of Pythagoras and Plato, now shows signs of supplanting all the older religions. Here we shall avoid theology and concentrate on strictly mundane activities such as engineering, surveying, building, carving, drawing, writing, reading, and counting. For although number is regarded as abstract, the things that we count can be seen or touched or heard, and so can the number-names we apply to them.

THE PRODUCTION OF FORMS

Since we cannot get far in these quantitative and structural activities without writing and drawing on paper, it is necessary to examine these documentary activities, and to ask what part they play in guiding our material constructions and our interpersonal communication. When we see someone writing a sentence or drawing a diagram, it is by no means easy to say where the shapes have come from. We suppose, vaguely, that they are stored in his head, but it seems very unlikely that they are merely copies of what is in the store. And when these graphic shapes are combined according to rules, how are the rules stored? Although mathematicians take some interest in the brain as a computer, and even as a pattern-recognition device, they seldom discuss its function as a form-producing device. But if we are to analyze the meaning of structure this is a very important question, for communication starts in one brain and ends in another.

FORMS AND VALUES

Now it will take a lot more neurophysiology than we, as yet, have available to explain in physiological terms just how a brain produces motor instructions that lead muscles to make forms on paper. We can observe the output itself, but not the process. What we can also observe, however, is the input. Unless the writer is merely a hack scribe or a copy typist, the input, in general, is widely different from the output, though not so different that the two have nothing in common. So we have a complex process in which certain input formations undergo certain transformations to yield an output, which we somewhat paradoxically refer to as "information." We can examine this at the level of letters, or of words, or of sentences. In each case, the rules are quite different. The strokes that make a letter have no literal value in themselves. The letters in a word have no verbal value. The words in a sentence have no sentential value.

STRUCTURAL TERMINOLOGY

Hearing the word *structure* used in many widely differing contexts, offering a promise of precise thinking, one is so frequently cheated by a failure to carry out the promise that one cultivates a habit of radical skepticism.

From this skeptical standpoint, let us examine whether "communication" can be said to have a "structure," and if so, in what precise terms this structure is to be presented. Must it necessarily be by means of a visual diagram, for example? Has music a structure? Can we assign a structure to social behavior, to a political constitution, to a military strategy? Does a dialogue have a structure, or a document, or a mathematical equation, or a recipe for baking a cake? In what terms can we speak of the structure of personality, or of the universe, or of the atom?

THE COMMUNICATION OF TIME

To make sense of the word *structure,* whether to be applied to communication or any other process, we must note that a process has a duration in time as well as a variation in space. However we define *time,* it remains invisible. Hence, any visual representation of time is necessarily symbolic and conventional. But if the convention is well chosen, it can direct the eye to make a movement and so reintroduce time into the experience of interpretation. But any symbol that directs a change of experience should serve just as well. Although visual communication is today the most vivid and most familiar mode, it is by no means the oldest, biologically speaking; and the blind, in spite of their affliction, are not *incommunicado.* Even the blind and deaf, as Helen Keller triumphantly demonstrated, can communicate.

TIME, TOUCH, AND MOVEMENT

For hundreds of millions of years before the evolution of ears and eyes, living creatures established communication with their environment by touch and movement. These two modes of experience are the foundations of consciousness itself. We could be *sans* eyes, *sans* ears, *sans* taste and smell, and still be conscious. But without skin and muscles, we could not survive. Thus touch and movement are, literally, the "touchstones" of communication. If we are to have a universal language of "structure," i.e., a vocabulary in which any structure whatever can be translated and interpreted by anyone living, this vocabulary must be built on the forms of experience that are common to all life. Here, in an English-speaking community, we can use familiar spoken or written words to *describe* these forms, but the forms themselves have to be experienced primarily by manipulation.

VALUE AND IMAGE

Many moments of experience are routine ephemeral trivialities, but others have a decisive value. They are decisive because they call for a decision. They have value because this decision costs the organism an effort. Subjectively, we describe these evaluations in emotive language such as "fear," "desire," "anger," etc. The evaluation process itself is a kind of computation in which the impact of incoming information on the current state of mobilization of the system of body processes creates a transitional state. We can describe this state emotively as "how we feel," or cognitively as "what we must do." But we have not yet done it; so it is not yet an action. It is the organic equivalent of potential energy. It is potential behavior. We can call it an "image" of incipient behavior, though it need not be a visual image.

IMAGE AND CONTROL

An "image" in this sense, while it may be subjectively described in terms of sight or sound, or some other sense, need not, in fact, be conscious at all. We can describe a body at high temperature as "hot," meaning that if we were in that state we should feel hot. But as a *state,* the temperature is a capacity for radiating heat. It is incipient thermal behavior. It differs from our own state when, for example, we are angry, in that we can, in fact, control our anger, whereas a hot body, unless insulated, cannot prevent itself radiating. The implication of this is that control depends on a kind of insulation. And it is precisely because every living organism *is* partially insulated, by its skin, that control has evolved.

SPACE AND FREEDOM

The insulation of the skin enables an organism to maintain a vastly complex system of autonomous processes that can continue at their own tempo for longer or shorter periods. The organism exists in a state of partial and intermittent disengagement from the tempo of surrounding events. We can describe this abstractly as the experience of pure space, i.e., a static state of consciousness free from the disturbance of alien variation. It may not last long, but while it lasts we can entertain what we call an "image." And we can decide whether to let the image evaporate or whether to behave in such a way to express it in material form. The experience of space is thus the condition for freedom of action.

ABSTRACT STRUCTURE

Our capacity for producing material forms, and our ability to refrain from producing them, is a demonstration both of our freedom and of the impossibility of separating the abstract concept of structure from its concrete expression. By "*the* concept," I mean a communicable mathematical form. After all, it is the mathematicians who have talked most about "abstract space." If this is a form that is never made concrete, it is an unsubstantiated subjective claim, not a communicable concept. For between one mathematician's skin and another mathematician's skin lies the space of concrete materials through which all their communication must pass.

CONDITION FOR ISOMORPHISM

We thus arrive at a concept of structure as an experience of one man which, through a concrete materialization, can give an experience to another man. These two experiences are private and mutually inaccessible. Since they can never be brought into juxtaposition, they cannot be compared. If we apply the adjective "isomorphic" to their relationship, it must mean not "the same form" but "elicited from the same formal object." But how can we know both that it *is* the same object and that its image is elicited in the same way? A fundamental principle arises here: *common knowledge of an object by two men can be ascertained by a third man only if their mutual knowledge of each other is established at the time of the knowing.*

THE PERSONAL PRONOUNS

The importance of this principle lies in the nature of language itself. An "ascertainment," i.e., a logical demonstration of the truth of a proposition, is a linguistic activity as well as a formal process. As a linguistic activity, it necessarily has an author. Hence logic can never be impersonal. Logic is simply the most formal mode of communication, in which persons are seeking to establish isomorphisms. The position and direction of any sign in this process is definable only by reference to the mutual positions of the two persons. Thus, the basis of all the so-called "logical constants" is to be found in the topological geometry of the personal pronouns. Since movement, contact, and radiation are all involved here, this must be a geometry of time as well as space.

LOGICAL IDENTITY

But the whole concept of structure is rooted in our demand for "constancy," for "invariance." And since time never ceases there is always variation. The way out of this dilemma is to be found in asking what we mean by "personal identity." I wake up in the morning and I seem to be still *me,* though I am several hours older than when I was last conscious. This subjective identity is a matter of having familiar images, i.e., feelings of sameness. This is enough for me, but it is not logic. If I wake up in a hospital and there is a need to establish my identity (i.e. to make a stable and verifiable statement of it), then communication becomes essential. Thus *logical identity requires communication between persons.*

THE SPACING OF TIME

This identity will involve not only persons and a flow of language, but recordings of past activity, whether in documentary form, or on tape, or in films, etc. In the long history of epistemology, which is itself a documentary activity, there has been a strange neglect of the fundamental role of the recording process in freezing time into space and making variation an invariant. If what I have said about the "structure of communication" can claim any novelty of approach, it is the introduction of a view of structure that sees it as a fossilization of interpersonal contacts as a means for satisfying a human need for the conservation of information. By freezing an image in space, we can contemplate its structure in our own time and at our own personal tempo.

Thomas E. Miller received his Ph.D. in Speech from North-western University in 1957. He has taught Human Relations, Organizational Behavior, and Communication at Northwestern University and the University of Kansas. He was a Training Fellow in Human Relations, Harvard Business School, 1952–54, and is currently Professor of Business Administration and Human Relations at the University of Missouri at Kansas City.

Bernard Sarachek received his Ph.D. in Business from the University of Illinois in 1962. He has taught Business, Economics and related areas at Clark University, University of Detroit and Rutgers. He is currently Professor of Administration at the University of Missouri at Kansas City.

32

MANAGEMENT BY UNDERSTANDING*

THOMAS E. MILLER and BERNARD SARACHEK

THERE are at least four different levels at which administrators may attempt to control or motivate subordinates:

1) Administrators may change the formal organization's structure, procedures, or rewards system. Such diverse plans as F. W. Taylor's "scientific management," the Scanlon Plan, traditional plans for decentralizing organizations, and various job enlargement schemes, all involve adjusting the formal organization in order to influence subordinates. This approach is based on two assumptions:
   a) the right formal rewards system will bring forth the right performance, and/or
   b) the failure to give the individual responsibility for a job large enough to be a meaningful challenge destroys his natural tendency toward high performance.

2) At a second level, attempts may be made to alter the environment in order to help the individual assimilate into his small informal group, while simultaneously encouraging the group to seek more complete

---

* The authors respectfully dedicate this article to the memory of Dr. Irving J. Lee of Northwestern University.

cooperation with other groups in the organization or society. This approach assumes that man has a natural propensity to form face-to-face groups that help define his social identity.

3) At a still more sophisticated level, the effort may be made to change the individual internally. The orientation here may be one of inducing change by forcing conformity—as the case of the "periodic evaluation" and "merit rating," or by setting forth the conditions under which he would voluntarily choose to change as a result of additional "self-knowledge"—as in the cases of "sensitivity training," "management-grid training," and individual counseling. Shame, guilt, acceptance, reward, and punishment are among the psychosocial pressures employed to induce a new conversion.

4) The fourth level that may be employed to influence others is probably the oldest—and most easily overlooked—approach to influencing human behavior. It is the approach of attempting to *understand* others. Every individual will seek to "size up" the important people in his life. A mere awareness of the existing style of operation of others could make a world of difference in our abilities to successfully interact with them.

While all four approaches may be useful, we are dealing only with that of simple understanding.[1] The other three approaches are mentioned merely to differentiate them from simple understanding—though admittedly, understanding is implicit as the first step in each of the other approaches. This article reflects the authors' faith that a host of interpersonal difficulties can be reduced or resolved by merely understanding one another without taking the further step of a conscious or concerted effort at reforming either the organization, group, or the individual.

THE INDIVIDUAL'S STYLE

An individual's style is that repertoire of attitudes and ways of behaving that he tends to use with particular frequency. Understanding the individual becomes a matter of learning his repertory, and learning how to draw forth those responses from that repertory that will continue and enhance the mutual benefits derived from our interactions with him.

We normally "size up the other fellow" by becoming aware of his characteristic ways of behaving, which are either too pronounced to ignore, or which complement our own needs and attitudes so well that we do not choose to ignore them. Our only refinement is the attempt at becoming more discerning by focusing on a few facets of behavior we ought to keep in mind as soon as we become aware of the need to obtain a greater understanding of the other fellow. The individual's style of approaching his life and his environment on or off the job may be categorized along three dimensions: his view of time, his view of the world, and his methods for engaging the world.

Time

In Dicken's *Christmas Carol,* Scrooge moved from spiritual void to full humanity as he successively encountered the spirits of the past, the present, and the future. Perhaps the most satisfying perceptions of time for most of us occur when we become capable of living *simultaneously* in all three periods—perceiving the past as a period of promise that is still being fulfilled in the present, and anticipating the future as the natural rewards (consequences) of the present, bearing with it a still higher level of fulfillment.[2] Despair, by contrast, is a feeling that one no longer has a meaningful future, and the present is a shabby substitute for a more satisfying past. For the escapist, the present may be a distasteful interlude between a romanticized past and a more satisfying future; or perhaps the future may be the revengeful vindication for the unpleasant inequities, frustrations, and humiliations of the present or past. How one weaves together his past, present, and future goes far to determine his self-image, and the valuation he places on his life. Rather like the Fates of Greek mythology, how *we* do our weaving patterns our future and our present.

View of the World

Each of us may have his own particular explanation of how and why the world is as it is. Understanding others starts with the attempt to comprehend their particular image of the world. Yet, though understanding implies acknowledging uniqueness, all different views of the world can be categorized to some degree. We may, for example, distinguish between those views that place relatively great trust in the yielding benevolence of the world, and those views which reflect fear and suspicion of the world. Some individuals are attuned to thinking in terms of a relativistic world, while others tend to bifurcate the world into two-valued exclusive categories of "good" and "bad," "men" and "women," "friends" and "enemies," etc.[3] Some tend to act in ways which are relatively consistent with their verbally expressed beliefs and attitudes, while others are much less consistent in word and deed.

Method of Engaging the World

The manner by which the individual engages the world depends first on his view of the world. But his view of the world is merely a prediction of how the world will respond to him. The particular choices of how to approach the world and engage it is much more directly a function of his personality and the history of environmental conditioning that went into the formulation of his personality structure. Thus, when we speak of a method of engaging the world, we are speaking of the types of choices the individual will normally tend to make within the range of choice his particular view of the world affords him.

A SAMPLER OF THREE CASES

We can more readily understand others if, when we approach them, we keep in mind the three questions: How do they relate their three time periods to one another? How do they view their world? What particular patterns do they follow when engaging the world? The true test of the worth of these three questions can only be determined by each of us in our particular real life situations and relationships. Yet we may simulate the process of understanding by presenting and discussing case reports of actual individuals, and in this way indicate how these three questions might be employed. The three cases we have chosen are actually tersely condensed portraitures based on much more elaborate field interview data.

John Winters

I came to work for this organization four years ago and have loved every minute of it. Here I can find challenge while at the same time maintain my integrity and perform a service to the company. Challenge, integrity, and reward for competence—that's tops in my book. What else does a man need?

Oh, I know you are going to hear a lot of complaints some people around here have about the work, long hours, and all the traveling that goes along with the job. These people who think they have to travel a lot, heck, they should have been in the military if they think this is anything. And work! If you start counting the hours on the clock you'll never get through the job. I say, go out and meet the assignment, do what it takes regardless of the hours, get the report written and get on to the next assignment. But, no, many of the guys around here complain about the "rotten" assignments, the long travel distances, and the lack of an eight-hour day. They like to be martyrs. But not for me, this martyr stuff!

Besides, the supervisors here will treat you right if you do the job right. They know what it was like to spend long hours working in the field, and, frankly, they haven't forgotten the heartaches in writing up long and complicated reports. If you do the job they expect without complaints and gripes, they'll see to it that you are treated right on assignments. Why some of the men around here will argue with a supervisor about every word on their reports. They get so upset when their bosses change words or phrases, even the whole report. I remember one supervisor telling me that I shouldn't use the word *reflect* in connection with evidence. He explained that *reflect* suggested a mirror approach to evidence, the "evidence shows" such and such, and does not "reflect." So, if he believed that, and wanted the report written that way, I say more power to him. Why should I argue or carry on? I try to find out what each one of my supervisors wants, what their favorite words and expressions are—and learn how they want the reports organized, and write them that way. Heck, they've been at this report writing a lot longer than I have, and I figure I've got lots to learn. So, why make a big production of a few changes? Besides, now that I've learned what they want, they hardly ever change my reports anymore.

Management, that's the secret to success. Management just doesn't stop with handling people—no, sir. It begins and ends with each person individually. That's why so many around here complain and believe they are getting a raw deal. They blame organizational management. The problem is their own personal management. If they would plan their work properly, figuring out their travel plans, decide a sequence of interviews, they needn't be out in the field six and seven weeks at a time. They could come home every third weekend, see the family, write up their reports, and get back in the field for the next assignment. But not some of these fellows.

Say, do you think a guy can be friendly with his supervisors and do a good job at the same time? I think so. My former boss and I were good friends. We went hunting and fishing together, and got into all sorts of social activities together. And we never had one bit of job-and-friendship trouble. No sir, I never took advantage of his friendship even once. Why, we even put on several skits together for the organization here at our annual Christmas party, and they went over big. Even the big boss said we did a good job. When my boss got promoted upstairs, I think he wanted me to go with him. But since everyone here has been so nice to me, and they offered me his job as a promotion, I felt proud and obligated to stay. Now I am responsible for the work of many others. Before, I was responsible only for my own behavior and assignments. I tell myself it's like when I graduated from fighter pilot to bombers. I went from a one-man show to a situation of responsibility for many. That's what I've got here, I guess—a crew to work with.

Oh, I'm going to enjoy it, I'm sure. I have every confidence everything will work out fine because as my new boss I've got the finest man in the world to work for—that's George Green. He has very high standards and doesn't believe in this equality stuff that's being preached around here. Green gives each man what he *earns* and can deliver. You treat George right and he'll treat you right. I think that is the secret, don't you? Don't ask for anything you haven't earned, and if you have earned it, you'll get it. Maybe not always right now, but in the long run. Lose some today and win some tomorrow. But, in the long haul, bosses will treat you right. I know that.

Winters' Uses of Time

For Winters, time usage has a relatively low priority. "Nonwork" time represents a *reserve* that can always be dipped into if the allotted amount of time is not enough for the job. Time is not a problem because Winters has mastered its uses so thoroughly that it bends to his will. By comparison, the individual who is obsessed with "saving time" is just the reverse of a John Winters. The "time saver" is apt to be a person who always feels that time is running ahead of him no matter how he tries or plans to keep up.

There is a sense of justice built into Winters' time perspective. The bosses help see to this. If you do things right today, you come out ahead in the long run. This belief is but one aspect of Winters' strong sense of continuity over time. The successes of today are not unlike his past military successes. The same style of performance is still working well. Winters' style is to manage. When he has no subordinates, he can still manage time, his job, and himself. Over time, the natural consequence of successful self management is to be given the opportunity to employ the same style of management over others.

Winters' View of the World

Winters trusts authority to be helpful, rewarding, and fair. His preoccupation with managers and the value of managing suggests that he views authority as being invested with the prime responsibility for running this world. The hard working competent people with integrity will find their interests served by management. Only the clock watchers who complain about giving their fair share of time to the job and who do not know how to manage time themselves will have difficulties dealing with authority. There are apparently only these two types of people in the world, and obviously to insist on equality between the competent people with integrity, and the inefficient clock watchers is to be unfair.

The job itself is seen as an opportunity rather than a burden. It can be used to learn and to prove one's integrity by being strong enough to meet challenges competently. Yet, at the same time, Winters is quite willing to set his feelings and investment in the job aside and accept without challenge whatever his superiors seem to want in the way of reports. What could be more upsetting than having to inject someone else's words and re-port style into the particular prose we might choose when communicating the results of a completed assignment in which we take pride? It would ap-pear that Winter's satisfactions are vested less in the pleasure of performing the task than in satisfying his superiors.

How Winters Engages His World

Winters is quite versatile in his dealings with authority. He has the emo-tional capability of not challenging authority when it does not want to be challenged. He handles authority by giving managers what they want, even friendship. He has learned how to incorporate their desires and expecta-tions into his own behavior and values. In short, he is willing to try every possible way to relate to his superiors.

The Prognosis for Winters

He has a winning style on the job. There is no reason to predict difficul-ties in his future relations with superiors, particularly if he remains in an organizational setting that is highly task oriented. If one would envisage one possible difficulty for Winters it would be most apt to occur in a much different organizational setting placing a high valuation on "subordinate oriented" human relations. In an organization emphasizing equalitarianism and democratic management, Winters may be faced with demands for changes in his values and behavior that exceed his capacity for adjustment. However, even this possibility is just a speculation since nothing in his record yields an example in which his flexibility was tested by such a situation.

John Winters has been quite successful in satisfying his need by adjust-ing to the demands made upon him by authority and by his job. In fact, he would fit very nicely the description of the "rate-buster." The next case, by contrast, is an example of an individual who has had some real difficulty adjusting to authority and, indeed, to the world in general.

Jim Miles

That boss of mine is destroying all confidence in myself and in my ability to write. No job is worth getting upset about every day. I think the only thing left is to look for another job—and the sooner the better. My boss, Park Lusk, has got such high standards. I don't mean to knock him. He knows his work and all that. I guess he does. But sometimes I just can't get to work. I'm all tied up inside. Nothing comes out. I can write and I know I can. I've got proof of that, but when I'm told I can't—well, I don't like it.

Of course, he's not the best writer who ever lived himself. Take the last issue we did—well, maybe I should say *he* did. At any rate, I submitted an article and he thought the ideas weren't bad, but then he proceeded to rewrite all my copy. He thinks he's improving it, but he's not as far as I'm concerned.

You know, he told me that my writing wasn't mature! Can you beat that? He told me I should read more poetry and great literature like T. S. Eliot. Then he started to quote from "The Love Song of [J.] Alfred Prufrock." I studied it in college just like he did, but I didn't say anything. That's the way I am when somebody gets on me. I get so boiled up inside that I can't talk or argue or anything. So I just sat there. But boy that made me mad. And then he criticized me because I don't take work home the way he does. He thinks you should work on the magazine 24 hours a day! You know, I haven't written a single thing to suit him since I started on the job.

Frankly, I don't think I should have ever gotten into the writing game anyway. I come from a small town. And, well, life was quite different when I got to the big city. I don't know quite how I got here. Well, of course, I do too. When the war was over, I had my G.I. bill, and I thought about going to school. I didn't want to go back to Easternville. You see, my father comes from the old country, and can't speak very good English. He's worked all his life sweeping floors in the local school. I guess I didn't want to wind up in a small town like my brothers and sisters—just rotting away being a storekeeper or janitor. Sweeping floors or delivering groceries wasn't my idea of a future. I did that after I got out of high school for a while. I helped my father sweep because he's old, and none of the other kids would. I don't guess they cared much, but I did.

But all the time I wanted something a little different. Is that so wrong? I guess I got into journalism because in high school a teacher used to encourage me to write. I once thought I could, just a little. At any rate, I started to school in New York City. I worked hard, tried to get along, and always tried to remain humble. That may sound kind of funny. Others laugh, but regardless of how many degrees I get, I don't ever want to forget where I came from, that I'm a janitor's son. But I also wanted to show Bill Jones and some others in my home town that I could amount to something. Bill runs one of the local drygoods stores, and was always a big shot in high school.

After school I worked in the city for one of the local stock journals. I continued to live near the campus. I guess I liked it there. The journal job wasn't too bad, but there weren't any possibilities for imagination of any sort. I hadn't planned to stay there very long anyway, so about a year after I started, I got a job working with the William Machinery Corporation on their personnel magazine. I didn't mind the work much, but no one seemed to pay me much mind, unless I was late or something like that. Then you heard about it but quick. Unless something like that happened, you were just a number.

It was after I moved to a room by myself that I met my future wife. I got acquainted with her through social activities in my church. I'm quite religious and take an interest in several of the church's activities. About a year later we were married, and that's one of the best decisions I ever made in my life. She encourages me a lot. Before I got married I never could save a dime. Now I take the paycheck home to her and we save a little from it each month.

I became a lot more settled after I married, and I've told my wife, jokingly of course, that we might go back to Easternville and I'll sweep floors in the local school. I tell her the big city is pretty cold. She understands and tells me we'll do what I think is best. She encourages me, and I need encouragement. For instance, I've always wanted to drive, but I never had an opportunity. My father never owned a car because they were so expensive, and there were so many children in the family. About six months ago, I mentioned to my wife that driving might be fun. Also with the baby and all, it would be easier if we had a car to drive to Easternville instead of taking a train. She said if I wanted a car and wanted to learn to drive, then I was to take driving lessons. I did, and that's worked out fine.

Miles' Uses of Time

Miles hints at a very typical response to present dissatisfaction when he starts to protest that he doesn't know how he got to the big city. He momentarily detaches the present from the past, for as Miles demonstrates by retracing his steps, he arrived where he is primarily because of his own choosing. If the present is a fulfillment of the promise of the past, continuity and one's share in making one's own present would be quite readily admitted.

Actually, Miles never really seemed to leave the past. Indeed he has mobilized his present and future to fight the battle of the past. Little is indicated of his attitude toward the future except his fantasy of returning to the past by going back to Easternville—driving a car—to sweep floors. When there is unfinished business from the past, there is a tendency to seek out or set up a situation in the present where the same drama can be replayed—hopefully to the end. Miles wanted to show the school big shot, Bill Jones, that he could amount to something, and journalism is one way to shout back to the small town from the big city that the janitor's son is better than the Bill Joneses of the world. Yet, when he seeks for a louder journalistic perch, Miles only runs into a new Bill Jones claiming intellectual superiority in the form of Park Lusk.

Miles' View of the World

To Miles the city, unlike Easternville, is a cold place. However, we don't know, as yet, exactly what he finds cold about it. We know more about his view of authority. Authority can be crippling and unreasonable. It can destroy Miles' self-confidence. Even though he would like to think that down deep he is just as good as a Park Lusk, he crumbles in the face of criticism. Authority is too threatening to answer directly.

How Miles Engages the World

Since Miles, the son of a foreign-speaking janitor, is too lacking in confidence or articulation to talk back directly to authority, he must disengage. Just as he left Easternville and the William Machinery Corporation, he is now preparing to escape Park Lusk and look for better footing in the world elsewhere. The only way he can talk back is to put distance between himself and authority, and shout back from afar through the medium of journalism. Words are power, and his words can overcome those of authority only if he can amplify them to carry so far that they overrun criticism without giving authorities' words an opportunity to reach back.

The Prognosis for Miles

If we wished to change Miles we might encourage him to alter his perceptions of time. In particular, we might encourage him to forget about his past "unfinished business" and begin to view the present and future as more meaningful. We might also attempt to alter Miles' view of authority so that Park Lusk's behavior is accounted for by Miles as learning opportunities at best or, at the worst, the personality peculiarities of Lusk to which Miles must adapt in a more mature manner. In short, to change Miles we would have to do a fairly complete job of overhauling his personality.

If we merely wish to understand Miles, we may start by accepting as given data the fact that he is holding to his particular mythologized image of time, authority, and the world. The problem, then, of helping him to be more effective in this world becomes one of affirming him and aiding him to work through his particular drama. This is what his high school teacher apparently did by directing his attention to journalism—the means by which he could reply to authority, and this appears to be what his wife did by affirming his religious values, encouraging him to learn how to drive, and encouraging him to do that which he thinks best.

The last case in this sampler deals with a young man, twenty-one years of age. Unlike the other two cases, this individual views superiors, peers, and lower status workers as opportunities to give and receive warmth and friendship. He has taken a humanistic "person oriented" approach to work. At the same time, however, this individual is similar to the other two cases insofar as he does find his task and authority relations to be particularly critical elements in achieving satisfaction in life.

Lynn Porter

When I first came to work here, Mr. Hansen, the boss, put me on special projects—that's a fancy name for doing all sorts of odd jobs and filling in for the girls when they are absent. I started with Rose Johnson in accounts receivable. I sat right next to her and watched her, and did everything she did. I learned her job and took over when she had her baby. When I was free from my work, I would run errands for Ann Clark, Mr. Hansen's secretary, or help her out when she was rushed with records. Also, I worked for Gloria Holman in payroll before she was made head bookkeeper. Then I handled accounts payable when that girl quit. I was always ready to pitch in where they needed me. I learned a lot that way. Even Mr. Hansen said that I could fill in anywhere in a pinch.

I started working on the computer as an assistant. Then one payroll period the regular operator failed to show for work and Mr. Hansen told me to get the payroll out. At the end of the day he told me that I was the computer operator from then on.

When they decided to get the bigger computer, Mr. Hansen sent me to an advanced computer school. It was rough. I couldn't sleep from worrying about the classes. I lost my dinner almost every night. But I was determined not to disappoint the company, and particularly Mr. Hansen, for showing such faith in me. I worked almost twenty hours every day, but at the end of two weeks I passed with flying colors.

It'll be a bit of a crisis for a time when the new computer comes. It's bigger than the present one, and we'll have to use both for about six months while we make the transfer and debug the new programs. But we'll make the transition okay. I've got confidence in that. I know the girls will cooperate. You see, here it isn't everyone for himself. Here we work together. Programming and running the computer isn't easy, and we are often racing with the clock to get certain jobs finished and on Mr. Hansen's desk on time. But I help the girls as much as I can to run their data through the computer, and they're always grateful for that. You know, in spite of the crises and hard work, we kid together and have a lot of fun. They're just about the nicest people I know.

I try to get along. You see my life before this was pretty hard. My mother and father divorced when I was four, and my sister and I were left pretty much alone because my mother worked. Mother used to say that I was the man of the house and would have to make decisions. But in spite of all her good intentions, I couldn't forget I didn't have a father. When I was eight mother remarried. That man beat me and my sister unmercifully. When I was twelve, he abandoned us—thank God! If I ever see him again, I'll beat him to a pulp.

I wanted to go to college, but there wasn't any money, and by then my mother was on her fourth husband and he wasn't interested in giving me any. So I went to work instead. I tried several jobs but I didn't like any of them. Finally I landed a selling job, but it was just too unethical for me. They expected me to take repossessed equipment and sell it for new. I told them I wouldn't do it. So they got mad and I quit. Then while I was waiting for something to turn up, I read this ad in the paper for a part-time person at this company. So I got an interview with Mr. Hansen. It was the greatest thing that ever happened to me.

I love my work so much I guess my wife thinks I live here. She still doesn't understand why I'm out at night so much. I frankly think I married too early. A man has a lot of living to do, and when he's married at twenty-one, it kind of puts a crimp in things, if you know what I mean. I engage in various activities because it helps my development. I recently joined the Lions Club, and Mr. Hansen was nice enough to get me into the Masons. I'm also a scoutmaster for the Boy Scout group that meets here at the company twice a month. And in addition to these activities. I've become interested in charity work. When Mr. Hansen asked me to help out with the United Fund—kind of be cochairman with him—I jumped at the opportunity since it is very good to be identified with community services, and also I want every kid to have the chances I didn't have, and that's why I think charities and scouting are so important.

I suppose my activities keep me out two or maybe three nights a week. Then, of course, sometimes I have to come in here and work on the computers if anything goes wrong. I've told the night operator I'm on call twenty-four hours a day to help. I sometimes get calls at 2:00 or 3:00 in the morning, but not frequently. And sometimes I come back to the building in the evenings to see that everything is going right. Occasionally I stop and talk with the janitors, the scrubwoman, or drop down to the snack shop to talk to people who are in the building working late. It's wonderful here at work. I guess you could call it my home in many ways.

I guess my only real problem now is my health. I guess that's hard to believe about anyone who looks as healthy as I do. But I've been having these bad burning pains in my stomach, and these sensations travel all the way up my esophagus and into my throat. I even went to a doctor to have X-rays made. I've told my wife about my stomach trouble and she is kind of sympathetic, but I guess she thinks I should be stoic and take everything in my stride.

Porter's Uses of Time

Porter's past environment is certainly quite different from his present. Unlike a Jim Miles, however, it was not Porter who chose to detach his past from his present. Porter was literally born anew, leaving behind a past of adversity for a present of personal growth and warmth.[4]

Despite the discontinuity in Porter's life between the past and present, he, like Jim Miles, appears to be using the present to handle the unfinished business of the past. Porter is using his current job, his boss, and his fellow workers to reconstruct a home and family life that will give him the security to grow to further maturity. While a Jim Miles merely replayed the drama of the past to the same unfortunate conclusion, Porter's new environment permits him to find a new and much more satisfactory conclusion. He has grasped the opportunity to finish his unfinished business, and he is prepared to move on to a newer stage of personal development.

Porter's present is a period of rapid ongoing personal development. Even in his future there does not appear to be any particular end or given level of achievement for him to take aim on. Porter's status, personality, and role are simply accelerating their growth without approaching any apparent limit.

Porter's View of the World

Porter has known the extremes of the world. His world can be categorized neither as entirely threatening not entirely accepting. Within the company—as within the ideal home—all he finds is a helpful benevolence. This company-home is a much warmer and more attractive place than the world he has encountered outside in the form of his past and present family life and his past jobs. The company has provided him with women who seem to fill him with sustenance. They teach him, and give him friendship and cooperation. Mr. Hansen, like a benevolent father, presents him with new challenges, opportunities, trust, responsibilities, and promotional rewards.

Even the computer has an almost familial role. He has tried hard to learn how to master it. It, like the women, is a dispenser of information and learning possibilities. It demands attendance at any possible hour. Though Porter (the son?) tends it, its output is ultimately destined for Mr. Hansen's desk (the father?). In short, he has more than humanized the job. He has familialized the job, the computer, his peers, and his boss.

His style of dealing with the job is anything but fatalistic. He has learned that plentiful opportunities exist, which one can use for personal growth. Indeed, he seems to be a master at recognizing opportunities and exploiting them without engendering hostilities or conflicts with others.

How Porter Engages the World

Porter values affection and growth opportunities. Consequently, he approaches the world with an eye toward gaining these. He engages the world as a learner and as a helper. As a learner he gives personal deference to those whom he engineers into the role of his teachers. As a helper he gives his service to others liberally. He will always "pitch in" where needed. To those whom he places in a teaching role he returns gratitude and status, and to both his teachers and those he aids he also passes along his affection in return for theirs.

In the process of learning and helping, Porter accumulates more responsibilities both on and off the job. His stature grows with the increased responsibilities he is able to assume. He begins to appear increasingly indispensable as a man who can always be counted upon.

The Prognosis for Porter

Psychiatrist Eric H. Erikson has classified the development of man's emotional maturity into "eight ages of man." Porter would seem to best fit Erikson's schema as having developed to an age of maturity well short of adolescence (i.e., the fifth state of maturation). The dominant characteristics of Porter's personality seem to have matured no further than Erikson's third age, the locomotor-genital age. At this emotional age,

> . . . the child is at no time more ready to learn quickly and avidly, to become bigger in the sense of sharing obligation and performance. . . . He is eager and able to make things cooperatively . . . he is willing to profit from teachers and to emulate ideal prototypes. He remains, of course, identified with the parent of the same sex, but for the present he looks for opportunities where work-identification seems to promise a field of initiative without too much infantile conflict or oedipal guilt and a more realistic identification based on a spirit of equality experienced in doing things together. . . .[5]

Porter has yet to outgrow his company-home. Eventually, as his role, status, and personality continue to expand, he will approach the limits of the sustenance that the company, the women, and Mr. Hansen can or will provide. At such a point, he must be prepared either to leave the company-home or start fighting for more developmental room within the company-home. He is entirely too young, and has moved too rapidly, to choose a third alternative of resigning himself to accepting either a relatively stationary or moderate, but steadily yielding, limit, to his further advancement.

In short, the possibilities of eventual oedipal tensions and even conflict between Porter and Mr. Hansen are quite high. Furthermore, Porter's opportunities of bypassing conflict by leaving the company as tensions arise are rather limited since he tends to lack the sorts of status that are easily transferable from one company to another. He is extremely young; he lacks a college degree; his existing on-the-job relations do not transfer with him; and his knowledge of the computer is rather limited, being particularly appropriate to the needs of his present company. In addition, as accident would have it, Mr. Hansen's immediate superior is in his late 20's, while Hansen himself is in his very early 40's. This age disparity may well be worked to Porter's advantage should he find himself eventually in a conflictful relationship with Hansen.

GENERAL SEMANTICS AND UNDERSTANDING

In this article, we have excluded until now almost all of the special terminology of general semantics and direct reference to general semantics theory. Teachers of general semantics have done superb jobs of translating the concepts of Korzybski, Whorf, Bridgman, and others into language that the average layman can comprehend and apply to his world. Yet, in the process, some writers and teachers have implicitly introduced two doctrinal biases that are quite opposite to the sort of flexible thinking one would expect of general semantics. Implicit in our discussion of simple understanding is a rejection of these two biases that some readers might mistakenly take as a rejection of the wisdom of general semantics. The two biases may be stated as follows: (1) Myths represent radical divergences between word-maps and life-fact territories. Therefore, we should not condone or reinforce the myths of others. (2) We should actively help others to remove divergences between their word-maps and life-fact territories by encouraging them to make more proper evaluations. We should aid others to become more effective in time-binding, nonallness, and nonidentification, avoiding the pitfalls of two-valued orientations, distinguishing between life-facts and word-maps, etc.

In short, these two biases imply a responsibility to attempt altering other individuals internally. By contrast, the notion of simple understanding, which we have discussed, implies a willingness to tolerate the mythical wishes and mythical time-world images of others. Rather than inducing others to "see the light," we are suggesting that much can be accomplished by interaction with others on the basis of *our* understanding of *their* myths, so as to aid those others to complete the dramas of their "unfinished business"—i.e., enable them to outgrow their myths rather than abandon them in midstream—and in this way mature to a saner relationship with us and their world.

If we attempt to *understand* others, it is we who are obliged to live by the wisdom of general semantics. We must be concerned about becoming "time-binders," and we must attempt to become more aware of the noncongruence between word-maps and life-fact territories. The more willing we are to employ the sort of wisdom indicated by general semantics, the more effective we will be in learning about the word-maps of others, and linking our interactions meaningfully to their wishes, their word-maps, and to our wishes. This does not mean, of course, that we should presume to become the judges of others. Rather, we hold with Carl R. Rogers the view that "understanding *with* a person, not *about* him—is such an effective approach that it can bring about major changes in personality."[6]

More than either of the other two cases, the Lynn Porter case suggests the positive force that can be unleashed by simple understanding, for purposes of helping the individual to develop. Largely by accident Porter found himself in a situation that coincided with his mythical wish for a rebirth into a new home-like and familial environment. As a consequence, he was well on his way toward developing to a higher stage of maturity. Most of this beneficial effect could have occurred just as easily as a consequence of his superior's understanding rather than the actual accidental congruity of Porter's wish and his superior's personal and task needs. Unlike Porter, Miles continued to encounter situations in which his mythical wish to prove himself to the high status Bill Joneses of the world remained unfulfilled either because of a lack of understanding or a lack of interest of his superiors in helping him to achieve its fulfillment.

The John Winters case indicates at least one danger in the approach of understanding. Unlike the other two cases, Winters was not faced with the dilemma of fulfilling a mythical wish. In other words, he did not find it necessary to contort the present in order to reenact the dramas appropriate to some quite different time period. Indeed, we get the impression that Winters has made every effort to drive out of his conscious mind any overall motivating wish. He seems to be saying that if he does not expose his wishes to himself or others, then the world and its administrators will see to it that he is properly treated. Any wish he otherwise might have had would be fulfilled by not wishing it. Of the three cases, only John Winters made an intensely self-controlled and concerted effort to understand others. He seemed to sacrifice excessively of himself in order to adapt to his understandings of his superiors. He forfeited not only his right to wish, but his right to complain, and even his right to express himself verbally on paper as he saw fit. To predicate our actions on an understanding of the views and wishes of others runs the risk of altering, forfeiting, or delaying some of our wishes in order to enhance the fulfillment of others' wishes. It is difficult not to feel that Winters has carried this to such an excess that he almost effaces his own personality in order to understand and relate to the needs of his superiors. Adjusting our behavior on the basis of our understandings of others should ideally be carried only so far as it enhances our personalities. Beyond this point, interactions based on understanding have been carried too far.

REFERENCES

1. F. J. Roethlisberger, in an early essay, stressed management's need to understand organizational behavior vis-à-vis the interviewing method. See his "Understanding: A Prerequisite to Leadership," recently reprinted in *Man-in-Organization: Essays of F. J. Roethlisberger*. Cambridge: Harvard University Press, pp. 20–34.
2. This view of time is totally consistent with Gordon W. Allport's psychology of "becoming." See Allport's book *Becoming: Basic Considerations for a Psychology of Personality*. New Haven: Yale University Press, 1955.
3. Korzybski's diagnosis of the two-valued pattern in intensional orientation and Mayo's observation of the false dichotomies in the thinking of obsessives were both helpful. See Alfred Korzybski, *Science and Sanity: An Introduction to Non-Aristotelian Systems and General Semantics*. Lakeville, Conn.: Institute of General Semantics, 1948; and Elton Mayo, *Some Notes on the Psychology of Pierre Janet*. Cambridge: Harvard University Press, 1948.
4. Porter's real life story is strikingly like a host of myths in the history of our society dealing with the second birth of the Hero. The Hero leaves behind a world of hardships and dangers to be reborn into a world of warmth replete with foster parents capable of providing wealth, wisdom, and happiness. Porter's experience of floating through several jobs, landing at a part-time job, and unexpectedly finding a home, is not unlike baby Moses' experience of floating downstream in a basket to the feet of his foster mother, the Pharoah's daughter. See Otto Rank, *The Myth of the Birth of the Hero*. New York: Robert Brunner, 1952. Translated by F. Robbins and S. E. Jelliffee. Martin Luther provides another case analysis of one "twice-born." See E. H. Erikson, *Young Man Luther: A Study in Psychoanalysis and History*. New York: W. W. Norton, 1962.
5. Erikson, Eric H. *Childhood and Society*. New York: W. W. Norton, 1963, p. 258.
6. Rogers, Carl R. *On Becoming a Person*. Boston: Houghton Mifflin Co., 1961, p. 332. See also Rogers' book *Client-Centered Therapy*. Boston: Houghton Mifflin Co., 1965.

Maurice B. Mitchell, formerly President and Editorial Director of Encyclopaedia Britannica, Inc., became the thirteenth Chancellor of the University of Denver in 1967. He is a member of the President's Committee on Civil Rights, has instituted formation of the National Citizens Committee for NDEA, serves on the Advertising Council's Public Policy Committee, and has been honored with the George Washington Honor Medal of the Freedoms Foundation.

33

OVER—, UNDER—, AND MISCOMMUNICATION IN OUR SOCIETY

MAURICE B. MITCHELL

I'VE given a lot of thought to the special effect that political activities of high density have on the whole field of communications. There are many examples of problems in communications that grow out of politics. One of the problems is that of translating the words of politicians who fracture the language beyond recognition.

A friend of mine related an extreme example: Finishing a political oration at a convention, one candidate drew himself up to his fullest height and concluded his remarks by saying, "And so we look down the untrod path of the future, seeing there the invisible footprint of some giant hand!"

Governor Brown, during his succesful campaign for the California state house, once exhorted his electorate to drive the Republicans out of the statehouse. "We will eliminate them from any position of power and significance in this state," he said, "and we will do this in one foul swoop."

During the first of the current series of Israeli–Arab conflicts, the United Nations Security Council held an emergency meeting. There was enormous tension, if you will remember. In silence and tension the Arabs arose and vilified the Israelis for an hour. The Israelis arose then and did the same to the Arabs. Then Warren Austin, U.S. Ambassador to the United Nations, said, "My country hears this exchange of bitterness with the deepest regret. We can only express the hope that both parties to this conflict will meet to resolve their problems in a spirit of true Christian brotherhood."

A man with whom I once worked provided another example: in the middle of a news program, he announced, "We interrupt our ordinary news to bring you a special bulletin. The prime minister of South Africa has just been assassinated." There was then a long pause, and as an old newsman I knew exactly what had happened. He couldn't find the rest of the copy. Finally he said, "The name is being withheld, pending notification of. . . ."

Each such example in its own way demonstrates some aspect of the communications problem.

As a University Chancellor, I find myself now making what is known as "remarks." That is the emission of preferably sterile air under circumstances that produce a kind of warm glow, but are not too distracting to the ongoing proceedings—very much like Ernie Byfield who ran the Pump Room in Chicago and served all his special dinners on a flaming sword. When he was asked why he did this, he said, "Well, it doesn't hurt the food any, and the customers like it."

But I would like to do a little bit more than simply make remarks.

The momentous problems in communications today hardly need restatement by me. We find ourselves in a unique moment in the history of civilization; we have come through a massive communications revolution, far beyond the wildest dreams of anyone who looked into the ages ahead. We have literally reappropriated for man those communications instruments that he lost in the earliest days of civilization—when the world got so big that he couldn't use his eyes anymore to see everything, or his ears to hear everything, when he found he couldn't talk to everybody. We are surrounded by those instruments. Nobody in the world lives beyond the range of them, and when men reach the planets, no one in outer space will live beyond the range of them, either. So we have an incredible array of facilities. Yet with all the rich instrumentation surrounding us, capable of drenching our society and penetrating its every crack and crevice, we seem at the same time to have managed to generate a series of problems for human beings far greater than any man has ever known. As we have eliminated one problem, it has given birth, in departing, to a multiplicity of others.

How it is possible to devise those skills, tools, and instruments to do all the things that we instinctively sense communications can and should do— and then have these tools do so little, prove so ineffective and, in fact, fall so easily into the hands of those who would use them for evil? I wonder if anyone ever worried about that in the earliest days, when the first spark sent sound around the world?

What are the problems we find ourselves faced with? We still haven't found a solution to the problems of peace. We are fighting wars, and there seems to be no early hope that we will stop fighting wars. No communication, no communications instrument, no language we have developed, no way of projecting ourselves beyond the boundaries of one kind of life into another, no look at the way other people live and what their problems are, has brought us any closer to the great Christian imperative that every man shall live in peace without fear, with enough to eat, and with a chance to rise to maturity in dignity and self-respect. Poverty abounds and, as a matter of fact, may very well win the "war on poverty." We are still groping for human purpose. I would still like to hear a clear definition of our national purpose in terms that would be understandable to the majority of our society. We're living in the midst of a kind of mixmaster of change, a rate of change which challenges our tolerance and that built-in speedometer that lies deep in the heart of every human being, which may now be indicating its outer limits in terms of accepting change.

We have race problems. There are men living in conditions that almost defy the imagination.

Crime seems constantly to increase. Only the statistics occasionally are manipulated to disguise the reality of the fact that we have achieved one thing; we have introduced people to crime earlier in life than many prior societies. There are many who feel that we have snapped, somewhere, the moral thread that has run through the existence of man since his beginning days.

All this in the face of the richest and widest resource of communications facilities that men have ever known.

At most universities in the United States (my own is always exempt from any of these comments), we are producing people who really can't read, who really can't write, who really cannot explain anything, who do not really understand and know the history of the country in which they live—much less the world in which it grew up—and who show shocking inadequacies in their ability to think rationally and intelligently. I have not, in over a year, had a single communication from a student that is grammatically correct, that is without misspellings, without poor usage, or that is not confusing and impossible to understand. I consider that to be a basic communications failure. Unless we find a way to solve that failure, many other kinds of communications in which we are going to engage are going to prove useless.

We're living in a world, of course, in which there is an enormous communications overload. Any system of communications that I can envisage has to have an overload point. Someone at Michigan is doing some research on the question of, "When does society reach an overload point in communications, and what is the effect on society when that overload point is reached?" The results will be interesting, the findings may be ominous.

We have in addition, as one of the broad problems in communication, the whole business of the development of special and new languages. For all of our sophistication in inventing computer languages, for example, we have developed no language that makes it possible for a person who has never lived in filth and deprivation and degradation to explain something important to someone who has, or vice-versa.

Not all of our languages, as you know, are verbal. Yet we have not taught the nonverbal languages. Basically, we are still teaching, in all of our school systems, reading and writing. But our students are surrounded by visual languages. Who is going to teach them the new languages?

All about us there are examples of overcommunications and undercommunications and miscommunications. As a matter of fact, there are times when all three are happening at the same time. Communication, as we all know, is not a simple path from someone to an audience. It is the path of a message of some kind to a large variety of people. For some of them, whatever is communicated is too much. For others, whatever is communicated is not enough. And for still others, whatever is communicated is a miscommunication, or an improper use of the communication form. The interesting thing is that it can be the same message in every case.

Harold Mendelssohn of our faculty says that the average person receives, in the course of a single day, some 1,500 messages. Somebody is exhorting each of us to do something, or warning us about something, or telling us to think about something, or trying to get our attention for some reason about 1,500 times a day. What kind of effect this is ultimately going to have on the society is worth studying.

Mendelssohn claims this overload makes most safety messages ineffective. The National Safety Council spends a fortune trying to get people to stop killing themselves in cars, yet people seem to be doing it more vigorously every year. What's happening? Why don't people avoid killing themselves when, in every medium we use, someone is explaining to them that the life they take may be their own, and when all sorts of communications impact is being made on them by people who are supposed to be good at communications?

You can get people, using very simple communication forms and techniques, to rush to centers to get polio vaccine. There is something about polio that catches our attention. As a matter of fact, people rushed to centers to get polio vaccine when it wasn't even clear whether the vaccine gave you polio or kept you from getting it. Many who had been vaccinated with one substance rushed to get vaccinated with another. In the process, they destroyed one of the greatest research potentials in all the history of medicine. No one today really knows whether it's the Salk or the Sabin vaccine that is providing immunity. If we'd had a little patience, and a little less communications (there's an example of overcommunications), we might have had the time to find out.

We're also assuming, when we overcommunicate, that communications alone will do the job—that if you just say something to somebody and he hears you, you're doing what has to be done to achieve the end result. I would argue that there is more to people than a pair of ears and a brain to process a message. People have demonstrated, by rushing to get polio vaccine and by paying no attention at all to the far more frequent message that a cigarette will kill you, that they are going to make distinctions in ways we don't fully understand. You can get people to take a polio shot who would violently oppose putting fluorine in the water. In people's minds, it is apparently a more serious thing to be a potential victim of polio than it is to be a walking victim of dental cavities. In people's minds, it is apparently more desirable to smoke cigarettes, develop emphysema, cancer of the lung, or heart disease than it is to get polio—which at any time in history has never involved more than two per cent of the population.

Communicators may be assuming that the communication itself is sufficient. I would argue that it is not, that a better understanding of the audience, of what happens to a generation of people who grow into a world that is reeling under the impact of new kinds of communication, is worthwhile, and that such an understanding may indicate to us that we are overkilling with communication.

Much of what I see today that I would categorize as overcommunication is an exercise in form rather than substance. There is an enormous temptation to do that.

How do we undercommunicate? The classic example of an undercommunication, for me, is a typical network documentary on radio or television that says, "In the next hour we will tell you about the race problem in the United States." This creates the great undercommunication—often, also, a miscommunication—that, by taking an hour out to listen thoughtfully while a few people oversimplify that vastly complex problem, you have achieved better understanding. What is often the case is that you thereby lose any sense of further responsibility to develop understanding, because somehow, in its highly persuasive and attractive way, the message seems to give us "the answers"; we've responded, and we are the better for it. The fact is that we're not usually the better for it.

I had a dramatic example of miscommunication some years ago in Liberia. I went with a USIA team down to a native tribe some distance from the capital. Malaria is rampant there. We had just done a film—a remarkable piece of color photography, close-up shots, screen-filling shots of a greatly magnified mosquito plunging its dagger into the human skin, sucking the blood, depositing the malaria virus. We were to show this to a native group. We got there quite late. It was dark. The group was sitting around a council fire, the chief telling tribal tales. We hooked up the screen on the back of the truck, turned on the generator, and projected our film on mosquitoes. When it was over, the chief came to me, patted me sympathetically on the shoulder and said, in effect, "I feel so sorry for you. Thank God we don't have mosquitoes that big here. Ours aren't nearly that big!"

We are seeing increasing evidence of the same problem in school children who watch animation in educational motion pictures, but who have never been taught the language of animation. I often wonder whether my 12-year-old daughter, when her mother has a headache, sits there and has a mental image of that rope unwinding in her mother's head.

Alexis de Tocqueville once said that among democratic nations, each new generation is a new people. As we move rapidly from one generation to another, in a world that changes so rapidly, we often forget that the languages that we're familiar with have changed. Even the words have different meanings.

Miscommunication: I saw a can of salmon once that was a classic example of that. Pink salmon is fashionable. White salmon can be a drug on the market when everybody wants pink salmon, so what one company did was put a little label on every can that said: "The white salmon in this can is positively guaranteed not to turn pink." I don't wish I'd said that, but some smart advertising man did.

How do you miscommunicate? For some years I helped edit an encyclopedia. A man named Herman Shumlin wrote to me one day. He had produced a play on Broadway that took a very dim view of the Pope's activities during World War II with respect to the treatment the Jews received. He argued that, in his opinion, the encyclopedia had in 25 years, year by year, minimized the guilt of the Nazis for what they did to the Jews.

This deeply concerned me. I went back over the years and studied the series of communications we had offered to the public and found that, on the face of it, it might appear to be just as he said. Then when I talked to historians, theologians, and specialists in this field, they made the obvious point that when something happens and you hold a "viewfinder" up to it, the event fills the screen completely. As an old photographer, I understand this communications problem. If you get up to a scene and stand close to it, you fill your view-finder. But as you move back from it, its size never changes, its facts don't change, but the amount of information input that pours in through the edges of the finder, just by virtue of the greater distance, creates a change of emphasis. Historically, simply substitute time for distance. Our here-and-now world is full of such miscommunications.

When I think about communications, I often think that we have God's palette at our disposal—the whole range of appeals to the senses and the minds of human beings. Yet we seem often to have such abysmal failures. What's the failure? What's the blindness? What's the inadequacy in communications skills?

I think the answers to these questions are going to have to be found at the university, in research, in meetings like this one, in broader recognition of the fact that communications is not any longer just something that happens when you drop a dime in a telephone or open a telegram; that it goes beyond all the conventional aspects of communications that we have come to recognize; that it's now projecting itself into worlds that are unknown; that it's creating new languages all the time; that the new inhabitants of our society, and those who will inhabit it in the future, are going to have needs beyond any machinery we have created to meet earlier demands.

Maybe the point can best be made by Carl Sandburg's words:

> In a Colorado graveyard, two men lie on one grave.
> They shot it out in a jam over who owned one corner lot,
>   over a piece of real estate.
> They shot it out. It was a perfect duel.
> Each cleansed the world of the other.
> Each horizontal, in an identical grave, had his bones
>   cleansed by the same maggots.
> They sleep now as two accommodating neighbors.
> They had speed and no control.
> They wanted to go and didn't know where.*

---

* Carl Sandburg, *The People, Yes,* New York: Harcourt Brace and World, 1936. Reprinted with permission.

Albert Upton, whose Ph.D. is from the University of California in Philology and Literature, was born in Denver in 1897. Dr. Upton taught at the University of California at Berkeley, the University of New Mexico, and the University of Southern California before he came to Whittier College, California, as Professor of English and Director of General Studies. His publications include *Design for Thinking,* and *Creative Analysis.*

34

ON THE "MATTER" OF FRESHMAN ENGLISH

ALBERT UPTON

THESE—ambiguity and metaphor—are the subjects of my story. If you ask me what is the matter *with* freshman English, I will not complain that it is too often taught by traditional old fogies or conventional young fogies who are still living in the not-so-sacred past; I will not view with alarm the barbarous invasion of the young Turks who charge upon us under the alien banner of anthropology; I will not add my voice to the indignant chorus of the *un*sane who resent the efforts of the non-Aristotelians to take us off the map and into the territory. On the contrary, I would staunchly defend the much maligned composition program even at its worst. No, if I were required to answer the question, "What is the matter with freshman English?" I should first have to answer, "Not so much in what it commits, but in what it omits."

One finds it difficult not to agree with Mr. Snow that our contemporary academic culture is schizoidal. Like the very brains in our skulls, we are split down the middle with a humanities lobe on one side and a science lobe on the other. And our gregarious fears and allegiances prompt us to keep the right lobe from knowing what the left is doing. Our scholastic problems of integration lie not only in the community, but in our heads! If language instruction is to continue as the vested interest of English and speech teachers, then I think we owe it to the student to prepare them to teach him the scientific as well as the artistic functions of language, and to help him realize that they may be complementary rather than antithetical components of his intelligent behavior.

I proceed on the assumption that the language of a civilized community is more an artifact than a natural growth in spite of its biological origins. I further hold that understanding of the nature of a tool is essential to its most effective use.

The language instrument seems to have three primary and two secondary function and the propaganda function. Whenever and whether the choice ment, and problem solving; the secondary functions I call the shibboleth function and the propaganda function. Whenever and wherever the choice of words, their spelling, punctuation, and arrangement become signs of status, the teaching of linguistic etiquette becomes a meaningful and sometimes vital enterprise—particularly in a democracy where a large contingent of the population desire to climb. From one point of view it may be opined that we still cling to the horse-and-buggy concept of correctness established by our rude forefathers who passionately desired to have a polish put upon their progeny.

When I speak of propaganda as a secondary function, I refer to that insidious kind of discourse in which an ulterior motive skulks behind an apparent intention. During the debunking era between the wars, many a quixotic English teacher went galloping about in the name of propaganda analysis, shattering lances on the windmills of hidden persuasion.

The etiquette function will probably be with us, and seem important to some of us until that heavenly day when the state has withered away and our descendants shall compose one big classless hungry family. Propaganda analysis, for some strange reason, went out of vogue with the arrival of the New Deal, and it is difficult to predict when we shall be bothered with *it* again.

It is with respect to problem solving, the third primary function just mentioned, that I find the most noteworthy omissions. When language is being seriously and competently employed in the problem solving process, definition, classification, and the formulation of working hypotheses are critically important linguistic functions, for which *heuristic* seems to be the best word in the language. But English teachers, like the fair Ophelia, generally are "unshifted in such perilous circumstance." Their discipline is artistically motivated; it has impatiently foregone the rigor of the tedious exercises necessary to conscious accuracy. Neither by theory nor practice do we train our students to trace the sometimes subtle shifts of a small but too too familiar portion of their enormous vocabularies; nor do we school them in the formulation of hypotheses and working classifications.

In a semantic count of the 600,000 terms of the Second International, an indefatigable student of mine once found that about 90% had but one "sense." *Pediculosis* means "infestation with lice," and that is all it means. The average word has about three senses. *Louse* has three; *lousy* has four, one of which is "abundantly provided with." Hence, it is appropriate to remark that a common little syllable like *set* is lousy with senses. Most language teachers do not behave as if they had explored the causes and implications of this fact; the vast majority do not know it. They do not realize that in order to have a language capable of meeting the needs and at the same time the limitations of a civilized intellect we must provide a very small corps of words with an ever-increasing and ever-changing equipment of more or less systematically related senses.

As things stand, it seems that just as our Puritan fathers joined in a fatuous conspiracy to keep their children from finding out where babies come from, so our scholastic fathers maintain a conspiracy of silence regarding the most pregnant subject of semantic propagation and the origins of meaning. If an aristocracy of a few experienced words didn't keep on having most of the babies, purists to the contrary notwithstanding, overpopulation of our vocabulary would set in and civilization would suffocate in a latter-day Babel. Looseness and obscurity born of the Bohemian union of *Roget's Thesaurus* and a handbook on style may be a bane, but disciplined control of the full semantic spectrum of a very small but essential portion of our total vocabulary is an inestimably precious boon. Some of our four-letter words get us into trouble because of their lack of ambiguity, but most of them get us into far more trouble and far more serious trouble because they have so many more senses than most of us know, or at least take into account.

This fact suggests the most adverse criticism that I am disposed to make of the present state of the teaching art. It is this: the concept of metaphor is but loosely and lightly considered among us, and the word *metaphor* therefore exemplifies what I would describe as an irrational ambiguity. My own inclination is to limit its use to what Aristotle called proportional metaphor because it can be analyzed in terms of the proportion $a:b::c:d$. The dictionaries are content to exemplify metaphor by two or three examples, such as the ship plows the sea, her marble brow, a volley of oaths, "all the world's a stage," he was a lion in the battle, and so forth. They are usually at pains to explain that the negative sign of the metaphor is the absence of the telltale *like* or *as* of the simile. *Webster's New World* defines *metaphor* metaphorically as "a compressed simile." That is to say, if one takes the expression, *her neck is like marble,* and squeezes it hard enough, he can express the word *like* and get a plain marble neck as the result. Such monstrosities are inevitable among grammar-minded rhetoricians who are not really concerned with what words mean.

The reason for the fundamental and everlasting importance of the competent interpretation of metaphor, however loosely defined, is this: sound education, as you will all agree, is not evaluated soundly by the student's demonstration that he can appropriately match words with words as the result of seeing or hearing them used together. We call this *verbal* learning and deplore it. Now metaphor, properly interpreted as metaphor, forces the interpreter to get out of the world of *words,* and into the world of *things—* off of the map into the territory. He cannot settle for the mere pattern $a:b::c:d,$ but must substitute for those logically useful little symbols the semantic actualities for which they stand.

My point is that professors of English ought to make up their minds whether you have to make up new stage directions to save the face of a simile or whether a metaphor can be a metaphor regardless of the presence of a *like* or *as.*

The all important thing is that the creator of a simile or a metaphor wants his interpreter to compare two scenes in his mind's eye, and the all important thing from the interpreter's point of view is to get the right scenes. In the simile, the two scenes tend to be strikingly similar; in the metaphor the striking thing is that they are so different.

Speaking generally, similes but lightly try our powers of abstraction. Metaphors may stretch them to their limits. This is why adding the interpretation and composition of metaphors to the scholastic diet of a metaphor-starved student registers a sudden and dramatic improvement in his scores on mental maturity and creativity scales.

I see no harm in regarding metaphors as examples of "more picturesque speech," and applaud the generosity of the *Reader's Digest,* which for years has been buying up at $10.00 apiece second-hand specimens in good condition. But there is one extremely unfortunate aspect of such encouragement. It helps to keep alive the erroneous idea that metaphors are merely literary ornaments, that, to use Pope's eloquent but ill-considered expression, "Good sense needs no flowers of speech." Metaphors may be flowers in the sense of the pretties and the beautifuls and the uniques at the flower show, but they are also the flowers (and this is far more important to you and me) in the sense that flowers are the strikingly apparent harbingers of the fruits to come. Deep thinkers, be they poets, philosophers, or scientists, have always used them for the purpose not only of *expressing* their thoughts but of *formulating* them. We acknowledge our debt to metaphor functioning as conceptual model for thinking about the meaning of life whenever we speak of the "symbolism" of a *Moby Dick* or an *Old Man and the Sea,* but do we recognize that contemporary physical science is what it is because of the *partial* success, at least, of the wave metaphor as it rolled progressively through the sciences of sound, sight, heat, and electrokinetic energy? The poet and the scientist at their best are equally creative for the simple reason that they both possess in marked degree man's most sublime capacity—the capacity to see analogies and create metaphors.

"O Nature, and O soul of man!" cries transcendentalist Ahab in the chapter on "They Sphynx" in *Moby Dick.* "How far beyond all utterance are your linked analogies; not the smallest atom stirs or lives on matter, but has its cunning duplicate in mind." Ishmael warns us in the "Whiteness" chapter that "in a *matter* like this [the tracing of the linkages], subtlety appeals to subtlety, and without imagination no man can follow another into these halls." Yet his is not a counsel of despair. "Let us try," he says

At my school (Whittier), we attempt to smuggle the scientific method into the belletristic English, and the forensic speech programs. The attempt, for example, at systematic analysis, which involves the painstaking effort to fill out all nine places in a standardized metaphor diagram, may appear upon casual notice to be an execellent way to destroy a student's interest in the poetry of Shakespeare's blank verse, or Melville's rhythmic prose. The results, however, are most convincingly to the contrary.

It was Aristotle himself who proposed this incipient "non-Aristotelianism" two thousand years ago: "It is by metaphor that we can best get hold of something fresh."

Part IV

APPENDIX

ALFRED KORZYBSKI: HIS CONTRIBUTIONS AND THEIR HISTORICAL DEVELOPMENT

CHARLOTTE READ*

ALFRED Habdank Skarbek Korzybski (1879–1950) came to the United States when he was thirty-six years old, during the First World War. Except for a year in the army in Canada, he lived in this country the second half of his life. Here he formulated and taught his life-work, which he called "the first non-Aristotelian system," with "general semantics" as its *modus operandi.*

In his first book, *Manhood of Humanity,* he gave a new definition of man.[1] After twelve years of study and writing, working out the development of the theory, he completed his second book, *Science and Sanity,* in which he laid a foundation for a science of man, and a positive theory of sanity based on the orientations of modern science and physico-mathematical methods.[2] He established and directed the Institute of General Semantics, now located in Lakeville, Connecticut, which continues to carry on his work.

Science and Sanity has been evaluated by some as "one of the ten most influential books of the twentieth century," by others as "among the least read and most criticized books." Other reactions ranged from regarding it as "a work of an inestimable and many-sided value," and "taken as a whole, beyond all comparison the most momentous single contribution that has ever been made to our knowledge and understanding of what is essential and distinctive in the nature of man," to "nothing new."

"The man comes before his work," Korzybski said. A few biographical details may help in understanding his aims, and reveal influences which determined the direction and form of his work.

Alfred Korzybski was born in Warsaw in 1879, the son of Ladislas Korzybski and Helena Rzewuska. His father was an engineer with the rank of General in the Ministry of Communication, a lover of mathematics and physics, and a pioneer in new methods of agriculture.

---

* See previous biographical sketch, Chapter 8.—EDITOR.

In Warsaw he lived with his parents and sister at 66 Wilcza Street, and in the country nearby on the family estate. While he was growing up he learned to speak four languages, a fact which proved helpful to him in his later work. For half of each day there was a French governess, for the other half a German governess. Russian and Polish were taught in the schools. He did not learn English until he came to America.

At his father's urging, he was trained as a chemical engineer at the Polytechnic Institute in Warsaw. But privately he developed an interest in law, mathematics, and physics instead, then found, too late, that he could not enter a university to pursue a career in such fields because his previous curriculum in the *Realschule* did not include certain prerequisites such as Greek, Latin, etc. This was an intense disappointment and frustration to him. In the meantime, he read constantly in the subjects of his special interests, including the philosophies of the day, and in history, history of cultures and of science, comparative religions, the literatures of Poland, Russia, France, and Germany. At one time he taught mathematics, physics, French, and German at a gymnasium in Warsaw.

Traveling as an eclectic scholar in Germany and Italy, he spent the major portion of this time in Rome and its university. He became friends with some of the Cardinals and others connected with the Vatican during the time of Pope Leo XIII. It was there, in his early twenties, before the Cardinals and the General of the Jesuits, that he made his first and only speech before coming to this country—on "The Relationship of the Polish Youth toward the Clergy, and the Clergy toward Polish Youth," criticizing the clergy for their treatment of Polish youths.

When he returned from Rome he was shocked with the realization that his former playmate, the gardener's son, as well as all the other peasants, could neither read nor write, yet their labor had for generations earned the money for the education and the freedom of travel of their landowners. He built a small schoolhouse for the peasants on the country estate, for which he was sentenced to Siberia by the Russian government, but his father managed to have the sentence suspended.

At the outbreak of the First World War, Korzybski immediately volunteered in Warsaw for service in the Second Russian Army, and was assigned to a special Cavalry Detachment of the General Staff Intelligence Department on the battlefields. In July, 1915, he was ordered "At the Disposal of the Minister of War," and sent to Petrograd, and in December of that year he was sent to Canada and the United States as an artillery expert. He served in various capacities here in the Russian Army until it collapsed, then lectured for the United States government. Later he became

Secretary of the French-Polish Military Commission, and Recruiting Officer for Ohio, Pennsylvania, and West Virginia.

These years of strain and suffering moved him to try to understand how such a world-wide catastrophe could happen, and with the Armistice he had no relief from his relentlessly prodding "why?" In November, 1918, he met Mira Edgerly, a native of Illinois and a portrait painter, in this country, France, and England, noted for her work on ivory. Recognizing in each other an intense concern for humanity, they immediately felt a mutual attraction. They were married two months later.

In groping for basic causes for our devastating human conflicts, Korzybski came to the deep questions he asked of himself: "What is life?" "Forms of life differ, but how?" With his engineering outlook, he was led to classify all forms of life in terms of what they *do*. Plants, he said, have the ability to transform energy from the sun into organic chemical energy. He called them the "chemistry-binding class of life." Animals have this capacity, but also are able to move about from one place to another. He called them the "space-binding class of life." Humans, together with these abilities, have a unique capacity which no other form of life has shown: They can use the accumulated achievements inherited from past generations, build upon them, and pass them on to the next generation. In doing so, they can begin where the former generation left off. He called this the "time-binding" capacity, which gave to man a different living dimension. He developed these formulations, with their depth of implication for human living, in his first book, *Manhood of Humanity: The Science and Art of Human Engineering,* published in 1921.

This definition of man as a "time-binding class of life" placed him within nature, not partly animal and partly supernatural, and gave him stature and dignity. The time-binding energy, Korzybski emphasized, was basically healthy and constructive. It functions autonomously if not obstructed. The progress men can achieve in the course of a generation grow sat an ever-increasing exponential rate in any given field, if it is not hindered by the creeds or mores of a society, or by other influences.

But there are two widely different laws of progress; they represent different rates of growth. Advancement in scientific fields and technological power has bounded ahead in a rapidly increasing geometrical progression, while progress in social fields has lagged behind, hampered by traditions and habits of bygone days. The great disparity in the rates of progress has created imbalances which result periodically in social cataclysms.

When men are no longer hindered by outdated creeds about their own nature, when they are not prevented from living in accord with the natural laws of human life, they will live in freedom to exercise their time-binding energies unobstructed. Humanity will then grow from its childhood to manhood. "I have no doubt," Korzybski wrote in 1921, "that that conception [of the human class of life] is to be the base, the guide, the source of light, of a new civilization."

Throughout this first book, and in his later work, Korzybski sought to follow the orientation of mathematics. His father had given him the *feel* of the calculus when he was five, and this had made a deep impression. Some of his reasons for a mathematical approach were that he desired to be clear, that mathematics is independent of hopes and selfishness and passions—it is impersonal. At that time he called his work "Human Engineering."

His good friend and mentor, Cassius Jackson Keyser, Adrian Professor of Mathematics at Columbia University, had given him invaluable editorial aid when his knowledge of the English language was new and limited. Keyser had laid aside work on his own book to help Korzybski, whose manuscript he considered urgent. Keyser's work in mathematical philosophy greatly influenced Korzybski, and during the following years as he developed his theory, it was one of the main foundation stones. In their writings in the early 1920's they both brought each other's work to public attention.

"If there is to be a science of human engineering," Korzybski wrote at that time, "it must be mathematical in spirit and in method and if we do not possess methods to apply mathematical thinking to human affairs, such methods must be discovered." [3]

The mathematical discoveries of the fifty to seventy-five years prior to 1920 impressed him with the power of rigorous thought, and revealed some processes of how it works. With the publication in 1854 of George Boole's *The Laws of Thought,* an internal revolution was started in logic and in mathematics. In this new scientific period, it was to become clear to many that all man can know is a joint phenomenon of the observer and the observed. Keyser had formulated the principle of "fate and freedom": we have the freedom (in accord with the laws of thought) to choose our assumptions, but once chosen, the consequences follow with a "logical fate." Since we are usually not aware of our silent assumptions, hidden in our language and underlying our actions, we must investigate our assumptions to ascertain whether they are based on facts.

In 1923, Korzybski wrote a rough outline of the principles on which the foundation of his future work, "the science and art of human engineering," would rest. [4] His main aim at that time was to give the practical applications of some of the great formulations of certain well known authors: Alfred Whitehead, Bertrand Russell, Henri Poincaré, Cassius J. Keyser, and Albert Einstein. The importance of correct symbolism appeared increasingly urgent as the need loomed larger for revising all our doctrines, bringing symbolism into accord with facts. This concern was expressed later in his formulation of structural similarity between language and what it represents. He concluded that mathematics is the only language which at present has a structure similar to that of the world and the human nervous system.

Korzybski was convinced that the new developments in logic and mathematics would demand scientific knowledge of human nature, and would make it imperative to adjust human beliefs, institutions, doctrines and conduct to what was discovered about the laws of human nature. The "brotherhood of man" he believed can be accomplished only and exclusively by the "brotherhood of doctrines." When we will investigate, many doctrines which still persist will be found to retard human progress, knowledge and happiness. The danger lies in that the majority of mankind is unaware of the doctrines that govern them.

In another year he had formulated in rough outline what he called "a general theory of time-binding" (dropping the name "human engineering" because of the way others used it).[5] It was based mainly on the mathematical foundations mentioned earlier, but also influenced by wide reading in the fields of scientific method, mathematics, mathematical philosophy, logic, the theories of relativity, the newer physics, psychiatry, biology, neurology, psychology, etc. He carried on an extensive correspondence with the leaders of the exciting new developments in these fields.

For two years, in 1925 and 1926, Korzybski studied psychiatry at St. Elizabeth's Hospital in Washington, D.C. There, working under the guidance of Dr. William Alanson White, the Superintendent, he shared with Dr. White his study of mathematical methods as applied to psychiatry. He was given the opportunity to observe the patients, attend meetings of the medical staff and participate in the programs of the psychiatric societies in Washington.[6]

"How does time-binding work?" he asked himself. Language seemed to be the main means of transmission. Hence the need for our language to correspond with what we were learning about the world. The old ways of speaking did not fit any more.

New and structurally different theories in biology and physiology were produced in the tropism theory (Jacques Loeb), and in the dynamic gradients formulations of Charles Child; W. E. Ritter and others were establishing that the organism must be considered "as-a-whole." The famous experiments of the physiologist Ralph Lillie showed that rhythmicity in life could not be explained by purely physical nor purely chemical means, but that it is more satisfactorily explained when treated as a physico-electro-chemical structural occurrence. There was growing recognition of the importance of colloidal science as it affects biology, psychiatry, and other sciences. These outlooks, so commonplace today but new in the 1920's, necessitated breaking down the old compartmentalized barriers that split one scientific study from another, and demanded the formulation of new studies in terms of the "organism-as-a-whole-in-its-environment," with the recognition that "everything" is affected by "everything else."

Einstein's revolutionary work in physics was one of the pillars on which Korzybski's new theory was built. Indeed in his "humanizing" of the theory, generalizing it to human behavior with its implications for changed relationships, he emphasized what a tremendous structural linguistic achievement Einstein's theories were.

He had to study and work out the psychological problems involved with the quantum mechanics, newly formulated in the 1920's, such as problems of causality, probability, etc., and clarify how they were expressions of a new way of relating to the world.

That the observer himself is an integral part of whatever he observes, that an observation cannot be "pure," but must be a *relation* between the observed and the observer's instruments, his language structure, his physiology, his habits of perception, the environmental conditions, etc., would have deep ramifications not only in scientific research but also in our daily lives.

Korzybski was in close touch with the physicist Percy Bridgman and with leading mathematicians in this country such as Eric Temple Bell, R. D. Carmichael, and E. V. Huntington, besides Cassius Keyser. He sought their evaluations of his work as his theory developed.

As new works appeared in different fields, dramatically breaking fresh ground, Korzybski saw that their approaches were somehow related in their underlying assumptions. He was faced with the necessity of searching out those assumptions and analyzing their structure, and the new structure of the language in which they were expressed (e.g. "space-time" instead of separate "space" *and* "time"). In unravelling the underlying structures, he found them to be aspects of one larger system embracing the new trends. "If we must label this system," Korzybski wrote in 1926, "*non-Aristotelian* probably would be the most appropriate."

The Aristotelian, Euclidean, and Newtonian systems were expressions of a structurally similar world view. The first science to break the traditional "structural ring" was geometry. When Gauss, Bolyai, Lobatchevsky, and Riemann formulated non-Euclidean geometries, it shook and freed the mathematical and scientific world, for now there was not only *the* one unique Euclidean geometry, but indefinitely many possible non-Euclidean geometries. Following these, non-Newtonian systems were built with Einstein's theories and the quantum.

Looking back over the development of this phase of his work, Korzybski wrote, "As soon as this new non-Aristotelian system was definitely formulated, a most curious, natural, and yet unexpected result became apparent; namely, that the three new systems, the non-*A*, non-*E*, and the non-*N* have *also* one underlying structure and metaphysics. . . . All these three new systems have been produced independently. They express between them the structural and semantic urge and longing of all modern science." [7] The new trilogy was *more general* than the old, and included the Aristotelian-Euclidean-Newtonian trilogy as a special case.

Korzybski had profound admiration for the work of Aristotle. He believed that the "non-Aristotelians" would carry forward the aims of Aristotle in modern times with the epistemological and scientific knowledge of the twentieth century.

To mention only a few of the characteristics of these contrasting metaphysics, it may be said that the Aristotelian included subject-predicate verbal structures, static, additive, linear, two-valued orientations. The non-Aristotelian may be characterized by relational methods, and dynamic, non-linear, functional, flexible, many-valued orientations.

Central to Korzybski's theory was his formulation of "consciousness of abstracting," to be achieved by developing an active awareness that a symbol is not to be considered the same in value as the nonverbal happening or person that it represents; that whatever we may *say* about a happening (or a person) can never cover "all,"; that we can abstract in higher and higher orders. Such awareness of our use of language and our reactions to language, involving our total functioning—including our everyday decisions, hopes, and fears—is vital to our well-being.

After the first draft of *Science and Sanity* was written, in which he set forth his new theory, Korzybski attended the Mathematical Congress of Slavic Countries at Warsaw in September, 1929. He had been impressed by the work of the Polish mathematicians, especially by the *restricted semantic* school represented by Leon Chwistek and his pupils, which was characterized mostly by the semantic approach. Up to this time he had called his work the "general theory of time-binding." By 1931, he decided to choose the term "general semantics" for his work. In later years, as the term "semantics" became more popular and became confused in public usage with "general semantics," he was to regret that he coined that name and used it for his work.

As a background for his selection, he had become acquainted with the work of Michel Bréal, who introduced the term "sémantique" into literature in 1883.[8] In his use, the term referred to a branch of philology. A few years later Lady Welby formulated a theory having to do with "signification," which she called "significs." Korzybski was also influenced by the use of the term "semantic" by certain Polish logicians. He selected the term "general semantics" for his theory for historical continuity. As he described his selection in 1948:

> The term "General Semantics" seemed most appropriate to me because of the derivation from the Greek *semainein*, "to mean," "to signify." A theory of evaluation seemed to follow naturally in an evolutionary sense from 1) "meaning" to 2) "signification" to 3) *evaluation, if we take into account the individual*, not divorcing him from his reactions, nor from his *neuro*-linguistic and *neuro*-semantic environments. Thus we allocate him in a *plenum* of some values, no matter what, and a *plenum* of language, which may be used to inform, or misinform by *commission* and/or *omission*, deceiving the individual himself and/or others. With such problems, without exception, the individual has to cope to be human at all. That's what I learned from the theory of time-binding, and what I tried to convey to others through General Semantics and psycho-biological non-Aristotelian considerations.[9]

Science and Sanity was published in 1933, and for the next seventeen years Korzybski devoted himself with great energy to teaching in his seminars (usually about forty hours each in duration), to lecturing, writing articles, and directing the Institute that he founded. He strongly emphasized that the principles must be applied, not merely talked about, and that they must be tested empirically. They would then, eventually, be manifested in our behavior, so that we would act more in accord with our potentialities as fully "human" persons.

Applications of his theory have been made in many professional fields —in medicine and psychiatry, law, engineering, architecture, etc.—in business and industry, international relations, as well as personal interrelationships, and in education at college, secondary and elementary levels. Besides his own writings, a large bibliography of books and articles have been written by others about his work, and it is being taught in many schools and colleges.

His formulations are still not accepted by some; others, while accepting "intellectually," have not followed through more deeply. The principles require self-discipline and perseverance before hindering habits of years' duration can be given up. The generality and simplicity of the theory are often deceptive. In action, we learn the discrepancy between principle and behavior and realize the inner transformation needed to bring them together. Although this is often difficult for adults, it is less so for children, who can still see with fresh eyes, and it was one of Korzybski's strongest hopes to bring his work to educators. For it is a *methodology* that lies at the heart of Korzybski's contributions, to help us to see more clearly and so to evaluate more appropriately. With our vision less distorted by prejudgments, we can become more open to continual growth.

REFERENCES

1. Korzybski, Alfred. *Manhood of Humanity: The Science and Art of Human Engineering.* New York: E. P. Dutton, 1921, 2d ed., 1950.
2. ———. *Science and Sanity: An Introduction to Non-Aristotelian Systems and General Semantics.* Lakeville, Conn.: International Non-Aristotelian Library Publishing Co., 1933; 4th ed., 1958. Distributed by the Institute of General Semantics.
3. ———. "Fate and Freedom," *The Mathematics Teacher.* Vol. XVI, No. 5 (May, 1923), pp. 274–290. Reprinted in *The Language of Wisdom and Folly,* ed. Irving J. Lee. New York: Harper & Row, 1949, p. 342.
4. *Ibid.*
5. ———. "Time-Binding: The General Theory." First Paper. Presented in abstract before the International Mathematical Congress, August, 1924, Toronto, Canada.
6. ———. "Time-Binding: The General Theory." Second Paper. Presented before the Washington Society for Nervous and Mental Diseases, June 25, 1925, and the Washington Psychopathological Society, March 13, 1926. Both "Time-Binding papers were published together by Institute of General Semantics, 1954.
7. ———. *Science and Sanity,* p. 91.
8. The word first appeared in an article in the annual of a society for Greek studies. It received wider attention later through the publication of Bréal's book, *Essai de sémantique: science des significations,* Paris, 1897, translated into English in 1900 under the title, *Semantics: Studies in the science of meaning.*
9. "Author's Note" in *Selections From Science and Sanity,* p. viii. Distributed by the Institute of General Semantics.